T0305763

The Science of Mistakes

of Mistakes

Lecture Notes on
Economic Data Engineering

World Scientific Lecture Notes in Economics and Policy

ISSN: 2630-4872

Series Editors: Felix Munoz-Garcia *(Washington State University, USA)*
Ariel Dinar *(University of California, Riverside, USA)*
Dirk Bergemann *(Yale University, USA)*
George Mailath *(University of Pennsylvania, USA)*
Devashish Mitra *(Syracuse University, USA)*
Kar-yiu Wong *(University of Washington, USA)*
Raghbendra Jha *(Australian National University, Australia)*
Richard Carpiano *(University of California, Riverside, USA)*
Chetan Dave *(University of Alberta, Canada)*
George C Davis *(Virginia Tech University, USA)*
Marco M Sorge *(University of Salerno, Italy)*
Ramon Fauli-Oller *(Universidad de Alicante, Spain)*

The World Scientific Lecture Notes in Economics and Policy series is aimed to produce lecture note texts for a wide range of economics disciplines, both theoretical and applied at the undergraduate and graduate levels. Contributors to the series are highly ranked and experienced professors of economics who see in publication of their lectures a mission to disseminate the teaching of economics in an affordable manner to students and other readers interested in enriching their knowledge of economic topics. The series was formerly titled World Scientific Lecture Notes in Economics.

Published:

Vol. 16: *The Science of Mistakes: Lecture Notes on Economic Data Engineering*
by Andrew Caplin

Vol. 15: *Economic Development, Agriculture and Climate Change*
by Antonio Yúnez-Naude and Jorge Mora-Rivera

Vol. 14: *Lectures in the Microeconomics of Choice: Foundations,
Consumers, and Producers*
by William David Anthony Bryant

Vol. 13: *Advanced Mathematical Methods in Environmental and
Resource Economics*
by Anastasios Xepapadeas

For the complete list of volumes in this series, please visit
www.worldscientific.com/series/wslnep

World Scientific Lecture Notes in Economics and Policy – Vol. 16

The Science
of Mistakes

Lecture Notes on
Economic Data Engineering

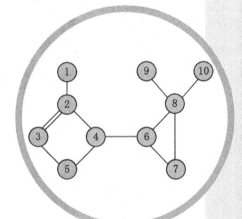

Andrew Caplin
New York University, USA

World Scientific

W JERSEY · LONDON · SINGAPORE · BEIJING · SHANGHAI · HONG KONG · TAIPEI · CHENNAI · TOKYO

Published by

World Scientific Publishing Co. Pte. Ltd.

5 Toh Tuck Link, Singapore 596224

USA office: 27 Warren Street, Suite 401-402, Hackensack, NJ 07601

UK office: 57 Shelton Street, Covent Garden, London WC2H 9HE

Library of Congress Cataloging-in-Publication Data
Names: Caplin, Andrew, author.
Title: The science of mistakes : lecture notes on economic data engineering /
    Andrew Caplin, New York University, USA.
Description: New Jersey : World Scientific, [2023] | Series: World scientific lecture notes in
    economics and policy, 2630-4872 ; Vol. 16 | Includes bibliographical references and index.
Identifiers: LCCN 2022042484 | ISBN 9789811262388 (hardcover) |
    ISBN 9789811262395 (ebook) | ISBN 9789811262401 (ebook other)
Subjects: LCSH: Economics--Study and teaching. | Econometric models. | Errors, Scientific.
Classification: LCC HB74.5 .C38 2023 | DDC 330.072--dc23/eng/20220915
LC record available at https://lccn.loc.gov/2022042484

British Library Cataloguing-in-Publication Data
A catalogue record for this book is available from the British Library.

For any available supplementary material, please visit
https://www.worldscientific.com/worldscibooks/10.1142/13026#t=suppl

Desk Editors: Aanand Jayaraman/Yulin Jiang

Typeset by Stallion Press
Email: enquiries@stallionpress.com

Printed in Singapore

This book is dedicated to my wife, Ruth Wyatt, who liberated me to depart from the academic straight and narrow. This book is an indirect result of our having met, as are our incredible children, Ann and Ollie, to whom love always. With deep love also to my brother Adam.

About the Author

Andrew Caplin is Silver Professor of Economics at New York University. He is a cognitive economist whose research covers such diverse topics as how to reduce legal and medical errors, and how best to understand life-cycle patterns of earnings, spending, and investing. The common feature is the central importance of reducing mistakes. He is a leader of the Sloan-NOMIS Program on the Cognitive Foundations of Economic Behavior, the Behavioral Macroeconomics research group at the National Bureau of Economic Research, and a member of the Center for Economic Behavior and Inequality at the University of Copenhagen. He has been working on modeling and measuring mistakes for some 15 years.

Acknowledgments

I thank Danny Goroff, Markus Reinhard, and Ruben Garcia Santos for supporting the Sloan-NOMIS Program on the Cognitive Foundations of Economic Behavior, which I head jointly with Ernst Fehr and Mike Woodford. I thank Soren-Leth Petersen and the Center for Economic Behavior and Inequality, as well as the NOMIS Foundation, the Alfred P. Sloan Foundation, and the National Science Foundation for their support. I thank Daniel Martin and Ruth Wyatt for pushing me to express ideas as personally as possible, and Val Whitten for teaching me how. Most of the theoretical material is written jointly with Daniel, Mark Dean, John Leahy, Stefan Bucher, Daniel Csaba, and Philip Marx. The experimental work is a collaboration not only with those mentioned above but also with Marina Agranov, Paul Glimcher, Robb Rutledge, Chloe Tergiman, Tom Tyler, and Oded Nov. The tradition continues with my current and recent PhD students advancing the science, including Sen Geng, Srijita Ghosh, Mateusz Gieszek, Eungik Lee, Giovanni Montonari, Isabelle Salcher, and Eric Spurlino. The applied lectures detail the work, complete and ongoing, with collaborators including John Ameriks, Joseph Briggs, Laura Bustamente, David Deming, Gunnar Epping, Paul Glimcher, Andrei Gomberg, Ivan Grahek, Victoria Gregory, Idda Hartmann, Ham Huang, Eungik Lee, Minjoon Lee, Soren Leth-Petersen, Shangwen Li, Sebastian Musslick, Robb Rutledge, Joyce Sadka, Johan Saeverud, Matthew Shapiro, Chris Tonetti, Jennifer Trueblood, Ben Weidmann and Kadachi Ye. In the broader profession, I am hugely indebted to Ernst Fehr and Mike Woodford for their intellectual companionship, and to Jim Poterba and the National

Bureau of Economic Research for helping me disseminate new ideas in their "mad scientist" phase. I owe a massive debt of gratitude to those who introduced me to economic research, in particular Frank Hahn and Hebert Scarf. Finally, I wish to acknowledge those who introduced the foundational ideas on which I build, in particular Paul Samuelson, Ernst Weber, Jacob Marschak, David Blackwell, Claude Shannon, and Chris Sims.

Contents

About the Author   vii

Acknowledgments   ix

Lecture 1: Overview   1

Part 1: The Operational Model   **25**

Lecture 2: Operationalizing the Blackwell Model   27

Lecture 3: Costly Information Representations and
    Attention Switches   53

Lecture 4: All Rationalizing Cost Functions   75

Lecture 5: Revealed Bayesian Learning: A Full
    Characterization   101

Lecture 6: Full Recovery of Costs and Welfare   137

Lecture 7: Comparison of Revealed Experiments   155

Lecture 8: Posterior-Separable Cost Functions and Behavior   185

Part 2: The Shannon Model of Rational Inattention   209

Lecture 9: Solving the Shannon Model   211

Lecture 10: Optimal Consideration Sets and the
        Invariant Likelihood Ratio Hyperplanes   233

Lecture 11: Equilibrium, Exchangeability, and Symmetry   247

Part 3: Applications   277

Lecture 12: Modeling Machine Learning   279

Lecture 13: Teaching, Testing, and Learning   307

Lecture 14: Management Skills and Productive Efficiency   323

Lecture 15: Decision-Making Skills, Job Transitions,
        and Income   337

Lecture 16: Communication Policies   353

Epilogue   373

Bibliography   375

Index   387

Lecture 1

Overview

This introductory lecture has four goals:

(1) To lay out the operational challenge in identifying mistakes;
(2) To present the "ideal data" method of responding to it;
(3) To explain the interwoven themes of the course:

  (a) the science of mistakes,
  (b) the economics of attention,
  (c) cognitive economics,
  (d) economic data engineering;

(4) To pique your interest in the lectures to come and in the many exciting research paths forward.

1.1 Guide to the Book

That mistakes are made is clear. What is meant by that is not. How to measure whatever might be meant less so. How to scientifically study even less so. In these lectures, I introduce an interdisciplinary science of mistakes to cut the Gordian knot.

While not previously so-named, the science of mistakes is of long-standing. Psychologists have studied mistakes and their sources at least since Weber (1834). Economic models of the past 70 years allow for imperfect information, hence also allowing for mistakes. In recent years, commonalities between economic and psychological conceptions have come to the fore, and it is this joint enterprise to which this book contributes. The key building blocks are model constructs drawn from the economic tradition, methods of measurement drawn from the psychometric tradition, and analytic methods drawn from economic theory. To do this burgeoning field justice would go far beyond my expertise and is, anyway, not the goal of these lecture notes. Instead, I focus on the core idea that has driven my personal research path: that of better operationalizing the essential constructs in formal models of choice, thereby to enrich the world of application. It is this approach that defines **economic data engineering**.

The lectures are largely self-contained and amenable to those with basic training in formal microeconomic theory. This first lecture is preparatory in nature and expands on the role of data engineering in defining my research path. Lectures 2–11 are, at heart, technical and cover completed research: I provide a guide at the end of this lecture once the groundwork has been covered. Lectures 12–16 cover applications. The ideas here are all subjects of ongoing research. The theme that is maintained is the need to deliberately engineer enriched data that are not contained in classical data sets of choices and outcomes.

1.2   Utility, Imperfect Information, and Costs of Learning

My central thesis is that the standard model of rational decision-making provides the three most essential constructs for the science of mistakes: Utility functions, imperfect information, and costs of learning.

1. **Modeling Mistakes Requires Utility**: In its essence, a mistake is a theoretical notion. It is by nature counterfactual. It involves comparing a decision that was taken to an alternative that could have been taken and identifying the former as **better from the perspective of the decision maker (DM)**. How are feasible alternatives identified? What do the words *better* and *worse* mean if we abandon *homo economicus* by giving up on the idea that there is some underlying utility function? The alternative decision would likely have produced a different outcome. Maybe even one that the observer believes that the DM is likely to have preferred. But all of this reasoning takes for granted that there is at least **some** underlying utility function. The economic analysis of mistakes relies centrally on the modeling abstraction that is a utility function.

I have no idea how to advance on the analysis of mistakes in a model in which the DM does not have a utility function. If others do, I am neither standing in their way nor standing in wait.

2. **Modeling Mistakes Requires Imperfect Information**: How can utility maximizers make mistakes? One obvious answer is that they don't know all that they would need to know to avoid them. Our students don't get exam answers wrong for fun. No more than our goal is to pick a piece of straw out of the haystack when looking for a needle. These mistakes and more result from gaps in knowledge. The minimal theory that captures this involves expected utility maximization in the face of information constraints. This is precisely the subject matter of the model of experimentation and choice of Blackwell (1953). I cannot think of better foundations on which to build the science of mistakes.

3. **Modeling Mistakes Requires Costs of Learning**: If mistakes would cause us less damage if we knew more, why don't we? The most essential reason is that learning is hard. If learning was costless, there would be far fewer mistakes. We would not need exams. Or teachers. Or computers. There would be no possibility of opaque presentations because we would know everything already. Theories of costly information acquisition and rational inattention would be irrelevant (Hayek, 1937, 1945; Stigler, 1961; Sims, 1998). The opposite is true in the story I tell and the world we inhabit.

1.3 The Operational Challenge

Never in history has anyone made a fully informed decision. Knowing all that could be known to make an unconditionally optimal decision is a platonic ideal. It does not survive contact with reality. The analysis of behavior is inseparable from the analysis of mistakes. Yet, decision-making mistakes have rarely been the focus of study in applied microeconomics. The fundamental reason for this is the operational challenge. Models alone do not make a science: There is a deep challenge of measurement. Mistakes are defined not by the choice that is made alone and its consequences for utility but by a comparison with a feasible choice that was not made and the counterfactual implications for utility. Rarely, if ever, is such counterfactual identification possible in standard behavioral data.

To highlight the depth of the measurement challenge, note that two of the most pivotal models in economics are of the essence in the science of mistakes: the expected utility model of experimentation and choice and models of costly information acquisition. The most basic construct in such models is an experiment, as formally defined by Blackwell (1953). This comprises a set of states, a set of signals, and a mapping that indicates for each state the probabilities over signals. The central idea of the model is that the experiment probabilistically produces signals that impact choice. The DM's goals are defined by an expected utility function over a prize space that indicates how good each available choice option is in each state. After receiving any particular signal, the DM updates from prior to posterior beliefs and chooses optimally among available options.

A moment's pause seems worthwhile. How many latent variables did I just name? Even if states and prizes can be agreed for the purposes of analysis, we are left with priors, signals, posteriors, experiments, and an expected utility function. What on earth do these translate to in terms of observations? The model has them play out in the DM's head. Fine. But if the result is to pick an apple, the evidence to separate out the constituent elements of this model seems limited. Given this, it is hard to think about what it would mean to identify a choice as mistaken in the sense that a different decision would have been taken had more been known that could have been. In the open field, on what basis can we identify one observed choice as a mistake, from the DM's viewpoint, and another as correct? And when we do call out a decision as mistaken, what exactly do we mean?

Sometimes, there seem to be common sense answers. There are many cases in which the outside observer, who I will call the econometrician, may feel that they know how to identify a DM as making a mistake when they see it: an incorrect medical diagnosis, a conviction overturned on later review, an incorrect sporting call, exam answer, etc. But stepping back to the bigger picture of decision-making, a problem of measurement emerges. As observers of the decisions people make, social scientists see what is chosen, not why. So, except in special cases, how do we know whether the choice of one alternative over another is optimal or reflects ignorance? A choice is a choice is a choice.

To appreciate the challenge and the method with which I address it in these lectures, we have to walk through some intellectual history.

The basic idea that these lectures follow up on is Samuelson's revolutionary operational approach to classical utility theory (Samuelson, 1938). The paragraphs with which Samuelson opened the article mark a dramatic turning point in social science. As necessary background, Samuelson was discussing the successive refinements of utility theory since economic theorists introduced it in the mid-nineteenth century, in large part to better understand the prices of commodities. For all that they refined the underlying logic of the theory, they left one key issue open: how to operationalize it. Samuelson started by setting the stage for his critique of the theory even in its (then and now) most modern form, with indifference curves having replaced cardinal utilities:

> From its very beginning the theory of consumer's choice has marched steadily towards greater generality, sloughing off at successive stages unnecessarily restrictive conditions. From the time of Gossen to our own day we have seen the removal of (a) the assumption of linearity of marginal utility; (b) the assumption of independence of utilities; (c) the assumption of the measurability of utility in a cardinal sense; and (d) even the assumption of an integrable field of preference elements.

> The discrediting of utility as a psychological concept robbed it of its only possible virtue as an explanation of human behaviour in other than a circular sense, revealing its emptiness as even a construction. As a result the most modern theory confines itself to an analysis of indifference elements, budgetary equilibrium being defined by equivalence of price ratios to respective indifference slopes.

With this backdrop, Samuelson posed his fundamental question concerning the operational content of the model. A utility function is latent: It is not stamped on the DM's forehead. So are indifference relations. Tired of the apparently circular notion that utility was revealed by choice while choice resulted from utility maximization, Samuelson drove to the heart of social science by questioning the operational status of utility theory (see Dixit, 2002, for a methodological background):

> ... just as we do not claim to know by introspection the behaviour of utility, many will argue we cannot know the behaviour of ratios of marginal utilities or of indifference directions. (Samuelson, 1938, p. 61)

Samuelson initiated a program of defining the theory of utility maximization by its observable consequences in ideal data. If the theory of utility maximization is intended to rationalize choice behavior, it must be defined by the properties of ideal choice data. Is it vacuous in these data, capable of explaining anything and therefore nothing, or does it have bite? Could one observe data that would lead one to have to enrich the theory or outright replace it?

We know now that the theory of utility maximization is equivalent to satisfaction of the strong axiom of revealed preference in an ideal data set on deterministic choice. The simplest statement involves a finite grand choice set X. A deterministic choice set is identified from all non-empty subsets of X. From this, we define x as strictly preferred to y if ever both are available but only x is chosen and indifferent to it if ever they are both chosen. The strong axiom of revealed preference says that such ideal choice data can result from the maximization of a utility function $u : X \to \mathbb{R}$ if and only if any string of preferred or indifferent relations that completes a cycle involves only indifference. A typical contradiction would be choosing only apple over a banana, only banana over a carrot, and only carrot over an apple.

For many economic theorists, revealed preference theory of this kind is something of a religious exercise undertaken as one technical exercise among many. I think that is most unfortunate. It is a dramatically different method of thought. In fact, this "revealed preference" method is very poorly served by its name. It should instead have been called "revealed chosen" method. Choice data are the basic given. Maximization of preferences is one possible model of these observations, albeit an important one. There are other theories that might better explain the data (e.g., Manzini and Mariotti, 2007), and there are other data sets that might allow richer theories to be tested. The latter is the path forward in the science of mistakes. It would have been unthinkable without Samuelson's method, based as it is on ideal data rather than directly on particular model constructs.

While beautiful and self-contained, classical utility theory is, of course, not a description of reality. A key condition of the simple utility model underlying classical revealed preference tests is that information is complete. The theory is easily rejected if information is incomplete. Operationalizing mistakes from choice data requires, at a minimum, separating out beliefs and utility. Addressing this challenge forms the centerpiece of the research that is covered in this book.

1.4 Random Utility or Random Perception?

Davidson and Marschak (1959) were among the first to conceive of measurements that reveal the scientific limits of classical utility theory. They took particular issue with the standard theory on the grounds that it is essentially inconsistent with commonly observed stochasticity in choice:

> Common experience suggests, and experiment confirms, that a person does not always make the same choice when faced with the same options, even when the circumstances of choice seem in all relevant respects to be the same. However, the bulk of economic theory neglects the existence of such inconsistencies and the best known theories for decision-making, for example, those of von Neumann and Morgenstern and Savage, base the existence of a measurable utility upon a pattern of invariant two-place relations, sometimes called preference and indifference. This raises a difficulty for any attempt to use such theories to describe and predict actual behavior. (Davidson and Marshak, 1959, p. 3)

In response to this challenge, Block and Marschak (1959) introduced a new class of what they called "basic observations," comprising ideal data in the form of stochastic rather than deterministic choice data. They also introduced a corresponding model to rationalize randomness in choice as resulting from randomness in utility. Their random utility model and its subsequent developments are now themselves standard in massive bodies of applied research, following the econometric work of McFadden (1974). The interpretation is typically based on unobserved population heterogeneity in preference rather than stochasticity across time. When performing comparative statics, it is traditional to use the uncovered parameters of the utility function to estimate demand as prices and product attributes change. This is justified by the identifying assumption that all consumers are perfectly informed (the consideration set model of Manzini and Mariotti, 2014, is a notable exception). If DMs were not perfectly informed, the idea that the distribution of utilities would stay the same for all changes in attributes and prices would be hard to maintain. This is part of a general issue in large swathes of discrete choice theory. Standard models of markets also typically impose complete information (e.g., Roth and Sotomayor, 1992).

There are strong *a priori* reasons to go beyond the assumption that information is complete. It is, in most cases, completely incompatible with common sense. In fact, the assumption of imperfect information is absolutely essential in almost all branches of economic theory. Beyond this, it is incompatible with what we know about the constraints imposed by the perceptual system, which relies on imperfectly encoding and decoding information about the external world. To give an economic example, Khaw *et al.* (2017) apply the principles of efficient coding to rationalize high apparent risk aversion in small-stakes gambles as resulting from imperfect perception. The assumption of perfect information also flatly contradicts the views of Block and Marschak themselves. Their work on stochastic choice data was based on the psychometric tradition. The Weber–Fechner laws of psychophysics and "psychometric curves" are the most basic constructs in many areas of psychology. These laws deal precisely with the limitations of sensory perception and characterize the proportion of time, e.g., the heavier of two weights is correctly identified. In this particular case, errors are primarily a function of the relative weight of the two objects and are largely independent of their absolute weights. Building on these psychometric foundations, Thurstone (1927, 1931) formulated stochastic choice data more than 30 years before it entered the economic canon. Luce (1956, 1958) also predated economists in introducing the logit model of stochastic choice. He called choice probabilities a "discrimination structure" to make clear the perceptual basis.

Being well schooled in this tradition, Block and Marschak never claimed to identify utility, contrary to the following work in discrete choice theory:

> Economists use the term "utility" as interchangeable with desirability (satisfaction), and thus independent of perceptibility. Our concept is coarser. All of the various definitions of utility given in this paper will be related to the empirical entities, called "alternatives". Each of these is identified precisely, but combines the information and the desirability aspect in some unknown though presumably not too changeable fashion. (Block and Marschak, 1959, p. 1.5)

They knew that separation of utility and beliefs would require altogether richer data:

> In particular, our operational approach seems to be unable to handle the following distinction that appears natural on grounds of common sense and may be important for predictions. If out of the pair $F = (a, b)$ of desirable objects a man chooses sometimes a and sometimes b, our introspection tells us that we may ascribe this to either or both of two different "causes":
>
> 1. He may have difficulty in perceiving all the relevant characteristics of the objects...
> 2. Even if he knew exactly the differences of the characteristics of the two objects, he might find them almost equally desirable ... and he will vacillate as a result. (Block and Marschak, 1959, p. 1.5)

To understand just how far economists who assume complete information in estimating models of discrete choice have departed from the psychological origins of the model of Block and Marschak, note that their primary example of stochastic choice was entirely perceptual: a wholesaler's repeated choice between two 10-ton carloads of the same merchandise in which

> the exact quantity (in pounds, net of package) or, for that matter, all the differences in quality, cannot be ascertained. (Block and Marschak, 1959, p. 1.7)

1.5 Basic Observations are Model Objects

From the viewpoint of the science of mistakes, one of the most important proposals of Block and Marschak was to make explicit the point that defining ideal data is a key step in scientific advance. In the science of mistakes that I outline, it is **the key step**, bar none.

In the words of Block and Marschak, "basic observations" are model objects to be specified to solve identification problems. They made a direct case for modeling and measuring other types of data to separate information from beliefs:

> Our particular way of defining the class of basic observations and, correspondingly, of the general testable conditions is to some extent arbitrary... The study may thus serve as a start when similar attempts are made under another definition of basic observations. (Block and Marschak, 1959, p. 1.5)

Noting the limits of stochastic choice data in resolving this belief-preference identification problem, they called for the development of new basic observations to resolve it. They argued that these should ideally be close to "the nature of economic observations", which presumably meant that one should include standard choice data at a minimum and make all further enrichment as close to this and as commonly available as possible.

This is the Block and Marschak challenge. How can we separately identify beliefs, experiments, and the costs of learning when utility functions themselves have to be inferred from choice data? The science of mistakes addresses this question head-on. As the book outlines, this has set up a highly promising and progressive scientific methodology for the analysis of mistakes.

1.6   Economic Data Engineering: General Principles

The point of method raised by Block and Marschak is entirely general. Theorists can "invent" new forms of data that are ideal for purposes of model identification. This is the method that I have pursued in the area of mistaken decisions and in other areas (Caplin, 2021). It is the method on which the research in this book is based. The goal of this form of research is to ensure that advances in economic modeling and in measurement are symbiotic. A strongly analogous case for model-based expansions in measurement is made in Orazio Attanasio's Presidential Address to the Econometric Society (Almas *et al.*, 2023). All forms of data engineering respond to identification problems in estimating economic models.

Before proposing the particular new class of basic observations that will dominate this book, let me first specify the engineering challenge somewhat abstractly. The first step is to define a "modeling and measurement framework" as a triple, (M, D, f), with M being an economic model class, D a corresponding data class, and the mapping f pinning down the implications of any standard model in standard data:

$$f : M \longrightarrow D.$$

The framework is, in principle, identified (e.g., Haavelmo, 1944; Koopmans, 1949; Marschak, 1953) if $f : M \longrightarrow D$ is one to one and is testable

(Samuelson, 1938) if the range $f(M)$ is a strict subset of D. In what follows, I superscript classes according to whether or not they are already in use and considered standard, which is obviously a moving target, particularly in the engineering research process.

The second step in the research process is to introduce a new standard modeling and measurement framework, (M^{NS}, D^{NS}, f^{NS}), ideally nesting the standard one, in which the new standard model is ideally well identified so that $f^{NS} : M^{NS} \longrightarrow D^{NS}$ is a one-to-one mapping and testable, with $f^{NS}(M^{NS})$ being a strict subset of D^{NS}. The third step is to implement the corresponding measurements and conduct empirical analyses. The fourth is to lay out next-level engineering challenges and reinitiate.

The work of Block and Marschak (1959), outlined above, well illustrates this process. They took as their standard modeling and measurement framework (M^S, D^S, f^S), the classical theory of utility maximization and deterministic choice data as conceptualized by Samuelson. As noted above, this involves some grand set of choices X and the theory that a choice from any subset of this choice set is guided by the maximization of a complete and transitive preference relation on the grand set. The standard data set involves observing the choice of elements from all subsets of X. The mapping implied by the theory is that these chosen elements comprise all maximal elements according to the fixed preference ordering. This is testable by the axioms of revealed preference and is identified since a unique preference ordering is picked out, with the caveat that one needs to observe sets of chosen actions to identify indifference.

The second step in Block and Marschak's research process was to introduce into the economic canon of D^{NS}, a new standard data set in the form of stochastic choice data and a corresponding new standard model class, M^{NS}, the random utility model. They studied the corresponding mapping $f^{NS} : M^{NS} \longrightarrow D^{NS}$ and used it to show that their model is in principle identified and testable.

The third step was implementation, which in this case came substantially later following the econometric work of McFadden (1974). The random utility model is itself now entirely standard and applied everyday, following the econometric work on the logit parametric form by McFadden, with important recent advances by Apesteguia and Ballester

(2018) and Manzini and Mariotti (2014). McFadden's pioneering work follows the standard econometric approach of finding a workable restricted model class, $M_R^{NS} \subset M^{NS}$, such that

$$f^{NS} : M_R^{NS} \longrightarrow D^{NS}$$

is one to one.

1.7   Application to Modeling Mistakes

As with random utility theory, the standard modeling framework (M^S, D^S, f^S) that calls for innovation in the case of identifying mistakes is the model of deterministic utility maximization, and the data come in the form of deterministic choice data, as conceptualized by Samuelson (1938). The spur to further innovation is discontent with the maintained assumption that information is complete.

The key step in the engineering process is the identification of a new standard modeling and measurement framework, (M^{NS}, D^{NS}, f^{NS}), nesting the standard one, in which the new standard model is ideally well identified so that $f^{NS} : M^{NS} \longrightarrow D^{NS}$ is one to one and testable, with $f^{NS}(M^{NS})$ a strict subset of D^{NS}. In the case of the science of mistakes, the new standard models are the Blackwell model of experimentation and the theory of costly learning. The new standard data set is specified in Lecture 2.

In these lecture notes, all mistakes will be "rationalized" in a model. In fact, the model in which they will be rationalized is highly standard. Of course, there is great room for richer models. But there is no free lunch. The more forces we wish to capture in our theory of mistakes, the harder it will be to operationalize these in any form of choice data. An imaginative economic theorist should be able to think of 100 latent factors, invisible not only to an outside observer but perhaps also to the DM, that impinge on any given behavior. A central challenge of social science is how to operationalize and tightly define some of the key forces. In my experience, conceptualizing a valuable new data set is far more challenging and impactful than building a model of choice with a new latent variable. It is the lack of ideas on data enrichment, not our lack of ability to imagine richer forces that might be at work, that limits the reach of economic theory. As a matter of personal choice, I am not comfortable modeling forces that I can see no clear path to measuring. More likely than not, advances in measurement technology will inspire modeling in the coming decades more than vice versa.

The third step in the engineering process is to implement the corresponding measurements and conduct empirical analyses. This is ongoing, as detailed in the applied lectures of the book that are outlined at the end of this first lecture.

The engineering method makes no explicit mention of preferences or beliefs (or economics for that matter). There are many other important models of behavior to posit as the new standard modeling framework, and each creates opportunity and need for new dedicated forms of theory-led data engineering. The key in each case is to define appropriate new standard observations.

1.8 My Path to Data Engineering

Before providing more granular details on the lectures themselves, I will outline the personal research journey that preceded them. Early in my academic career, I noticed, as do many, the rigid boundaries within and between social scientific disciplines. I saw them then, as I do now, as at once deep, pervasive, and scientifically bankrupt. A particular limitation is the extent to which theory and measurement advance in separate silos. It is with great deliberation that I rejected this approach and walked a different path.

I began my research career as an essentially pure theorist with a strong desire to interact in real time with measurement. Intuitions about fundamental forces can get you only so far. I was also struck by how relatively easy it was to name and model a new latent force or interact previously modeled forces without ever specifying how to measure them. Far easier than correspondingly advancing measurement. This created a deep tension that I found hard to resolve. It prevented me from wanting to join any of the existing subdisciplines of economics and social science more broadly.

I fought hard to keep much of my theoretical research close to application. But my frustration with the divide between model and measurement grew steadily stronger as my research advanced. A case in point relates to my early research on indivisibilities. John Leahy and I were struck by the extent to which inertia might prevent information from being transmitted and thought this might underlie many market crashes. We developed a corresponding model (Caplin and Leahy, 1994). I hoped that this would be followed by rich efforts on the part of more applied economists to measure information. Seeing this not happen gave me a first insight into the difficulty in identifying informational constraints. The research described herein reflects my continued focus on this issue.

The second push in this direction derived from theoretical work on psychology and economics, beginning with psychological expected utility theory (Caplin and Leahy, 2001). We modeled preferences over psychological states associated with subjective uncertainty, naming such examples as anxiety, love of surprise, etc. We got methodological pushback on the operational content of the theory. We were asked a reasonable question: What precisely is the operational imprint of psychological states in behavior (Kang and Camerer, 2018, illustrate how this can be done with additional physiological measurements)? Technically, what behavior reveals whether rejection of information is due to a love of surprise or the additional worry that learning might cause (Caplin and Leahy, 2004)? An example of the former might be wanting to not be told about a birthday present until the day itself and of the latter the desire to avoid learning potentially worrying facts about health about which little can be done (Oster *et al.*, 2013).

I took the operational challenge to heart but understood it to be much deeper. What behavior reveals what people know? What behavior reveals asymmetry in what two people know? What behavior reveals an out-of-equilibrium strategy? How about ambiguity *per se* and possible aversion to it? How can we insist that states of anxiety be operationalized without insisting on the same for imperfect information, asymmetric information, costs of learning, ambiguity, or out-of-equilibrium strategies? This is transparently a matter of academic convention rather than scientific integrity.

There is something liberating about calling scientific incoherence by its name. Of course, the challenge is to move beyond discontent to liberate new forms of scientific progress. In my case, that process started in neuroeconomics and on the dopamine system (Caplin *et al.*, 2010). That involved the explicit expansion of data to include dopaminergic signals to characterize dopaminergic reward prediction error theory (Schultz *et al.*, 1997; Bayer and Glimcher, 2005). With ideal measurement, the theory could be of massive value for separate identification of beliefs and rewards. Unfortunately, at this stage, measurement is far too crude and cumbersome.

The next steps in my research progress involved efforts to identify promising enhancements of standard choice data to separate out knowledge and beliefs from utility. This is in itself a lightly trodden path. An early example, due to Ericsson and Simon (1980), involves recording and analyzing verbal statements descriptive of the process of learning: the so-called verbal protocol analysis. Likewise concerned with procedure, Payne *et al.* (1993) introduced data on mouse clicks to understand information search and choice. Other search-related psychological data include eye tracking and even neural activity. Johnson *et al.* (2002) showed the value of this data in uncovering information that is simply not accessed and hence cannot have produced any updating.

The challenge from an engineering perspective is that no one has tightly modeled the words that are spoken, the precise pattern of mouse-click activity, or eye movements and their relationship to standard choice behavior. These data are also far removed from the Block and Marschak ideal of staying close to "the nature of economic observations." What then to do?

The first ideas I focused on that hold promise relate formally to one of the most prominent theories of costly learning: the theory of search due to Stigler (1961). In its standard form, it specifies a fixed cost of understanding each available option in a choice set. Once the fixed cost is paid, that option is fully internalized and understood at no additional cost. Hence, it involves full information among searched options, and only the information that prior beliefs reveal for those that are not searched. In this sense, it is a hybrid of complete and incomplete information. The behavioral essence of the theory is that the DM either maximizes utility among those items considered or chooses an outside option about which they learn nothing. In this sense, it links to recent bounded rationality models that allow for the DM to stop searching according to a simple rule, as in Manzini and Mariotti (2014) and also as in the "consideration set" model of marketing.

While search models are appealing and important, there is a clear operational problem in standard behavioral data. Any choice can be rationalized in a model in which what is chosen is the only object searched with unsearched alternatives believed to be worse. There are no restrictions whatever. As Block and Marschak stated, the goal of the researcher in the face of such a fundamental identification problem is to design and generate a richer data set in which the theory has bite. The question from a data engineering perspective is how to enhance this data set to make the theories of search falsifiable. If these broad tests are passed, one can specialize in particular models of search. If not, one can explore less restrictive models, for example, in which options are, partially understood.

Precisely to this end, Mark Dean, Daniel Martin, and I proposed the use of choice process data, which captures provisional choices during the search process, to better identify theories of learning (Caplin and Dean, 2011; Caplin *et al.*, 2011). Such choice process data can be gathered experimentally by randomizing the time at which an item in the shopping basket will be recorded as purchased so that it is always optimal to place in the shopping basket the item currently regarded as the best. The real idea here is that one gets to see the decision to continue as well as to stop.

We published the first experimental implementation in Caplin *et al.* (2011), in which we incentivized subjects to continuously update their perceived optimal choice and then choose when to stop searching. In that implementation, we asked subjects to choose the largest of a set of arithmetic operations in word form (e.g., four plus eight minus three minus six plus twelve). We varied complexity and choice set size. In all cases, we broadly confirmed the basic prediction of search theory that chosen options should be replaced by others of higher value. Furthermore, the data were consistent, to a first order, with a satisficing stopping rule by which the search stopped when the value rose above a threshold determined by the complexity of the decision problem.

There are two particular limitations of choice process data that drove us to return to the drawing board to engineer an additional data set. First, choice process data is of most value in a limited class of learning models involving sequential search. In these cases, and only in these cases, can one infer that replacement of one option with another implies a preference for the newly picked one. With other forms of learning, prevarication is likely and is indeed common in applications, as in Agranov *et al.* (2015) related to the guessing game (Nagel, 1995). In brief, we found that subjects moved back and forth to some extent as if changing their opinion about all options over time. Such partial understanding is the rule, and the prevarication it produces provides a limited and intricate window on learning. The second factor that limits the appeal of choice process data as a launching pad for the science of mistakes is that it is too far from the Block and Marschak ideal of being close to the nature of standard economic observations so that it is rarely available in practice. It was this continued discontent with choice process data that spurred the data innovations that are central to these lectures.

1.9 Guide to the Lectures

In closing this lecture, I present a brief guide to those that remain. Lectures 2–8 introduce and analyze precisely the ideal data set that has been central to recent progress. Lectures 9–11 are more traditional and solve a canonical model based on costs of learning: the Shannon model. The remaining lectures lay out research agendas that translate the theory to applied settings in data science, economics, and psychology. Some of these agendas are well under way, and others are in the initiation phase.

The material in the early lectures is highly abstract and technical. Key definitions are provided. In some cases, proofs are provided. In others, the reader is left either to prove the result themselves or to refer to the named sources. The former might be preferable, in part because it will uncover shortcomings. Please let me know. But the larger value is that what is known at this point is so very limited, and new perspectives are of potentially great scientific value.

(1) **Part 1: The Operational Model of Mistakes**: Lectures 2–8 introduce and analyze the basic observations that allow us to model and measure errors.

    (a) **Lecture 2: Operationalizing the Blackwell Model**: The basic economic model that separates utility and mistakes is the Bayesian expected utility model of experimentation and choice due to Blackwell (1953). This lecture operationalizes the model in ideal behavioral data. The linear **no improving action switches** (NIAS) inequalities of Caplin and Martin (2011, 2015) are introduced.

    (b) **Lecture 3: Costly Information Representations and Attention Cycles**: Mistakes in the basic model arise because DMs don't know everything that they in principle could. Implicitly, this is due to costs of learning. This lecture introduces the model of costly learning and the linear **no improving attention cycles** (NIAC) inequalities of Caplin and Dean (2015) and their role in characterizing what the DM wants, what they know, and patterns in their mistakes. Results of Rockafellar (2015) are of great value in the analysis of learning costs.

(c) **Lecture 4: All Rationalizing Cost Functions**: Costs of learning are of equivalent importance to costs of production. Just as in the case of production, learning costs come in all flavors and types. We have just seen the tip of this particular iceberg. The fact that it is hard to specify costs of learning *a priori* raises the importance of research to better measure such costs. Methods are outlined for recovering all cost functions that can rationalize observed data for any given utility function. These draw from Caplin and Dean (2015) and Caplin *et al.* (2023c).

(d) **Lecture 5: Revealed Bayesian Learning: A Full Characterization**: Following Caplin *et al.*, 2023c, this lecture provides a complete characterization of utility functions, forms of learning, and cost functions that can rationalize state-dependent stochastic choice data (SDSC) from a set of decision problems as resulting from rational inattention. In doing this, it also provides methods for identifying precisely when learning may be explained by fixed capacity constraints rather than as a result of a flexible investment in learning. I also characterize models of fixed information, in which learning is fixed and essentially independent of the decision context. Important fixed information models in psychology include signal detection theory (Green and Swets, 1966). In economics, information is treated as fixed in various decision-theoretic models and in models of incomplete and asymmetric information, in which private knowledge is pre-specified by the model builder rather than being endogenous to incentives. The implied restrictions on data turn out to be a variation on the Blackwellian theme.

(e) **Lecture 6: Full Recovery of Costs and Welfare**: This lecture shows that when utility is known, the cost function can be fully recovered in suitably designed data (Caplin *et al.*, 2020).

The method is readily implemented experimentally. Methods of recovering welfare are also outlined.

(f) **Lecture 7: Comparison of Revealed Experiments**: In this lecture, I provide a revealed preference refinement of Blackwell (1953) on the comparison of experiments. There are no cost considerations in this comparison. Rather, behavioral data are used to welfare rank different presentations of the same information, following Caplin and Martin (2021).

(g) **Lecture 8: Posterior-Separable Cost Functions and Behavior**: This lecture summarizes the results of Caplin *et al.* (2022a) that behaviorally characterize the Shannon model of rational inattention (Sims, 2003, 2010) and some key generalizations: posterior separability, uniform posterior separability (Morris and Strack, 2019; Hébert and Woodford, 2019; Bloedel and Zhong, 2021), and invariant posterior separability (Hebert and La'O, 2020; Angeletos and Sastry, 2019).

(2) **Part 2: The Shannon Model of Rational Inattention**: The second part of the book introduces and illustrates methods for solving the paradigmatic model of flexible optimal learning: the Shannon model. While special, this will continue to be of great importance due to its sophistication, subtlety, and the reasonable nature of the qualitative answers it provides. I believe it will be of equivalent importance to the theory of sequential search.

(a) **Lecture 9: Solving the Shannon Model**: This lecture introduces two very different methods of solution (Mattsson and Weibull, 2002; Matejka and McKay, 2015; Caplin *et al.*, 2019) and provides a series of examples that illustrate the valuable interplay between them.

(b) **Lecture 10: Optimal Consideration Sets and the ILR Hyperplanes**: This lecture introduces and illustrates a method of solving for optimal strategies for all priors due to Caplin *et al.* (2019).

(c) **Lecture 11: Equilibrium, Exchangeability, and Symmetry**: Equilibrium conditions are applied to settings in which solutions can be found. Of most interest are the symmetry conditions introduced by Bucher and Caplin (2021), which included the exchangeability of prior beliefs. These play a powerful role in rational inattention theory and, to some extent, substitute for the i.i.d assumption that makes search theory tractable. The central application characterizes strategic uncertainty in matching markets. Other applications are waiting in the research wings.

(3) **Part 3: Applications**: The third part of the book presents applied research on mistakes that leans heavily, but far from exclusively, on the theoretical approach developed in prior lectures. In all cases, new data are deliberately engineered to better understand mistakes. This third part is entirely distinct in style and in intent from the first two parts in several respects. It is essentially a series of research agendas that are in their early stages. To the extent possible, each lecture is self-contained and can be read without deep engagement with prior technical material. In making the transition to applications, I make opening and closing remarks in Part 3 about the definition of a "state" in applied settings. The availability of SDSC depends on this definition, which is more flexible in application than one might imagine as a pure theorist.

(a) **Lecture 12: Modeling Machine Learning**: If machines are not already the most important learners and DMs in the world, they soon will be. Yet, machine learning algorithms are effectively black boxes that elude interpretation. I outline the research of Caplin *et al.*, 2022b that develops and tests an **as if** representation of what machines learn and why. Our model precisely mirrors the approach of Part 1 in treating learning as a process of signal gathering, belief formation, and choice. If anything, the application to machine learning is tighter than to human learning since ideal data are available, and few would want to argue that algorithms have immutable biases as may be the case for humans. The key methodological device involves applying a standard decision-theoretic method to algorithmic performance by deliberately varying the loss function that the algorithm is minimizing. We characterize two models that involve different conditional performance as the loss function is varied. In **feasibility-based machine learning**, the machine chooses among a feasible set of Blackwell experiments as it seeks to learn about observations in the test set. In **cost-based machine learning**, the algorithm trades off the benefits of conducting a more informative experiment against additional (and not directly observable) costs of learning. In a first test case, the manner in which machine predictions change as the loss function is manipulated is consistent with cost-based learning, but not with feasibility-based learning. Using the methods of Part 1, we recover sharp bounds on the structural cost parameters.

(b) **Lecture 13: Teaching, Testing, and Learning**: Human learning, no less than machine learning, requires advances in the science of mistakes. A key role of teaching is surely to lower costs for as yet unrealized future decision problems. Incentives for students to learn depend on methods of testing and teaching, which depend, in turn, on what tests reveal. De Finetti (1965) and Savage (1971) proposed that **proper scoring rules**, which incentivize truthful revelation of subjective probabilities, should play a prominent role in human learning. Following the encouraging findings of Bickel (2010), I make the case for further experimentation with such protocols. Each class provides a natural opportunity for such experimentation. A key to the possible value of proper scoring rules in the teaching process is the information they reveal on students' degree of **calibration**: their accuracy in understanding their level of uncertainty. Calibration is important in the field: Currie and MacLeod (2017) show that physicians not only have diverse **task** skills in operating procedure but also have diverse **decision-making** skills. An important open question that requires combined modeling and measurement is the extent to which such calibration is itself teachable, as Savage himself believed.

(c) **Lecture 14: Management Skills and Productive Efficiency**: We don't stop making mistakes when we leave school. We just stop measuring them. In rare cases, ideal SDSC data, or a close approximation to it, are available (e.g., sporting events, medical diagnoses, and quality control). In more typical cases, behavioral data alone do not allow clean identification of errors. In this lecture, I focus on the development and deployment of cognitive instruments that help identify poor decisions in important domains, as in the work of Lusardi and Mitchell on financial literacy and financial outcomes. I outline ongoing research with David Deming,

Soren Leth-Petersen, and Ben Weidmann that applies analogous methods to the study of management skills and business performance. Recent research has indicated the profound role that "good management" plays in improving productive efficiency. In a first research stage, we build a rational inattention model of the manager's job as being to efficiently allocate resources in a complex and changing environment. We then develop and deploy corresponding experimental protocols, ranging from the abstract to the realistic. We are planning to deploy a corresponding short survey instrument into the Danish population registries, together with additional survey questions directly related to management experience. The final stage will be to link the survey-measured management skills with the measures of actual management performance in the registries.

(d) **Lecture 15: Decision-Making Skills, Job Transitions, and Income**: Decision-making skills matter in all phases of life. While being a manager of a fixed group of workers is a particularly salient example of this, there is no realm of behavior in which such skills are irrelevant. Deming (2021) hypothesized that decision-making skills are of growing importance in determining life-cycle income. I outline planned research to operationalize Deming's hypothesis, focusing on labor market transitions: decisions on whether and how to search for jobs, including when to quit, what to do in the face of an impending layoff, when to take time out of the labor force and retool, and when to retire. When and how such transitions are made is much studied in administrative data. However, decision quality is as much about actions that were **not** taken as much as those that were and about what was **not** known as what was. To make such transitions effectively requires workers to be well informed, realistic about options, and to have relevant search skills. In addition to designing instruments to measure these skills and fielding them in administrative data, research in this area requires a detailed study of the beliefs that guide behavior. I outline the Copenhagen Life Panel, a new panel implemented in the Danish Population Registries, designed precisely to measure beliefs about possible job transitions (Caplin *et al.*, 2023b). I outline planned research, combining the resulting panel data on the evolution of beliefs with measures of relevant cognitive skills to parse out the importance of various decision-making skills in making effective job transitions not only during the standard career but also when the career job has terminated. Recent research shows that many retirees would like to return to work (Ameriks *et al.*, 2020a). For how many was the initial retirement based on illusory beliefs about a possible later return to work?

(e) **Lecture 16: Communication Policies**: The rational inattention revolution was launched, in part, to capture cognitive constraints relevant to monetary policy design (Sims, 1998, 2010). In that arena, important lessons have been learned about the need for clear communication of policy intent (e.g., forward guidance). In the case of monetary policy, the policy tools are incomprehensible to the public at large, which makes communication inherently challenging. Caplin *et al.* (2022c) show that limits in comprehension apply even to the simplest and most personally relevant policies. We find a large gap between public policy plans and public perception about the age at which those of working age will become eligible for social security. This appears largely to be a result of passive rather than active policy communication: when relevant information is actively provided the gap between plan and perception essentially disappears. The need for active communication is far broader than this. I outline the case of cognitive decline. Recent evidence shows that those in the pre-decline phase are worried not only above possible future decline but also about possible future unawareness of that decline (Ameriks *et al.*, 2023). The policy challenge is for financial institutions and the social security administration to develop communication strategies before decline has gone too far and to set in place appropriate protective measures. The final case study shows that clear communication improves the quality of justice (Caplin *et al.*, 2023a). A key step in the judicial process is a formal review of a complex case file to extract key legal "facts" that determine the initial verdict. In a field study, we are able to add an index to make the file easier to navigate prior to extraction of these facts. Perhaps not surprisingly, this resulted in significantly fewer successful appeals. After diligent research into how clarity of the case file improved the quality of justice, we now have an answer. Rather than listing more facts, fewer were listed, clearly more to the legal point.

4. **Epilogue**: There is a genre called social science fiction that speculates on the future of society. I end instead with social-science fiction. I envision a future in which social science evolves far more rapidly as data and model interact in closer to real time. The key to such a progressive future is institutional change that promotes increased teamwork across key academic and applied fields.

Part 1

THE OPERATIONAL MODEL

Lecture 2

Operationalizing the Blackwell Model

The goals of this lecture are:

1. To formally introduce the Blackwell model of experimentation, expected utility maximization, and the space of strategies as suited to purpose.
2. To formalize the Block and Marschak identification challenge and to understand why it calls for data engineering with new basic observations.
3. To introduce state-dependent stochastic choice data (SDSC), the basic observations that form the analytic core of the book, as well as revealed posteriors, experiments, and strategies.
4. To precisely pose the question of what it means for SDSC to be rationalized by the Blackwell model and to illustrate data sets that can and cannot be so rationalized.
5. To introduce and illustrate the no improving action switch (NIAS) characterization of such rationalizable data sets.
6. To prove the resulting characterization theorem.

Delivering all of this material in a single lecture is excessive. So, the real goal of this lecture is to permit students to review the material *ex post* and accomplish the above goals by themselves. This comment applies to all of the lectures that follow.

2.1 Blackwell Experiments and Bayes' Plausibility

An experiment, as defined by Blackwell, comprises a finite set of states $\omega \in \Omega$, a finite set of signals $s \in S$, and a mapping $\pi : \Omega \longrightarrow \Delta(S)$ that

27

indicates for each state the probabilities over signals. A trivial case involves two states and two signals, the first of which is more likely in state 1 and the second in state 2:

$$\pi(s_1|\omega_1) = \pi(s_2|\omega_2) = 0.8,$$
$$\pi(s_2|\omega_1) = \pi(s_1|\omega_2) = 0.2.$$

Updating is Bayesian. Given a prior μ over states with both states equiprobable, Bayes' rule implies that the two signals are equiprobable. Applying Bayes' rule directly, we can derive the posterior belief after signal 1 as $(0.8, 0.2)$ and that after signal 2 as $(0.2, 0.8)$. This is a standard Blackwell experiment in that each distinct signal gives rise to a distinct posterior. This is far from general. For example, in models of continuous learning, many different paths of learning can produce the same posterior belief.

In the developments that follow, it is more useful to bypass the subjective signals, which are particularly hard to operationalize, and instead define an experiment as a Bayes' plausible distribution of posteriors, as in Kamenica and Gentzkow (2011). Given $\mu \in \Delta(\Omega)$, we define $Q(\mu)$ as all those distributions of posteriors with finite support that satisfy Bayes' rule:

$$Q(\mu) \equiv \{Q \in \Delta(\Delta(\Omega)) | \sum_{\gamma \in \text{supp} Q} \gamma Q(\gamma) = \mu\}. \tag{1}$$

For our purposes going forward, an experiment comprises a prior $\mu \in \Delta(\Omega)$ and a Bayes' consistent distribution of posteriors $Q \in Q(\mu)$. Where possible, the prior is suppressed for notational simplicity.

Note that one can directly map any standard Blackwell experiment into its corresponding posterior-based experiment. In the simple example above, each posterior, 0.8 and 0.2, is equally likely under the Bayesian operator. Hence, the definition in terms of posteriors is simply

$$Q(0.8, 0.2) = Q(0.2, 0.8) = 0.5.$$

2.2   Choices and Utility Maximization

The Blackwell model includes a choice stage. There is a finite set of actions A and a finite prize space Z. Whenever we take the DM's perspective, we include in the model an expected utility function $u : Z \longrightarrow \mathbb{R}$. The

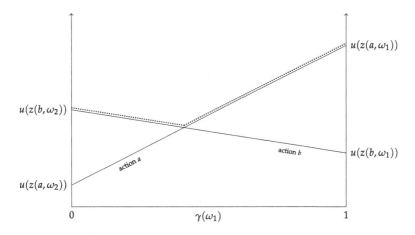

Figure 2.1 Geometry of action choice.

Blackwell model is then closed with the assumption that choices maximize expected utility at each posterior. Technically, at each posterior belief $\gamma \in \Delta(\Omega)$, the DM solves the optimal action choice problem. Figure 2.1 illustrates the standard geometry of optimization in a case with two actions and two states, with action a offering a higher payoff in state 1 and action b in state 2. The horizontal axis records the probability of state 1. Action a pays off strictly more than action b in state 1, and vice versa in state 2. The linearity of the payoff to each action reflects the linearity of expected utility in beliefs. The posterior at which the actions are indifferent (where the expected utility lines cross) is strictly interior to the unit interval. Action b is optimal when state 1 is believed to be less likely than this, and action a when it is more likely. The expected utility of better choice is therefore defined by the upper envelope indicated by the dashed line in the figure.

2.3 Strategies of Learning and Choice

Given our operational perspective, there are many cases in which the utility function is unknown and also in which learning strategies are chosen. For that reason, when formalizing the strategy space in an arbitrary decision problem, it is best to separate out beliefs and actions choices from the utility they produce. Fixing in the background a finite state space Ω, a decision problem is a pair (μ, A), with $\mu \in \Delta(\Omega)$ specifying the prior probabilities of the states and A specifying the finite set of available actions $a \in A$. The strategy space comprises Bayes' consistent distributions of posteriors with finite support and corresponding mixed action strategies. We call this space $\Lambda(\mu, A)$, the posterior-based strategies of learning and choice:

$$\Lambda(\mu, A) \equiv \{(Q, q) | Q \in Q(\mu), q : \operatorname{supp} Q \longrightarrow \Delta(A)\}. \tag{2}$$

Given $(Q, q) \in \Lambda(\mu, A)$ and $u : Z \longrightarrow \mathbb{R}$, $G(Q, q|u)$ is defined as the corresponding gross expected utility:

$$G(Q, q|u) \equiv \sum_{\gamma \in \operatorname{supp} Q} \sum_{a \in A} Q(\gamma) q(a|\gamma) \sum_{\omega \in \Omega} \gamma(\omega) u(z(a, \omega)). \tag{3}$$

The right-hand side (RHS) is the expected utility of action a given the posterior γ, multiplied by $q(a|\gamma)$, the probability of choosing action a given γ, and by $Q(\gamma)$, the probability of posterior γ. The summation is over all actions in A and posteriors in the support of Q.

The objective of the DM in the Blackwell model is to identify optimal strategies, which is where the prizes Z and the expected utility function $u : Z \longrightarrow \mathbb{R}$ enter the picture. The DM is hypothesized to pick expected-utility-maximizing actions at each posterior. Figure 2.2 illustrates an experiment with interior prior μ, in which the strategy involves two surrounding posteriors $\gamma < \mu < \gamma'$ and corresponding optimal choices: action b at γ and action a at γ'. The overall level of expected utility in this strategy is defined by the height of the corresponding line between the posteriors as it crosses the prior: This is marked as point v in Figure 2.2.

Given a distribution of posteriors, Bayesian expected utility (BEU) maximization is assumed: Optimal strategies are all those at which optimal actions are chosen at all posteriors.

If this was a standard course in economic theory, I would now go on to work further on the logic of optimization. The first concern would be to verify that optimal strategies exist. But that is not at all my research goal. The key question is not about existence but rather about how one can, taking this model as given, find a data set in which to operationalize it. We are on the hunt for a data set in which this standard Blackwell model is testable. If such a data set can be found, our second goal will be to recover all possible rationalizations. In particular, we are interested in what can be learned about the underlying experiment and utility function. It is to that basic challenge we now turn after making precise the Block and Marschak

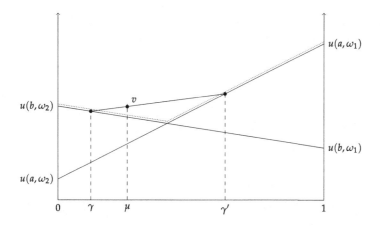

Figure 2.2 Geometry of total expected utility.

call for new basic observations to operationalize models in which beliefs and utilities are both of the essence, most essentially the Blackwell model itself.

A word on this form of inverse reasoning. My co-authors and I have often felt that we are swimming against the tide. The tradition is to start with a model, work out its internal logic, and only then (if ever) pin down its observable consequences. Following Samuelson, the method we employ to a large extent inverts this. The goal is to imagine a set of basic observations in which to operationalize the Blackwell model in the senses specified in the last paragraph.

2.4 The Block and Marschak Identification Challenge

To formalize the operational challenge, let's take up Block and Marschak's primary example of stochastic choice: repeated choice between two 10-ton carloads of uncertain merchandise. To state this formally, consider a retailer choosing two 10-ton carloads of perishable inspection goods. The choice set for the retailer is one of the two suppliers: Call them a and b. In state ω_1, a is better, and in state ω_2, b is better. Suppose further that the retailer is a risk-neutral, expected profit maximizer and, for simplicity, that one and only one of the truckloads is of a fixed high rather than low value:

$$v^H > v^L.$$

Note that in this case, we are allowing ourselves to identify one prize as better than the other *a priori*. In the more general treatment later, there will be no such luxury: Utilities themselves need to be jointly operationalized with the experiment.

The reason for starting with this simple example is that it allows us to get to the heart of the operational challenge in short order. What is the standard choice data that the econometrician gets to see if they follow the Block and Marschak formulation involving stochastic choice data? All they see in this case is the proportion of the time that supplier *a* is chosen. To be concrete, suppose that supplier *a* is chosen 80% of the time and supplier *b* 20% of the time. What does this teach the econometrician about how well informed the DM might have been, how many mistakes they made, and of what form?

One obvious possibility, implicit in current methods in the literature on discrete choice, is that the choice is perfectly informed and reflects the underlying truth. So, the data are consistent with there being no mistakes whatsoever. In this world of perfect information with the subjective prior $\mu(\omega_1) = 0.8$, the perfect signals will deliver the two possible posteriors as $(1,0)$ with probability 0.8, at which action *a* maximizes the expected profit and is hence chosen, and $(0,1)$ with probability 0.2, at which action *b* maximizes the expected profit and is hence chosen. Assuming that all subjective probabilities in the theory are objective, this is a clear candidate explanation for the observed stochastic choice behavior.

The challenge is that we can construct infinitely many other rationalizations. For example, suppose *a* is good 60% of the time and there is perfect information half of the time. In this case, *a* is always chosen when nothing is learned due to the asymmetric prior. In the 50% of the time in which information is perfect, *a* is better and hence chosen 60% of the time, and *b* the remaining 40%. Note that there are three possible posteriors. At posteriors $(1,0)$ and $(0.6,0.4)$, *a* is chosen. At posterior $(0,1)$, action *b* is chosen. Overall, *a* is chosen with a probability of 0.8, just as in the case of perfect information with the prior belief that *a* is good being 0.8. There are infinitely many other possible explanations for precisely the same choice probabilities. All that is required is that possible signals make *a* the better choice 80% of the time and *b* 20% of the time. This is precisely the Block and Marschak identification problem. Many standard Bayesian *EU* theories might produce the same stochastic choice data. In what data set and to what extent can these different theories be separately identified? To quote Samuelson:

> Just as we do not claim to know by introspection the signals people are seeing, many will argue that we cannot know their posteriors either just by observing what they choose in a given situation.

What to do? The challenge is to specify a choice-based data set that helps in separately identifying utilities over prizes and beliefs about the states of the world.

2.5 State-Dependent Stochastic Choice Data

The research in these lectures is based on what I believe to be the simplest and most central answer to the Block and Marschak challenge. In applied work, the smoking gun for inattention is the apparent failure to respond to underlying realities: sales taxes (Chetty *et al.*, 2009), available scholarships in school choice (Hastings and Weinstein, 2008; Hoxby and Turner, 2015), etc. This key idea also lies behind the psychometric tradition dating back to Weber (1834). With handheld weights, for example, the ability to correctly identify the heavier object has been shown to be based on their relative magnitudes. Figure 2.3 shows a typical psychometric curve, with the horizontal axis showing the difference in the objective weights between the left and right hands and the vertical axis showing the proportion of the time that the right hand is selected as having the heavier weight. The standard interpretation of this curve is that it reveals perceptual randomness, in that when weights are close together, mistaken choices are frequent, while when they are far apart, mistaken choices are rare.

What makes the psychometric interpretation compelling is the obvious theory that a failure to identify the heavier weight reflects the mistaken belief that it is, in fact, heavier rather than a desire to get the answer wrong. What makes it harder to identify mistakes in general decision problems is that, in addition to information being imperfect, preferences are unknown to the econometrician. The challenge is to specify a choice-based data set that helps in separately identifying utilities over prizes and beliefs about the states of the world.

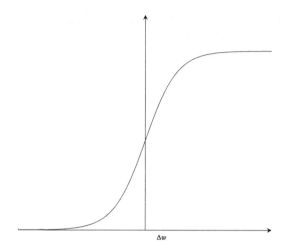

Δw

Figure 2.3   Generic psychometric curve.

The key idea on which these lectures are based is to abstract the essentials of the psychometric method for broader application. Viewed abstractly, psychometric experiments measure how patterns of stochastic choice respond to changes in the underlying state of the world. The natural generalization is then to measure how patterns of stochastic choice depend on the underlying state of the world as observed by the econometrician.

State-dependent stochastic choice (SDSC) data is no more and no less than the generalized version of the standard psychometric data set. Given states $\omega \in \Omega$ and actions $a \in A$, SDSC comprises a joint distribution over actions and states, $\mathbf{P}(a, \omega)$. Where possible, I mark data objects in bold and theory objects in plain. This is important to keep track of since we will really be dealing with two distinct worlds, that of theory and that of data, and considering how to move back and forth between them.

Abstractly, for any (μ, A), we can derive the correspondingly possible data sets as $\mathcal{P}(\mu, A)$. It is taken that the econometrician knows the choice set (hence all state-dependent prizes) and has seen a particular data set $\mathbf{P}(a, \omega)$.

SDSC was formally introduced by Caplin and Martin (2011, 2015). We used it to define revealed experiments and to better operationalize the Blackwell model. Since then, it has been established that this form of data can be further engineered to recover utility and beliefs, to test the general theory of costly information acquisition, to identify the form of the cost function, and even to recover costs and welfare. The results are far stronger than anticipated at the start of the research journey, which makes me optimistic that there is much more to be found both in theory and in application. The material is excellent for experimental design, as I will illustrate. It is also available, or at least partially so, in myriad applications. When the data are more limited, an appropriately operational definition of the state or econometric innovation will be in order: See Part 3 on the state space in particular.

2.6 Revealed Prior

There are two ground rules in formalizing the use of SDSC to operationalize the expected utility model. First, some key model elements are treated as commonly understood by the DM and the econometrician: the possible states Ω, the available actions A, and the state-dependent prizes $z(a, \omega)$. Second, the econometrician is assumed to observe choices from this fixed decision setting infinitely often, with different realized states of the world drawn from a fixed prior μ. With this, note that there is a natural candidate for the prior that is revealed in the data. We call this the **revealed prior** $\mu_{\mathbf{P}}(\omega) \in \Delta(\Omega)$:

$$\mu_{\mathbf{P}}(\omega) \equiv \sum_{a \in A} \mathbf{P}(a, \omega).$$

When looking to rationalize observed data, we impose a form of rational expectations. We equate the prior and action set as observed by the econometrician with that hypothesized to have been faced by the DM. This means that the empirical frequency of states defines the DM's subjective prior: Indeed, it means that we are going to think about the DM as having faced precisely the decision problem $(\mu_{\mathbf{P}}, A)$. While we maintain this assumption throughout the book, it is easy to imagine important situations where it is likely to be false. What comes most directly to mind are "interference" tasks, such as the Stroop task, in which there is a first instinctual response that may be driven by a prior that is hard to overturn. This is a very interesting road to travel, and indeed, this particular research journey is in its earliest stages. That said, we retain a standard form of rational expectations throughout this lecture series. There is quite enough to be done even within the resulting structure. Note that what this effectively means is that the decision problem (μ, A) is agreed upon between the DM and the econometrician.

What remains is to think about what the data say about the posterior-based strategy (subjective signals are of no use *per se* in this data-based perspective) that the DM adopted. To that end, we now revisit the truck example with SDSC in mind. Recall the challenge. Two suppliers have been picked repeatedly, with supplier a picked with a probability of 0.8 and supplier b with a probability of 0.2 We noted that this might be explained if, in fact, supplier a is better 80% of the time and information is perfect. But there are infinitely many other explanations: All the data reveal is that a is believed to be at least as good as b at least 80% of the time and b to be at least as good as a at least 20% of the time. One such possibility is a world in which a is good 60% of the time and there is perfect information half of the time. In this case, a is always chosen when nothing is learned due to the asymmetric prior. In the 50% of the time in which information is perfect, a is better and hence chosen 60% of the time, and b the remaining 40%. Note that there are three possible posteriors. At posteriors $(1,0)$ and $(0.6, 0.4)$, a is chosen. At posterior $(0,1)$, action b is chosen. Overall, a is chosen with a probability of 0.8, just as in the case of perfect information, with the prior belief that a is good being 0.8.

The state of the world in the eyes of an ideal observer identifies the true high-value supplier. In the example, what more can SDSC reveal that stochastic choice data alone cannot? Clearly, the econometrician would now notice the difference between perfect and imperfect information in priors as revealed to the observer. With perfect information,

$$\mu_{\mathbf{P}}(\omega_1) = \mathbf{P}(a, \omega_1) + \mathbf{P}(b, \omega_1) = 0.8.$$

In the three posterior cases possible, the posteriors are $(1,0)$ with a probability of 0.3, $(0,1)$ with a probability of 0.2, and $(0.6, 0.4)$ otherwise, so that the revealed prior is 0.6:

$$\mu_{\mathbf{P}}(\omega_1) = \mathbf{P}(a, \omega_1) + \mathbf{P}(b, \omega_1) = 0.6.$$

The proportion of errors is visible in this simple example, given that we observe both when a choice is appropriate and when it is not. It is this feature that underlies the great value of SDSC for the science of mistakes. Yet, there are limits on what SDSC allows us to infer that need to be understood since there is still averaging involved, as we now analyze.

2.7 From Strategy to SDSC

In order to work analytically with SDSC and relate it to the Blackwell model, we must think about the SDSC that any strategy $(Q, q) \in \Lambda(\mu, A)$ would generate. Indeed, there are times in which one treats the strategy space precisely as the choice of SDSC as a strategy: In particular, this is the approach of Matejka and McKay (2015). Note that this is a theory object and, as such, is not in bold. Technically, we define $P_{(Q,q)} \in \mathcal{P}(\mu, A)$ by

$$P_{(Q,q)}(a, \omega) = \sum_{\gamma \in \text{supp } Q} q(a|\gamma) Q(\gamma) \gamma(\omega). \tag{4}$$

Note that the mapping is not one to one. Many different strategies produce the same data, as the following examples illustrate.

Example A. Consider a two-equiprobable-state, two-action-world, and posterior-based strategy (Q^A, q^A) with only one possible posterior. For Bayes' consistency, this posterior is 0.5 for sure, $Q^A(0.5) = 1$. Suppose further that a and b are equally likely chosen at this posterior:

$$q^A(a|0.5) = q^A(b|0.5) = 0.5.$$

One can now apply formula (4) to work out the corresponding SDSC as

$$
\begin{aligned}
P_{(Q^A, q^A)}(a, \omega_1) &= 1 * 0.5 * 0.5 \\
&= 0.25 = P_{(Q^A, q^A)}(a, \omega_2) \\
&= P_{(Q^A, q^A)}(b, \omega_1) = P_{(Q^A, q^A)}(b, \omega_2).
\end{aligned}
$$

Example B. Now, consider an alternative strategy, (Q^B, q^B), in this same decision problem, with two possible posteriors 0.25 and 0.75 so that $Q^B(0.25) = Q^B(0.75) = 0.5$ and with b and a chosen with equal probability in both states:

$$q^B(a|0.25) = q^B(b|0.25) = q^B(a|0.75) = q^B(b|0.75) = 0.5.$$

Applying (4) again, we get

$$
\begin{aligned}
P_{(Q^B, q^B)}(a, \omega_1) &= Q^B(0.25) * 0.5 * 0.25 + Q^B(0.75) * 0.5 * 0.75 \\
&= 0.25 = P_{(Q^B, q^B)}(a, \omega_2) \\
&= P_{(Q^B, q^B)}(b, \omega_1) = P_{(Q^B, q^B)}(b, \omega_2).
\end{aligned}
$$

The above clearly makes the point that many distinct posterior-based strategies correspond to the same SDSC strategy:

$$P_{(Q^A, q^A)} = P_{(Q^B, q^B)}.$$

This raises an interesting question. Which such strategy should we be thinking about when we take an SDSC data set as the given object? Intuitively, it seems that we don't want to unduly complicate so that the first posterior-based strategy seems like the one to pick out in this case. Another example illustrates a different form of ambiguity, which may be important in practice.

Example C. Consider again a two-equiprobable-state, two-action-world, and posterior-based strategy (Q^C, q^C) with posteriors 0.8 and 0.2 of state 1 being equiprobable, $Q^C(0.2) = Q^C(0.8) = 0.5$, and with deterministic choice of a at 0.8 and b at 0.2:

$$q^C(a|0.8) = q^C(b|0.2) = 1.0.$$

Example D. Consider now (Q^D, q^D) with four equiprobable posteriors of state 1,

$$Q^D(1) = Q^D(0.6) = Q^D(0.4) = Q^D(0),$$

and with deterministic choice of a at 1.0 and 0.6 and b at 0.4 and 0.0,

$$q^D(a|1) = q^D(a|0.6) = q^D(b|0.4) = q^D(b|0) = 1.$$

Both examples C and D look entirely sensible and distinct if one thinks of the geometry of the tracking problem and in terms of actual learning. But in terms of the SDSC strategy to which they correspond, they are the same:

$$P_{(Q^C, q^C)}(a, \omega_1) = 0.8 * 0.5 = 0.4,$$
$$P_{(Q^C, q^C)}(b, \omega_1) = 0.2 * 0.5 = 0.1,$$
$$P_{(Q^C, q^C)}(a, \omega_2) = 0.2 * 0.5 = 0.1,$$
$$P_{(Q^C, q^C)}(b, \omega_2) = 0.8 * 0.5 = 0.4.$$

Likewise,

$$P_{(Q^D,q^D)}(a,\omega_1) = 1.0*0.25 + 0.6*0.25 = 0.4,$$

$$P_{(Q^D,q^D)}(b,\omega_1) = 0.4*0.25 + 0.0*0.25 = 0.1,$$

$$P_{(Q^D,q^D)}(a,\omega_2) = 0.0*0.25 + 0.4*0.25 = 0.1,$$

$$P_{(Q^D,q^D)}(b,\omega_2) = 1.0*0.25 + 0.6*0.25 = 0.4.$$

Which of these is most appropriate for analytic purposes and why?

2.8 Revealed Posteriors, Experiment, and Strategy

To answer the question of how to work out a particular strategy from SDSC, consider first the psychometric case in which what is measured is not directly a belief but rather the proportion of times the heavier weight is chosen. Suppose that the choice of left or right hand correctly identifies the heavier weight 90% of the time. With rational expectations, the average belief of the subject that their choice is correct at the point of decision-making can be inferred as 90%. Note that there may well, in fact, be cases in which they were sure and other cases in which they were less sure, but this is not revealed in the data set. That is exactly the substantive point in comparing C and D above. In one case, there is a fixed level of confidence when making a given decision; in the other, there are variations in confidence. What they share is the average belief when making a given choice, and this therefore seems like the best version of an inferred strategy.

Caplin and Martin (2011, 2015) provide the general decision-theoretic translation of this simple method of inference. The econometrician uses the data to construct the revealed posteriors associated with any chosen action a. The possible posteriors are all those associated with chosen actions. Note that example A above, in which there is a single posterior and a mixed action strategy, shows that the general formulae must allow for revealed posteriors that are common across chosen actions.

The revealed experiment is then defined as the associated probabilities over revealed posteriors which satisfy the Bayesian constraint by construction. Given that we have seen the action choices also, we can also specify the revealed (posterior-based) strategy.

Definition 1: Given SDSC $\mathbf{P} \in \mathcal{P}(\mu_{\mathbf{P}}, A)$, we define the **revealed action probabilities** $\mathbf{P}(a) = \sum_{\omega \in \Omega} \mathbf{P}(a, \omega)$. When $\mathbf{P}(a) > 0$, we define also **revealed posterior** $\gamma_{\mathbf{P}}^a \in \Delta(\Omega)$ by

$$\gamma_{\mathbf{P}}^a(\omega) = \frac{\mathbf{P}(a, \omega)}{\mathbf{P}(a)}.$$

We define the **revealed experiment** $(\mu_{\mathbf{P}}, \mathbf{Q_P})$ by

$$\mathbf{Q_P}(\gamma) = \sum_{\{a \in A \mid \gamma_{\mathbf{P}}^a = \gamma\}} \mathbf{P}(a).$$

To define the **revealed strategy** $(\mathbf{Q_P}, \mathbf{q_P}) \in \Lambda(\mu_{\mathbf{P}}, A)$, we specify, in addition, the implied mixed-action strategy:

$$\mathbf{q_P}(a|\gamma) = \begin{cases} \frac{\mathbf{P}(a)}{\mathbf{Q_P}(\gamma)} & \text{if } \gamma_{\mathbf{P}}^a = \gamma, \\ 0 & \text{if } \gamma_{\mathbf{P}}^a \neq \gamma. \end{cases}$$

There are several observations that can be made about the revealed strategy that are good for the reader to confirm:

1. This strategy generates the data

$$P_{(\mathbf{Q_P}, \mathbf{q_P})} = \mathbf{P}.$$

2. $(\mathbf{Q_P}, \mathbf{q_P})$ is the unique strategy that generates the data with each action chosen at one and only one posterior. All others have the same average posterior associated with each action.
3. Caplin and Dean (2015) show that $(\mathbf{Q_P}, \mathbf{q_P})$ is uniquely the least Blackwell informative strategy that generates the data. We follow up on this point at some depth in Lecture 5, in which we characterize all strategies that might have produced the given data.

Note that this pins down a particular strategy that would produce the observed data in the hypothetical decision problem (μ, A) in which the theoretical and revealed prior are the same, $\mu = \mu_{\mathbf{P}}$, and in which the action set is commonly held by the DM and the econometrician. This assumption is maintained in the current versions of the theory–data map.

Note that in the first of the two examples above, which involves the same data produced by $(Q^A, q^A), (Q^B, q^B)$, the revealed strategy would be strategy A rather than B. The revealed posteriors associated with both actions are 0.5. Hence, the revealed strategy involves this posterior for sure, with a and b equally likely: $(\mathbf{Q_P}, \mathbf{q_P}) = (Q^A, q^A)$. In the second of the two examples above, which involves the same data produced by $(Q^C, q^C), (Q^D, q^D)$, the revealed strategy is (Q^C, q^C). The reason for this is that the key defining feature of the revealed strategy is that no action is chosen at more than one posterior. Hence, when an SDSC strategy specifies the choice of an action at distinct posteriors, one simply averages the posteriors according to their relative likelihoods.

2.9 Testing the Blackwell Model

We continue now to think of an econometrician who knows the decision problem (μ, A), and hence all possible states, all possible actions, and their state-dependent prizes, and has seen repeated choice and, from it, found $\mathbf{P}(a, \omega)$. Note that we have seen above some data-based constraints on what must have been learned under rational expectations, but these are far from precise. We also saw choices. The key questions are as follows:

1. What does this tell us about utility?
2. As in the classical theory of choice, global indifference can rationalize any behavior. What does one do to break the indifference as a rationalization for anything?
3. If global indifference is ruled out, is the Blackwell model of BEU maximization refutable in the data?

Caplin and Martin (2011, 2015) answer the question of what patterns in observed SDSC are equivalent to a non-vacuous (not always indifferent among ever-chosen actions) theory in which there exists a strategy (Q, q) that produces the data and a utility function such that the patterns that are observed reflect the optimal choice. Technically, we are given an SDSC data set for a given decision problem. Given this data set, we want to see if there is some utility function over prizes $u : Z \to \mathbb{R}$ and a strategy of learning and choice $(Q, q) \in \Lambda(\mu, A)$ that produces the observed data and in which all action choices maximize utility at the posteriors at which they are chosen. There must be a strict preference for some chosen action over another to make the conditions non-vacuous.

Definition 2: $(Q,q) \in \Lambda(\mu,A)$ and $u : Z \longrightarrow \mathbb{R}$ provide a **BEU** representation of $\mathbf{P} \in \mathcal{P}(\mu,A)$:

1. **Data Matching:** For all $\omega \in \Omega$ and $a \in A$,

$$P_{(Q,q)}(a,\omega) = \mathbf{P}(a,\omega). \tag{5}$$

2. **Non-Vacuous Optimality:** For all $\gamma \in \operatorname{supp} Q$ and $a \in A$ with $q(a|\gamma) > 0$,

$$\sum_{\omega} \gamma(\omega)u(z(a,\omega)) \geq \sum_{\omega} \gamma(\omega)u(z(b,\omega)) \text{ all } b \in A, \tag{6}$$

with the inequality strict for some $\gamma \in \operatorname{supp} Q$ and $a,b \in A$.

What makes a weak version of this (no insistence on strict inequality) of less interest for testing the model is that global indifference provides such a representation for any SDSC.

A nice point to note is that the value is the same for all strategies that produce the given data: Their value is, in fact, precisely implied by that data. Given any $(Q,q) \in \Lambda(\mu,A)$ that satisfies the data-matching condition (5) has total expected utility that can be computed using the SDSC itself:

$$\sum_{a \in A} \sum_{\omega \in \Omega} P_{(Q,q)}(a,\omega)u(z(a,\omega)) = \sum_{a \in A} \sum_{\omega \in \Omega} \mathbf{P}(a,\omega)u(z(a,\omega)).$$

So, this means that for value purposes, there is no difference between learning and choice strategies that produce the same SDSC. When we are given both SDSC **P** and a utility function and are considering the learning and choice strategies that give rise to them, we can infer the corresponding common valuation as the **revealed value** of the SDSC according to the utility function.

2.10   A Simple Tracking Problem

The workhorse in this body of theory is a tracking problem, as now introduced. There is what the data will reveal to be a good prize and a bad prize and as many actions as states. We work with the case of two actions a,b, two states (ω_1,ω_2), and two prizes z_1,z_2, noting that, as yet, we cannot know which prize is good: The data will have to tell us that. We present all information in the following tabular format, which should be self-explanatory.

Action	State 1	State 2
a	z_1	z_2
b	z_2	z_1

The only feature we vary is an interior prior parametrized by $\mu \in (0,1)$ the probability of state 1: For now, we set $\mu \geq 0.5$.

To feel our way forward, we describe the observed SDSC data in a traditional psychometric manner. The data reveal that the prize z_1 is received with the same probability of $r > 0.5$ in either state. Our question is naturally whether or not this data has a BEU representation.

Technically, we have the following data:

$$\mathbf{P}(a, \omega_1) = r\mu \Longrightarrow \mathbf{P}(b, \omega_1) = (1 - r)\mu,$$
$$\mathbf{P}(b, \omega_2) = r(1 - \mu) \Longrightarrow \mathbf{P}(a, \omega_2) = (1 - r)(1 - \mu).$$

This would seem to suggest that the prize z_1 is strictly preferred to z_2 in any BEU representation. How might one argue this?

We first directly compute the total *ex ante EU* of the whole strategy as

$$[\mathbf{P}(a, \omega_1) + \mathbf{P}(b, \omega_2)]u(z_1) + [\mathbf{P}(a, \omega_2) + \mathbf{P}(b, \omega_1)]u(z_2)$$
$$= ru(z_1) + (1 - r)u(z_2).$$

Given that we are ruling out indifference, we can normalize the expected utility of the better prize to 1 and the worse to 0. *Ex ante*, there are two possibilities:

1. $u(z_1) = 1$ and $u(z_2) = 0 \Longrightarrow EU = r > 0.5.$
2. $u(z_1) = 0$ and $u(z_2) = 1 \Longrightarrow EU = 1 - r.$

The second seems ridiculous. What is the mode of argument?

2.11 Counterfactual Action Switches

The trick is to pursue a clearly informationally feasible strategy. One thing that the model implies is that there are subjective contingencies in which a is chosen. In the general model, this happens with a mixed strategy in the face of various possible posteriors. In principle, with these same posteriors and mixing devices, the DM could always switch actions completely. Suppose they did this and always reversed their choice to b in place of a and a in place of b. We let EU' denote the resulting expected utility. Directly:

1. $u(z_1) = 1$ and $u(z_2) = 0 \implies EU' = 1 - r < 0.5 < r.$
2. $u(z_1) = 0$ and $u(z_2) = 1 \implies EU' = r > 0.5 > 1 - r.$

What makes the second look wrong is that this strategy raises EU. No Bayesian expected utility maximizer would make this mistake. We can conclude that $u(z_1) = 1$ and $u(z_2) = 0$.

With this knowledge, we can work forward to see what data sets can be rationalized. What we will do is think about the two revealed posteriors separately and use the same trick of reversing actions. Again, these wholesale action switches should not strictly increase the probability of getting the good prize, which in this case is expected utility. The revealed posterior associated with the observed choice of action a is

$$\gamma_P^a = \frac{\mathbf{P}(a, \omega_1)}{\mathbf{P}(a, \omega_1) + \mathbf{P}(a, \omega_2)} = \frac{r\mu}{r\mu + (1-r)(1-\mu)} > 0.5$$

since $r > 0.5$ and $\mu \geq 0.5$. We now compute the expected utility associated with the choice of action a as

$$EU(a) = \gamma_P^a u(a, \omega_1) + [1 - \gamma_P^a]u(a, \omega_2) = \gamma_P^a > 0.5.$$

Suppose now that we reverse and switch from action a to b. This would have given an expected utility $EU'(a)$:

$$EU'(a) = \gamma_P^a u(b, \omega_1) + [1 - \gamma_P^a]u(b, \omega_2) = 1 - \gamma_P^a < 0.5.$$

To be consistent with optimization, this must not be improving: Indeed, it is not a given that it lies below $EU(a)$.

We now repeat this exercise for the posterior associated with action b:

$$\gamma_P^b = \frac{\mathbf{P}(b, \omega_1)}{\mathbf{P}(b, \omega_1) + \mathbf{P}(b, \omega_2)} = \frac{(1-r)\mu}{(1-r)\mu + r(1-\mu)}.$$

We compute EU associated with action b as

$$EU(b) = \gamma_P^b u(b, \omega_1) + [1 - \gamma_P^b]u(b, \omega_2) = 1 - \gamma_P^b.$$

Again, consider the wholesale switch of actions at this revealed posterior, in which action b is switched to a, and compute the corresponding expected utility $EU'(b)$:

$$EU'(b) = \gamma_{\mathbf{P}}^b u(a, \omega_1) + [1 - \gamma_{\mathbf{P}}^b] u(a, \omega_2) = \gamma_{\mathbf{P}}^b.$$

To be consistent with the optimization, this must not be improving:

$$EU(b) \geq EU'(b) \Longleftrightarrow 1 - \gamma_{\mathbf{P}}^b \geq \gamma_{\mathbf{P}}^b$$

$$\Longleftrightarrow \gamma_{\mathbf{P}}^b = \frac{(1-r)\mu}{(1-r)\mu + r(1-\mu)} \leq \frac{1}{2}.$$

Equivalently,

$$(1-r)\mu \leq r(1-\mu)$$

$$\Longleftrightarrow \mu \leq r,$$

otherwise a switch to action a whenever b was taken would be improving. Note that this is unrestrictive when $\mu = 0.5$ but increasingly restrictive as $\mu \nearrow 1$. In retrospect, this is obvious: The prior can make it such that correctly choosing b with a high probability in the unlikely state 2 is swamped by choosing b incorrectly in the far more likely state 1.

The example illustrates a method for working out precisely which data sets are, and which are not, consistent with Bayesian expected utility maximization. It all rests on a simple method of switching actions from taken to untaken and insisting that no such switches raise expected utility. The logic seems more general. Indeed it is.

2.12 No Improving Action Switches: Characterization

Caplin and Martin (2011, 2015) show that this method can be generalized to characterize precisely those SDSC data sets that have a BEU representation. We require that chosen actions be optimal at all corresponding revealed posteriors in which they are revealed as chosen $\gamma_{\mathbf{P}}^a \in \Delta(\Omega)$:

$$\sum_{\omega} \gamma_{\mathbf{P}}^a(\omega) u(z(a, \omega)) \geq \sum_{\omega} \gamma_{\mathbf{P}}^a(\omega) u(z(b, \omega)),$$

for all $a \in A$, $b \in A$. Since

$$\gamma_{\mathbf{P}}^a(\omega) = \frac{\mathbf{P}(a, \omega)}{\mathbf{P}(a)},$$

we can state this without conditioning by multiplying both sides by $\mathbf{P}(a)$. This also handles unchosen actions since then both sides are zero. For non-vacuous optimality, recall that we impose that the DM has strict preference for some chosen action over some alternative action: This aspect shows up in the definition. When characterizing all rationalizing utility functions, as done in lectures 6 and 7, we can get rid of this additional clause. So, we define both a condition that does and one that does not impose strictness.

Definition 3: the Utility function $u : Z \longrightarrow \mathbb{R}$ satisfies **no improving action switches (NIASs)** for SDSC **P** if, given $a, b \in A$,

$$\sum_\omega \mathbf{P}(a, \omega)u(z(a, \omega)) \geq \sum_\omega \mathbf{P}(a, \omega)u(z(b, \omega)). \qquad (7)$$

It satisfies **strict NIAS** if the inequality is strict for some $a, b \in A$.

The main result is that NIAS is not only necessary but also sufficient for the existence of a BEU. Necessity is essentially definitional. Sufficiency is direct once one has the definition of revealed strategy. In fact, the definition was introduced precisely to prove sufficiency.

Theorem 1 (Caplin and Martin, 2011, 2015) *Existence of a utility function satisfying strict NIAS for* **P** *is equivalent to* **P** *having a BEU representation.*

Proof 1 (i) BEU implies strict NIAS: A first observation is that if the utility function $u : Z \longrightarrow \mathbb{R}$ and the information structure $(Q, q) \in \Lambda(\mu, A)$ constitute a BEU of **P**, then the same utility function and the revealed strategy, $(Q_\mathbf{P}, q_\mathbf{P}) \in \Lambda(\mu, A)$, also provide a BEU representation since the only change is to the average of the posteriors among those in which a is chosen: Being optimal at each implies being optimal at the average. What this means is that, for all chosen actions with $\mathbf{P}(a) > 0$,

$$\sum_\omega \gamma_\mathbf{P}^a(\omega)u(z(a, \omega)) \geq \sum_\omega \gamma_\mathbf{P}^a(\omega)u(z(b, \omega)) \text{ all } b \in A,$$

with the inequality strict for some $a, b \in A$. Multiplying by $\mathbf{P}(a)$ yields

$$\sum_\omega \mathbf{P}(a, \omega)u(z(a, \omega)) \geq \sum_\omega \mathbf{P}(a, \omega)u(z(b, \omega)) \text{ all } b \in A,$$

with the inequality strict for some $a, b \in A$, establishing (7).

(ii) Strict NIAS implies BEU: By definition, given **P** that satisfies (7), we know that

$$\sum_{\omega} \mathbf{P}(a,\omega)u(z(a,\omega)) \geq \sum_{\omega} \mathbf{P}(a,\omega)u(z(b,\omega)) \text{ all } b \in A,$$

with the inequality strict for some $a, b \in A$. Now, given any chosen action with $\mathbf{P}(a) > 0$, we can divide by $\mathbf{P}(a)$ to arrive at the revealed posterior so that

$$\sum_{\omega} \gamma_{\mathbf{P}}^a(\omega)u(z(a,\omega)) \geq \sum_{\omega} \gamma_{\mathbf{P}}^a(\omega)u(z(b,\omega)) \text{ all } b \in A,$$

with the inequality strict for some $a, b \in A$. Hence, the revealed strategy $(Q_{\mathbf{P}}, q_{\mathbf{P}}) \in \Lambda(\mu, A)$ itself satisfies the non-vacuous optimality condition (6). What remains is to show that the revealed strategy satisfies data matching (5) in that

$$P_{(Q_{\mathbf{P}}, q_{\mathbf{P}})} = \mathbf{P}.$$

By way of confirmation,

$$
\begin{aligned}
P_{(Q_{\mathbf{P}}, q_{\mathbf{P}})}(a,\omega) &= \sum_{\gamma \in supp Q_{\mathbf{P}}} q_{\mathbf{P}}(a|\gamma) Q_{\mathbf{P}}(\gamma)\gamma(\omega) \\
&= q_{\mathbf{P}}(a|\gamma_{\mathbf{P}}^a) Q_{\mathbf{P}}(\gamma_{\mathbf{P}}^a)\gamma_{\mathbf{P}}^a(\omega) \\
&= \frac{\mathbf{P}(a)}{Q_{\mathbf{P}}(\gamma_{\mathbf{P}}^a)} Q_{\mathbf{P}}(\gamma_{\mathbf{P}}^a)\gamma_{\mathbf{P}}^a(\omega) \\
&= \mathbf{P}(a)\gamma_{\mathbf{P}}^a(\omega) = \mathbf{P}(a,\omega),
\end{aligned}
$$

thus completing the proof.

The result is clear once the basic ideas and definitions have been introduced. The creative steps lie in introducing the objects and posing the question precisely.

2.13 Arbitrary SDSC in the Tracking Problem

To illustrate the value of characterization, we now allow for a completely general SDSC in the two-state tracking problem and identify necessary and sufficient conditions for there to be a BEU representation: In the first example, we worked with the special case of being correct with a probability of $r > 0.5$ in either state. Recall the example.

Action	State 1	State 2
a	z_1	z_2
b	z_2	z_1

Take as given the SDSC $\mathbf{P} \in \Delta(A \times \Omega)$ with both actions chosen and both states possible (this allows for any prior). NIAS states:

$$\mathbf{P}(a,\omega_1)u(z_1) + \mathbf{P}(a,\omega_2)u(z_2) \geq \mathbf{P}(a,\omega_1)u(z_2) + \mathbf{P}(a,\omega_2)u(z_1),$$

$$\mathbf{P}(b,\omega_1)u(z_2) + \mathbf{P}(b,\omega_2)u(z_1) \geq \mathbf{P}(b,\omega_1)u(z_1) + \mathbf{P}(b,\omega_2)u(z_2),$$

with at least one strict.

We are looking for the utility numbers $u(z_1)$ and $u(z_2)$ that rationalize this as a BEU representation. The non-triviality condition says that $u(z_1) \neq u(z_2)$. WLOG, set $u(z_1) = 1$ and $u(z_2) = 0$ and identify the rationalizable data sets. The strict NIAS conditions now assert:

$$\mathbf{P}(a,\omega_1) \geq \mathbf{P}(a,\omega_2),$$

$$\mathbf{P}(b,\omega_2) \geq \mathbf{P}(b,\omega_1),$$

with at least one strict.

Note that these conditions imply that the converse specification, $u(z_1) = 0$ and $u(z_2) = 1$, does not rationalize the data. Hence, any rationalizing utility function is unique. We can translate this into the revealed posteriors of state 1 (for simplicity, we simplify, where convenient, by suppressing the state ω_1 parentheses on posterior beliefs hereinafter when discussing the geometric approach):

$$\mathbf{P}(a,\omega_1) \geq \mathbf{P}(a,\omega_2) \Leftrightarrow \gamma_{\mathbf{P}}^a = \frac{\mathbf{P}(a,\omega_1)}{\mathbf{P}(a,\omega_1) + \mathbf{P}(a,\omega_2)} \geq 0.5,$$

$$\mathbf{P}(b,\omega_2) \geq \mathbf{P}(b,\omega_1) \Leftrightarrow \gamma_{\mathbf{P}}^b = \frac{\mathbf{P}(b,\omega_1)}{\mathbf{P}(b,\omega_1) + \mathbf{P}(b,\omega_2)} \leq 0.5,$$

with at least one strict.

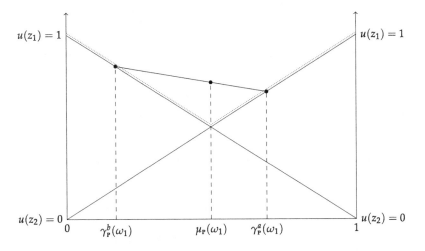

Figure 2.4 Evaluating the revealed experiment.

Identify the revealed prior probability of state 1 in the data as

$$\mu_{\mathbf{P}}(\omega_1) = \mathbf{P}(a, \omega_1) + \mathbf{P}(b, \omega_1).$$

Bayes' consistency is then implied:

$$[\mathbf{P}(a, \omega_1) + \mathbf{P}(a, \omega_2)] \gamma_{\mathbf{P}}^a + [\mathbf{P}(b, \omega_1) + \mathbf{P}(b, \omega_2)] \gamma_{\mathbf{P}}^b = \mu_{\mathbf{P}}(\omega_1).$$

As again illustrated in Figure 2.4, this value can be considered in the geometric picture of *EU* in the tracking problem by plotting the *EU* to each action as a function of $\gamma(\omega_1) \in (0, 1)$, the probability of state 1. In our two-prize case, the expected utility of a posterior-based strategy is found geometrically at the point where the line joining $(\gamma_{\mathbf{P}}^b(\omega_1), \bar{u}^b(\gamma_{\mathbf{P}}^b(\omega_1)))$ with $(\gamma_{\mathbf{P}}^a(\omega_1), \bar{u}^a(\gamma_{\mathbf{P}}^b(\omega_1)))$ passes above the prior, where $\bar{u}^{a/b}$ denotes the expected utility at the corresponding posterior.

The corresponding payoffs at these posteriors are $\gamma_{\mathbf{P}}^a$ for a and $1 - \gamma_{\mathbf{P}}^b$ for b. The line joining these has weights of $\mathbf{P}(a)$ on $\gamma_{\mathbf{P}}^a$ and $\mathbf{P}(b)$ on $\gamma_{\mathbf{P}}^b$. Hence, the corresponding *EU* is

$$\mathbf{P}(a)\gamma_{\mathbf{P}}^a + \mathbf{P}(b)\left(1 - \gamma_{\mathbf{P}}^b\right) = \mathbf{P}(a, \omega_1) + \mathbf{P}(b, \omega_2).$$

Obviously, we can, likewise, find all data sets that rationalize the opposite strict preference $u(z_1) = 0$ and $u(z_2) = 1$.

At the end of this process, we can precisely identify all data sets for which a BEU exists in this two-prize, two-state, and two-action decision problem. The process is general, as a second example illustrates.

2.14 Safe vs. Risky

We now use geometry to explore a case with two states and more than two prizes. We have one safe and one risky action in a world with two possible states.

Action	State 1	State 2
a	z_1	z_2
b	z_s	z_s

We have seen **P** with both states possible and both actions picked with a positive probability. To avoid trivia, we insist that the revealed posteriors of state 1 associated with the actions are both interior to the unit interval. The strictness aspect of the BEU representation implies that they must be distinct.

Our goal is to identify what the NIAS inequalities teach us about the underlying set of possible utility functions and to illustrate any degrees of freedom. To work this out, it is convenient to use two normalizations. WLOG, set $u(z_s) = 0$. For interior posteriors, we know that the utilities $u(z_1)$ and $u(z_2)$ must have the feature that one is strictly below and the other strictly above zero. WLOG, set $u(z_1) > u(z_2)$. The second normalization is to set their first difference as 1. Overall,

$$u(z_1) = u_1 = u(z_2) + 1.$$

Note that what this has done is make state 1 favorable to the risky action and state 2 unfavorable to it. We now explore what the NIAS inequalities imply for the value of $u_1 > 0$. With these normalizations, the strict NIAS inequalities assert:

$$\mathbf{P}(a, \omega_1)u_1 + \mathbf{P}(a, \omega_2)(u_1 - 1) \geq \mathbf{P}(b, \omega_1)u_1 + \mathbf{P}(b, \omega_2)(u_1 - 1),$$

with at least one strict. We divide by unconditional action probabilities to get expressions in terms of the revealed posteriors:

$$\gamma_{\mathbf{P}}^{a} u_1 + (1 - \gamma_{\mathbf{P}}^{a})(u_1 - 1) \geq \gamma_{\mathbf{P}}^{b} u_1 + (1 - \gamma_{\mathbf{P}}^{b})(u_1 - 1),$$

with at least one strict. Simplifying, these read, respectively,

$$1 - \gamma_{\mathbf{P}}^{a} \leq u_1 \leq 1 - \gamma_{\mathbf{P}}^{b},$$

with at least one strict. Hence, NIAS allows us to strictly order the revealed posteriors:

$$\gamma_{\mathbf{P}}^{a} > \gamma_{\mathbf{P}}^{b}.$$

An important point to note here is that the NIAS constraints provide **quantitative** constraints on expected utilities rather than just an ordering of prizes. This will show up again and again in examples.

There is a clear geometric translation of all of these that also reveals the degrees of freedom with NIAS satisfied. What one needs is simply that the line representing the expected utility of action a at different beliefs about the probability of state ω_1 passes through the origin somewhere in

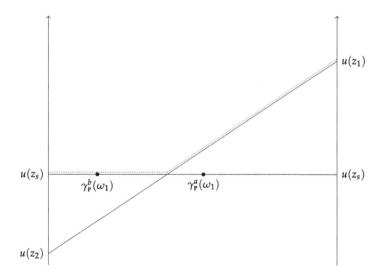

Figure 2.5 Revealed posteriors bounding utility.

the closed interval $\left[\gamma_{\mathbf{P}}^{b}, \gamma_{\mathbf{P}}^{a}\right]$, as in Figure 2.5. This identifies the degrees of freedom with NIAS.

This is clearly general for the two-action, two-state case, even with four distinct prizes. We can always orient things in such a way that state 1 favors action a: This means $u(z(a, \omega_1)) \geq u(z(b, \omega_1))$ and $u(z(b, \omega_2)) \geq u(z(a, \omega_2))$, with at least one strict, so that there is an interior intersection. Note that if either was an equality, then the other action would be weakly dominant, and the revealed posterior associated with the other would be either 0 or 1, which we have assumed it is not. The same geometric observation applies to the freedom to adjust slopes, provided each action is maximal at its revealed posterior. This is the general geometry in any number of dimensions for any number of actions. Each chosen action must be among those with the highest utility at the revealed posterior at which it is picked. This is precisely what the NIAS inequalities convey.

In Lecture 6, we introduce a very different method for understanding the NIAS constraints, which has value for a number of questions.

2.15 Closing Remarks

As stated at the outset, the goals of this lecture were:

1. to formally introduce the Blackwell model.
2. to formalize the Block and Marschak identification challenge.
3. to introduce SDSC data.
4. to precisely pose the question of what it means for SDSC to be rationalized by the Blackwell model.
5. to provide and prove the NIAS characterization.

In closing, I pose an obvious open question that will be addressed in many of the ensuing lectures: What exactly can SDSC reveal to us about what people learn before deciding and why?

Lecture 3

Costly Information Representations and Attention Switches

The goals of this lecture are:

1. To formally define costs of learning and rational inattention theory.
2. To precisely specify what it means for SDSC from various decision problems to be consistent with a particular cost function and hence to have a costly information representation (CIR).
3. To illustrate cases in which such a CIR exists and cases in which no non-trivial CIR exists and to make intuitive progress in understanding the underlying logic.
4. To introduce the counterfactual attention switches that play a key role in the examples and to construct matrices of the resulting direct and indirect value switches.

3.1 Learning Costs and Rational Inattention Theory

As indicated in the introduction, the most important and global reason for a DM's information being imperfect is that it is hard to know everything. The importance of this fact for social science was stressed by Hayek (1938, 1944). Since that time, models of costly learning have proliferated. Many different models have by now been presented. As noted above, the theory of search initiated by Stigler (1961) is particularly central. Others involve paying a cost for full state revelation (e.g., Mankiw and Reis, 2001), choosing from a set of available partitions (e.g., Ellis, 2012), and choosing the variance of the normal signal (e.g., Verrecchia, 1982).

In recent years, the literature has expanded dramatically and opened up to far more subtle and sophisticated formalizations of learning costs. The key is complete flexibility in the degree of partial information, as introduced by Sims (1998) in his seminal model of rational inattention. There are now massive classes of such universal cost functions that generalize the Shannon model in key ways (see Lecture 8 for key examples). I believe this additional flexibility in modeling is of vital importance. **Costs of learning are of equivalent importance to the costs of production.** Just as in the case of production, learning costs come in all flavors and types. We have just seen the tip of this particular iceberg. The fact that it is hard to specify the costs of learning *a priori* raises the importance of research to better measure such costs. That is the challenge to which we now turn. The research detailed in this lecture has as its primary source, Caplin and Dean (2015).

Solving a model with the costs of learning involves identifying a precise pattern of ultimate learning and decision-making. Such learning produces a Blackwell experiment. A key first step is to identify a suitable domain for the cost function. I want to emphasize just how many options there are in this regard. One might wish to specify costs on the domain of Blackwell experiments: Many do this. One might want to specify it in the space of SDSC strategies: Many do this, and indeed, I will use this method many times as it becomes convenient. In this lecture, I use a different domain, as now detailed. A researcher in this area should have all domains in mind since the most convenient one for analytic purposes depends on the question to be addressed.

In this lecture, we start with a finite state space Ω. We specify a prior over these states: $\mu \in \Delta(\Omega)$. Costs will be specific to both. Any change in the state space may obviously change the ease or difficulty of learning. Likewise for any change in the prior. There is a lot to learn when states start out equiprobable, possibly less when there is a strong prior that one of the states will eventuate. Of course, there are likely to be links between the costs of learning across distinct priors, and these may be of first-order importance in applications. A precise formulation of possible such links is given in Lecture 8.

As usual, a decision problem will be defined by a finite action set *A*, in addition to the prior. The key exclusion restriction in the theory is that this action set *per se* has no effect on the costs of learning. The formalism nicely supports this assumption. The choice of action depends only on beliefs about the state. So, all the effort is devoted appropriately to learning about the state. From this perspective, a natural domain for the cost function is the class of Bayes' consistent distributions of posteriors, $\mathcal{Q}(\mu)$, with the generic element $Q \in \Delta(\Delta(\Omega))$, with a finite support that is Bayes' consistent with the prior. Note that there are no general cross-prior restrictions on the cost function, so we fix the prior as $\mu \in \Delta(\Omega))$ in what follows and suppress it wherever no confusion would result. Note also that the range of the cost function allows for infinite costs, so the mapping is to the extended real line $\overline{\mathbb{R}}$.

Definition 4:   Given prior $\mu \in \Delta(\Omega)$, we define $\mathcal{K}(\mu)$ as the set of all **attention cost functions** $K : \mathcal{Q}(\mu) \to \overline{\mathbb{R}}$.

The definition of what it means to be rationally inattentive is to maximize net utility.

Definition 5:   Given decision problem (μ, A) and strategy $(Q, q) \in \Lambda(\mu, A)$ and $u : Z \longrightarrow \mathbb{R}$, compute $G(Q, q|u)$, as in equation (2.3), as the corresponding expected utility:

$$G(Q, q|u) \equiv \sum_{\gamma \in \text{supp } Q} \sum_{a \in A} Q(\gamma) q(a|\gamma) \sum_{\omega \in \Omega} \gamma(\omega) u(z(a, \omega)). \qquad (8)$$

Given also $K \in \mathcal{K}(\mu)$, the value of the strategy is

$$V(\mu, (Q, q)|u, K) \equiv G(Q, q|u) - K(\mu, Q).$$

The value function of the decision problem (μ, A) *is then defined as*

$$\hat{V}(\mu, A|u, K) \equiv \sup_{\{(Q, q) \in \Lambda(\mu, A)\}} V(\mu, (Q, q)|u, K).$$

The set of **rationally inattentive strategies** comprise all that achieve the supremum

$$\hat{\Lambda}(\mu, A|u, K) \equiv \left\{ (Q, q) \in \Lambda(\mu, A) \,|\, V(\mu, (Q, q)|u, K) = \hat{V}(\mu, A|u, K) \right\}.$$

As noted before, in a standard course on the costs of learning, it would be key to impose conditions that imply the existence of optimal strategies. Given the very different goals in what follows, which relate to analyzing the properties of data sets consistent with such optimization, the issue of existence is moot: It is included as a key hypothesis in trying to rationalize the data.

3.2   Ideal Data and CIRs

In terms of the theory that the costs of learning constrain what can be observed in the data, distinct decision problems will need to be observed in order to have a testable theory of costly information acquisition. Otherwise, the theory that all unobserved forms of learning are infinitely costly can trivially rationalize what was seen. Hence, we need to observe SDSC for many decision problems. In what follows, we follow Caplin and Dean (2015) and consider a finite set of M non-trivial decision problems (more than one action) and corresponding data sets. For simplicity, we index the choice sets and the corresponding SDSC by $1 \leq m \leq M$. Hence, what we have in hand is a set of pairs $(A^m, \mathbf{P}^m)$ detailing the action sets and the observed SDSC data sets, respectively.

Definition 6: Fixing prior $\mu \in \Delta(\Omega)$, a data set $\{(A^m, \mathbf{P}^m)\}_{m=1}^M$ comprises M pairs of finite choice sets A^m and the corresponding SDSC data sets $\mathbf{P}^m$.

Our goal is to rationalize $\{(A^m, \mathbf{P}^m)\}_{m=1}^M$ based on some unknown but fixed utility and learning cost functions. To formalize, I now specify what it means for a pair $u : Z \longrightarrow \mathbb{R}, K \in \mathcal{K}(\mu)$ to provide a CIR of such a data set. The idea is that in each decision problem, the DM picks the strategy (Q^m, q^m) to maximize expected utility net of attention costs and that this strategy produces what is seen in the data. We are also interested in distinguishing between utility functions that admit such a CIR and those that do not.

Definition 7: $\{(A^m, \mathbf{P}^m)\}_{m=1}^M$ have a **costly information representation** if there exist u, K, and $(Q^m, q^m) \in \hat{\Lambda}(A^m | u, K)$ for $1 \leq m \leq M$ such that $\mathbf{P}^m = P_{(Q^m, q^m)}$. u **admits** a CIR of $\{(A^m, \mathbf{P}^m)\}_{m=1}^M$ if there exist K and $(Q^m, q^m) \in \hat{\Lambda}(A^m | u, K)$ that in combination with u provide a CIR. We define $\mathcal{U}^{CIR}$ as the class of such utility functions.

Note that we are here allowing the trivial case of a utility function with global indifference and all learning being costless, which will rationalize anything. In the following, we identify cases in which the only CIRs are trivial in this sense. We describe these as having no costly information representation (CIR) to convey our disinterest.

Definition 8: Data set $\{(A^m, \mathbf{P}^m)\}_{m=1}^{M}$ **admits** a CIR if there exists a non-trivial utility function (one in which there is no global indifference) that admits a CIR.

The general definition reveals that the unobservables to be recovered from the data to the extent possible are the utility function u, the information cost function K, and the strategies (Q^m, q^m). As we will see later, the revealed experiment introduced above will play a key role. In fact, it is clear that much of the logic of the previous lecture applies. In particular, it is necessary for a CIR that the utility function satisfy NIAS in all data sets. If this does not hold, one can find a strictly higher utility switch in the strategy using precisely the revealed information structure by performing the corresponding value-increasing holistic action switch.

Comment 3.1: If $u : Z \longrightarrow \mathbb{R}$ and $K \in \mathcal{K}(\mu)$ provide a CIR of $\{(A^m, \mathbf{P}^m)\}_{m=1}^{M}$, then u must satisfy NIAS for each $\mathbf{P^m}$, $1 \leq m \leq M$.

Given that the NIAS constraints will have to be satisfied in each data set, what we are left is to find any **additional conditions** that are required for such representations to exist.

Note that the domain of learning costs comprises Bayes' consistent distributions of posteriors. For convenience, it is simpler at this stage to conceive of learning costs as being defined directly on SDSC, with $K(P)$ as comprising the minimum cost among all the distributions of posteriors for all strategies that are capable of producing the performance data P. Essentially, this is the revealed posterior distribution $Q_{\mathbf{P}}$. With this understanding, identifying the learning cost functions that explain the data boils down to identifying a suitable learning cost $K^m = K(\mathbf{P}^m)$ for each data set; worrying about how that relates to costs defined on Bayes' consistent information structures comes later. In the following lecture, we formalize our interest in these **qualifying costs of revealed learning**. We return to the original domain of information structures in Lecture 5, but this is all we need for now.

3.3 A Two-by-two-by-two Case

Possibly the simplest way to generate a data set for which a CIR exists involves a pair of decision problems with a clear prize that will be revealed to be bad, in which one of the data sets reveals that more is learned in the corresponding tracking problem. In that case, one would expect this to be consistent with a CIR, provided the cost of the increased information is no higher than the increased reward required to rationalize the additional learning. To formalize, consider a two-equiprobable-state world with the following action sets.

Choice Set A^1

Action	State ω_1	State ω_2
a_1	z_1	z_0
b_1	z_0	z_1

Choice Set A^2

Action	State ω_1	State ω_2
a_2	z_2	z_0
b_2	z_0	z_2

The corresponding data sets $\mathbf{P}^1, \mathbf{P}^2$ are

$$\mathbf{P}^1(a_1, \omega_1) = 0.4 = \mathbf{P}^1(b_1, \omega_2),$$

$$\mathbf{P}^1(a_1, \omega_2) = 0.1 = \mathbf{P}^1(b_1, \omega_1),$$

$$\mathbf{P}^2(a_2, \omega_1) = 0.3 = \mathbf{P}^2(b_2, \omega_2),$$

$$\mathbf{P}^2(a_2, \omega_2) = 0.2 = \mathbf{P}^2(b_2, \omega_1).$$

Hence, the revealed attention strategy in $(A^1, \mathbf{P}^1)$ involves the following probabilities of state ω_1:

$$\gamma_{\mathbf{P}^1}^{a_1} = 0.8 \text{ and} \gamma_{\mathbf{P}^1}^{b_1} = 0.2,$$

with choice probabilities

$$\mathbf{Q}^1\left(\gamma_{\mathbf{P}^1}^{a_1}\right) = \mathbf{Q}^1\left(\gamma_{\mathbf{P}^1}^{b_1}\right) = 0.5.$$

The revealed attention strategy in $(A^2, \mathbf{P}^2)$ involves the state ω_1 probabilities of

$$\gamma_{\mathbf{P}^2}^{a_2} = 0.6 \text{ and } \gamma_{\mathbf{P}^2}^{b_2} = 0.4,$$

with choice probabilities

$$\mathbf{Q}^2\left(\gamma_{\mathbf{P}^2}^{a_2}\right) = \mathbf{Q}^2\left(\gamma_{\mathbf{P}^2}^{b_2}\right) = 0.5.$$

The NIAS constraints are simple in the two decision problems separately: NIAS in A^1 implies $u(z_1) \equiv u_1 \geq u(z_0) \equiv u_0$ since the action switch in either case raises the probability of getting prize z_0. Likewise, NIAS in A^2 implies $u(z_2) \equiv u_2 \geq u_0$. In essence, this is all that NIAS can teach us.

We now work this through in a simple example that is consistent with what NIAS applies, in which we set $u_1 = 1, u_2 = 0.5$, and $u_0 = 0$. We show that this will allow us to rationalize the above, provided it does not cost too much more to learn the extra amount that is learned in A^1. What exactly does this tell us about costs, and how can we formalize this intuition?

One interesting thought experiment is to imagine switching action set A^1 to data set $\mathbf{P}^2$ associated with the action set A^2 using holistic action switches and by maximizing. If one did that, it is clearly optimal to pick the action more likely to yield the better prize. The result would be getting prize z_1 with a probability of 0.6 rather than 0.8 as in the actual data set $\mathbf{P}^1$. With $u_1 = 1$, this switch would lower expected utility by 0.2, with a cost difference of $K^1 - K^2$. So, the following comparison of net utilities must hold:

$$0.8u_1 - K^1 = 0.8 - K^1 \geq 0.6u_1 - K^2 = 0.6 - K^2 \implies K^1 - K^2 \leq 0.2.$$

By analogous reasoning, we need to be careful not to make K^1 too low; otherwise, it would be worth switching in the reverse direction. By a precisely analogous logic, imagine switching action set A^2 to the data set $\mathbf{P}^1$ associated with action set A^1 using holistic action switches and maximizing. Again, it is clearly optimal to pick the action more likely to yield the better prize. The result would be getting prize z_2 with a probability of 0.8 rather than 0.6 as in the actual data set $\mathbf{P}^2$. Given that $u_2 = 0.5$, there would be a gain of utility involved, amounting to $0.2u_2 = 0.1$ with a cost difference of $K^2 - K^1$. Again, this cannot be worthwhile:

$$0.6u_2 - K^2 = 0.3 - K^2 \geq 0.8u_2 - K^1 = 0.4 - K^1 \implies K^1 - K^2 \geq 0.1.$$

Taking both of these inequalities into account seems possible, provided we obey both constraints on costs, $K^1 - K^2 \in [0.1, 0.2]$. So, here is our first example of intuitively constructing a CIR, which also reveals interesting constraints on cost.

Note that the above constraints were for a specific utility function. If we change utilities, we correspondingly change the constraints. This will be dealt with formally in the next lecture. For now, what we want to show is that not all utilities that pass the NIAS constraints permit non-trivial CIRs. To see this, let's set utilities $u_1 = 0.5, u_2 = 1$, and $u_0 = 0$ and see what is implied by insisting that there is no benefit to switching attention. By an exactly analogous reasoning for $\mathbf{P}^1$, as opposed to $\mathbf{P}^2$, to be maximal with A^1 requires

$$0.8u_1 - K^1 = 0.4 - K^1 \geq 0.6u_1 - K^2 = 0.3 - K^2 \implies K^1 - K^2 \leq 0.1.$$

Conversely, for $\mathbf{P}^2$, as opposed to $\mathbf{P}^1$, to be maximal with A^2 requires

$$0.6u_2 - K^2 = 0.6 - K^2 \geq 0.8u_2 - K^1 = 0.8 - K^1 \implies K^1 - K^2 \geq 0.2.$$

The fact that the last two inequalities are contradictory rules out this utility function providing a CIR in combination with any cost function.

There is a good intuitive reason for this: More is learned in A^1 in an intuitive and a formal sense based on the Blackwell ranking of information structures (see Lecture 5). In A^1, 80% of the uncertainty is resolved, but in A^2, only 60% of the uncertainty is resolved. It would seem irrational to learn more when it is less important. In fact, it is useful to make an analogy with production theory. A competitive firm would not want to produce less output with a lower price of output than with a higher price of output. The reason is that if it switched the uses, it would not change the total cost since this was just rotated but would receive higher revenue. Surely, an analogous logic can be used to indicate that it is not rational to give more attention to the less important problem. This is precisely what played out in this example. We found that no costs of learning exist that would make it rational to invest less in knowledge in the more important setting. This is the flavor of the overall restrictions we will uncover.

3.4   Adding a Third Decision Problem: Case 1

There are now three two-state, two-action, and two-prize decision problems with prior $\mu = (0.5, 0.5)$ and three possible prizes z_0, z_1, and z_2 with the following prize structure. The pairs $(A^1, \mathbf{P}^1)$ and $(A^2, \mathbf{P}^2)$ are as above so that, by NIAS, we know $u_1 \geq u_0$ and $u_2 \geq u_0$. Here is the third decision problem and corresponding data.

Choice Set A^3

Action	State ω_1	State ω_2
a_3	z_2	z_1
b_3	z_1	z_2

$$\mathbf{P}^3(a_3, \omega_1) = 0.15 = \mathbf{P}^3(b_3, \omega_2),$$
$$\mathbf{P}^3(a_3, \omega_2) = 0.35 = \mathbf{P}^3(b_3, \omega_1).$$

Hence, the revealed attention strategy involves state ω_1 probabilities of

$$\gamma_{\mathbf{P}^3}^{a_3} = 0.3 \text{ and } \gamma_{\mathbf{P}^3}^{b_3} = 0.7,$$

with choice probabilities of

$$\mathbf{Q}^3\left(\gamma_{\mathbf{P}^3}^{a_3}\right) = \mathbf{Q}^3\left(\gamma_{\mathbf{P}^3}^{b_3}\right) = 0.5.$$

The new pair $(A^3, \mathbf{P}^3)$ implies that $u_1 \geq u_2$ since, after learning, at each resulting posterior, the DM picks the action that is more likely to yield that prize. Overall, the data remain consistent with the expected utility maximization for any utility function with $u_1 \geq u_2 \geq u_0 = 0$. For non-triviality, it suffices that $u_1 > 0$ so that we can use our second normalization to set $u_1 = 1$, leaving $u_2 \in [0, 1]$ as the only unknown.

We now want to think about the inequalities on costs K^1, K^2, and K^3. To be specific, we fix $u_1 = 1, u_2 = 0.5$, and $u_3 = 0$ and consider what makes it better to choose K^1 rather than either K^2 of K^3 in A^1 and likewise for the other choices. Note that expected utility in A^1 with data $\mathbf{P}^1$ produces gross expected utility of 0.8 while a switch to data $\mathbf{P}^2$ produces gross expected utility of 0.6 and to $\mathbf{P}^3$ produces gross expected utility of 0.7 due to the respective 80%, 60%, and 70% chance of identifying the better prize. For the observed choice to be optimal, it requires the net utility to be maximal. Reasoning analogously about all other choices and possible switches produces the following three inequalities:

$$0.8 - K^1 \geq \max\{0.6 - K^2, 0.7 - K^3\},$$
$$0.3 - K^2 \geq \max\{0.4 - K^1, 0.35 - K^3\},$$
$$0.85 - K^3 \geq \max\{0.9 - K^1, 0.8 - K^2\}.$$

As we will establish formally and with great generality in the following lecture, these inequalities do indeed characterize the possible costs of revealed learning.

3.5   Adding a Third Decision Problem: Case 2

In our second case, we reverse the SDSC in A^3 as follows:

$$\mathbf{P}^3(a_3, \omega_1) = 0.35 = \mathbf{P}^3(b_3, \omega_2),$$
$$\mathbf{P}^3(a_3, \omega_2) = 0.15 = \mathbf{P}^3(b_3, \omega_1).$$

In this case, the standard NIAS argument implies that $u_2 \geq u_1$ since, after learning, at each resulting posterior, the DM picks the action that is more likely to yield that prize. Taken alone, the three decision problems are consistent with NIAS, provided only $u_2 \geq u_1 \geq 0$, so again, for such a non-trivial case, we can normalize to $u_2 = 1$, leaving $u_1 \in [0, 1]$ as the only unknown.

Now, there is reason to suspect that $u_1 < 1$ will not work. Why is this? Intuitively, it is because in such a case, less is learned in a decision problem in which the choice is between the best and the worst prizes than when it is between the second best and the worst prizes. This does not seem reasonable. Again, it appears irrational to give more attention to the less important decision.

One key insight from the first example is that the complete attention strategies are in principle movable between decision problems. Making any such switch simultaneously in both directions should not allow an improvement in total expected utility. What we do, in particular, is to switch between A^1 and A^2 in light of what we know from A^3 about the preferences as between prizes 1 and 2.

Making this switch should not allow an improvement in the total *EU*. What we do is to add up the total *EU* in the data as observed. We should then switch the attention strategies between problems and maximize. Rationality demands that this would not be a winning move. To check this, we first compute the actual revealed expected utility for the given utility function in $(A^1, \mathbf{P}^1)$; it is $0.8u_1$, while in $(A^2, \mathbf{P}^2)$ it is 0.6. The sum of the utilities is therefore $0.6 + 0.8u_1$.

The key computation involves swapping data sets again. What is the highest possible expected utility in A^1 with data set $\mathbf{P}^2$? It involves replacing a_1 with a_2 and b_1 with b_2. This yields in total utility of 0.8. What is the maximum that can be earned in A^2 with data set $\mathbf{P}^1$? It involves replacing a_2 with a_1 and b_2 with b_1. This yields in total $0.6u_1$. The reason this utility specification is not consistent with a CIR is that the total expected utility with the switch adds to more than the total *EU* in the data:

$$0.8 + 0.6u_1 > 0.6 + 0.8u_1.$$

An obvious necessary condition for the existence of a CIR is that this should not be possible. We conclude that

$$u_1 \geq 1.$$

So, we have as our only candidate $u_1 = u_2 = 1$ and $u_3 = 0$.

How well does this fit with the need to find costs that rationalize all choices? As before, the expected utility in A^1 with data $\mathbf{P}^1$ produces gross expected utility of 0.8 so that the first inequality is unchanged. However, the second equality changes because $u_2 = 1$ so that EU reflects precisely the probability of correctly identifying the state. Finally, in A^3, all data sets allow maximal expected utility of 1 since both prizes have this maximal EU. Putting together all constraints associated with the optimality of the chosen data set, as opposed to alternatives in light of cost, we get

$$0.8 - K^1 \geq \max\{0.6 - K^2, 0.7 - K^3\},$$
$$0.6 - K^2 \geq \max\{0.8 - K^1, 0.7 - K^3\},$$
$$1 - K^3 \geq \max\{1 - K^1, 1 - K^2\}.$$

Note that there are **no** cost functions satisfying all of these constraints. In particular, note the comparisons between K^2 and K^3 in the last two inequalities:

$$K^3 \geq K^2 + 0.1,$$
$$K^3 \leq K^2,$$

which are inconsistent. The reason intuitively is that learning was irrelevant in A^3, so it had to cost no more than learning less, while learning was important in A^2, so should have been undertaken there if no more expensive than the low level of learning in that case.

3.6   Two Decision Problems with No CIR

The above case has no CIR, but the logic is a bit particular and required three decision problems. This example and the next build on the approach to find more generalizable examples with no CIR. In this first example, there are two decision problems, in each of which the data are better matched to the other decision problem in the sense that switching to it would raise utility. This is not trivial to accomplish given that all features, including utilities, must themselves be recovered from the data itself. What we want the data to reveal is that A^1 is best suited to $\mathbf{P}^2$ and that A^2 is best suited to $\mathbf{P}^1$. The challenge is that any inequalities on utilities must also derive from the SDSC in the set of observed decision problems. It is not appropriate simply to assume features of utility. These must be inferred.

How then can we ensure that the data reveal learning about states that are payoff irrelevant? For example, to reveal that data set $\mathbf{P}^2$ is better for A^1, we need that data set to reveal learning about states that are payoff irrelevant in decision problem A^2. It is tempting to have several prizes with different utility differences. But then, one has to ensure that the data reveal a ranking of utility differences, which is relatively hard work. It is much easier to work on cases in which there are only two prizes, as in the simple tracking problem.

The solution adopted in this example and the one to follow is to add more prizes and actions to each decision set to reveal information but to ensure that all prizes are indifferent except for one. That is accomplished based on ensuring that the corresponding action choices cycle so that the NIAS constraints, which will effectively rank prizes, hold with equality.

The first example of this kind involves three prizes: one that will be revealed good, prize z_G, and two that will be revealed bad and also revealed indifferent, z_{B1} and z_{B2}. There are four equiprobable states. Note that in describing the data, it is easiest to show how this works by working with the revealed posteriors associated with the actions: These will be weighted so that their average will reproduce the uniform prior for Bayes' consistency.

Choice Set A^1

Action	ω_1	ω_2	ω_3	ω_4
a_1	z_G	z_{B1}	z_{B1}	z_{B1}
a_2	z_{B1}	z_G	z_{B1}	z_{B1}
b_1	z_{B1}	z_{B1}	z_{B1}	z_{B1}
b_2	z_{B2}	z_{B2}	z_{B2}	z_{B2}

Here are the corresponding revealed posteriors in $\mathbf{P}^1$.

	ω_1	ω_2	ω_3	ω_4
$\gamma_{\mathbf{P}^1}^{a_1}$	0.75	0.25	0	0
$\gamma_{\mathbf{P}^1}^{a_2}$	0.25	0.75	0	0
$\gamma_{\mathbf{P}^1}^{b_1}$	0	0	1	0
$\gamma_{\mathbf{P}^1}^{b_2}$	0	0	0	1

All chosen actions are equiprobable to reproduce the uniform prior.

Choice Set A^2

Action	ω_1	ω_2	ω_3	ω_4
a_3	z_{B1}	z_{B1}	z_G	z_{B1}
a_4	z_{B1}	z_{B1}	z_{B1}	z_G
b_1	z_{B1}	z_{B1}	z_{B1}	z_{B1}
b_2	z_{B2}	z_{B2}	z_{B2}	z_{B2}

Revealed Posteriors in $\mathbf{P}^2$

	ω_1	ω_2	ω_3	ω_4
$\gamma_{\mathbf{P}^2}^{a_3}$	0	0	0.75	0.25
$\gamma_{\mathbf{P}^2}^{a_4}$	0	0	0.25	0.75
$\gamma_{\mathbf{P}^2}^{b_1}$	1	0	0	0
$\gamma_{\mathbf{P}^2}^{b_2}$	0	1	0	0

Again, all actions are equiprobable to reproduce the prior.

Note in this case that when we apply NIAS to both decision problems, we arrive at effectively a single non-trivial utility function. For example, the distinct choices in decision problem A^1 in states ω_3 and ω_4 reveal that prizes z_{B1} and z_{B2} are indifferent since the constant actions b_1 and b_2 made it feasible to get each prize in each case, and these distinct choices were both made. The remaining choices reveal that $u(z_G) \geq u(z_{B1})$ since an action switch could have earned a higher probability of the latter while the chosen action yielded the former with higher probability. Hence, for non-triviality, NIAS has the simple implication:

$$u(z_G) > u(z_{B1}) = u(z_{B2}).$$

Precisely the same logic applies in A^2. Hence, NIAS is satisfied non-trivially if and only if this holds. We normalize to $u(z_G) = 1, u(z_{B1}) = u(z_{B2}) = 0$.

With this simple utility function, in which the only good prize is z_G, it is easy to work out the optimal choices for any of the action sets in any of the data sets corresponding to other decision problems. First, we can directly compute expected utility in action set A^1 as observed in data set $\mathbf{P}^1$ as $\frac{3}{8}$ since the two actions allow a good prize to be selected only when the state is either ω_1 or ω_2, which occurs with a probability of 0.5, and even in these cases, the state is identified only $\frac{3}{4}$ of the time. Likewise, expected utility in action set A^2, as observed in data set $\mathbf{P}^2$, is $\frac{3}{8}$. Yet, with the switch in either case, the expected utility of $\frac{1}{2}$ could have been realized since $\mathbf{P}^2$ allows the perfect separation of states ω_1 and ω_2 that are payoff relevant for action set A^1, while $\mathbf{P}^1$ allows the perfect separation of states ω_3 and ω_4 that are payoff relevant for action set A^2. Adding together the results of both switches yields a total counterfactual utility of 1, as opposed to the actual utility of $\frac{3}{4}$, contracting optimality.

What the above implies is that thinking about attention switching between decision problems pushes up directly against the NIAS constraints. To make switches of attention not raise utility requires z_G and (z_{B_1}), contra NIAS. So, there is no CIR in which prizes are other than indifferent, which is the trivial case and of no interest.

3.7 Longer Cycles

In the above example of a direct cycle, we ruled out utility functions by first applying NIAS to get some necessary inequalities and then doing a direct pair-wise swap of what was learned between decision problems. Not surprisingly, for students of standard revealed preference theory, it is not enough to limit attention to pairs: We have to consider longer cycles, just as we need to impose the strong rather than the weak axiom of revealed preference in classical revealed preference theory. Note that the trouble with a direct Condorcet cycle is that it creates a contradiction with NIAS alone: If the choice of prize cycles, then the only representation is global indifference. But building on the previous example, one can find cases in which there are non-trivial utilities that derive from all NIAS conditions, yet in which existence of a CIR rules them out.

There will be three key decision problems A^i and 15 states ω_k. In A^1, all that matters will be separating states $\omega_1, \omega_2, \omega_3, \omega_4,$ and ω_5 due to five actions that involve a particularly high reward in each such state. In A^2, all that matters will be separating states ω_6–ω_{10} due to five actions that pick out the reward in these states. In A^3, all that matters will be separating states ω_{11}–ω_{15} since five of the actions pick out the reward in these states.

What we want the data to reveal is that A^1 is best suited to $\mathbf{P}^2$, A^2 is best suited to $\mathbf{P}^3$, and A^3 to $\mathbf{P}^1$ in classic Condorcet style. This will be an improving cycle. But we need to rule out improving swaps: In fact, we want to make them strictly utility lowering. Hence, A^1 must be significantly better suited to $\mathbf{P}^1$ than to $\mathbf{P}^3$, A^2 must be significantly better suited to $\mathbf{P}^2$ than to $\mathbf{P}^1$, and A^3 must be significantly better suited to $\mathbf{P}^3$ than to $\mathbf{P}^2$.

There are six prizes: one that will be revealed good, prize z_G, and five that will be revealed bad and also revealed indifferent, $z_{B1}, z_{B2}, z_{B3}, z_{B4},$ and z_{B5}.

Choice Set A^1

	ω_1	ω_2	ω_3	ω_4	ω_5	ω_6	ω_7	ω_8	ω_9	ω_{10}	ω_{11}	ω_{12}	ω_{13}	ω_{14}	ω_{15}
a_1	z_G	z_{B1}	z_{B1}	z_{B1}	z_{B1}	z_{B1}	z_{B1}	z_{B1}	z_{B1}	z_{B1}	z_{B1}	z_{B1}	z_{B1}	z_{B1}	z_{B1}
a_2	z_{B1}	z_G	z_{B1}	z_{B1}	z_{B1}	z_{B1}	z_{B1}	z_{B1}	z_{B1}	z_{B1}	z_{B1}	z_{B1}	z_{B1}	z_{B1}	z_{B1}
a_3	z_{B1}	z_{B1}	z_G	z_{B1}	z_{B1}	z_{B1}	z_{B1}	z_{B1}	z_{B1}	z_{B1}	z_{B1}	z_{B1}	z_{B1}	z_{B1}	z_{B1}
a_4	z_{B1}	z_{B1}	z_{B1}	z_G	z_{B1}	z_{B1}	z_{B1}	z_{B1}	z_{B1}	z_{B1}	z_{B1}	z_{B1}	z_{B1}	z_{B1}	z_{B1}
a_5	z_{B1}	z_{B1}	z_{B1}	z_{B1}	z_G	z_{B1}	z_{B1}	z_{B1}	z_{B1}	z_{B1}	z_{B1}	z_{B1}	z_{B1}	z_{B1}	z_{B1}
b_1	z_{B1}	z_{B1}	z_{B1}	z_{B1}	z_{B1}	z_{B1}	z_{B1}	z_{B1}	z_{B1}	z_{B1}	z_{B1}	z_{B1}	z_{B1}	z_{B1}	z_{B1}
b_2	z_{B2}	z_{B2}	z_{B2}	z_{B2}	z_{B2}	z_{B2}	z_{B2}	z_{B2}	z_{B2}	z_{B2}	z_{B2}	z_{B2}	z_{B2}	z_{B1}	z_{B2}
b_3	z_{B3}	z_{B3}	z_{B3}	z_{B3}	z_{B3}	z_{B3}	z_{B3}	z_{B3}	z_{B3}	z_{B3}	z_{B3}	z_{B3}	z_{B3}	z_{B3}	z_{B3}
b_4	z_{B4}	z_{B4}	z_{B4}	z_{B4}	z_{B4}	z_{B4}	z_{B4}	z_{B4}	z_{B4}	z_{B4}	z_{B4}	z_{B4}	z_{B4}	z_{B4}	z_{B4}
b_5	z_{B5}	z_{B5}	z_{B5}	z_{B5}	z_{B5}	z_{B5}	z_{B5}	z_{B5}	z_{B5}	z_{B5}	z_{B5}	z_{B5}	z_{B5}	z_{B5}	z_{B5}

As in the earlier example of a direct swap, the first five actions make it important in utility terms to identify the corresponding states. The last five are designed for informational purposes: Their choice in any payoff-irrelevant state reveals preferences among bad prizes. These will cycle, establishing indifference. Again, we work with the revealed posteriors associated with the actions: These will be weighted so that their average will reproduce the uniform prior for Bayes' consistency.

Revealed Posteriors in $\mathbf{P}^1$

	ω_1	ω_2	ω_3	ω_4	ω_5	ω_6	ω_7	ω_8	ω_9	ω_{10}	ω_{11}	ω_{12}	ω_{13}	ω_{14}	ω_{15}
$\gamma_{\mathbf{P}^1}^{a_1}$	1	0	0	0	0	0	0	0	0	0	0	0	0	0	0
$\gamma_{\mathbf{P}^1}^{a_2}$	0	1	0	0	0	0	0	0	0	0	0	0	0	0	0
$\gamma_{\mathbf{P}^1}^{a_2}$	0	0	1	0	0	0	0	0	0	0	0	0	0	0	0
$\gamma_{\mathbf{P}^1}^{a_4}$	0	0	0	$\frac{1}{7}$	$\frac{1}{7}$	$\frac{1}{7}$	$\frac{1}{7}$	$\frac{1}{7}$	$\frac{1}{7}$	$\frac{1}{7}$	0	0	0	0	0
$\gamma_{\mathbf{P}^1}^{a_5}$	0	0	0	$\frac{1}{7}$	$\frac{1}{7}$	$\frac{1}{7}$	$\frac{1}{7}$	$\frac{1}{7}$	$\frac{1}{7}$	$\frac{1}{7}$	0	0	0	0	0
$\gamma_{\mathbf{P}^1}^{b_1}$	0	0	0	0	0	0	0	0	0	0	1	0	0	0	0
$\gamma_{\mathbf{P}^1}^{b_2}$	0	0	0	0	0	0	0	0	0	0	0	1	0	0	0
$\gamma_{\mathbf{P}^1}^{b_3}$	0	0	0	0	0	0	0	0	0	0	0	0	1	0	0
$\gamma_{\mathbf{P}^1}^{b_4}$	0	0	0	0	0	0	0	0	0	0	0	0	0	1	0
$\gamma_{\mathbf{P}^1}^{b_5}$	0	0	0	0	0	0	0	0	0	0	0	0	0	0	1

To reproduce the prior, actions $a_1, a_2, a_3, b_1, b_2, b_3, b_4$, and b_5 each have a probability of $\frac{1}{15}$, while actions a_2 and a_3 each have a probability of $\frac{7}{30}$. The idea is that this data set reveals that states $\omega_1, \omega_2, \omega_3$, and all states

ω_{11}–ω_{15} are cleanly identified, while nothing is learned about how to separate states ω_4–ω_{10}. Before outlining the rest of the data, I apply NIAS to the above data to see what it teaches us about utility.

As in the earlier case, note that the distinct choices in states ω_1–ω_5 reveal that prizes $z_{B1}, z_{B2}, z_{B3}, z_{B4}$, and z_{B5} are indifferent since the constant actions $b_1, \ldots, b_5$ made it feasible to get each prize in each case, and these distinct choices were all made. Finally, the remaining choices reveal that $u(z_G) \geq u(z_{B1})$ since an action switch could have earned the latter while the chosen action yielded the former. Hence, for non-triviality, NIAS has the following simple implication:

$$u(z_G) > u(z_{B1}) = u(z_{B2}) = u(z_{B3}) = u(z_{B4}) = u(z_{B5}).$$

We normalize to $u(z_G) = 1, u(z_{B1}) = u(z_{B2}) = u(z_{B3}) = u(z_{B4}) = u(z_{B5}) = 0$.

The remaining choice sets A^2 and A^3 are highly analogous. Each has 10 actions. I will not write them out in full but rather specify their differences from A^1. Action set A^2 contains actions a^6–a^{10} that payout the good prize only in the correspondingly indexed state. It also contains all actions b_1–b_5. Here are the revealed posteriors.

Revealed Posteriors in $\mathbf{P}^2$

	ω_1	ω_2	ω_3	ω_4	ω_5	ω_6	ω_7	ω_8	ω_9	ω_{10}	ω_{11}	ω_{12}	ω_{13}	ω_{14}	ω_{15}
$\gamma_{\mathbf{P}^2}^{a_6}$	0	0	0	0	0	1	0	0	0	0	0	0	0	0	0
$\gamma_{\mathbf{P}^2}^{a_7}$	0	0	0	0	0	0	1	0	0	0	0	0	0	0	0
$\gamma_{\mathbf{P}^2}^{a_8}$	0	0	0	0	0	0	0	1	0	0	0	0	0	0	0
$\gamma_{\mathbf{P}^2}^{a_9}$	0	0	0	0	0	0	0	0	$\frac{1}{7}$	$\frac{1}{7}$	$\frac{1}{7}$	$\frac{1}{7}$	$\frac{1}{7}$	$\frac{1}{7}$	$\frac{1}{7}$
$\gamma_{\mathbf{P}^2}^{a_{10}}$	0	0	0	0	0	0	0	0	$\frac{1}{7}$	$\frac{1}{7}$	$\frac{1}{7}$	$\frac{1}{7}$	$\frac{1}{7}$	$\frac{1}{7}$	$\frac{1}{7}$
$\gamma_{\mathbf{P}^2}^{b_1}$	1	0	0	0	0	0	0	0	0	0	0	0	0	0	0
$\gamma_{\mathbf{P}^2}^{b_2}$	0	1	0	0	0	0	0	0	0	0	0	0	0	0	0
$\gamma_{\mathbf{P}^2}^{b_3}$	0	0	1	0	0	0	0	0	0	0	0	0	0	0	0
$\gamma_{\mathbf{P}^2}^{b_4}$	0	0	0	1	0	0	0	0	0	0	0	0	0	0	0
$\gamma_{\mathbf{P}^2}^{b_5}$	0	0	0	0	1	0	0	0	0	0	0	0	0	0	0

To reproduce the prior, actions $a_6, a_7, a_8, b_1, b_2, b_3, b_4$, and b_5 each have a probability of $\frac{1}{15}$, while actions a_9 and a_{10} each have a probability of $\frac{7}{30}$. The idea is that this data set reveals that states $\omega_6, \omega_7, \omega_8$, and all states ω_1–ω_5 are cleanly identified, while nothing is learned about how to separate states ω_9–ω_{15}.

Finally, we turn to action set A^3. This contains actions a^{11}–a^{15} that pay-out the good prize only in the correspondingly indexed state as well as all actions b_1–b_5. I again specify revealed posteriors in data set $\mathbf{P}^3$.

Revealed Posteriors in $\mathbf{P}^3$

	ω_1	ω_2	ω_3	ω_4	ω_5	ω_6	ω_7	ω_8	ω_9	ω_{10}	ω_{11}	ω_{12}	ω_{13}	ω_{14}	ω_{15}
$\gamma^{a11}_{\mathbf{P}3}$	0	0	0	0	0	0	0	0	0	0	1	0	0	0	0
$\gamma^{a12}_{\mathbf{P}3}$	0	0	0	0	0	0	0	0	0	0	0	1	0	0	0
$\gamma^{a13}_{\mathbf{P}3}$	0	0	0	0	0	0	0	0	0	0	0	0	1	0	0
$\gamma^{a14}_{\mathbf{P}3}$	$\frac{1}{7}$	$\frac{1}{7}$	$\frac{1}{7}$	$\frac{1}{7}$	$\frac{1}{7}$	0	0	0	0	0	0	0	0	$\frac{1}{7}$	$\frac{1}{7}$
$\gamma^{a15}_{\mathbf{P}3}$	$\frac{1}{7}$	$\frac{1}{7}$	$\frac{1}{7}$	$\frac{1}{7}$	$\frac{1}{7}$	0	0	0	0	0	0	0	0	$\frac{1}{7}$	$\frac{1}{7}$
$\gamma^{b1}_{\mathbf{P}3}$	0	0	0	0	0	1	0	0	0	0	1	0	0	0	0
$\gamma^{b2}_{\mathbf{P}3}$	0	0	0	0	0	0	1	0	0	0	0	1	0	0	0
$\gamma^{b3}_{\mathbf{P}3}$	0	0	0	0	0	0	0	1	0	0	0	0	0	0	0
$\gamma^{b4}_{\mathbf{P}3}$	0	0	0	0	0	0	0	0	1	0	0	0	0	0	0
$\gamma^{b5}_{\mathbf{P}3}$	0	0	0	0	0	0	0	0	0	1	0	0	0	0	0

Analogous to the other data sets, to reproduce the prior, actions $a_{11}, a_{12}, a_{13}, b_1, b_2, b_3, b_4$, and b_5 each have a probability of $\frac{1}{15}$, while actions a_{14} and a_{15} each have a probability of $\frac{7}{30}$. The idea is that this data set reveals that states $\omega_{11}, \omega_{12}, \omega_{13}$, and all states ω_6–ω_{10} are cleanly identified, while nothing is learned about how to separate states ω_{14}, ω_{15}, and ω_1–ω_5.

With this simple utility function, in which the only good prize is u_G, it is easy to work out the optimal choices for any of the action sets in any of the data sets corresponding to other decision problems. First, we can directly compute the expected utility as observed in the data as $\frac{4}{15}$ since three of the five important states are picked out, and the other two are each picked with a probability of $\frac{1}{2}$ in the other two states in which they alone yield the high payoff. By contrast, action set A^1 yields a higher utility of $\frac{1}{3}$ when shifted to data set $\mathbf{P}^2$ since this data set allows full revelation of the five payoff relevant states. Likewise, action set A^2 yields a higher utility of $\frac{1}{3}$ when shifted to data set $\mathbf{P}^3$, as does action set A^3 when shifted to data set $\mathbf{P}^1$. Conversely, action set A^1 yields a lower utility of $\frac{1}{7}$ when shifted to data set $\mathbf{P}^2$ since this data set randomizes all five good actions and also mixes in two payoff-irrelevant states. Likewise, action set A^2 yields a lower utility of $\frac{1}{15}$ when shifted to data set $\mathbf{P}^3$, as does action set A^3 when shifted to data set

$\mathbf{P}^1$. Note, therefore, that each of the direct swaps leave the corresponding sum of utilities from $\frac{8}{15}$ to $\frac{1}{3} + \frac{1}{7} < \frac{8}{15}$.

Hence, what this data set reveals is that there is an improving cycle. To show that this is inconsistent with the existence of a rationalizing cost function, note that this requires existence of numbers K^1, K^2, and K^3 such that it is best in all cases to choose what was chosen rather than the alternative.

To formalize the implications, we introduce important general definitions starting with the gross expected utility implied by the data for any given utility function.

Definition 9: Given $A^m, \mathbf{P}^m$, and $u : Z \longrightarrow \mathbb{R}$, the corresponding total utility is

$$G^m(u) \equiv \sum_{a \in A^m} \sum_{\omega \in \Omega} u(a, \omega) \mathbf{P}^m(a, \omega). \tag{9}$$

A key part of the logic involves putting together information on all swaps. We formalize this in the direct value difference matrix. This is an $M \times M$ matrix of value differences D_0, with element D_0^{mn} in row m column n and specifying the change in maximized utility when decision set A^m is moved away from data set $\mathbf{P}^m$ to data set $\mathbf{P}^n$. To specify it, we first define the value switch matrix which specifies the maximum expected utility when decision set A^m is used in data set $\mathbf{P}^n$.

Definition 10: Given $\{(A^m, \mathbf{P}^m)\}_{m=1}^{M}$ and $u : Z \longrightarrow \mathbb{R}$, define the $M \times M$ **value switch matrix**

$$G^{mn}(u) \equiv \sum_{a \in A^n} \max_{a' \in A^m} \sum_{\omega \in \Omega} u(z(a', \omega)) \mathbf{P}^n(a, \omega), \tag{10}$$

for $1 \leq m, n \leq M$. Define the $M \times M$ **direct value difference matrix** D_0 by

$$D_0^{mn}(u) \equiv G^{mn}(u) - G^{mm}(u). \tag{11}$$

Note that the operation on the RHS of (10) measures the optimal utility that can be achieved using action choices from A^m in the data $\mathbf{P}^n$ associated with A^n. The idea is that, given any action $a \in A^n$, one picks some action $a' \in A^m$ to replace it wholesale and computes the corresponding expected utility. One then adds this up across all actions that are chosen in the data in set A^n. Any such set of wholesale action replacements is feasible.

The optimal replacement is the one that maximizes expected utility among all such options. The finiteness of the set of such switches ensures that the maximum is achieved.

Considering only the switches above, we need that

$$G^1 - K^1 \geq G^{12} - K^2,$$
$$G^2 - K^2 \geq G^{23} - K^3,$$
$$G^3 - K^3 \geq G^{31} - K^1.$$

Adding these three inequalities, we see that total costs are the same on the left-hand side (LHS) and the RHS so that we derive the implication

$$G^1 + G^2 + G^3 \geq G^{12} + G^{23} + G^{31}.$$

This directly contradicts what the improving cycle reveals:

$$G^{12} + G^{23} + G^{31} = 1 > \frac{12}{15} = G^{11} + G^{22} + G^{33} = G^1 + G^2 + G^3.$$

Hence, no such representation exists.

3.8   Value Switch and Direct Value Difference Matrices

The above example reveals several key features of the analytic approach to CIRs. First, it is important to think about the total utility in the data and to check that it is maximal in satisfaction of NIAS. Second, one needs to think about reallocation of attention strategies. What the above example has shown is that a key operation in identifying whether or not $u : Z \longrightarrow \mathbb{R}$ permits a CIR involves swapping what is learned between decision problems and evaluating the corresponding change in the total utility. Third, the basic logic involves working first with the attention strategies seen in the data and making sure that there are no improvements to be found by making feasible cyclic switches. These have echoes in the general arguments that follow. First, we define the total utility implied by the observed data for any given utility function.

Note that $G^{mm}(u)$ defines the maximal gross expected utility associated with the given data:

$$G^{mm}(u) \equiv \sum_{a \in A^m} \max_{a' \in A^m} \sum_{\omega \in \Omega} u(z(a', \omega)) \mathbf{P}^m(a, \omega).$$

Note also that NIAS is satisfied by u if and only if this is precisely the same as expected utility in the actual data.

Comment 3.2: $u : Z \longrightarrow \mathbb{R}$ satisfies NIAS in $\mathbf{P}^m$ if and only if

$$G^m(u) = G^{mm}(u). \tag{12}$$

3.9 The Indirect Value Difference Matrix

It should be clear to students of revealed preference that the process we are going through is strongly analogous. In fact that is directly hinted at by the name of the matrix as involving **direct** value differences: It involves only direct paths of attentional change. What we do now, in further pursuit of the analogy, is to construct an **indirect value difference matrix**. To that end, we define the arbitrary sequences of indices $\vec{h} = (h(1), h(2), \ldots, h(J(\vec{h})))$, with $1 \leq h(j) \leq M$, allowing for cycles but no other repetition so that the first $J(\vec{h}) - 1$ entries are distinct. We define H as the set of all such vectors. Note that included in the set are direct cycles of length 2 starting and stopping at the same index. We then define the set that starts at m and end at n for arbitrary $1 \leq m, n \leq M$:

$$H(m, n) = \{\vec{h} \in H | h(1) = m, h(J(\vec{h})) = n)\}.$$

We use this to define the maximum sum of utility changes along such a path and arrange them in an $M \times M$ matrix, which will be key in what follows. We call this the indirect value difference matrix. It is derived from the direct value matrix as now specified.

Definition 11: Given $\{(A^m, \mathbf{P}^m)\}_{m=1}^{M}$ and $u : Z \longrightarrow \mathbb{R}$, the corresponding $M \times M$ **indirect value difference matrix** $D(u)$ with entry in row m and column n is defined by

$$D^{mn}(u) \equiv \max_{\{\vec{h} \in H(m,n)\}} \sum_{j=1}^{J(\vec{h})-1} D_0^{j(j+1)}(u). \tag{13}$$

This is called the indirect value difference matrix because it sums up the changes in the maximized expected utility along a path in which each decision problem $A^{h(i)}$ is shifted to data set $\mathbf{P}^{h(i+1)}$ corresponding to one higher index. It is intuitive that this matrix plays an important role in identifying whether or not a CIR exists. As we will see, it does a great more besides. In fact, the central point of the following lecture is showing that essentially everything of interest concerning CIRs is contained in the $D(u)$ matrix.

Lecture 4

All Rationalizing Cost Functions

In this lecture, I follow Caplin and Dean (2015) and Caplin *et al.* (2023c) not only to characterize CIRs but also to precisely show how to recover all rationalizing cost functions for any such utility function. All results are organized around matrices introduced at the end of the previous lecture. Before plunging into the general results, I open by restating the key objects and providing a number of illustrative examples that point the path forward.

The goals of the lecture are:

1. To introduce qualifying costs of revealed learning.
2. To show why they are central to the existence and characterization of a CIR.
3. To work with the value switch, direct and indirect value difference matrices in the examples to look for regularities and conjectures in terms of what they reveal about these qualifying costs.
4. To produce the full characterization of the qualifying costs of revealed learning.
5. To introduce the no improving attention cycles (NIAC) condition of Caplin and Dean (2015) and to establish their result that NIAS and NIAC together characterize the existence of a CIR.
6. To introduce the learning cost polyhedron and the representative cost.
7. To make explicit the analogy between the direct and indirect value switch matrices with the direct and indirect affordability matrices that are central to classical revealed preference theory and to establish applicability of the Floyd–Warshall algorithm to compute the indirect value

difference matrix from the direct value difference matrix, just as it is used to compute the indirect from the direct affordability matrix.
8. To introduce the variational lower bound on costs.

There is a caveat to the lecture. What we are doing is identifying all cost functions for which what is learned in each data set is precisely the revealed information structure. This is precisely what is learned when the learning cost function is strictly increasing in the Blackwell order so that more learning is strictly more costly. As we will see in the following lecture, there are other possibilities for what might have been learned. Caplin *et al.* (2023c) showed that the material in this lecture can be adapted for those cases. But there is a notational and conceptual cost.

For ease of reference, I restate the key objects to open the lecture. Given $\{(A^m, \mathbf{P}^m)\}_{m=1}^M$ and $u : Z \longrightarrow \mathbb{R}$, define the $M \times M$ value switch matrix:

$$G^{mn}(u) \equiv \sum_{a \in A^n} \max_{a' \in A^m} \sum_{\omega \in \Omega} u(z(a', \omega)) \mathbf{P}^n(a, \omega).$$

The direct value difference matrix D_0 is defined by

$$D_0^{mn}(u) \equiv G^{mn}(u) - G^{mm}(u).$$

The indirect value difference matrix $D(u)$ is defined by

$$D^{mn}(u) \equiv \max_{\{\vec{h} \in H(m,n)\}} \sum_{j=1}^{J(\vec{h})-1} D_0^{j(j+1)}(u),$$

where $H(m,n)$ is defined as all sequences of set indices that start at m and end at n for arbitrary $1 \leq m, n \leq M$, in which all indices are distinct (except for the first and last when $m = n$).

4.1 Qualifying Costs of Revealed Learning and Costly Information Representations

As noted above, a central goal is to characterize all qualifying costs of revealed learning which are vectors of costs, one per action set, $\vec{K} = (K^1, \ldots, K^M) \in \mathbb{R}^M$, such that the net utility based on these costs cannot be raised by any switch across decision problems. Here is the formal definition.

Definition 12: Given $\{(A^m, \mathbf{P}^m)\}_{m=1}^M$ and utility function u, $\vec{K} \in \mathbb{R}^M$ are the **qualifying costs of revealed learning** if

$$G^{mm}(u) - K^m \geq G^{mn}(u) - K^n, \tag{14}$$

or, equivalently,

$$K^n - K^m \geq D_0^{mn}(u). \tag{15}$$

We define $\mathcal{K}^R(u) \subset \mathbb{R}^M$ as the set of such vectors $\vec{K}$.

It is intuitive that the existence of such costs is crucial to the existence of a CIR. We now formalize this point. Necessity is direct: If there are no such costs, then we will be able to identify some switch that is beneficial for any proposed cost function. For sufficiency, we impose also the condition that NIAS be satisfied so that actual utility in the data corresponds to the maximum as in Comment 3.2:

$$G^{mm}(u) = G^m(u).$$

Theorem 2: *A necessary condition for u to admit a CIR of $\{(A^m, \mathbf{P}^m)\}_{m=1}^M$ is that $\mathcal{K}^R(u) \neq \emptyset$. Together with u satisfying NIAS for each $\mathbf{P}^m$, this is also sufficient for it to admit a CIR of $\{(A^m, \mathbf{P}^m)\}_{m=1}^M$.*

Proof 2: The proof of necessity works by contradiction. Suppose to the contrary that there there exists a CIR but that there are no qualifying costs of revealed learning. Based on the proposed CIR, we can identify the corresponding cost function (u, K) that constitutes a CIR and define the vector of costs $(K^1, \ldots, K^M) \in \mathbb{R}^M$ for the corresponding revealed information structures

$$K^m = K(Q_{\mathbf{P}^m}).$$

Given that there are no qualifying costs of revealed learning, we know that we can identify $1 \leq m \neq n \leq M$ such that

$$G^{mm}(u) - K^m < G^{mn}(u) - K^n. \tag{16}$$

The contradiction is that this implies that there is a feasible strategy in decision problem A^m that has a higher net utility than can be achieved with the revealed information structure, which contradicts the optimality condition of the CIR. Specifically, we take the information structure to be the revealed information structure associated with P^n, $Q_{\mathbf{P}^n}$, which by definition has cost K^n. As for the mixed action strategy, we take it to be any strategy that achieves the maximum gross utility of G^{mn}:

$$G^{mn}(u) \equiv \sum_{a \in A^n} \max_{a' \in A^m} \sum_{\omega \in \Omega} u(z(a', \omega)) \mathbf{P}^n(a, \omega).$$

Formally, one can rewrite this to involve deterministic choice of any action $a' \in A^m$ at any of the possible posteriors, given information structure $Q_{\mathbf{P}^n}$. By construction, this achieves precisely the RHS in equation (16), contradicting the optimality condition in a CIR.

Turning to sufficiency, the proof is constructive. Take the qualifying costs of revealed learning $\vec{K} \in \mathcal{K}^R(u)$, set $(Q^m, q^m) = (Q_{\mathbf{P}^m}, q_{\mathbf{P}^m})$, and define the cost function by

$$K(Q) = \begin{cases} K^m & \text{if } Q = Q_{\mathbf{P}^m}, \\ \infty & \text{else.} \end{cases}$$

The claim is that these constitute a CIR if NIAS is satisfied.

A preliminary requirement is that the definition is legitimate in that it successfully defines a function. This follows from equation (15): If $Q_{\mathbf{P}^m} = Q_{\mathbf{P}^n}$ and $\vec{K}$ are qualifying costs, then $K^m = K^n$. This is clear since, otherwise, the switch to the cheaper is improving since $G^{mm} = G^{mn}$. With this in place, the first condition for a CIR is that the proposed strategies produce the data: This is clear since we established globally that

$$P_{(Q_{\mathbf{P}}, q_{\mathbf{P}})} = \mathbf{P}.$$

All that is left is optimality. With u satisfying NIAS w.r.t $\mathbf{P}^m$, we know that

$$G^m(u) = G^{mm}(u) = \sum_{a \in A^m} \max_{a' \in A^m} \sum_{\omega \in \Omega} u(z(a', \omega)) \mathbf{P}^m(a, \omega).$$

Note that no strategy $(Q^m, q^m) \in \Lambda(\mu, A^m)$ that generates the data can yield higher gross utility than this since they all produce the data and $G^{mm}(u)$ is maximal subject to this constraint. Given that costs are infinite elsewhere, the only possible improvements in net utility involve switching to the revealed experiments associated with other actions sets $Q_{\mathbf{P}^n}$ and thereafter optimizing. For any such choice to be a strict improvement requires

$$G^{mn} - K^n > G^{mm} - K^m,$$

which directly contradicts $\vec{K} \in \mathcal{K}^R(u)$, completing the proof.

With this, the characterization of when a utility function admits a CIR of $\{(A^m, \mathbf{P}^m)\}_{m=1}^M$ with NIAS satisfied is equivalent to the existence of qualifying costs of learning for that utility function. Identifying conditions guaranteeing the existence of qualifying costs of revealed learning and identifying all such costs are the remaining tasks.

4.2 Revisiting the First Example

Recall the first example of a two-state tracking problem in which prize z_1 is picked over prize z_0 80% of the time in $(A^1, \mathbf{P}^1)$, while prize z_2 is picked over prize z_0 60% of the time in $(A^2, \mathbf{P}^2)$. As we noted, taken alone, the NIAS constraints imply that $\min\{u_1, u_2\} \geq u_0$. But we made the argument that existence of a CIR requires also $u_1 \geq u_2$ since more is learned in A^1 than in A^2. What we now show is how to read this argument from the value switch and value difference matrices. I do this first for a case that satisfies the conditions and then for one that passes NIAS but not NIAC.

Take first a utility function that satisfies these conditions: $u_1 = 1, u_2 = 0.5$, and $u_0 = 0$. In this case, direct computation reveals the 2×2 $G(u)$ matrix as

$$G(u) = \begin{pmatrix} \overset{\mathbf{P}^1}{0.8} & \overset{\mathbf{P}^2}{0.6} \\ 0.4 & 0.3 \end{pmatrix} \begin{matrix} A^1 \\ A^2 \end{matrix}.$$

The reason for this is simple: Data set $\mathbf{P}^1$ identifies the true state 80% of the time and data set $\mathbf{P}^2$ only 60% of the time. The first row shows that in choice set A^1, in which the good prize has a utility of $u_1 = 1$ and the bad $u_0 = 0$, the counterfactual switch to worse state identification produces a utility of 0.6 rather than 0.8. In choice set A^2, in which the good prize has a utility of $u_2 = 0.5$ and the bad $u_0 = 0$, the counterfactual switch to better state identification produces a utility of 0.4 rather than 0.3.

Direct computation from the T matrix shows that this is a case in which the direct and indirect value switch matrices are the same

$$D_0(u) = D(u) = \begin{pmatrix} \overset{\mathbf{P}^1}{0} & \overset{\mathbf{P}^2}{-0.2} \\ 0.1 & 0 \end{pmatrix} \begin{matrix} A^1 \\ A^2 \end{matrix}.$$

The computation for $D_0(u)$ is immediate while that for $D(u)$ involves thinking also about the indirect cycle, e.g., with A^1 switched to $\mathbf{P}^2$ simultaneously with the reverse switch. The reason that this leaves the matrix unchanged is that, the indirect cycle in either direction on net reduces the total maximal utility by 0.1. One more feature of the example is worth noting. For a CIR, the diagonal elements of the $G(u)$ matrix have to be maximal in their rows with costs netted out:

$$0.8 - K^1 \geq 0.6 - K^2,$$

$$0.3 - K^2 \geq 0.4 - K^1.$$

Combining these, we see that $K^1 - K^2 \in [0.1, 0.2]$ is necessary and sufficient for a qualifying cost function. We will soon see how to read this information directly out of the corresponding $D(u)$ matrix.

We now stay with the same data set but take a case that we ruled out as having a CIR in the direct argument in the previous lecture: $u_1 = 0.5, u_2 = 1$, and $u_0 = 0$. In this case, direct computation reveals the 2×2 $G(u')$ matrix as

$$G(u') = \begin{array}{cc} \mathbf{P}^1 & \mathbf{P}^2 \end{array} \\ \begin{pmatrix} 0.4 & 0.3 \\ 0.8 & 0.6 \end{pmatrix} \begin{array}{c} A^1 \\ A^2 \end{array}.$$

Again, the reasoning is direct and involves applying the fact that $\mathbf{P}^1$ identifies the true state 80% of the time and data set $\mathbf{P}^2$ only 60% of the time. The key change is that in this case, the D_0 and D matrices differ. D_0 is read directly off G by subtracting the main diagonal element from each row:

$$D_0(u') = \begin{array}{cc} \mathbf{P}^1 & \mathbf{P}^2 \end{array} \\ \begin{pmatrix} 0 & -0.1 \\ 0.2 & 0 \end{pmatrix} \begin{array}{c} A^1 \\ A^2 \end{array},$$

where the D matrix differs in that it also requires us to consider indirect cycles. In this case, both of the indirect cycles end up raising the total utility by 0.1. When A^1 is switched to $\mathbf{P}^2$ simultaneously with the reverse switch, there is first a fall of 0.1 in expected utility, then an increase of 0.1, accounting for the 0.1 value of D^{11}, and likewise for D^{22}:

$$D(u') = \begin{matrix} & \mathbf{P}^1 & \mathbf{P}^2 & \\ & \begin{pmatrix} 0.1 & -0.1 \\ 0.2 & 0.1 \end{pmatrix} & \begin{matrix} A^1 \\ A^2 \end{matrix} \end{matrix}.$$

What is it about this matrix $D(u')$ that reveals that there is no CIR?

4.3 Revisiting the Second Example

Our second example involved adding a third choice set. We consider the following case in which we showed that NIAS implies $u(z_1) \geq u(z_2) \geq u(z_0) = 0$.

Choice Set A^3

Action	State ω_1	State ω_2
a_3	z_2	z_1
b_3	z_1	z_2

$$\mathbf{P}^3(a_3, \omega_1) = 0.15 = \mathbf{P}^3(b_3, \omega_2),$$

$$\mathbf{P}^3(a_3, \omega_2) = 0.35 = \mathbf{P}^3(b_3, \omega_1).$$

Here is the corresponding value switch matrix $\tilde{G}(u)$ corresponding to the expected utility in all switches with $u_1 = 1, u_2 = 0.5$, and $u_3 = 0$:

$$\tilde{G}(u) = \begin{matrix} & \mathbf{P}^1 & \mathbf{P}^2 & \mathbf{P}^3 & \\ & \begin{pmatrix} 0.8 & 0.6 & 0.7 \\ 0.4 & 0.3 & 0.35 \\ 0.9 & 0.8 & 0.85 \end{pmatrix} & \begin{matrix} A^1 \\ A^2 \\ A^3 \end{matrix} \end{matrix}.$$

To understand this, one can look down the columns. The expected utilities in column 1 reflect an 80% chance of identifying the true state. This gives rise to an expected utility of 0.8 in A^1 when the good and bad prizes have utilities of 1 and 0, respectively, 0.4 in A^2 when the good and bad prizes have utilities of 0.5 and 0, respectively, and 0.9 in A^3 when the good and bad prizes have utilities of 1 and 0.5, respectively. Other columns are correspondingly explained.

The direct value switch matrix is derived straightforwardly by subtracting the main diagonal from each row:

$$\tilde{D}_0(u) = \begin{pmatrix} 0 & -0.2 & -0.1 \\ 0.1 & 0 & 0.05 \\ 0.05 & -0.05 & 0 \end{pmatrix} \begin{matrix} A^1 \\ A^2. \\ A^3 \end{matrix}$$

with column headers $\mathbf{P}^1$, $\mathbf{P}^2$, $\mathbf{P}^3$.

The $\tilde{D}(u)$ matrix can be derived from this by direct computation as

$$\tilde{D}(u) = \begin{pmatrix} 0 & -0.15 & -0.1 \\ 0.1 & 0 & 0.05 \\ 0.05 & -0.05 & 0 \end{pmatrix} \begin{matrix} A^1 \\ A^2. \\ A^3 \end{matrix}$$

with column headers $\mathbf{P}^1$, $\mathbf{P}^2$, $\mathbf{P}^3$.

To understand this, note that there are losses from a direct shift of A^1 to $\mathbf{P}^2$ and $\mathbf{P}^3$, with the maximized expected utility falling from by 0.2 from 0.8 to 0.6 in the first case and by 0.1 from 0.8 to 0.7 in the second. The first step of the indirect path from A^1 to $\mathbf{P}^2$ involves shifting A^1 to $\mathbf{P}^3$ and hence lowering the maximized expected utility by 0.1. The second step from A^3 to $\mathbf{P}^2$ involves a further lowering of maximized utility by 0.05. The sum of these is above -0.15 so that the maximum reflects the indirect path change of -0.15. To compare the direct and indirect paths from A^1 to $\mathbf{P}^3$, note that the former involves a utility reduction of 0.1 and the latter involves first reducing utility by 0.2 and then raising it by 0.05 for a net utility loss of 0.15. The smallest loss is therefore on the direct path as reflected in the matrix. Finally, note that the entry $D_{11} = 0$ on the main diagonal reflects the fact that no indirect cycles increase utility while the direct cycle leaves utility unchanged.

The other two rows have corresponding explanations. With regard to the second row, the gain from a direct shift of A^2 to $\mathbf{P}^1$ and $\mathbf{P}^3$ involves the maximized expected utility rising by 0.1 and 0.05, respectively. The first step of the indirect path from A^2 to $\mathbf{P}^1$ involves shifting A^2 to $\mathbf{P}^3$ and hence raising the maximized expected utility by 0.05. The second step from A^3 to $\mathbf{P}^1$ involves a further raising of the maximized utility by 0.05. The sum of these is precisely 0.1, equal to that of the direct shift and therefore corresponding to the maximum, as reflected in D_{21}. The change in utility on the indirect path from A^2 to $\mathbf{P}^3$ involves a utility increase of 0.1 in the first place and a loss of 0.1 in the second stage, giving rise to a sum of 0, which is lower than that in the direct switch, explaining $D_{23} = 0.1$. Again, note that the entry $D_{22} = 0$ on the main diagonal reflects the fact that no indirect cycles increase utility, while the direct cycle leaves utility unchanged.

With regard to the third row, the gain from a direct shift of A^3 to $\mathbf{P}^1$ is 0.05, while the loss from the direct switch of A^3 to $\mathbf{P}^2$ is correspondingly 0.05. The first step of the indirect path from A^3 to $\mathbf{P}^1$ involves shifting A^3 to $\mathbf{P}^2$ and hence lowering the maximized expected utility by 0.05. The second step from A^2 to $\mathbf{P}^1$ raises it by 0.1. The sum of these is 0.05, which is equal that of the direct shift and therefore corresponding to the maximum, as reflected in $D_{31} = 0.05$. The change in utility on the indirect path from A^3 to $\mathbf{P}^2$ involves a utility increase of 0.05 in the first place and a loss of 0.2 in the second stage, giving rise to a loss of 0.15, which is higher than the loss in the direct switch, as reflected in $D_{31} = -0.05$. Finally, note once again that the entry $D_{11} = 0$ on the main diagonal reflects the fact that no indirect cycles increase utility, while the direct cycle leaves utility unchanged.

Much information is contained in the $D(u)$ matrix that relates to CIRs. Particularly salient is that the main diagonal is zero. This is in fact necessary and sufficient for a CIR due to the NIAC condition of Caplin and Dean that we formally introduce in the following.

4.4 No CIR: The Final Example

As a final illustration of the construction of key matrices, we turn to the final example of the previous lecture with three action sets and 15 states constructed so that the only utility function consistent with NIAS involved the utility of the good prize of 1 and that of all others as 0. Here is the corresponding matrix G with the u argument suppressed since there is only one non-trivial rationalization of the data in a BEU in which the utility of the good prize can be normalized to 1 and that of all bad prizes to 0.

First, we compute the direct value switch matrix, as indicated in the example:

$$G = \begin{array}{ccc} \mathbf{P}^1 & \mathbf{P}^2 & \mathbf{P}^3 \\ \begin{pmatrix} \frac{4}{15} & \frac{1}{3} & \frac{1}{7} \\ \frac{1}{7} & \frac{4}{15} & \frac{1}{3} \\ \frac{1}{3} & \frac{1}{7} & \frac{4}{15} \end{pmatrix} & \begin{array}{c} A^1 \\ A^2. \\ A^3 \end{array} \end{array}$$

Subtracting the diagonal, we get the D_0 matrix:

$$D_0 = \begin{pmatrix} \mathbf{P}^1 & \mathbf{P}^2 & \mathbf{P}^3 \\ 0 & \frac{1}{15} & -\frac{13}{105} \\ -\frac{13}{105} & 0 & \frac{1}{15} \\ \frac{1}{15} & -\frac{13}{105} & 0 \end{pmatrix} \begin{matrix} A^1 \\ A^2 \\ \end{matrix}.$$

The indirect value difference D matrix can be found by direct computation as

$$D = \begin{pmatrix} \mathbf{P}^1 & \mathbf{P}^2 & \mathbf{P}^3 \\ \frac{3}{15} & \frac{1}{15} & \frac{2}{15} \\ \frac{2}{15} & \frac{3}{15} & \frac{1}{15} \\ \frac{1}{15} & \frac{2}{15} & \frac{3}{15} \end{pmatrix} \begin{matrix} A^1 \\ A^2 \\ A^3 \end{matrix}.$$

To understand this, we consider all non-repeating paths and maximize the resulting change in utility. Reading from the D_0 matrix, we see that the direct paths from action set A^1 to $\mathbf{P}^2$, from action set A^2 to $\mathbf{P}^3$, and from action set A^3 to $\mathbf{P}^1$ each result in the maximized utility increasing by $\frac{1}{15}$ from $\frac{4}{5}$ to $\frac{1}{3}$. The corresponding indirect paths, for example, from A^1 to $\mathbf{P}^3$ and from A^3 to $\mathbf{P}^2$, successively lower the maximized utility: in each move, from $\frac{4}{15}$ to $\frac{1}{7}$. Hence, the sum of these changes is negative, and the indirect paths in this case play no role in the maximization and hence in the D matrix. This explains why $D_{12} = D_{23} = D_{31} = \frac{1}{15}$. The three entries $D_{13} = D_{21} = D_{33} = \frac{2}{15}$ stem from the indirect paths rather than from the direct path, which would instead result in a reduction in utility in each case from $\frac{4}{15}$ to $\frac{1}{7}$. The entries of $\frac{2}{15}$ can be understood by thinking of the indirect paths, e.g., getting from A^1 to $\mathbf{P}^3$ indirectly by first shifting A^1 to $\mathbf{P}^2$ and then A^2 to $\mathbf{P}^3$, each of which increases the maximized utility by $\frac{1}{15}$. The complete cycle of A^1 to $\mathbf{P}^2$, A^2 to $\mathbf{P}^3$, and A^3 to $\mathbf{P}^1$ explains the main diagonal of $D_{11} = \frac{3}{15}$ and correspondingly the rest of the main diagonal. These are clearly higher than the corresponding direct cycles, which leave the total utility unchanged, and the two-step cycles, which lower total utility.

Again, we see a main diagonal that is strictly positive. In what follows, we learn how to read the D matrix to understand not only existence but also the set of rationalizing costs when the existence test is passed.

4.5 Characterization of Qualifying Costs

In this section, we establish a number of other important features that are revealed in the $D(u)$ matrix. The following result shows how to recover all qualifying costs of revealed learning from the indirect value difference matrix D.

Theorem 3: *Given* $\{(A^m, \mathbf{P}^m)\}_{m=1}^{M}$, $\vec{K} \in \mathcal{K}^R(u)$ *if and only if,*

$$K^n - K^m \geq D^{mn}(u), \tag{17}$$

for all $1 \leq m, n \leq M$.

Proof 3: To establish that (17) is necessary for $\vec{K} \in \mathcal{K}^R(u)$, find a path $\vec{h}^*$ from m to n that achieves the maximum. By definition,

$$D^{mn}(u) = \sum_{j=1}^{J(\vec{h}^*)-1} D_0^{h^*(j)h^*(j+1)}(u).$$

Now, suppose $\vec{K}$ are qualifying costs of revealed learning that satisfy equation (15):

$$K^{h^*(j+1)} - K^{h^*(j)} \geq D_0^{h^*(j)h^*(j+1)}(u).$$

Summing across the path and noting that only the first and last terms on the LHS do not cancel and that $h^*(1) = m$ and $h^*(J(\vec{h})) = n$, we conclude that

$$K^n - K^m \geq \sum_{j=1}^{J(\vec{h}^*)-1} D_0^{h^*(j)h^*(j+1)}(u) = D^{mn}(u),$$

completing the proof of necessity.

To establish sufficiency, suppose that $\vec{K} \in \mathbb{R}^M$ are **not** qualifying costs of revealed learning. In this case, there exists $1 \leq m \neq n \leq M$ for which

$$K^n - K^m < D_0^{mn}(u) \leq D^{mn}(u),$$

where the second inequality follows since $D_0^{mn}(u)$ corresponds to the direct path from m to n and $D^{mn}(u)$ is a maximum across all paths, including the direct path. Hence, for $\vec{K}$ not to define a qualifying learning cost function requires that at least one inequality $K^n - K^m \geq D^{mn}(u)$ is violated, completing the proof that (17), for all $1 \leq m,n \leq M$, is sufficient.

An interesting and open technical question concerns identifying the set of all indirect value switch matrices consistent with the existence of a CIR for some $\{(A^m, \mathbf{P}^m)\}_{m=1}^M$.

4.6   NIAC and CIRs

We have now backed in to the CD15 characterization of (Caplin and Dean, 2015) based on NIACs in addition to NIAS.

Definition 13: Given $\{(A^m, \mathbf{P}^m)\}_{m=1}^M$, utility function u satisfies **no improving attention cycles** if given any cyclic list of decision problems that is not a direct cycle, $\vec{h} = (h(1), h(2), \ldots, h(J(\vec{h})) \in H(m,m)$, for some m:

$$\sum_{j=1}^{J(h)-1} G^{h(j)}(u) \geq \sum_{j=1}^{J(h)-1} G^{h(j)h(j+1)}(u). \tag{18}$$

Note that LHS is in the data. As noted, when introducing the value switch matrix, the RHS operation expresses the optimal utility that can be achieved using action choices from $A^{j(h)}$ in the data associated with $A^{j(h+1)}$. One then adds the impact of this replacement all across the cycle and rules out improvement.

Comment 4.1: There are many different ways to specify NIAS and NIAC. For example, one can unify them in an inclusive version of NIAS and NIAC by noting that NIAS is itself equivalent to the direct cycle version of the above with $J(h) = 2$. The reason for specifying as above is that NIAS alone is important for its role in the BEU representation, so one wants to keep NIAC distinct. But from the viewpoint of the CIR, one can note that NIAS and NIAC together corresponds to

$$\sum_{j=1}^{J(h)-1} G^{h(j)}(u) \geq \sum_{j=1}^{J(h)-1} G^{h(j)h(j+1)}(u), \tag{19}$$

for all $\vec{h} = (h(1), h(2), \ldots, h(J(\vec{h})) \in H(m,m)$ for any m. There are other valuable ways to think of the combined impact of NIAS and NIAC. NIAS and NIAC together is equivalent to NIAS, which relates to the data and says that $G^m(u) = G^{mm}(u)$ and an alternative version of NIAC that is focused purely on the value switch matrix and makes no reference to the actual choices in the data:

$$\sum_{j=1}^{J(h)-1} G^{h(j)h(j+1)}(u) - \sum_{j=1}^{J(h)-1} G^{h(j)h(j)}(u) = \sum_{j=1}^{J(h)-1} D_0^{h(j)h(j+1)}(u) \leq 0. \quad (20)$$

Given the direct cycle $h(1) = h(2) = m$ for which the above sum is zero, for a utility function that satisfies NIAS, NIAC is equivalent to the diagonal of the indirect value switch matrix D comprising all zeroes.

$$\sum_{j=1}^{J(h)-1} D^{h(j)h(j+1)}(u) = 0. \quad (21)$$

With this, the theorem of Caplin and Dean is that together with NIAS, NIAC characterizes whether or not a utility function admits a CIR comes down entirely to finding conditions equivalent to the existence of qualifying costs of revealed learning, which is straightforward given Theorem 3.

Theorem 4 (Caplin and Dean, 2015): *Given* $\{(A^m, \mathbf{P}^m)\}_{m=1}^M$, *utility function* $u : Z \longrightarrow \mathbb{R}$ *admits a CIR if and only if it satisfies NIAS and NIAC.*

Proof 4: Sufficiency: Comment 4.2 shows that with NIAS satisfied, NIAC implies that $D^{mm}(u) = 0$, for all m. What we do is show that this implies that there exist qualifying revealed learning costs. To this end, note that for any $1 \leq m, n \leq M$, there are two inequalities that come from (15) on $K^n - K^m$, one from reversing order:

$$-D^{nm}(u) \geq K^n - K^m \geq D^{mn}(u),$$

Hence, these permit a solution, provided

$$D^{mn}(u) + D^{nm}(u) \leq 0, \quad (22)$$

for all $1 \leq m, n \leq M$. We now show that this is implied by $D^{mm}(u) = 0$ for all m. To that end, consider the optimal paths from m to n and back again that, respectively, achieve $D^{mn}(u)$ and $D^{nm}(u)$. Note that putting together these paths defines a cycle from m to m. If this path contains no sub-cycle, then it is direct that

$$D^{mn}(u) + D^{nm}(u) \leq D^{mm} = 0.$$

This is because the path is a non-repeating cycle, and $D^{mm}(u) = 0$ is the maximum across all such non-repeating cycles. If there is an inner cycle because of repetition, this can add a non-positive amount since the maximum among all cycles is zero under NIAC, completing the proof of sufficiency.

Turning to the necessity proof, note that the necessity of NIAS for a CIR is established in Comment 3.1. Now, suppose that NIAS is satisfied but that NIAC is not. What this means is that there exists some m such that $D^{mm} > 0$ (it can't be less with NIAS holding and direct cycles being permitted). Note that $D^{mm} > 0$ requires that there exist some paths from m to n and from n to m that achieve the maximum

$$D^{mn}(u) + D^{nm}(u) = D^{mm} > 0.$$

Note that this directly means from inequality (22) that there are no qualifying revealed costs of learning, completing the proof.

4.7   Inattention is Free and the Weak Blackwell Property

Whenever **any** CIR exists, there exists a CIR that has some properties that might be attractive. There are two properties in particular that can be added without any further constraints on data sets:

1. **The Weak Blackwell Property**: It is natural to think of learning more as more costly in typical applications in which the goal is to make well-informed decisions (there are, of course, other interesting motives but no reason to muddy the waters at this stage). In particular, if $Q, Q' \in \mathcal{Q}(\mu)$ satisfy $Q' \succsim_B Q$ (at least as Blackwell informative as), then we would want $K(\mu, Q') \geq K(\mu, Q)$. Note that we will have more to say about the Blackwell order in Lectures 5 and 7.
2. **Inattention is Free**: $K(\mu, Q) = 0$ for inattentive strategies in which $Q(\mu) = 1$, with all other costs non-negative.

Caplin and Dean (2015) show that both conditions can be imposed WLOG for purposes of existence. The basic idea is that one can take any cost function that does not satisfy Blackwell dominance and reduce the costs of all too costly Blackwell-dominated options to the minimum cost of any option that Blackwell dominates them. This cannot replace any prior optimal choice since the Blackwell-dominant one is at least as valuable in all decision problems. With this, one can simply subtract from the entire cost function the cost of the inattentive option, noting that this will set its cost to zero, that all others will be non-negative (by the weak Blackwell property), and that the optimal choices are invariant.

4.8 Revisiting the Examples in Light of the Theorem

We apply the result in the examples with CIRs to see what the additional conditions imply and what more might be learned. Here is the first D matrix:

$$D(u) = \begin{array}{cc} \mathbf{P}^1 & \mathbf{P}^2 \\ \begin{pmatrix} 0 & -0.2 \\ 0.1 & 0 \end{pmatrix} & \begin{array}{c} A^1 \\ A^2 \end{array} \end{array}.$$

We know about the diagonal of zero. The theorem asserts that this is equivalent to the off-diagonal elements having a non-positive sum, which is true above. Then, there is the additional condition on cost differences, $K^n - K^m \geq D^{mn}(u)$, which translates to

$$K^2 - K^1 \geq D^{12}(u) = -0.2,$$
$$K^1 - K^2 \geq D^{21}(u) = 0.1.$$

Putting these together, we get $K^1 - K^2 \in [0.1, 0.2]$, which we had previously identified directly from the G matrix in this simple case.

Consider now the three-by-two-by-two example:

$$D(u) = \begin{array}{ccc} \mathbf{P}^1 & \mathbf{P}^2 & \mathbf{P}^3 \\ \begin{pmatrix} 0 & -0.3 & -0.2 \\ 0.2 & 0 & 0.1 \\ 0.1 & -0.1 & 0 \end{pmatrix} & & \begin{array}{c} A^1 \\ A^2 \\ A^3 \end{array} \end{array}.$$

Confirming again the application of Theorem 2, we note that the condition on all cross sums $D^{mn}(u) + D^{nm}(u) \leq 0$ is satisfied. With regard to the full characterization of all cost functions, the inequalities are as follows:

$$K^2 - K^1 \geq D^{12}(u) = -0.3,$$
$$K^1 - K^2 \geq D^{21}(u) = 0.2,$$

$$K^3 - K^1 \geq D^{13}(u) = -0.2,$$

$$K^1 - K^3 \geq D^{31}(u) = 0.1,$$

$$K^3 - K^2 \geq D^{23}(u) = 0.1,$$

$$K^2 - K^3 \geq D^{32}(u) = -0.1.$$

Putting the last two conditions together, we get that $K^3 - K^2 = 0.1$, as we had identified directly from the G matrix. The prior two inequalities specify $K^1 - K^3 \in [0.1, 0.2]$, making the first pair, which specify $K^1 - K^2 \in [0.2, 0.3]$, redundant. Putting these together, we conclude that

$$K^2 - K^3 = 0.1,$$

$$K^1 - K^3 \in [0.1, 0.2]$$

are necessary and sufficient conditions for qualifying cost functions.

The examples reveal additional information that can be identified from the D matrix. This relates to its rows and columns. It turns out that each of these identifies the qualifying costs of revealed learning when read appropriately.

Consider first the two-by-two case:

$$D(u) = \begin{pmatrix} \mathbf{P}^1 & \mathbf{P}^2 \\ 0 & -0.2 \\ 0.1 & 0 \end{pmatrix} \begin{matrix} A^1 \\ A^2 \end{matrix}.$$

The first row specifies $D^{11}(u) = 0$ and $D^{12}(u) = -0.2$. Note that $K^1 = D^{11}(u)$ and $K^2 = D^{12}(u)$ are themselves the qualifying costs of revealed learning since $K^1 - K^2 \in [0.1, 0.2]$ (noting that only differences in the costs are irrelevant at this stage). Likewise, setting the costs according to the second row, $K^1 = D^{21}(u) = 0.1$ and $K^2 = D^{12}(u) = 0$ define a cost function since $K^1 - K^2 \in [0.1, 0.2]$. Let's now turn this around and look at the columns. The first column specifies $D^{11} = 0$ and $D^{21} = -0.1$. In this case, if we flip the sign and set $K^1 = -D^{11}(u)$ and $K^2 = -D^{21}(u) = -0.1$, we again have the qualifying costs of revealed learning. The same trick works in the second column, which specifies $D^{12}(u) = -0.2$ and $D^{22}(u) = 0$, so that flipping the sign and setting $K^1 = -D^{12} = 0.2$ and $K^2 = -D^{22} = 0$ yet again identifies the qualifying costs of revealed learning function.

Consider now the three-by-two-by-two example:

$$D(u) = \begin{matrix} & \mathbf{P}^1 & \mathbf{P}^2 & \mathbf{P}^3 & \\ & \begin{pmatrix} 0 & -0.15 & -0.1 \\ 0.1 & 0 & 0.05 \\ 0.05 & -0.05 & 0 \end{pmatrix} & & & \begin{matrix} A^1 \\ A^2 \\ A^3 \end{matrix} \end{matrix}.$$

What about the rows and columns? Reading first across the rows and then down the columns with the flipped sign, we get the following conjectured cost functions:

$$R1 : (K^1, K^2, K^3) = (0, -0.15, -0.1),$$
$$R2 : (K^1, K^2, K^3) = (0.1, 0, 0.05),$$
$$R3 : (K^1, K^2, K^3) = (0.05, -0.05, 0),$$
$$C1 : (K^1, K^2, K^3) = (0, -0.1, -0.05),$$
$$C2 : (K^1, K^2, K^3) = (0.15, 0, 0.05),$$
$$C3 : (K^1, K^2, K^3) = (0.1, -0.05, 0).$$

Note that in all cases, indeed, $K^3 - K^2 = 0.1$ and $K^1 - K^2 \in [0.1, 0.15]$ in confirmation that these are the qualifying cost of revealed learning.

One final additional feature to note is that in all cases, the costs identified by flipping the sign in a given column are at least weakly higher than those identified in the corresponding row. In the two-by-two case, the first-row costs of $(0, -0.2)$ are lower than the sign-flipped first-column costs of $(0, -0.1)$. Likewise, the second-row costs of $(0.1, 0)$ are lower than the sign-flipped second-column costs of $(0, 0.2, 0)$. In the three-by-two case, the dominance of the sign-flipped column over the row is clear:

$$(0, -0.15, -0.1) \le (0, -0.1, -0.05),$$
$$(0.1, 0, 0.05) \le (0.15, 0, 0.05),$$
$$(0.05, -0.05, 0) \le (0.1, -0.05, 0).$$

4.9   Qualifying Cost Functions in the *D(u)* Matrix

All of the results above are general. The next theorem by Caplin *et al.* confirms that qualifying cost functions can be read out directly from the rows and columns of the $D(u)$ matrix.

Theorem 5: *Consider the indirect value difference matrix $D(u)$ for $\{(A^m, \mathbf{P}^m)\}_{m=1}^M$ that has a CIR. Given $1 \leq q \leq M$, both $\{D^{qm}(u)\}_{m=1}^M$ and $\{-D^{mq}(u)\}_{m=1}^M$ are qualifying learning costs, with*

$$D^{qm}(u) \leq -D^{mq}(u).$$

Proof 5: We show first that $D^{qm}(u)$ defines a qualifying learning cost function. Given $1 \leq m, n \leq M$, find a sum-maximizing path of length J from q to m that evaluates to $D^{qm}(u)$ and append to it a direct final leg from m to n. By definition, this adds the term

$$G^{h(J)h(J+1)}(u) - G^{h(J)h(J)}(u) = G^{mn}(u) - G^{mm}(u)$$

to $D^{qm}(u)$. This identifies a feasible path from q to n, which has precisely the following RHS value that is a lower bound on $D^{qn}(u)$ as the maximum across paths:

$$D^{qn}(u) \geq D^{qm}(u) + G^{mn}(u) - G^{mm}(u).$$

Rearrangement yields

$$G^{mm}(u) - D^{qm}(u) \geq G^{mn}(u) - D^{qn}(u).$$

This directly implies that $\{D^{qm}(u)\}_{m=1}^M$ are the qualifying costs of revealed learning.

To show that $\{-D^{mq}(u)\}_{m=1}^M$ are qualifying learning costs, consider $1 \leq m, n \leq M$ and find a sum-maximizing path of length J from n to q that evaluates to $D^{nq}(u)$ and append to it a new initial leg from m to n. By definition, this adds the term

$$G^{h(0)h(1)}(u) - G^{h(0)h(0)}(u) = G^{mn}(u) - G^{mm}(u)$$

to $D^{nq}(u)$. This identifies a feasible path from m to q which has precisely the RHS value. Hence, the maximizing path from m to n must have a value at least this high:

$$D^{mq}(u) \geq D^{nq}(u) + G^{mn}(u) - G^{mm}(u).$$

Rearrangement yields

$$G^{mm}(u) - (-D^{mq})(u) \geq G^{mn}(u) - (-D^{nq}(u)).$$

This directly defines $\{-D^{mq}(u)\}_{m=1}^{M}$ as the qualifying costs of revealed learning.

The final part of the theorem asserts that these costs are ordered as

$$D^{qm}(u) \leq -D^{mq}(u),$$

for $\{(A^m, \mathbf{P}^m)\}_{m=1}^{M}$ with a CIR. This is an immediate consequence of (22), which establishes that $D^{qm}(u) + D^{mq}(u) \leq 0$ is necessary for a CIR to exist.

4.10 Extremal Learning Costs and the Learning Cost Polyhedron

There is one final point to make about the costs associated with the rows and columns of the D matrix. These have an interpretation as minimal and maximal in a well-defined sense. We formalize this in a geometric manner using convex analysis. As a first step, we normalize. At this stage, there is one degree of freedom in constructing qualifying learning costs since the defining property

$$K^m - K^n \leq G^{mm}(u) - G^{mn}(u) = -D^{mn}(u)$$

or, equivalently,

$$K^n - K^m \geq D^{mn}(u)$$

is based on first differences. This means that any qualifying cost of revealed learning lies in an equivalent set of such costs defined by arbitrarily adding or subtracting a constant. In the next result, we show that arbitrarily setting one of the costs to zero gives rise to qualifying costs that form a convex polyhedron.

In stating the main result, we fix $K^M = 0$ to keep this simple. Note that the row M of the matrix and sign-flipped column M define two such normalized costs: By Theorem 3, we know that $\{D^{Mm}(u)\}_{m=1}^{M}$ and

$\{-D^{mM}(u)\}_{m=1}^{M}$ are qualifying learning costs, and in both cases, their last element is $D^{MM}(u)$. By Theorem 2, $D^{MM}(u) = 0$. But to identify other normalized cost functions requires subtracting the value of K^M: For example, this applies to all of the rows and sign-inverted columns of the matrix identified as cost functions by Theorem 3. Mechanically, this normalization requires subtracting $D^{qM}(u)$ from each of the first $M - 1$ other elements $D^{qm}(u)$ of row q to get the M-normalized row and, conversely, adding $D^{Mq}(u)$ to each of the first $M - 1$ other elements $D^{mq}(u)$ of column q to get the corresponding normalized column.

Given that we are going to apply convex analysis, it is convenient to identify normalized costs geometrically as points in $\mathbb{R}^{M-1}$. With that geometric interpretation, the next theorem shows that the set of qualifying normalized costs when a CIR exists is a convex polyhedron in $\mathbb{R}^{M-1}$. It shows also that the first row and sign-inverted first column of the D matrix are extreme points of this polyhedron.

Theorem 6: *Consider utility difference matrix D for $\{(A^m, \mathbf{P}^m)\}_{m=1}^{M}$ with a CIR. Normalizing to $K^M = 0$, the set of qualifying learning costs is a convex polyhedron in $\mathbb{R}^{M-1}$ of which $(D^{M1}(u), \ldots, D^{M(M-1)}(u))$ and $(-D^{1M}(u), \ldots, -D^{(M-1)M}(u))$ are extreme points.*

Proof 6: Note first that, by Theorem 3, substituting $m = M$ and $n = q$, then $m = q$ and $n = 1$ into the defining inequalities

$$K^n - K^m \geq D^{mn}(u)$$

yields, respectively, the upper and lower bounds on each K^q relative to K^M for $1 \leq q \leq M - 1$:

$$K^q \geq K^M + D^{Mq}(u),$$

$$K^q \leq K^M - D^{qM}(u).$$

Normalizing to $K^M = 0$, the inequalities become

$$D^{Mq}(u) \leq K^q \leq -D^{qM}(u).$$

The set that satisfies this for all $1 \leq q \leq M - 1$ is a hyperrectangle in $\mathbb{R}^{M-1}$. Note that all other inequalities $K^n - K^m \geq D^{mn}(u)$ for $1 \leq m \neq n \leq M - 1$ define half spaces and that the set of qualifying learning cost functions is therefore the intersection of a finite set of half spaces with a convex polyhedron, hence itself a convex polyhedron.

With Theorem 3, we know that both $(D^{M1}(u), D^{M2}(u), \ldots, D^{M(M-1)}(u))$ and $(-D^{1M}(u), \ldots, -D^{(M-1)M}(u))$ are qualifying learning costs. To prove that these are extreme points requires us to identify a normal vector such that this point is uniquely maximal in the set, the defining characteristic of an extreme point of a convex set.

For $(D^{M1}(u), \ldots, D^{M(M-1)}(u))$ we use normal vector $(-1, -1, \ldots, -1) \in \mathbb{R}^{M-1}$. To confirm that $(D^{M1}(u), \ldots, D^{M(M-1)(u)})$ is the unique maximizer of the dot product, suppose to the contrary there exists some $x = (x^1, x^2, \ldots, x^{M-1}) \in \mathbb{R}^{M-1}$ that defines the qualifying costs of revealed learning that has at least as high a dot product. Inverting the sign, this implies

$$\sum_{m=1}^{M-1} x^m \le \sum_{m=1}^{M-1} D^{Mm}(u).$$

For this to be true with $x \ne (D^{M1}(u), \ldots, D^{M(M-1)}(u))$ requires that it be strictly lower in at least one argument, say the first:

$$x^1 < D^{M1}(u).$$

This is inconsistent with $x = (x^1, x^2, \ldots, x^{M-1}) \in \mathbb{R}^{M-1}$ defining the qualifying costs of revealed learning since one of the defining inequalities of Theorem 3 with $K^M = 0$ is

$$K^1 \ge D^{M1}(u).$$

Finally we show that $(-D^{1M}(u), \ldots, -D^{(M-1)M}(u))$ is the unique maximizer when we use normal vector $(1, 1, \ldots, 1) \in \mathbb{R}^{M-1}$. If not, we could find $x = (x^1, x^2, \ldots, x^{M-1}) \in \mathbb{R}^{M-1}$ that defines a qualifying normalized cost function for which

$$\sum_{m=1}^{M-1} x^m \ge \sum_{m=1}^{M-1} -D^{mM}(u).$$

This requires that it is strictly higher in some argument: say,

$$x^1 > -D^{1M}(u).$$

This is inconsistent with $x = (x^1, x^2, \ldots, x^{M-1}) \in \mathbb{R}^{M-1}$ defining a qualifying cost of revealed learning since one of the defining inequalities of Theorem 3 with $K^M = 0$ is

$$K^1 \le -D^{1M}(u),$$

completing the proof.

4.11   Revisiting the Examples

Consider again the two-by-two case with a CIR:

$$
\begin{matrix} & \mathbf{P}^1 & \mathbf{P}^2 & \\ D(u) = & \begin{pmatrix} 0 & -0.2 \\ 0.1 & 0 \end{pmatrix} & \begin{matrix} A^1 \\ A^2 \end{matrix} \end{matrix}.
$$

Theorem 4 implies directly that -0.2 and -0.1 are extreme points of the cost polyhedron normalized to $K^2 = 0$, which is a line segment. Of course, there is nothing special about normalizing the second cost to zero. If we normalized the first cost to zero, we would use the second row and the sign-inverted second column to conclude that 0.2 and 0.1 are extreme points of the cost polyhedron normalized to $K^1 = 0$. This identifies the same set of cost functions.

Consider now the three-by-three case with a CIR:

$$
\begin{matrix} & \mathbf{P}^1 & \mathbf{P}^2 & \mathbf{P}^3 & \\ D(u) = & \begin{pmatrix} 0 & -0.15 & -0.1 \\ 0.1 & 0 & 0.05 \\ 0.05 & -0.05 & 0 \end{pmatrix} & & \begin{matrix} A^1 \\ A^2 \\ A^3 \end{matrix} \end{matrix}.
$$

In this case, Theorem 4 implies directly that $(0.05, -0.05)$ and $(0.1, -0.05)$ are extreme points of the cost polyhedron normalized to $K^3 = 0$. The entire polyhedron involves also the upper and lower bounds on $K^1 - K^2$:

$$
K^1 - K^2 \geq D^{12}(u) = -0.15,
$$

$$
K^2 - K^1 \geq D^{21}(u) = 0.1.
$$

4.12   A Representative Cost Function

It may be of interest to identify some concept of a representative cost function. One way of looking at this is to note that the center of the hyperrectangle associated with normalizing to $K^M = 0$ is a qualifying cost function as the average of such. The idea of using this as an average is uncomfortable since it involves an arbitrary normalization. An interesting alternative is to define a representative cost $\overline{K}$ as the average of the centers of the normalized hyperrectangles. An appealing feature of this is that it can be rationalized and computed in an entirely direct manner as the average of the extremal qualifying learning costs identified in Theorem 6. It is just the average of the rows minus the average of the columns of the D matrix:

$$\overline{K} = \frac{\sum_{m=1}^{M} D^{Mm}(u) - \sum_{m=1}^{M} D^{mM}(u)}{M}.$$

One can also set bounds on the set of qualifying cost functions. Note that normalizing to $K^q = 0$ the hyperrectangle of costs has a volume of

$$V_q = \Pi_{m \neq q}(D^{qm}(u) + D^{mq}(u)).$$

For each $1 \leq q \leq M$, this is a superset of the convex cost polyhedron normalized to that cost $K^q = 0$. Hence, the smallest such value is also an upper bound.

4.13 Floyd–Warshall Algorithm

Readers aware of revealed preference theory will see very strong analogies that are reflected in the names of the given matrices. In the case of revealed preference theory, the strong axiom of revealed preference asserts that there can be no cycles of affordability among chosen bundles of goods that are strict in any way. This generalizes the observation that one should not have been able to buy all goods for strictly less in total by cycling chosen bundles between decision problems (although it is not stated this way). The way in which this is implemented in practice is to compute the pair-wise affordability matrix, which is essentially the change in cost when the optimal purchases in one bundle are purchased at the prices and income levels that generated other bundles. This matrix is obviously trivial to compute. To derive the indirect affordability matrix, one applies the Floyd–Warshall algorithm to the direct affordability matrix and thereby derive the indirect affordability matrix. This matrix cannot have any strictly negative entries on the diagonal as the test of the classical deterministic theory of utility maximization.

The results above show that the direct and indirect value switch matrices play **precisely** the same role in the theory of CIRs as do the direct and indirect affordability matrices in classical revealed preference theory.

The key difference is that the counterfactual comparison that is required involves switching the choice of information structure between action sets and optimizing. Once that more intricate operation has been carried out, the remaining logic is essentially identical. That means we can use the Floyd–Warshall algorithm, which identifies the minimal cost of weighted paths between nodes in a weighted directed graph, to identify if any diagonal element of $D(u)$ is less than zero (indicating failure of NIAC) and can be used to generate the $D(u)$ matrix when a CIR exists. Perhaps, the most important point is that this well-known algorithm is polynomial: It has a complexity of $O(V^3)$.

The Floyd–Warshall algorithm takes as an input a directed graph with weight $W(i,j)$ on the vertex from node i to node j and cycles through these weights for all $1 \leq i,j,k \leq M$, identifying when $W(i,j) > W(i,k) + W(k,j)$ and correspondingly reducing it to equality, setting $W'(i,j) = W(i,k) + W(k,j)$. The key step in using the Floyd–Warshall algorithm is to construct a complete weighted directed graph with M nodes, with the weight $W(m,n) = -D_0^{mn}(u)$ on the directed edge from node m to node n. By definition,

$$D^{mn}(u) \equiv \min_{\{\vec{h} \in H(m,n)\}} \sum_{j=1}^{J(\vec{h})-1} -D_0^{mn}(u).$$

In graph-theoretic terms, $H(m,n)$ identifies the set of all non-repeating directed paths from node m to node n in the graph. For any such path, the sum on the RHS is precisely the sum of these weights. Hence, $D^{mn}(u)$ defines the minimal sum of weights on all directed paths from m to n, and the Floyd–Warshall algorithm efficiently identifies all such paths.

4.14 The Variational Lower Bound on Costs

From the recovery viewpoint, we need to go beyond information structures revealed in the data and fill in costs on the full domain. The key is a lower bound on the costs on information structures that are not revealed in the data. To that end, we take as given both a utility function that satisfies NIAS and NIAC and the qualifying costs of revealed learning for that utility function, $\vec{K} \in \mathcal{K}^R(u)$. Key computations relate to maximized expected utility.

Definition 14: Given $u \in \mathcal{U}^{NIAC}$ and $Q \in \mathcal{Q}$, we define $G^m(Q|u)$ as the maximal utility of Q in A^m as

$$G^m(Q|u) = \sum_{\gamma \in \text{supp } Q} Q(\gamma) \max_{a \in A^m} \sum u(a, \omega) \gamma(\omega),$$

for all $1 \leq m \leq M$.

Consider any $Q \in \mathcal{Q}(\mu)$. Our job is to make sure that none strictly dominates those that are chosen: This also applies to those that are chosen so that the inequalities are universal. We now compute, for any cost $K(Q)$, the corresponding net utility in decision problem A^m as

$$G^m(Q|u) - K(Q).$$

For optimality of what is chosen, we need this to be no lower than the net utility that is revealed in the data and by the specified cost

$$G^m(Q|u) - K(Q) \leq G^m(u) - K^m,$$

where recall that $G^m(u)$ on the RHS is identifiable by combining the data with the given utility function. Rearranging and noting that this must be true for all m produces the implied lower bound on costs given in (23) as follows.

It is important to note that the variational lower bound on costs depends on **both** the utility function **and** a specific vector of costs of revealed learning. Note also that the variational lower bound in combination with standard functional forms assumptions on costs, in particular posterior separability (see Lecture 6), can be extremely restrictive. In fact, in such cases, it is by far the most powerful constraint on costs since it is the only constraint that compares what was chosen in the data with **unchosen** strategies and, in that sense, contains far richer information. The key to inference in the case of posterior-separable cost functions is the Lagrangean lemma of Lecture 8, which reveals a common tangency condition that ties together derivatives of the cost function at distinct chosen posteriors. There are also powerful restrictions on the cost difference that can tighten the general constraints above. Application to this case is outlined in the following lecture.

4.15   Complete Characterization

We close the lecture by summarizing what we have uncovered in this section. For a utility function that admits a CIR, we can use the above to precisely identify all cost functions strictly increasing in the Blackwell order that can rationalize it by computing the matrix $D(u)$, using it to compute the set of all qualifying costs of revealed learning $\mathcal{K}^R(u)$, and then, given both u and $\vec{K} \in \mathcal{K}^R(u)$, closing out the characterization with the corresponding variational lower bound on costs. We define this set to close the lecture.

Definition 15:   Given $u \in \mathcal{U}^{CIR}$, we define $\mathcal{K}^{SB}(u)$ as all the costs of learning strictly increasing in the Blackwell order such that (u, K) constitute a CIR. The set $\mathcal{K}^{SB}(u)$ is defined in two steps as follows:

1. In the first step, we compute the indirect value switch matrix D and use it to identify the set of qualifying costs of revealed learning $\vec{K} \in \mathcal{K}^R(u)$ according to Theorem 3.
2. Given u and any $\vec{K} \in \mathcal{K}^R(u)$, we fill in the full cost function by imposing the **variational lower bound on costs** associated with u and $\vec{K}$:

$$K(Q) \geq \max_{1 \leq m \leq M} [G^m(Q|u) - G^m(u) + K^m]. \tag{23}$$

Lecture 5

Revealed Bayesian Learning: A Full Characterization

5.1 Introduction

This lecture presents a full characterization of what can be inferred about utility, learning, and costs and constraints on learning from the SDSC data set $\{(A^m, \mathbf{P}^m)\}_{m=1}^{M}$ based on Caplin *et al.* (2023c). The lecture contains a great deal of material. What makes it difficult on first encounter is the need to change point of view several times to gain understanding. The first portion of the lecture introduces the guiding question, which I believe to be fundamental to social scientific inference. If one gathers ideal data in the form of SDSC, to what extent does it allow separate identification of what the DM likes, what they know, and why they don't know more? The centrality of this question is clear given that Bayesian models are dominant in so much of economics, cognitive science, and neuroscience. Prior lectures have provided partial answers which are invoked in providing the full characterizations, but there are several conceptual innovations involved in providing the definitive answers of this lecture. There are several distinct lines of attack, as indicated in this summary of the goals of the lecture:

1. The lecture opens by broadening our perspective on Bayesian learning to allow for different forms of models that play an important role in modern social science: capacity-constrained representations (CCRs) and fixed information representations (FIRs), in addition to CIRs.
2. I introduce a simple motivating example in which I lay out the questions of interest. It makes clear how much more we need to know

before definitively answering the question of this lecture concerning the separate identification of utility, comprehension, and barriers to comprehension.

3. I introduce and illustrate the CCR and CIR **utility cones**, which identify all utility functions that admit the corresponding representations.

4. I informally introduce **posterior-separable costs** and comment on the power of the variational lower bound on costs when combined with the hypothesis that costs are posterior separable.

5. I introduce **garblings** and **mean-preserving spreads** (MPSs), which define the Blackwell order on the informativeness of different information structures and establish their role in permitting a strategy to generate the data.

6. I introduce and illustrate **mean- and optimality-preserving spreads** (MOPS), which impose an additional optimality condition over the standard MPS that allows them to preserve optimality while generating the data. They play a key role in characterizing for information structures that might have given rise to the data and, thereby, possible learning.

7. I discuss the full characterization theorems summarizing all that can be recovered from the data in a CIR, a CCR, and an FIR. The full formal statements are in Caplin *et al.* (2023c).

In fairness to students, I stress again that the material is excessive for a single lecture. In fact, this is essentially two lectures in one. My choice is to end the first lecture after having introduced the Blackwell order, leaving its role in completing the characterization to the ensuing lecture.

5.2   Three Bayesian Model Classes

We now introduce the three Bayesian model classes of interest. While Bayesian learning models form a bedrock of modern social science and are ubiquitous in economic, psychological, and neuroscientific analyses, they come in different flavors. They largely fall into one of three large and nested classes: fixed information, capacity-constrained learning, and costly learning.

In **fixed information models**, learning is not impacted by the payoffs available but is instead determined by the features of the mind or environment without reference to the particular decision context that is to be faced. Examples include the dominant signal processing model of psychometric data due to Green and Swets, 1996 classic exogenous information market models of incomplete information, auctions, observational learning, etc. When data are consistent with a fixed information model, we say that they have a **fixed information representation**.

In **capacity-constrained** learning models, there is a fixed feasible set of information structures, and the role of the utility function is to pick among this set to best match the payoffs available. This form of learning underlies vast literatures in psychology, cognition, and neuroscience and has entered economics as fixed capacity rational inattention (Sims, 2003) and efficient coding (Woodford, 2020). When data are consistent with a capacity-constrained model, we say that they have a **capacity-constrained representation** (CCR).

In costly information models of the form we have been considering heretofore, information structures carry different costs and are chosen given the tradeoffs with the payoffs available. Examples include sequential search, bandit problems, and standard models of rational inattention.

5.2.1 *Costly information representation*

It is simplest to state the definitions in order of restrictiveness, starting first with the most general, the CIR, followed by the CCR and finally the FIR, which is the most restrictive. In addition to stating all definitions, we provide the characterization of a CIR in its simplest form by combining NIAS and NIAC into a single condition, which we call condition CIR. We also introduce a correspondingly simple condition for a CCR, which we naturally call condition CCR. The FIR does not have such a direct translation. In fact, the analysis of an FIR involves quite distinct logic that is more information theoretic in nature and is covered in the later parts of the lecture.

We open by restating the definition of a CIR and defining the set of utility functions that admit such a representation.

Definition 16: $\{(A^m, \mathbf{P}^m)\}_{m=1}^{M}$ have a **costly information representation** if there exist u, K, and $(Q^m, q^m) \in \hat{\Lambda}(A^m | u, K)$ for $1 \leq m \leq M$ such that $\mathbf{P}^m = P_{(Q^m, q^m)}$. u **admits** a CIR of $\{(A^m, \mathbf{P}^m)\}_{m=1}^{M}$ if there exists K and $(Q^m, q^m) \in \hat{\Lambda}(A^m | u, K)$ that in combination with u provide a CIR. We define $\mathcal{U}^{CIR}$ as the class of utility functions that admit a CIR.

A key result from the previous lecture, Theorem 4, proves the result of Caplin and Dean (2015) that NIAS and NIAC together are equivalent to $u \in \mathcal{U}^{CIR}$. For present purposes, it is best to present them jointly as what we will call condition CIR. As indicated in Comment 4.1, from the viewpoint of the CIR, one can note that NIAS and NIAC together correspond to a version of NIAC in which there is no restriction on cycle length: including the direct cycles of length 2, which are excluded in the standard NIAC statement, is equivalent to adding NIAS. Given that CIR is equivalent to NIAS and NIAC, it is equivalent to a utility function admitting a CIR.

Definition 17:   Utility function u satisfies **condition CIR** and hence admits a CIR, $u \in \mathcal{U}^{CIR}$, if and only if

$$\sum_{j=1}^{J(h)-1} G^{h(j)}(u) \geq \sum_{j=1}^{J(h)-1} G^{h(j)h(j+1)}(u), \tag{24}$$

for all $\vec{h} = (h(1), h(2), \ldots, h(J(\vec{h})) \in H(m,m)$, for any m with any cycle length $2 \leq J(\vec{h})) \leq M + 1$ and with $h(j) \neq h(j')$ except for first and last in cycle.

Note that, as stated, to check whether or not a utility function satisfied $u \in \mathcal{U}^{CIR}$ involves performing a somewhat intricate set of operations on a function by function basis. What we show in the following is that this search has a simple structure and that the full set $\mathcal{U}^{CIR}$ can be recovered in relatively simple fashion. The constructive procedure we introduce for identifying $\mathcal{U}^{CIR}$ stems from a switch in perspective, as detailed in the following. Given any such utility function, we then characterize all possible learning. We conclude with a full characterization, which indicates in full, the sequential structure to the logic: One first identifies all utility functions. Based on this, one identifies all possible forms of learning. Only at this point can one identify the class of all rationalizing cost functions.

5.2.2 *Capacity-constrained representation*

In a CCR, the available modes of learning are not *per se* impacted by incentives but rather are limited by a fixed capacity constraint. In such cases, the only role of incentives is to pick from this feasible set, the mode of learning best suited to the decision at hand. Technically, data admit a CCR if the learning in each decision problem is optimal for some fixed feasible set of experiments $Q^* \subset Q$. Given decision set A, the feasible set of learning strategies is defined by Q^* as

$$\Lambda(A, Q^*) \equiv \{(Q, q) \in \Lambda(A) | Q \in Q^*\}.$$

Optimal strategies are those that maximize the prize-based expected utility in this set:

$$\hat{V}(A|u, Q^*) \equiv \sup_{\{(Q,q)\in\Lambda(A,Q^*)\}} \sum_{\gamma\in\mathrm{supp}\,Q} \sum_{a\in A} Q(\gamma)q(a|\gamma) \sum_{\omega\in\Omega} \gamma(\omega)u(z(a,\omega));$$

$$\hat{\Lambda}(A|u, Q^*) \equiv \{(Q,q) \in \Lambda(A, Q^*) | V(Q,q|u,K) = \hat{V}(A|u, Q^*)\}.$$

Definition 18: $\{(A^m, \mathbf{P}^m)\}_{m=1}^{M}$ have a **capacity-constrained representation** if there exist $u : Z \longrightarrow \mathbb{R}$, $Q^* \subset Q$, and $(Q^m, q^m) \in \hat{\Lambda}(A^m|u, Q^*)$ for all $1 \leq m \leq M$ such that $\mathbf{P}^m = P_{(Q^m, q^m)}$. Utility function $u : Z \longrightarrow \mathbb{R}$ **admits** a CCR of $\{(A^m, \mathbf{P}^m)\}_{m=1}^{M}$ if there exist $Q^* \subset Q$ and $(Q^m, q^m) \in \hat{\Lambda}(A^m|u, Q^*)$ that in combination with u provide a CCR. We define $\mathcal{U}^{CCR}$ as the class of such utility functions.

In order to characterize $\mathcal{U}^{CCR}$, we introduce the equivalent to the NIAS- and NIAC-based characterization of a CIR. The result here is intuitive, and we refer to the corresponding condition as condition CCR. Rather than considering action switches and attention cycles, we need to consider switches of **both** action and attention. With all revealed information structures feasible for all action sets, it is clearly necessary that the chosen structures are optimal among all that are available. That this necessary condition is sufficient is clear from constructing the feasible set to include only the revealed information structures.

Definition 19: Utility function u satisfies **condition CCR** and hence admits a CCR, $u \in \mathcal{U}^{CCR}$, if and only if

$$G^m \geq G^{mn}, \tag{25}$$

for all $1 \leq m, n \leq M$.

Note that this definition subsumes NIAS, which corresponds to the case in which $m = n$, in which the condition must be met with equality. Note also that there is a clear alternative definition that reveals this to be a harder condition to satisfy than a CIR: It says that a data set has CCR if and only if it has a CIR in which costs are equal for information structures that are chosen. Hence, $\mathcal{U}^{CCR} \subset \mathcal{U}^{CIR}$.

5.2.3 *Fixed information representation*

The final representation of interest is an FIR. This is a special case of a CCR in which the feasible set of learning strategies is a singleton. It is simplest to express this in terms of the twin conditions of the mixed action strategies picking out optimal actions and combining with the common information structure to produce the data. For this purpose, it is valuable to define the set of posteriors for which each action $a \in A^m$ is optimal given utility function u in the data set as $\hat{\Gamma}^m(a|u)$:

$$\hat{\Gamma}^m(a|u) \equiv \left\{ \gamma \in \Delta(\Omega) \middle| \sum_{\omega \in \Omega} \gamma(\omega)u(z(a,\omega)) \right.$$
$$\left. \geq \sum_{\omega \in \Omega} \gamma(\omega)u(z(b,\omega)) \text{ for all } b \in A^m \right\}$$

Definition 20: $\{(A^m, \mathbf{P}^m)\}_{m=1}^M$ have a **fixed information representation** if there exist $u : Z \longrightarrow \mathbb{R}$, $Q \in \mathcal{Q}$, and $\{q^m\}_{m=1}^M$, with $q^m : \text{supp } Q \longrightarrow \Delta(A^m)$ satisfying:

1. $q^m(a|\gamma) > 0 \implies \gamma \in \hat{\Gamma}^m(a|u)$ for all $1 \leq m \leq M$ and $a \in A^m$;
2. $\mathbf{P}^m = P_{(Q,q^m)}$.

u **admits** an FIR of $\{(A^m, \mathbf{P}^m)\}_{m=1}^M$ if there exists $Q \in \mathcal{Q}$ and q^m that in combination with u provide an FIR. We define $\mathcal{U}^{FIR} \subset \mathcal{U}^{CCR}$ as the set of such utility functions.

We will have much more to say about this representation, but the critical discussion is information theoretic and is therefore delayed until after we have discussed utility functions at some depth.

5.3 Example 5.1

We illustrate the identification challenge that we address in the lecture with unknown utility and unobserved information in the following simple example. Two decision problems are faced: $A^1 = \{a_1, a_2\}$ and $A^2 = \{a_1, a_2, a_3\}$. Actions can yield one of three prizes, z_1, z_2, z_3, depending on the state as follows.

Action	State ω_1	State ω_2
a_1	z_1	z_3
a_2	z_3	z_1
a_3	z_2	z_2

Choice data $\mathbf{P}^1$ from the first decision problem is summarized by the following joint distribution over actions (a_1, a_2) and states (ω_1, ω_2):

$$\mathbf{P}^1 = \begin{array}{cc} & \begin{array}{cc} \omega_1 & \omega_2 \end{array} \\ \begin{pmatrix} 0.4 & 0.1 \\ 0.1 & 0.4 \end{pmatrix} & \begin{array}{c} a_1 \\ a_2 \end{array} \end{array}.$$

Clearly, this exhibits symmetric choice patterns. The choice data $\mathbf{P}^2$ observed from the second decision problem is somewhat asymmetric:

$$\mathbf{P}^2 = \begin{array}{cc} & \begin{array}{cc} \omega_1 & \omega_2 \end{array} \\ \begin{pmatrix} 0.25 & 0 \\ 0.05 & 0.2 \\ 0.2 & 0.3 \end{pmatrix} & \begin{array}{c} a_1 \\ a_2 \\ a_3 \end{array} \end{array}.$$

In the first state, the first and third actions are selected more often, and in the second state, the second and third actions are selected more often. Note that data set $\mathbf{P}^1$ has two equiprobable revealed posteriors of state ω_1, which are recorded with their unconditional probabilities as:

$$\gamma_{\mathbf{P}^1}^{a_1} = 0.8; \text{ and } \mathbf{P}^1(a_1) = 0.5$$

$$\gamma_{\mathbf{P}^1}^{a_2} = 0.2; \text{ and } \mathbf{P}^1(a_2) = 0.5.$$

In contrast, data set $\mathbf{P}^2$ has three revealed posteriors of state ω_1 again recorded with their unconditional probabilities as:

$$\gamma_{\mathbf{P}^2}^{a_1} = 1 \text{ and } \mathbf{P}^2(a_1) = 0.25,$$

$$\gamma_{\mathbf{P}^2}^{a_2} = 0.2 \text{ and } \mathbf{P}^2(a_2) = 0.25,$$

$$\gamma_{\mathbf{P}^2}^{a_3} = 0.4 \text{ and } \mathbf{P}^2(a_2) = 0.5.$$

We show that we can infer an enormous amount about utility, learning, and the costs of learning from the behavioral data $\mathbf{P}^1$ and $\mathbf{P}^2$. We find out that the data admit not only CIRs but also CCRs and FIRs. The implied conditions on utility are increasingly stringent: There is effectively a unique utility function that can rationalize these data in an FIR. The specifics of what is learned depend intricately on the rationalizing utility function.

5.4   The CCR Utility Cone

To make analytic headway in the general case, we introduce a geometric approach to visualize and compute the restrictions that the SDSCs impose on prize utilities. Spiritually, we follow Caplin and Martin (2021) in moving to the space of prize lotteries (their work is limited to NIAS alone and considers welfare: see Lecture 7). Recall that there are K prizes that have been correspondingly indexed as z_k. The objects of interest will all be found in this space. To understand why this plays such a key role, note that this is precisely the space in which expected utility functions are to be found as vector $\vec{u} \in \mathbb{R}^K$, where u_k specifies the expected utility of prize z_k. Taking the prize-based perspective leads to a thoroughgoing restatement of all of the inequalities characterizing CCR and CIR representations as now specified.

As an aside, while we work forward with $\{A^m, \mathbf{P}^m\}_{m=1}^M$ based on a single prior, the underlying logic does not need for the priors or even the state space to be the same. The only necessary common element is the prize space $Z = \{z_k\}_{k=1}^K$.

As the CCR conditions show, the characterization of utility functions that admit a CCR of $\{(A^m, \mathbf{P}^m)\}_{m=1}^M$ is based on ruling out a set of changes in action choices and learning strategies, those that are feasible according to the theory, as improving. The comparison of interest involves the following steps:

1. For each m, we define the lottery associated with the actual observed data L^m by $L^m = (L_1^m, \dots, L_K^m) \in \Delta(Z)$ so that for each prize z_k,

$$L_k^m = \sum_{\{a \in A^m, \omega \in \Omega \mid z(a,\omega) = z_k\}} \mathbf{P}^m(a, \omega).$$

2. We generate a comparison lottery in several steps. Starting with any given decision problem A^m, we select a target data set $\mathbf{P}^n$. There are no restrictions: All that is needed is that $1 \leq m, n \leq M$. In particular, it is allowed that $m = n$.

3. Consider the set of actions that are **chosen** in the SDSC for data set $\mathbf{P}^n$: the set $A_{\mathbf{P}^n}$. Map this set to any **feasible** actions in set A^m according to $f : A_{\mathbf{P}^n} \longrightarrow A^m$.

4. Given any triple (m, n, f), define the corresponding SDSC on $a \in A^m$ as

$$\mathbf{P}^{(m,n,f)}(a, \omega) \equiv \sum_{\{b \in A_{\mathbf{P}^n} | f(b) = a\}} \mathbf{P}^n(b, \omega).$$

This defines the data set corresponding to a set of holistic switches of actions from A^m into the data set $\mathbf{P}^n$ associated with alternative action set A^n.

5. Define the lottery associated with the data set after all defined adjustments, $L^{(m,n,f)}$, so that for each prize z_k,

$$L_k^{(m,n,f)} = \sum_{\{a \in A^m, \omega \in \Omega | z(a, \omega) = z_k\}} \mathbf{P}^{(m,n,f)}(a, \omega).$$

6. Define the difference in the lottery as between the chosen and counterfactual as $C^{(m,n,f)} \in \mathbb{R}^K$:

$$C_k^{(m,n,f)} = L_k^m - L_k^{(m,n,f)},$$

for $1 \leq k \leq K$.

7. With all of these steps completed for a single specification (m, n, f), we repeat them for all such triples. To simplify notation for this large set of counterfactual switches, we index all distinct triples (m, n, f) by $1 \leq i \leq I$ and define the corresponding lottery change as $C^i \equiv C^{(m(i), n(i), f(i))}$.

8. As a final preparatory step, we think about positively weighted combinations of these vectors C^i. We call the convex cone defined by all such lottery changes the CCR cone.

Definition 21: We call the convex cone formed by all C^i the **CCR cone**:

$$\mathcal{C}^{CCR} = \left\{ C = \sum_{i=1}^{I} \alpha^i C^i \in \mathbb{R}^K | \alpha^i \in \mathbb{R}_+ \right\}.$$

Regarding the name, this set being a cone is clear since it comprises half lines through the origin. It being convex is also clear.

The defining feature of a CCR is that each of C^i reflects the choice of a particular feasible strategy over an alternative that could have been generated by the corresponding switch of $A^m(i)$ to $\mathbf{P}^{n(i)}$ so that for the utility function to have a CCR, staying with the chosen lottery cannot result in a reduction in expected utility. In fact, according to condition CCR, a **necessary and sufficient** condition for $u \in \mathcal{U}^{CCR}$ is that the utility function has a non-negative dot product with all vectors C^i:

$$\sum_{k=1}^{K} u_k C_k^i \geq 0.$$

Given that the CCR cone comprises only positively weighted combinations of the C^i, this inequality extends to the entire cone. This gives rise to the key observation, which is essentially immediate in light of the above, that having a positive dot product with all vectors in the CCR cone is equivalent to a utility function admitting a CCR.

Proposition 1:   *Utility function $u : Z \longrightarrow \mathbb{R}$ admits a CCR, $u \in \mathcal{U}^{CCR}$, if and only if*

$$\sum_{k=1}^{K} u_k C_k \geq 0$$

all $C \in \mathcal{C}^{CCR}$.

Note that this proposition reveals the set $\mathcal{U}^{CCR}$ itself to be a convex cone. We therefore call it **the CCR utility cone**.

5.5   The CIR Utility Cone

As with the CCR, for a utility function to satisfy condition CIR and hence admit a CIR requires a set of corresponding changes in prize lotteries to be non-improving. However, the construction is more elaborate since a significant amount of processing of the data is necessary to translate conditions on cyclic changes in information structures into statements about changes in prize lotteries. The basic idea involves taking the action set at each stage in the cycle and shifting it to the data set that follows it and then averaging appropriately to compare the average lottery in each given cycle with the alternative average lottery defined by the objects specified in the cycle. Here are the steps involved:

1. As a first preparatory step, we construct the full set of cycles of attention switches with arbitrary action choices during the course of the cycle. Technically, recall that a cycle is defined by its length $2 \le J \le M + 1$ and a corresponding vector of indices $\vec{m} = (m(1), \ldots, m(J))$, with $1 \le m(j) \le M$ with $m(1) = m(J)$ but $1 \le m(j) \ne m(j') \le M$ otherwise.

2. As for the action choices in the cycle, we need to specify a set of corresponding functions mapping from action set $A^{m(j)}$ at each stage $1 \le j \le J - 1$ in the cycle based on the learning revealed in data set $\mathbf{P}^{m(j+1)}$. As in the case of a CCR, we replace each of the chosen actions in decision problem $A^{m(j+1)}$ with a feasible action in the preceding choice set $A^{m(j)}$ according to corresponding stage j action mapping $f^j : A_{\mathbf{P}^{m(j+1)}} \longrightarrow A^{m(j)}$ that specifies a holistic replacement for each chosen action $a \in A_{\mathbf{P}^{m(j+1)}}$ in the successor set with an action $a' \in A^{m(j)}$ available in the predecessor. With all such mappings specified, we have defined the **cycle of attention and action switches** $(J, \vec{m}, \{f^j\}_{j=1}^{J-1})$.

3. Given cycle $(J, \vec{m}, \{f^j\}_{j=1}^{J-1})$, we can, at each stage in the cycle $1 \le j \le J - 1$, compute the corresponding lottery over prizes induced by the mapping using precisely the same logic as in the CCR. Technically, given $m(j)$, we define the lottery associated with the actual observed data $L^{m(j)} \in \Delta(Z)$ so that for each prize z_k,

$$L_k^{m(j)} = \sum_{\{a \in A^{m(j)}, \omega \in \Omega | z(a, \omega) = z_k\}} \mathbf{P}^{m(j)}(a, \omega).$$

4. We then define the **unweighted average** of these lotteries across the cycle, which is itself a lottery, $\bar{L}^{\vec{m}} \in \Delta(Z)$, on a prize-by-prize basis,

$$\bar{L}_k^{\vec{m}} = \frac{\sum_{1 \le j \le J-1} L_k^{m(j)}}{J - 1}.$$

5. We generate the comparison average lottery in cycle $(J, \vec{m}, \{f^j\}_{j=1}^{J-1})$ in several steps. We begin by computing the lottery associated with

the stage j action switch mapping f^j as $L^{f^j} \in \Delta(Z)$. This specifies the probability of each prize z_k as

$$L_k^{f^j} = \sum_{\{a \in A_{\mathbf{P}^{m(j+1)}} \,|\, f^j(a)=a'\}} \sum_{\{\omega \in \Omega \,|\, z(a',\omega)=z_k\}} \mathbf{P}^{m(j+1)}(a,\omega).$$

6. We then define the unweighted average lottery associated with full cycle of switches $\bar{L}^{\{f^j\}_{j=1}^{J-1}} \in \Delta(Z)$ on a prize-by-prize basis,

$$\bar{L}_k^{\{f^j\}_{j=1}^{J-1}} = \frac{\sum_{1 \leq j \leq J-1} L_k^{f^j}}{J-1}.$$

7. Having computed both the factual and counterfactual average lotteries in the given cycle, we can also compute the difference between the actual and the counterfactual average lottery as $\bar{C}^{(J,\vec{m},\{f^j\}_{j=1}^{J-1})} \in \mathbb{R}^K$ with component k as

$$\bar{C}_k^{(J,\vec{m},\{f^j\}_{j=1}^{J-1})} \equiv \bar{L}_k^{\vec{m}} - \bar{L}^{(J,\vec{m},\{f^j\}_{j=1}^{J-1})}$$

so that the sum of the elements is zero as the difference between two vectors of numbers that have the same sum.

8. The NIAS and NIAC characterizations of a CIR derives precisely from the observation that any cycle of attention and action switches is in principle feasible at no additional cost and so cannot be improving. Hence, a clear necessary condition for $u : Z \longrightarrow \mathbb{R}$ to admit a CIR is that no such change raises the utility summed over the cycle, which is equivalent to the unconditional average lottery change induced by the switch to the counterfactual average lottery $\bar{C}^{(J,\vec{m},\{f^j\}_{j=1}^{J-1})} \in \mathbb{R}^K$ not improving

$$\sum_{k=1}^{K} u_k \bar{C}_k^{(J,\vec{m},\{f^j\}_{j=1}^{J-1})} \geq 0.$$

9. We repeat all of the above steps for all triples $(J,\vec{m},\{f^j\}_{j=1}^{J-1})$. To simplify notation, for this large set of counterfactual switches, we index all distinct triples $(J,\vec{m},\{f^j\}_{j=1}^{J-1})$ by $1 \leq l \leq L$ and define the corresponding lottery change as $\bar{C}^l \equiv \bar{C}^{(J(l),\vec{m}(l),\{f^j(l)\}_{j=1}^{J-1})}$.

10. As a final preparatory step, we think about positively weighted combinations of these vectors $\bar{C}^l$. We call the convex cone defined by all such lottery changes the CIR cone.

Definition 22: We call the convex cone formed by all $\bar{C}^l$ the **CIR cone**:

$$\bar{C}^{CIR} = \{\bar{C} = \sum_{l=1}^{L} \alpha^l \bar{C}^l \in \mathbb{R}^K | \alpha^l \in \mathbb{R}_+\}.$$

As with the CCR cone, this set being a cone is clear since it comprises half lines through the origin. Its being convex is also clear.

As noted above, as an alternative average lottery that would have been generated by the corresponding cycle, for a utility function to admit a CIR implies that none of these switches can raise expected utility. In fact, according to condition CIR, a **necessary and sufficient** condition for $u \in \mathcal{U}^{CIR}$ is that the utility function has a non-negative dot product with all vectors C^l:

$$\sum_{k=1}^{K} u_k \bar{C}_k^l \geq 0.$$

Given that the CIR cone comprises only positively weighted combinations of the C^l, this inequality extends to the entire cone. This gives rise to the key observation, which is essentially immediate in light of the above, that having a positive dot product with all vectors in the CIR cone is equivalent to a utility function admitting a CIR.

Proposition 2: *Utility function* $u : Z \longrightarrow \mathbb{R}$ *admits a CIR,* $u \in \mathcal{U}^{CIR}$, *if and only if*

$$\sum_{k=1}^{K} u_k C_k \geq 0,$$

for all $\bar{C} \in \bar{C}^{CIR}$.

As with the CCR, this proposition reveals the set $\mathcal{U}^{CIR}$ itself to be a convex cone. We therefore call it **the CIR utility cone**.

5.6 Utility Cones in Example 5.1

We now illustrate the utility cones in Example 5.1. Note that both CCR and CIR require NIAS, so we start there as the common base and illustrate how this constrains utilities in the example. Within A^1, the possible action switches are choosing a_2 in place of a_1 and vice versa. What we do in each case is to translate this into a condition on prize lotteries. To that end, note first that either actual choice yields lottery probabilities $(p_1, p_2, p_3) = (0.8, 0, 0.2)$ over the three prizes $z_k, 1 \leq k \leq 3$. Both of the counterfactual lotteries attained by action switches yield $(p_1, p_2, p_3) = (0.2, 0, 0.8)$. The option of switching hence changes the received lottery by $(0.6, 0, -0.6)$. Given that choices are optimal, we conclude that prize utilities (u_1, u_2, u_3) must have a positive dot product with this vector so that $u_1 \geq u_3$.

In choice set A^2, consider first action switches of choosing either a_2 or a_3 in place of a_1. When chosen a_1 produces $(p_1, p_2, p_3) = (1, 0, 0)$. Switching to a_3 cannot be improving since it yields $u_3 \leq u_1$. Switching to a_2 would yield z_2 for sure so that the corresponding NIAS inequality implies that $u_1 \geq u_2$. Switching from a_2 to a_1 cannot be improving since all it does is lower the probability of receiving z_1 rather than z_3. For it to be non-improving, not to switch from a_2 to a_3 requires that the resulting lottery $(0.8, 0, 0.2)$ be at least as good as pure prize z_2 achievable by switching to a_3:

$$0.8u_1 + 0.2u_3 \geq u_2.$$

Finally, consider possibly switching from a_3 to a_2 or a_1. For what was chosen, which produced the pure prize z_2, to be at least as good as the best alternative, which would be to switch to a_3 and get the lottery $(0.6, 0, 0.4)$, therefore, requiring

$$u_2 \geq 0.6u_1 + 0.4u_3.$$

Combining the above inequalities, we confirm that the only non-trivial rationalization involves $u_1 > u_2 > u_3$ so that we normalize to $u_1 = 1$ and $u_3 = 0$ with $u_2 \in [0.6, 0.8]$.

Of the additional conditions to add, the simpler is no improving attention switches. The basic operations are switching A^1 to $\mathbf{P}^2$ and then optimizing and, likewise, switching A^2 to $\mathbf{P}^1$ before optimizing. As a first step in this direction, we compute the full-prize lotteries from the actual choices. In choice set A^1, the realized lottery in $\mathbf{P}^1$ is $(0.8, 0, 0.2)$. In choice set A^2, the realized lottery in $\mathbf{P}^2$ is $(0.45, 0.5, 0.05)$.

The implications of switching A^1 to $\mathbf{P}^2$ are straightforward. At each posterior, it is best to choose the action that is more likely to yield prize

z_1 rather than z_3. The average such probability in $\mathbf{P}^2$ is 0.75 rather than 0.8. Hence, sticking with the chosen attention yields a lottery change of $(0.05, 0, -0.05)$ relative to the best alternative. The CCR utility cone condition to which this corresponds is that $u_1 \geq u_3$, which is already implied by NIAS. The implications of switching A^2 to $\mathbf{P}^1$ are equally simple: In either case, the maximum utility derives from picking the action that yields lottery $(0.8, 0, 0.2)$, given that we have already established $u_2 \leq 0.8$. Hence, the difference between sticking with the actual attention strategy rather than switching is defined by lottery difference $(-0.35, 0.5, -0.15)$. For this to be advantageous, as required in the CCR cone, tighten bounds on utility to include

$$u_2 \geq 0.7.$$

Putting all conditions together, we see that the condition for a CCR is $u_1 = 1$ and $u_3 = 0$ with $u_2 \in [0.7, 0.8]$.

As the general logic suggests, the CIR utility cone involves somewhat more intricate logic that is not obviously related to a single change in lottery. The corresponding NIAC constraint prevents utility rising when **both switches happening simultaneously** since such a cycle is feasible since costs are taken out of the equation. While either one of the switches might be improving in isolation, they cannot be improving when carried out simultaneously. One way to work our what this implies is to follow the general averaging process illustrated in the general case and to take the arithmetic average of the change in lottery when A^1 is switched to $\mathbf{P}^2$ with subsequent optimization and when A^2 is switched to $\mathbf{P}^1$ with subsequent optimization. Based on the separate implications of each such switch in data set, the averaged lottery change is

$$\frac{(-0.35, 0.5, -0.15) + (0.05, 0, -0.05)}{2} = (-0.15, 0.25, -0.1).$$

The corresponding inequality on utilities that make this have positive utility given what is already known is

$$u_2 \geq 0.6,$$

which adds no new constraints over those for NIAS alone. Putting these together, we see that the condition for a CCR is $u_1 = 1$ and $u_3 = 0$ with $u_2 \in [0.6, 0.8]$.

5.7 Cost of Revealed Learning in Example 5.1

In terms of characterizing costs, we first apply the characterization of costs of revealed learning from Theorem 3 for any of the utility functions that admit a CIR. Given $u_1 = 1$, $u_3 = 0$, and $u_2 \in [0.6, 0.8]$, the NIAC logic corresponds to the costs of revealed learning satisfying

$$0.8 - K^1 \geq 0.75 - K^2,$$

$$0.45 + 0.5u_2 - K^2 \geq 0.8 - K^1.$$

To understand the top inequality, note that the odds of getting the good prize are 80% in data set $\mathbf{P}^1$ and, with only the first two actions available, would be 60% with a probability of 0.5 and 80% and 100% each with a probability of 0.325 in data set $\mathbf{P}^2$. Overall, this corresponds to odds of 0.75, as reflected on the RHS of the top inequality. With regard to the second inequality, the prizes received in the observed data are the medium prize with a probability of 0.5 and the good one with a probability of 0.25 when action a_1 is chosen and with a probability of 0.2 when action a_2 is chosen. That accounts for the LHS. On the RHS, with the utility of the medium prize being no higher than 0.8, a switch to the second data set would involve getting the good prize with a probability of 80%, just as when the action set was A^1.

In combination, we have the following:

$$K^1 - K^2 \in [0.35 - 0.5u_2, 0.05].$$

Note that this set is non-empty for all $u_2 \in [0.6, 0.8]$. When $u_2 = 0.8$, there is a wide range of rationalizing costs:

$$K^1 - K^2 \in [-0.05, 0.05].$$

When $u_M = 0.6$, the only rationalizing cost is $K^1 - K^2 = 0.05$.

Note that the logic of a CCR is equivalent to there being a CIR with equal costs, so we need a rationalization in which $K^1 = K^2$. This is possible only if $u_2 \in [0.7, 0.8]$. This is the second approach and, of course, an equivalent approach to identifying the tighter constraints on utility associated with a CCR.

5.8 The Variational Lower Bound and Posterior Separability

We turn now to the variational lower bound and indicate that it is extremely informative in this case, particularly if we are willing to work within the posterior-separable class of Lecture 8, which is previewed now in part to understand its analytic value. We start with a given finite set of states Ω and a prior $\mu \in \Delta(\Omega)$ that assigns strictly positive probability to all of them. In simple terms, an attention cost function K is posterior separable if, given $\mu \in \Delta\Omega$ and any Bayes' consistent posteriors $Q \in \mathcal{Q}(\mu)$,

$$K(\mu, Q) = \sum_{\gamma \in \text{supp } Q} Q(\gamma) T_\mu(\gamma),$$

for some convex function $T_\mu : \Delta(\Omega) \to \bar{\mathbb{R}}$. A fuller definition is given in Lecture 8. For present purposes, we assume also that T is differentiable.

The essence of posterior separability is that the cost function is equal to the expectation of some convex function of the individual posteriors T_μ. This creates a wonderful geometry of optimization with powerful analytic content. Define the net utility of action a and posterior γ:

$$N_\mu^a(\gamma) \equiv \sum_{\omega \in \text{supp } \gamma} \gamma(\omega) u(z(a, \omega)) - T_\mu(\gamma).$$

Note that since $T_\mu(\gamma)$ depends on μ, so does $N_\mu^a(\gamma)$. One can express the rationally inattentive decision problem in terms of maximizing a weighted average of net utilities. This allows a simple geometric interpretation of the solution. Maximizing the value function is equivalent to maximizing a Bayes' consistent weighted average of net utilities. Net utilities are concave since net utility is the difference between expected utility, which is linear in the probabilities, and the cost of information, which is convex. These curves differ in the utility that they assign to each state and action. Any finite set of posteriors that include the prior in their convex hull is feasible. The optimal action at each posterior provides the highest net utility. This is identified as the upper envelope of all net utility functions.

The value of choosing any set is of posteriors can be identified geometrically as the height of the hyperplane joining the points on the upper envelope of net utility curves as it passes over the prior. To find the maximal such height geometrically is to find the highest such point above the prior.

In technical terms, the entire operation revolves around the construction of the concavified net utility function, which is defined as the minimal concave function that majorizes all net utilities (Rockafellar, 1970). In standard cases, the highest chord lies on the line tangent to the lower epigraph at the prior. The optimal posteriors are the points at which this tangent plane meets the net utilities. All other net utilities lie (weakly) below this tangent plane. This gives rise to the Lagrangean lemma (see Caplin *et al.*, 2022, and Lecture 8), which implies that all net utility functions have the same slope at optimal choices.

It is shocking how profoundly this limits cost functions in our simple two-action set example. In brief, we know from the revealed posteriors of state 1 being 0.2 and 0.8 in A^1 that the difference in the slope of the T function as between posteriors 0.2 and 0.8 is precisely the same as the difference in the slopes of the lines that give the corresponding state-dependent payoffs of each action. This difference in slope is precisely 2 so that it is precisely the difference in the derivative (more precisely subdifferentials) of the T function. From A^2, in which there are two new revealed posteriors of state 1, 0.4 and 1, we learn two more facts about the derivative of the T function: At posterior 0.4, it is equidistant between the slopes at 0.2 and 0.8, while at 1, it is precisely the same as at 0.8. Finally, we note that since there is a common revealed posterior involving the probability of state 1 being 0.2, the two supporting hyperplanes to maximal net utility in action sets A^1 and A^2 are precisely the same. Hence, the difference in revealed costs must be precisely the same as the difference in net utility:

$$K^1 - K^2 = 0.8 - (0.45 + 0.5u_2) = 0.35 - 0.5u_2.$$

Apparently, there is much more to learn about this subject than is currently known.

5.9   Blackwell's Comparison of Experiments

Our next goal is to understand what might have been learned. Technically, given generic $(A, \mathbf{P})$, our key goal is to find out what the data say about what might have been learned. For reasons that will be clear, before doing that, we step back and present the basics of Blackwell informativeness. Recall that a Blackwell experiment is defined by a finite set of states, a finite set of (mutually exclusive) signals, and a function $\pi : \Omega \longrightarrow \Delta(S)$ that specifies in each state the likelihood with which each signal is seen. It is this function that can be used to update beliefs using Bayes' rule.

A key operation for our later purposes will be to compare experiments in terms of how informative they are. What we will do is to consider a simple example in which it seems clear that one experiment is more informative than another and use it to illustrate three equivalent methods of validating this intuition that Blackwell showed to be one and the same.

Example 5.2: There are two equiprobable states of the world. Experiment π involves two possible signals, the first of which has probabilities of 0.8 in state ω_1 and 0.2 in state ω_2 and the second of which has the converse probabilities of 0.2 in state ω_1 and 0.8 in state ω_2. To specify π in standard form, we name signals in the obvious manner as s_1, s_2 and probabilities in a matrix with the row sums 1 corresponding to states and with the columns relating to the two possible signals in π:

$$\pi = \begin{matrix} & s_1 & s_2 & \\ \begin{bmatrix} 0.8 & 0.2 \\ 0.2 & 0.8 \end{bmatrix} & & \begin{matrix} \omega_1 \\ \omega_2 \end{matrix} \end{matrix}.$$

Experiment π' involves three permissible signals, s_1', s_2', s_3', and we go straight to expressing it in standard matrix form:

$$\pi' = \begin{matrix} & s_1' & s_2' & s_3' & \\ \begin{bmatrix} 0.3 & 0.5 & 0.2 \\ 0.2 & 0.5 & 0.3 \end{bmatrix} & & \begin{matrix} \omega_1 \\ \omega_2 \end{matrix} \end{matrix}.$$

Looking across the rows and thinking about the corresponding updating from a uniform prior, note that signal s_2' induces no updating, while signals s_1', s_3' update the probability of state ω_1 to 0.6 and 0.4, respectively. In contrast, in experiment π, signals s_1, s_2 update the probability of state ω_1 to 0.8 and 0.2, respectively. Hence, it seems clear that π is more informative than π', but what exactly does that mean? One answer given by Blackwell is to transform the signals in the more informative experiments into the less informative ones by mixing them up. Technically, a garbling matrix will take the two signals in the more informative experiment and mix them up to arrive at the less informative one. So, the only issue is what weights to use in doing this. That must be defined by a 2×3 matrix specifying how to transform the good into the bad signals.

In the context of Example 5.2, a garbling matrix is a non-negative 2×3 stochastic matrix G with row sums 1 (so that each signal in S is stochastically mapped into each signal in S' such that $\pi G = \pi'$. Note that we are not *per se* mentioning posteriors. This just operates in abstract signal space, but of course, the weights are going to reflect the updating. For example, since $0.6 = 2/3(0.8) + 1/3(0.2)$, it looks like the two equiprobable signals s_1 and s_2 will need relative weights 2:1 to produce the information that s_1' contains: equal relative weights to produce s_2' and 1:2 to produce the information that s_3' produces. To work out the full matrix, we have to produce the corresponding unconditional probabilities with s_2' twice as likely overall as either s_1' or s_3'. Here then is the proposed garbling matrix:

$$
G = \begin{bmatrix} \dfrac{1}{3} & \dfrac{1}{2} & \dfrac{1}{6} \\ \dfrac{1}{6} & \dfrac{1}{2} & \dfrac{1}{3} \end{bmatrix}.
$$

For example, to check $\pi'(s_1 | \omega_1)$,

$$
\pi'(s_1 | \omega_1) = \frac{8}{30} + \frac{2}{60} = \frac{9}{30} = 0.3.
$$

Here, we have found a garbling matrix which definitely suggests that π is more informative than π'. The garbling operation is illustrated in Figure 5.1, which is intended to be self-explanatory. Blackwell reasonably proposed this as the necessary and sufficient condition for one experiment to be more informative than another. If there is no such garbling, then the experiments cannot be unequivocally ranked in terms of informativeness.

One of Blackwell's equivalent alternative definitions works through Bayes' consistent information structures. Note that we know precisely what that looks like in the case above. All we need to do is to compare Q, Q', which are both Bayes consistent information structures defined by

$$
Q(0.8) = Q(0.2) = Q'(0.5) = 0.5,
$$
$$
Q'(0.6) = Q'(0.4) = 0.25.
$$

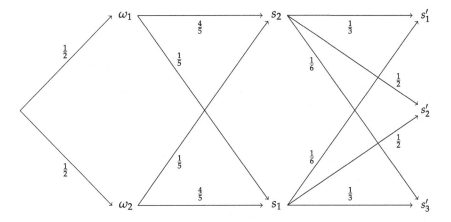

Figure 5.1   A garbling.

It feels now like we can build up the more informative using MPSs of the posteriors of the less informative. This is pretty clear geometrically. Map posterior 0.6 to 0.8 with a probability of 2/3 and 0.2 with a probability of 1/3, and the mean posterior is preserved. Likewise, map 0.5 to 0.8 with a probability of 1/2 and 0.2 with a probability of 1/2, and map 0.4 to 0.8 with a probability of 1/3 and 0.2 with a probability of 2/3. This is certainly an MPS of each posterior. Also, it is clear from the overall symmetry that in the end, this renders the two posteriors 0.8 and 0.2 equiprobable (see Figure 5.2):

$$Q(0.8) = \frac{2}{3}Q'(0.6) + \frac{1}{2}Q'(0.5) + \frac{1}{3}Q'(0.4)$$

$$= \frac{1}{3}Q'(0.6) + \frac{1}{2}Q'(0.5) + \frac{2}{3}Q'(0.4) = Q(0.2) = 0.5.$$

We call experiment Q more informative than Q' precisely because it can be derived by an MPS of the posteriors.

The final alternative definition is that a more informative experiment produces a higher maximized utility for any expected utility-maximizing DM regardless of the particulars of the utility function. We return to this in the next lecture. For now, we focus only on garblings and MPSs.

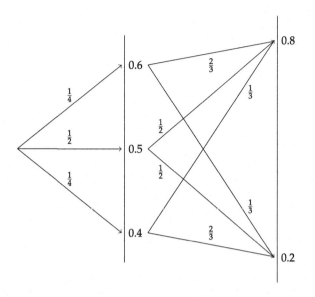

Figure 5.2   A mean-preserving spread.

5.10   Generating the Data

As indicated, our real interest is to find information structures that can explain observed SDSC. As part of that, they must be informative enough to generate the data.

Definition 23:   Information structure Q can **generate** $(A, \mathbf{P})$ if there exists $q : \operatorname{supp} Q \longrightarrow \Delta(A)$ such that $P_{(Q,q)} = \mathbf{P}$.

It is intuitively clear that a mixed strategy provides a garbling device. Blackwell's theorem shows that Q being more informative than $\tilde{Q}$, in the sense that the latter is a garbling of the former, is equivalent to the former being an MPS of the latter. This means that it is intuitive that a distribution of posteriors can generate the data if and only if the data set is more Blackwell informative than the revealed information structure. Caplin and Dean (2015) established that being at least as Blackwell informative as the revealed posterior distribution is necessary to generate the data. Here, we strengthen that to necessary and sufficient using the general definition of an MPS. Here is the theorem that Caplin *et al.* (2023c) prove.

Theorem 7: *Q can generate* $(A, \mathbf{P})$ *if and only if it is more Blackwell informative than $Q_{\mathbf{P}}$.*

To state the result precisely, I first state the definition of an MPS specialized to this application.

Definition 24: *Q* is a **mean-preserving spread** of $Q_{\mathbf{P}}$ if and only if there exists an $I \times J$ non-negative matrix B, where $1 \leq i \leq I$ indexes posteriors $\tilde{\gamma}^i$ in the support of $Q_{\mathbf{P}}$ and $1 \leq j \leq J$ indexes posteriors in the support of Q such that:

1. It is a Markov matrix so that row sums are 1:

$$\sum_{j=1}^{J} B_{ij} = 1. \tag{26}$$

2. For each $1 \leq j \leq J$, the unconditional probabilities in Q are generated as $Q_{\mathbf{P}}$ implies

$$\sum_{i=1}^{I} Q_{\mathbf{P}}(\tilde{\gamma}^i) B_{ij} = Q(\gamma^j). \tag{27}$$

3. The posteriors $\tilde{\gamma}^i$ are generated as Q, B imply

$$\tilde{\gamma}^i = \sum_{j=1}^{J} B_{ij} \gamma^j. \tag{28}$$

Proof 7: To establish sufficiency, we use the existence of the B matrix that is defining of Q being an MPS of $Q_{\mathbf{P}}$ to construct a mixed strategy $q : \text{supp} Q \longrightarrow \Delta(A)$ such that

$$P_{(Q,q)}(a, \omega) = \mathbf{P}(a, \omega),$$

for all $a \in A$ and $\omega \in \Omega$. To specify, note first that by construction, each chosen action $a \in A_{\mathbf{P}}$ has a strictly positive probability of being chosen at one and only one of the revealed posteriors whose index is denoted $i(a)$. With this, we establish that the following mixed strategy $q : \text{supp} Q \longrightarrow \Delta(A)$ has the property that it combines with Q to generate the data:

$$q(a|\gamma^j) = \frac{\mathbf{P}(a) B_{i(a)j}}{Q(\gamma^j)}. \tag{29}$$

The first issue is to confirm that q, as defined in (34), are mixed strategies. What we need to show is that summing the numerators across actions yields the denominator. To confirm, note that

$$\sum_{a \in A} \mathbf{P}(a) B_{i(a)j} = \sum_{i=1}^{I} \sum_{a:i(a)=i} \mathbf{P}(a) B_{ij}$$

$$= \sum_{i=1}^{I} Q_{\mathbf{P}}(\tilde{\gamma}^i) B_{ij}$$

$$= Q(\gamma^j),$$

where the first line is definitional, the second because $Q_{\mathbf{P}}(\gamma^i) = \sum_{a:i(a)=i} \mathbf{P}(a)$ by construction of the revealed posteriors and the revealed experiment, and the third from equation (27). It remains to confirm that $P_{(Q,q)} = \mathbf{P}$. To see this, note that given any action $a \in A_{\mathbf{P}}$ and state ω:

$$P_{(Q,q)}(a, \omega) = \sum_{j=1}^{J} q(a|\gamma^j) Q(\gamma^j) \gamma^j(\omega)$$

$$= \sum_{j=1}^{J} \mathbf{P}(a) B_{i(a)j} \gamma^j(\omega) = \mathbf{P}(a) \sum_{j=1}^{J} B_{i(a)j} \gamma^j(\omega)$$

$$= \mathbf{P}(a) \gamma^{i(a)}(\omega)$$

$$= \mathbf{P}(a) \gamma_{\mathbf{P}}^{a}(\omega)$$

$$= \mathbf{P}(a, \omega),$$

where the first line is definitional, the second line follows from equation (34), the third from equation (28), the fourth since $i(a)$ it is the only posterior at which a is chosen, so is the revealed posterior associated with action a, and the last from the definition of the revealed posterior, completing that the given strategy generates the data.

To prove necessity, suppose there exists an information structure and strategy (Q, q) such that $P_{(Q,q)}(a, \omega) = \mathbf{P}(a, \omega)$. We will verify that the matrix

$$B_{ij} = \frac{\sum_{a:i(a)=i} q(a|\gamma^j) Q(\gamma^j)}{\sum_{a:i(a)=i} \mathbf{P}(a)} \tag{30}$$

satisfies the requisite properties to establish Q as an MPS of $Q_{\mathbf{P}}$.

To show that B is a Markov matrix, it is useful to first note that

$$\sum_{j=1}^{J} q(a|\gamma^j)Q(\gamma^j) = \sum_{j=1}^{J} q(a|\gamma^j)Q(\gamma^j)\left[\sum_{\omega}\gamma^j(\omega)\right]$$

$$= \sum_{\omega}\sum_{j=1}^{J} q(a|\gamma^j)Q(\gamma^j)\gamma^j(\omega)$$

$$= \sum_{\omega} P_{(Q,q)}(a,\omega) = P_{(Q,q)}(a)$$

$$= \mathbf{P}(a),$$

where the first line follows from expanding $\sum_{\omega}\gamma^j(\omega) = 1$ and rearranging, the second by definition, and the third by the fact that $P_{(Q,q)}(a,\omega) = \mathbf{P}(a,\omega)$. Then,

$$\sum_{j=1}^{J} B_{ij} = \sum_{j=1}^{J}\left[\frac{\sum_{a:i(a)=i} q(a|\gamma^j)Q(\gamma^j)}{\sum_{a:i(a)=i}\mathbf{P}(a)}\right] = \frac{\sum_{a:i(a)=i}\sum_{j=1}^{J} q(a|\gamma^j)Q(\gamma^j)}{\sum_{a:i(a)=i}\mathbf{P}(a)}$$

$$= \frac{\sum_{a:i(a)=i}\mathbf{P}(a)}{\sum_{a:i(a)=i}\mathbf{P}(a)} = 1,$$

where the first line follows by the definition of B and rearrangement and the second by the preceding observation.

Next, we verify that B combined with the distribution of revealed posteriors $Q_{\mathbf{P}}$ generates the distribution of posteriors Q:

$$\sum_{i=1}^{I} Q_{\mathbf{P}}(\gamma^i)B_{ij} = \sum_{i=1}^{I} Q_{\mathbf{P}}(\gamma^i)\left[\frac{\sum_{a:i(a)=i} q(a|\gamma^j)Q(\gamma^j)}{\sum_{a:i(a)=i}\mathbf{P}(a)}\right]$$

$$= \sum_{i=1}^{I}\sum_{a:i(a)=i} q(a|\gamma^j)Q(\gamma^j)$$

$$= \sum_{a\in A} q(a|\gamma^j)Q(\gamma^j) = Q(\gamma^j)\sum_{a\in A} q(a|\gamma^j)$$

$$= Q(\gamma^j),$$

where the first line follows by definition, the second because $Q_{\mathbf{P}}(\gamma^i) = \sum_{a:i(a)=i}\mathbf{P}(a)$ by construction of the revealed posteriors and revealed experiment, the third by collecting sums and rearranging, and the fourth because $\sum_{a} q(a|\gamma^j) = 1$.

Third, B recovers the revealed posteriors. For any $\omega \in \Omega$,

$$\sum_{j=1}^{J} B_{ij}\gamma^j(\omega) = \sum_{j=1}^{J}\left[\frac{\sum_{a:i(a)=i}q(a|\gamma^j)Q(\gamma^j)}{\sum_{a:i(a)=i}\mathbf{P}(a)}\right]$$

$$\gamma^j(\omega) = \frac{\sum_{a:i(a)=i}\sum_{j=1}^{J}q(a|\gamma^j)Q(\gamma^j)\gamma^j(\omega)}{\sum_{a:i(a)=i}\mathbf{P}(a)}$$

$$= \frac{\sum_{a:i(a)=i}\mathbf{P}_{(Q,q)}(a,\omega)}{\sum_{a:i(a)=i}\mathbf{P}(a)}$$

$$= \frac{\sum_{a:i(a)=i}\mathbf{P}(a,\omega)}{\sum_{a:i(a)=i}\mathbf{P}(a)}$$

$$= \frac{\sum_{a:i(a)=i}\mathbf{P}(a)\gamma_{\mathbf{P}}^a(\omega)}{\sum_{a:i(a)=i}\mathbf{P}(a)} = \frac{\sum_{a:i(a)=i}\mathbf{P}(a)\gamma^i(\omega)}{\sum_{a:i(a)=i}\mathbf{P}(a)} = \gamma^i(\omega),$$

where the first line follows by definition and rearrangement, the second by the definition of $P_{(Q,q)}$, the third by the assumption that $P_{(Q,q)}(a,\omega) = \mathbf{P}(a,\omega)$, and the fourth by the definition of the revealed posterior and the summation over actions inducing the same revealed posterior.

5.11   Rationalizability: Mean- and Optimality-Preserving Spreads

Just because an information structure could, in principle, have generated the data for **some** mixed strategy does not mean that it could do so while obeying rationality. To identify learning, given a utility function $u \in \mathcal{U}^{NIAC}$, we wish to identify the set of possible information structures Q for which there exists an optimal mixed strategy q such that (Q,q) generate the observed data P.

Definition 25: Given $u \in \mathcal{U}^{NIAC}$, information structure Q can **rationalize** $(A,\mathbf{P})$ if there exists a mixed strategy $q : \operatorname{supp} Q \longrightarrow \Delta(A)$ that generates the data optimally:

$$P_{(Q,q)} = \mathbf{P} \tag{31}$$

$$Q(\gamma) > 0, q(a|\gamma) > 0 \implies \gamma \in \hat{\Gamma}(a|u,A). \tag{32}$$

As established above, a necessary condition for Q to rationalize $\mathbf{P}$ is that Q must be at least as Blackwell informative as the revealed experiment $Q_{\mathbf{P}}$, which corresponds to condition (31). Yet, Blackwell dominance is not sufficient for rationalization because it does not guarantee consistency with utility maximization, as summarized in condition (32). For example, it is possible for information structures to reveal "too much" about certain states or attributes to rationalize the data $\mathbf{P}$ for a given utility function. In Example 5.1, to which we return in the following, full learning would allow both data sets to be generated but in neither case would the SDSC result from an optimal fully informed strategy which would produce an expected utility of 1 by always picking the best prize.

To find the right conditions, we introduce a variation of the Black-wellian theme. We now define an MOPS by insisting that there exists an optimality-preserving matrix that has the MPS property of the revealed posterior strategy. Note that, in the definition, we use the observation that each chosen action $a \in A_{\mathbf{P}}$ has a strictly positive probability of being chosen at one and only one of the revealed posteriors.

Definition 26: Given $(A, \mathbf{P})$ and $u \in \mathcal{U}^{NIAC}$, consider any information structure Q. Let I be the cardinality of the support of $Q_{\mathbf{P}}$ and index-revealed posteriors as $\gamma_{\mathbf{P}}^i$, J that of Q with possible posteriors indexed as γ^j. Q is a **mean- and optimality-preserving spread** (MOPS) of $\mathbf{P}$ if there exists a $I \times J$ non-negative matrix B that defines Q as an MPS of $Q_{\mathbf{P}}$ and if, in addition, given $a \in A_{\mathbf{P}}$ and defining $i(a)$ as the index of the revealed posterior at which it is chosen,

$$B_{i(a)j} > 0 \implies \gamma^j \in \hat{\Gamma}(a|u, A). \tag{33}$$

The key result in relation to what might have been learned is that ratio-nalizability is equivalent to a MOPS. A subtlety is that rationalizability does not require actions with the same revealed posteriors to be chosen at the same posteriors in Q; in contrast, the MOPS does this implicitly because the B matrix maps revealed posteriors rather than actions. This gives rise to the key insight in the equivalence theorem, which is that any posterior distribution for which there exists a mixed strategy that differenti-ates among actions with the same revealed posterior permits an alternative mixed strategy that is symmetric among such actions, as required in the MOPS construction. This, in turn, requires establishing that optimality is preserved **across** actions that induce the same revealed posteriors, which is the centerpiece of the proof.

Theorem 8:   *Given $u \in \mathcal{U}^{NIAC}$, information structure Q can rationalize $(A, \mathbf{P})$ if and only if it is an MOPS of $\mathbf{P}$.*

Proof 8: To show that Q being an MOPS of $\mathbf{P}$ for $u \in \mathcal{U}^{NIAC}$ is sufficient for it to rationalize $(A, \mathbf{P})$, consider the mixed strategy introduced in the previous theorem:

$$q(a|\gamma^j) = \frac{\mathbf{P}(a)B_{i(a)j}}{Q(\gamma^j)}. \tag{34}$$

We have shown that this generates the data. All that is left to show is that actions are chosen only at posteriors at which they are optimal. We need that

$$q(a|\gamma^j) > 0 \implies \gamma^j \in \hat{\Gamma}(a|u, A).$$

By construction,

$$q(a|\gamma^j) = \frac{\mathbf{P}(a)B_{i(a)j}}{Q(\gamma^j)} > 0 \implies B_{i(a)j} > 0.$$

By property (4) of the MOPS, this directly implies $\gamma^j \in \hat{\Gamma}(a|u, A)$, completing the proof.

In terms of the necessity proof, we again know that being an MPS is necessary from the previous theorem so that all that is left is to prove that preservation of optimality is necessary. By definition (30) of B, it suffices to show that for any actions $a, a' \in A$,

$$Q(\gamma^j) > 0, \; q(a|\gamma^j) > 0, \text{ and } \gamma_{\mathbf{P}}^a = \gamma_{\mathbf{P}}^{a'} \implies \gamma^j \in \hat{\Gamma}(a'|u, A).$$

To establish this, consider a mixed strategy q that generates the data optimally, i.e., it satisfies (31) and (32). Invoking (31) to replace the $\mathbf{P}$ terms in the definition of the revealed posterior with their counterparts $P_{(Q,q)}$, we can express the revealed posterior for any action a as a convex combination of posteriors in the support of Q:

$$\gamma_{\mathbf{P}}^{a} = \sum_{j=1}^{J} \rho^{a}(\gamma^{j})\gamma^{j}, \tag{35}$$

where

$$\rho^{a}(\gamma^{j}) = \frac{q(a|\gamma^{j})Q(\gamma^{j})}{\sum_{k=1}^{J} q(a|\gamma^{k})Q(\gamma^{k})}.$$

By optimality (32) of q, the weights ρ are positive only at posteriors where a is optimal:

$$\rho^{a}(\gamma^{j}) > 0 \implies \gamma^{j} \in \hat{\Gamma}(a|u,A). \tag{36}$$

This implies that the action a is also optimal at its revealed posterior:

$$\gamma_{\mathbf{P}}^{a} \in \hat{\Gamma}(a|u,A). \tag{37}$$

We close the proof by establishing a key fact that, given two actions a, a' with the same revealed posteriors, $\gamma_{\mathbf{P}}^{a} = \gamma_{\mathbf{P}}^{a'}$, both are optimal at any posterior at which either is chosen. Suppose to the contrary that there exists a posterior γ^{j} for which $Q(\gamma^{j}) > 0$ and $q(a|\gamma^{j}) > 0$ so that $\rho^{a}(\gamma^{j}) > 0$, but for which $\gamma^{j} \notin \hat{\Gamma}(a'|u,A)$. Then,

$$\sum_{\omega} u(a',\omega)\gamma_{\mathbf{P}}^{a'}(\omega) = \sum_{\omega} u(a',\omega)\gamma_{\mathbf{P}}^{a}(\omega)$$

$$= \sum_{j=1}^{J} \rho^{a}(\gamma^{j}) \sum_{\omega} u(a',\omega)\gamma^{j}(\omega)$$

$$< \sum_{j=1}^{J} \rho^{a}(\gamma^{j}) \sum_{\omega} u(a,\omega)\gamma^{j}(\omega)$$

$$= \sum_{\omega} u(a,\omega)\gamma_{\mathbf{P}}^{a}(\omega) = \sum_{\omega} u(a,\omega)\gamma_{\mathbf{P}}^{a'}(\omega),$$

where the first and second equalities follow, respectively, from equal posteriors and (35), the third inequality follows from optimality (36) of a combined with our assumed **strict** suboptimality of a' for some γ^{j} with $\rho^{a}(\gamma^{j}) > 0$, and the fourth and fifth equalities follow again from (35) and equal posteriors. Thus, $\gamma_{\mathbf{P}}^{a'} \notin \hat{\Gamma}(a'|u,A)$, contradicting (37). It follows that $\gamma^{j} \in \hat{\Gamma}(a'|u,A)$, completing the proof.

5.12   Possible Learning in Example 5.1

Applying Theorem 8 to characterize possible learning in Example 5.1 above and beyond the revealed information structure generally requires specifying the utility function $u \in \mathcal{U}^{NIAC}$, which by the characterization of the previous section reduces to picking $u_2 \in [0.6, 0.8]$ with the normalization $u_1 = 1, u_3 = 0$. However, the characterization of possible learning in decision problem A^1 is independent of this value u_2 because the corresponding prize z_2 is never attained by actions a^1 and a^2. Given that only actions a^1 and a^2 are available in A^1, the key sets of posteriors at which each action is optimal are given by:

$$\hat{\Gamma}^1(a_1|u) = [0.5, 1.0],$$

$$\hat{\Gamma}^2(a_2|u) = [0, 0.5].$$

Theorem 8 states that an information structure can rationalize the data if and only if it can be obtained by spreading the revealed posteriors across posteriors that preserve optimality at each associated action. More specifically, the posteriors that a Markov matrix B permits from revealed posterior $\gamma_{\mathbf{P}^1}^{A_1} = 0.8$ must all preserve optimality of a_1 and hence be in the range $[0.5, 1.0]$, while those permitted from revealed posterior $\gamma_{\mathbf{P}^1}^{A_2} = 0.2$ must all preserve optimality of a_2 and hence be in the range $[0, 0.5]$. Thus, the MOPS equivalence of Theorem 8 leads to a succinct characterization of information structures Q that rationalize the data $\mathbf{P}^1$.

Proposition 3: *Given $u_1 = 1, u_3 = 0$, Q can **rationalize** $(A^1, \mathbf{P}^1)$ if and only if there exists $p \in [0, 1]$ such that the following equations hold:*

$$\sum_{\gamma > 0.5} Q(\gamma) + pQ(0.5) = 0.5, \tag{38}$$

$$\sum_{\gamma > 0.5} \gamma Q(\gamma) + 0.5 pQ(0.5) = 0.4, \tag{39}$$

$$\sum_{\gamma < 0.5} \gamma Q(\gamma) + 0.5(1-p)Q(0.5) = 0.1. \tag{40}$$

The main subtlety in Proposition 3 arises at posterior 0.5. Because both actions a_1 and a_2 are optimal at this posterior, it can be "reached" (in the sense of B) from either revealed posterior. The fraction of the probability

$Q(0.5)$ stemming from $\gamma_{\mathbf{P}^1}^{a_1}$ is parameterized by the additional variable p. That is, assuming $Q(0.5) > 0$ and letting $j(0.5)$ denote the index of posterior 0.5,

$$p = \frac{\mathbf{P}^1(a_1)B_{1j(0.5)}}{Q(0.5)}.$$

The key distinction in decision problem A^2 is that feasible learning depends on the utility parameter u_2 through the sets of posteriors inducing optimal actions:

$$\hat{\Gamma}^2(a_1|u_2) = [u_2, 1],$$

$$\hat{\Gamma}^2(a_3|u_2) = [1 - u_2, u_2],$$

$$\hat{\Gamma}^2(a_2|u_2) = [0, 1 - u_2].$$

Again, Theorem 8 states that an information structure can rationalize the data $\mathbf{P}^2$ if and only if it can be obtained by spreading the revealed posteriors across posteriors that preserve optimality at each associated action.

5.13 Full Characterizations

5.13.1 *Costly information representations*

Appropriately combining elements from the previous section, we can fully characterize all utility functions and information structures $u, \{Q^m\}_{m=1}^M$ for which a cost function exists that provide a CIR of $\{(A^m, \mathbf{P}^m)\}_{m=1}^M$. Utility function u and learning $\{Q^m\}_{m=1}^M$ are such that there exists a learning cost function K that provides a CIR of $\{(A^m, \mathbf{P}^m)\}_{m=1}^M$ if and only if

1. u is in the CIR cone associated with $\{(A^m, \mathbf{P}^m)\}_{m=1}^M$.
2. Given u, each Q^m is a MOPS of $(A^m, \mathbf{P}^m)$, $1 \leq m \leq M$.

There is a subtlety in relation to the set of cost functions that can provide such a rationalization. In Lecture 4, we identified all such rationalizing cost functions that are strictly increasing in the Blackwell order. There are subtle adjustments to allow for cost functions that are only weakly increasing in the Blackwell order: see Caplin *et al.* (2023c).

5.13.2   *Capacity-constrained representations*

Recall that a CCR comprises a triple u, $\{Q^m\}_{m=1}^{M}$ and Q^*. The condition on utilities is defined by the cone and the conditions on $\{Q^m\}_{m=1}^{M}$ from the MOPS section. What is left is to identify all possible constraint sets Q^*. Here, the key observation is that this builds off the section on the variational lower bound on costs. As noted, when introduced, this depends both on a utility function in the CIR Utility cone and a corresponding vector of revealed learning costs. Recall the two-step definition in which we start with $u \in \mathcal{U}^{NIAC}$ and then identify possible revealed costs of learning from the $D(u)$ matrix $\vec{K} \in \mathcal{K}^R(u)$. In the second step, one identifies possible costs on the full domain $Q \in \mathcal{Q}$ which are characterized by the variational lower bound on costs:

$$K^{\min}(Q|u,\vec{K}) = \max_{1 \leq m \leq M} [G^m(Q|u,A^m) - G^m(u) + K^m]. \qquad (41)$$

What makes this particularly simple in a CCR is that the cost of all revealed information structures can be set equal at zero WLOG. This means that the inequalities on costs simplify to

$$K^{\min}(Q|u,0) = \max_{1 \leq m \leq M} [G^m(Q|u,A^m) - G^m(u)]. \qquad (42)$$

This function plays a key role in the characterization since anything for which this minimum is non-positive would not be chosen even if available, while any information structure for which it is strictly positive would, by definition, replace a chosen information structure if available. This has strong implications for what might have been feasible to learn in a CCR: It corresponds precisely to those information structures for which this function is non-positive.

By way of summary, utility function u, learning $\{Q^m\}_{m=1}^{M}$, and learning cost function K provide a CCR of $\{(A^m, \mathbf{P}^m)\}_{m=1}^{M}$ if and only if:

1. u is in the CCR utility cone associated with $\{(A^m, \mathbf{P}^m)\}_{m=1}^{M}$;
2. given u, each Q^m is a MOPS of its revealed information structure $Q_{\mathbf{P}^m}$;
3. $\cup_m Q^m \subset Q^* \subset \{Q \in \mathcal{Q} | K^{\min}(Q|u,0) \leq 0\}$.

5.14   Fixed Information Representations

An FIR is a special case of a CCR. Hence, the restrictions on utility to admit an FIR will be even stronger. It turns out that they are best characterized directly using the concept of an MOPS that characterize the possible forms of learning consistent with data. What is different about an FIR from all others is that it is focused not on the costs of what is chosen but rather must specify that one thing and only one thing is learnable. This means that it must have been learnable in all pairs $(A^m, \mathbf{P}^m)$. This is precisely what characterizes the existence of an FIR.

By way of summary, utility function u, learning $\{Q^m\}_{m=1}^{M}$, and learning cost function K provide an FIR of $\{(A^m, \mathbf{P}^m)\}_{m=1}^{M}$ if and only if:

1. u is in the CCR utility cone associated with $\{(A^m, \mathbf{P}^m)\}_{m=1}^{M}$;
2. given u, each Q^m is a MOPS of its revealed information structure $Q_{\mathbf{P}^m}$;
3. Q^* itself is a MOPS of all $(A^m, \mathbf{P}^m)$ given u.

5.15   FIR in the Example

To identify when a utility function that admits a CCR also admits an FIR requires identification of a common distribution of posteriors Q and optimizing mixed action strategies q^1, q^2 from all possible posteriors $\gamma \in$ supp Q, which can be distinct between decision problems, that in each case generates the data in the example. This turns out to be very restrictive. In fact, there is one and only one utility specification in which this is possible: It involves $u_2 = 0.8$.

Not only is the utility function pinned down but also there are powerful constraints on the common information structure Q. Here is the simplest possible information structure that allows the data to be rationalized. Defining this structure by the posterior probability of state ω_1, we have

$$Q(1) = Q(0.6) = 0.25, Q(0.2) = 0.5.$$

In this case, the unique strategies that rationalize the data are

$$q^1(a_1|1) = q^1(a_1|0.6) = q^1(a_2|0.2) = 1,$$

$$q^2(a_1|1) = q^2(a_3|0.6) = 1,$$

$$q^2(a_2|0.2) = q^2(a_3|0.2) = 0.5.$$

That the above strategies are optimizing is clear. All deterministic strategies involve actions that are uniquely optimal at the corresponding posterior, while the mixed strategy in data set A^2, in which both a_2 and a_3 are chosen when the probability of state ω_1 is 0.2, reflects the fact that both yield an equal utility of $u_2 = 0.8$ at this posterior. To confirm that this produces the data, consider by way of illustration, the choice of action a_1 in data set $\mathbf{P}^1$:

$$P_{(Q,q^1)}(a_1, \omega_1) = Q(1)q^1(a_1|1) * 1 + Q(0.6)q^1(a_1|0.6) * 0.6$$
$$= 0.4 = \mathbf{P}^1(a_1, \omega_1),$$
$$P_{(Q,q^1)}(a_1, \omega_2) = Q(0.6)q^1(a_1|0.6) * 0.4 = 0.1 = \mathbf{P}^1(a_1, \omega_2),$$

with the precisely analogous logic for action a_2 in data set $\mathbf{P}^1$. With regard to data set $\mathbf{P}^2$,

$$P_{(Q,q^2)}(a_1, \omega_1) = Q(1)q^2(a_1|1) = \frac{1}{4} = \mathbf{P}^2(a_1, \omega_1),$$
$$P_{(Q,q^2)}(a_1, \omega_2) = 0 = \mathbf{P}^2(a_1, \omega_2),$$
$$P_{(Q,q^2)}(a_2, \omega_1) = Q(0.2)q^2(a_2|0.2) * 0.2 = 0.05 = \mathbf{P}^2(a_2, \omega_1),$$
$$P_{(Q,q^2)}(a_2, \omega_2) = Q(0.2)q^2(a_2|0.2) * 0.8 = 0.2 = \mathbf{P}^2(a_2, \omega_2),$$
$$P_{(Q,q^2)}(a_3, \omega_1) = Q(0.6)q^2(a_3|0.6) * 0.6 + Q(0.2)q^2(a_3|0.2) * 0.2$$
$$= 0.2 = \mathbf{P}^2(a_3, \omega_1),$$
$$P_{(Q,q^2)}(a_3, \omega_2) = Q(0.6)q^2(a_3|0.6) * 0.4 + Q(0.2)q^2(a_3|0.2) * 0.8$$
$$= 0.3 = \mathbf{P}^2(a_3, \omega_2).$$

This completes the demonstration that these together define an FIR.

To illustrate the MOPS operation, consider that the simplest information structure Q that defines an MPS of $\mathbf{P}^1$ and $\mathbf{P}^2$ is $Q(1) = Q(0.6) = 0.25$ and $Q(0.2) = 0.5$. The 2×3 transition matrix B^1 with the probability of state ω_1 in the corresponding rows and columns is:

$$B^1 = \begin{matrix} & 0.2 & 0.8 & 1 & \\ \begin{pmatrix} 1 & 0 & 0 \\ 0 & 0.5 & 0.5 \end{pmatrix} & & & & \begin{matrix} 0.2 \\ 0.8 \end{matrix} \end{matrix}.$$

The transition matrix B^2 is the identity matrix.

Why is there no utility level other than $u_2 = 0.8$ for which an FIR exists? The key is the need to rationalize the combination of unconditional action probabilities and revealed posteriors of chosen actions. Data set $\mathbf{P}^1$ has two equiprobable revealed posteriors of state ω_1, which are recorded with their unconditional probabilities as

$$\gamma_{\mathbf{P}^1}^{a_1} \equiv 0.8 \text{ and } \mathbf{P}^1(a_1) = 0.5,$$

$$\gamma_{\mathbf{P}^1}^{a_2} \equiv 0.2 \text{ and } \mathbf{P}^1(a_2) = 0.5.$$

In contrast, data set $\mathbf{P}^2$ has three revealed posteriors of state ω_1 again recorded with their unconditional probabilities as

$$\gamma_{\mathbf{P}^2}^{a_1} \equiv 1 \text{ and } \mathbf{P}^2(a_1) = 0.25,$$

$$\gamma_{\mathbf{P}^2}^{a_2} \equiv 0.2 \text{ and } \mathbf{P}^2(a_2) = 0.25,$$

$$\gamma_{\mathbf{P}^2}^{a_3} \equiv 0.4 \text{ and } \mathbf{P}^2(a_2) = 0.5.$$

This combination of observations restrict not only the utility function but also any rationalizing information structure. The first key observation relates to the fact that the choice of action a_2 in both choice sets A^1 and A^2 has a common revealed posterior probability of state ω_1 of 0.2 but a probability of 0.5 rather than 0.25 in A^1 rather than in A^2. Hence, there must be some posterior at which a_2 can be in A^1 at which a_3 was chosen in A^2. By optimality, these have to be the higher posteriors in the range, if any. If indeed there were any possible posteriors in the range $(0.2, 0.5]$ at which a_3 was chosen in A^2 while a_2 was in A^1, their removal would strictly lower the revealed posterior of that action in decision problem A^2, which they do not.

The conclusion, therefore, is that 0.2 must be the only possible posterior in the range $[0, 0.5)$ and that it must have unconditional probability $Q(0.2) = 0.5$. To explain the data, we then need the mixed strategy at this posterior to assign equal probability to actions a_2, a_3. It is precisely the need for this to be consistent with an optimal strategy that pins down $u_2 = 0.8$ as necessary for an FIR.

To round off the example, we identify the necessary and sufficient conditions on the information structure Q and the corresponding mixed strategies that produce the data and that in combination with $u_M = 0.8$ provide an FIR. The remaining logic again involves the combined weight of the information that can be inferred from the revealed posteriors and their unconditional probabilities in the two data sets. With regard to the common information structure, note that $Q(1) = 0.25$. It must be at least that high to explain $\gamma_{\mathbf{P}2}^{A_1} \equiv 1$ and $\mathbf{P}^1(a_1) = 0.25$. It cannot be higher since it is strictly optimal to choose a_1 at this posterior. We are left only to find the final 0.25 uncommitted posterior probabilities. In data set $\mathbf{P}^1$, we know that the average posterior when a_1 is chosen is 0.8 and that it is chosen with a probability of 0.5. Since we also know that the posterior is precisely 1 with a probability of 0.25, it must average precisely 0.6 otherwise. A second immediate observation is that there is no possible posterior in the range $(0.8, 1]$ for precisely the same reason that if there were, then optimality would imply a strictly higher probability of choosing action a_1 in data set $\mathbf{P}^2$. To state this succinctly, the remaining 0.25 probability must all be assigned to posteriors at which a_1 is optimal in data set A^1 and a_3 is optimal in action set A^2. This sets the support as $[0.5, 0.8]$. Furthermore, we know that in this range, the average posterior must be 0.6.

The above arguments have left out one final piece of the puzzle, which is that the average posterior other than 0.2 at which a_3 is chosen in data set $\mathbf{P}^2$ must be 0.6 to rationalize the revealed posterior of 0.4. But this is already implied above, so it adds now new conditions. We conclude that there are indeed no more restrictions. What this means is that we can generalize the particular example in which $Q(0.6) = Q(1) = 0.25$ and $Q(0.2) = 0.5$ in only one respect. We can replace $Q(0.6)$ with any set of posteriors on the support $[0.5, 0.8]$ that average to 0.6 and then set the corresponding strategy of deterministically choosing a_1 at all such posteriors in A^1 and a_3 at all such posteriors in A^2.

Lecture 6

Full Recovery of Costs and Welfare

In terms of how to do applied research, the central idea in these lectures is that rich data about decisions in a fixed learning environment with very different incentives to learn allows rich inference about utility, learning, and the costs of learning. In this lecture, I take this point to its limit and consider a researcher who is able to vary incentives widely and otherwise to design the decision-making environment. In addition to laying out some particularly insightful variations in the learning environment and decision problem, I present an experiment designed around the main recovery result. The attentive reader will note that the results in this section are illustrative rather than fully definitive. There are many ways to design experimental choice environments that generate insightful SDSC. Many of these have, in fact, been pioneered in psychometrics, which routinely generates such data. I focus on the few cases that have been formally studied in detail. The result is partial rather than complete recovery. It is clear that one can drive far further forward on this road, and I close the lecture by pointing out a few valid directions forward.

Here are the goals of this lecture:

(1) Taking some utility function $u : Z \longrightarrow \mathbb{R}$ as known, I introduce the method of Caplin, Csaba, Leahy, and Nov (henceforth CCLN) for pinning down the costs of learning using a particularly simple class of decision problems. A very strong analogy with competitive supply guides this particular conceptual design. While the basic idea of this portion of the lecture is drawn from CCLN, the result is more powerful. CCLN establish a result that recovers utility from a continuum of

experiments: The result in this lecture shows rapid convergence with a more realistic finite set of experiments. In addition, the proof of the result is more direct.

(2) I introduce a corresponding experimental design from CCLN in which these costs are measured. Of particular interest is a device introduced therein for scaling incentives, which has many potential applications in psychometrics.

(3) The second recovery result in this section involves the use of test functions introduced by Lu (2016). I show how these can be used to recover welfare without knowing separately either the utility function or the cost function.

(4) I close the section by discussing entirely different experimental approaches to measuring net welfare. If the theoretically implied equality were to fail (I have little doubt that it would), it would point the path forward toward next-generation modeling, which in turn would require further data engineering. In this particular case, the most obvious theoretical gap relates to metacognition: To what extent are DMs aware of the mistakes they make and their costs of learning? This is a wonderful open question for theory and measurement that I revisit in Lecture 13.

6.1 Recovery: The Analogy with Competitive Supply

CCLN introduce a simple method of recovering costs of learning from choice data under the assumption that the utility function is known: Otherwise, one can regard it as specifying a unique cost function, given a utility function that permits a CIR in the data. By analogy with competitive supply, the recovery theorem identifies the equivalents of total revenue, total cost, and producer surplus for the attentional problem.

The starting point is standard, with the DM choosing from a finite set A of $N \geq 2$ actions. Action a yields known utility $u(a, \omega)$ in state $\omega \in \Omega$. Note that at this point, the prize space is suppressed, given that utilities are known. The key idea is to scale attentional incentives linearly by constructing a family of decision problems A^π, indexed by $\pi > 0$. We enumerate actions in A by $a(n)$ for $1 \leq n \leq N$ and correspondingly each action in A^π

by $a^\pi(n)$. Utility for each action is proportionate to that for action $a(n)$ with factor of proportionality π. This defines the equivalent of price for a firm.

Definition 27: The **linear family of decision problems** generated by A is a set of decision problems, $\{A^\pi\}_{\pi>0}$, with A^π having N actions $a^\pi(n)$ with state-dependent utility for $1 \leq n \leq N$ satisfying

$$u(a^\pi(n), \omega) = \pi u(a(n), \omega) \geq 0.$$

Note that there is a normalization imposed: There is effectively a utility of zero in a base case with $\pi = 0$. So, this is essentially the prize that is received independent of attention. In implementing this experimentally, the idea is that choice is relevant to the prize with a probability of π, otherwise the prize is choice independent. Note that there is no implied restriction on how good is the choice independent prize, but there are very different implications for total utility if prizes are bad relative to the default. So, in what follows, we think of them as better, but this does not impact the formal analysis.

As detailed in the following, one can use lottery prizes to generate such a linear family. But this is not essential: One can equally recover costs in the appropriate expected utility units by applying a risk-aversion correction when monetary rewards are scaled up and down.

The ideal data comprise the observation of SDSC for each $\pi > 0$. Let $\mathbf{P}^\pi(n, \omega) \geq 0$ specify the probability of choosing each possible action $a^\pi(n) \in A^\pi$ in each possible state. For each $\pi > 0$, we use this data set to compute the corresponding revealed expected utility:

$$G(\pi) := \sum_\omega \sum_n u(a^\pi(n), \omega) \, \mathbf{P}^\pi(n, \omega).$$

Our goal is to record the quality of the decision-making. To that end, we divide expected utility by π. This is equivalent to recording the expected utility that results from using the strategy for decision problem A^π with the rewards associated with A:

$$\bar{G}(\pi) := \frac{G(\pi)}{\pi} = \sum_\omega \sum_n \frac{u(a^\pi(n), \omega)}{\pi} \mathbf{P}^\pi(n, \omega) = \sum_\omega \sum_n u(a(n), \omega) \mathbf{P}^\pi(n, \omega).$$

The maintained assumption is that the full data set is consistent with rational inattention, albeit with an unknown cost function. The recovery theorem will identify the costs associated with the learning involved in producing each data set $\mathbf{P}^\pi$. We denote this cost $K(\pi)$. On a technical note, NIAC applied to **all finite cycles** is necessary and sufficient for a CIR when one observes an infinite number of distinct decision problems, as in the current case. This is established in the online appendix to Caplin *et al.* (2019). A second technical note: As always, in this form of analysis, the existence of optimal strategies is implied by the terms of the recovery exercise. A prerequisite for the data to be consistent with rational inattention is that optimal strategies exist. We normalize the function so that inattention is free.

6.2   Two Simple Observations

The special structure of the linear class of decision problems has two important implications. The first is that the function $G(\pi)$ is non-decreasing in π. CCLN call this non-decreasing function the incentivized psychometric curve for the obvious reason that it is a version of the psychometric curve in which incentives operate to leverage up the extent to which the truth is understood.

Theorem 9: *With NIAC, $\bar{G}(\pi)$ is non-decreasing in π.*

Proof 9: Take $\pi_2 \neq \pi_1 > 0$ with NIAC satisfied. NIAC directly implies that switching data between decision problems cannot be improving. This swap mechanically changes the total utilities achieved. The use of $\mathbf{P}^{\pi_1}$ with action set A^{π_2} yields a precise gross expected utility of $\frac{\pi_2}{\pi_1}G(\pi_1)$, while correspondingly, using $\mathbf{P}^{\pi_2}$ with action set A^{π_1} yields a precise gross expected utility of $\frac{\pi_1}{\pi_2}G(\pi_2)$. Since NIAC holds, this joint swap cannot raise total utility:

$$G(\pi_1) + G(\pi_2) \geq \frac{\pi_2}{\pi_1}G(\pi_1) + \frac{\pi_1}{\pi_2}G(\pi_2).$$

Direct subsitution yields

$$\pi_1 \bar{G}(\pi_1) + \pi_2 \bar{G}(\pi_2) \geq \pi_2 \bar{G}(\pi_1) + \pi_1 \bar{G}(\pi_2)$$

or, equivalently,

$$(\pi_1 - \pi_2)(\bar{G}(\pi_1) - \bar{G}(\pi_2)) \geq 0,$$

establishing that $\pi_1 > \pi_2$ implies $\bar{G}(\pi_1) \geq \bar{G}(\pi_2)$, establishing the result.

Note that this result holds even if the prizes in the attentional lottery realized with a probability of π are worse than the prize that is independent of attention. While total utility might diminish, not so normalized utility, which will increase due to the increased incentive as π increases to avoid the worst of prizes.

The second important observation concerns the value of the optimal strategy for one value π in the data associated with π', which is key to the construction of the G matrices that played a key role in cost recovery in the previous section. As is standard, we define the optimal utility that can be achieved using action choices from one set, A^π, with data from the other, $\mathbf{P}^{\pi'}$, as

$$G^{\pi\pi'} \equiv \sum_{a\in A^{\pi'}} \max_{a'\in A^\pi} \sum_{\omega\in\Omega} u(a',\omega)\mathbf{P}^{\pi'}(a,\omega).$$

The key observation is that in the linear family, an optimal switch is trivial: It is to keep the same action index as in the original data and therefore multiply up or down rewards mechanically according to the ratio of π to π'. Technically, given π and π',

$$G^{\pi\pi'} = \frac{\pi}{\pi'}G(\pi') = \pi\bar{G}(\pi'). \qquad (43)$$

The reason is clear. If the inequality was strict in either direction, it would be improving to correspondingly switch strategy.

6.3 Bounds on Costs and Full Recovery

The above observation allows us not only to prove the existing recovery result from CCLN but also to do one better by showing bounds on costs that shrink to zero with the grid size in an extremely simple and usable manner. As a prelude, we consider what a CIR allows us to say based on data only for $\pi = 0, 1$, where recall that the cost of the SDSC in an optimal strategy for a given level of π as $K(\pi)$. Here are two inequalities that can be computed based on these two alone and the fact that with a CIR, it cannot be possible to switch to the other data at its cost, reoptimize, and raise utility:

$$\bar{G}(1) - K(1) = G(1) - K(1) \geq \bar{G}(0) - K(0) = \bar{G}(0). \qquad (44)$$

Here we use the facts that $K(0) = 0$ since there is no reward to compensate and that the inattentive strategy is always available and costless, it is optimal to apply (anything else is, at least, as costly in the representation). Combining this with monotonicity, we get simple bounds on $K(1)$:

$$0 \leq K(1) \leq \bar{G}(1) - \bar{G}(0).$$

What we now do is to consider, for any M, the subset of π values that are of the form $\frac{m}{M}$ for $0 \leq m \leq M$ and the corresponding action and data sets:

$$\{(A^{\frac{m}{M}}, \mathbf{P}^{\frac{m}{M}})\}_{m=0}^{M}.$$

The key observation is that the observation of this collection provides a proportionate tightening in the difference between the upper and low bounds on costs and also produces the recovery result.

Theorem 10: *Given a CIR and data set* $\{(A^{\frac{m}{M}}, \mathbf{P}^{\frac{m}{M}})\}_{m=0}^{M}$, *cost* $K(1)$ *can be bounded above and below as*

$$K(1) \geq \sum_{j=0}^{M-1} \frac{j}{M} \left[\bar{G}\left(\frac{j+1}{M}\right) - \bar{G}\left(\frac{j}{M}\right) \right] \equiv K^{\min}(M), \qquad (45)$$

$$K(1) \leq \sum_{j=0}^{M-1} \frac{j+1}{M} \left[\bar{G}\left(\frac{j+1}{M}\right) - \bar{G}\left(\frac{j}{M}\right) \right]] \equiv K^{\max}(M). \qquad (46)$$

Hence, the difference between the upper and lower bounds shrinks precisely in proportion with M:

$$K^{\max}(M) - K^{\min}(M) = \frac{\bar{G}(1) - \bar{G}(0)}{M}. \qquad (47)$$

Finally, taking the limit with M *produces the recovery result:*

$$K(1) = \bar{G}(1) - \int_0^1 \bar{G}(\pi) d\pi. \qquad (48)$$

Proof 10: Pick $0 \leq j \leq M - 1$, and note that given this is a CIR, we know that costs K^j, K^{j+1} must be such that swapping data between A^j and A^{j+1}

and paying the corresponding cost cannot raise net utility:

$$G\left(\frac{j}{M}\right) - K\left(\frac{j}{M}\right) = \frac{j}{M}\bar{G}\left(\frac{j}{M}\right) - K\left(\frac{j}{M}\right)$$

$$\geq \frac{j}{M}\bar{G}\left(\frac{j+1}{M}\right) - K\left(\frac{j+1}{M}\right).$$

Rearranging, we conclude that

$$K\left(\frac{j+1}{M}\right) - K\left(\frac{j}{M}\right) \geq \frac{j}{M}\left[\bar{G}\left(\frac{j+1}{M}\right) - \bar{G}\left(\frac{j}{M}\right)\right].$$

Adding up and noting that $K(0) = 0$ yields

$$K(1) = \sum_{j=0}^{M-1}\left[K\left(\frac{j+1}{M}\right) - K\left(\frac{j}{M}\right)\right]$$

$$\geq \sum_{j=0}^{M-1}\frac{j}{M}\left[\bar{G}\left(\frac{j+1}{M}\right) - \bar{G}\left(\frac{j}{M}\right)\right],$$

establishing the claimed lower bound.

Regarding the upper bound, we consider the opposite switch that cannot be improving:

$$G\left(\frac{j+1}{M}\right) - K\left(\frac{j+1}{M}\right) = \frac{j+1}{M}\bar{G}\left(\frac{j+1}{M}\right) - K\left(\frac{j+1}{M}\right)$$

$$\geq \frac{j+1}{M}\bar{G}\left(\frac{j}{M}\right) - K\left(\frac{j}{M}\right).$$

Rearranging, we conclude that

$$K\left(\frac{j+1}{M}\right) - K\left(\frac{j}{M}\right) \leq \frac{j+1}{M}\left[\bar{G}\left(\frac{j+1}{M}\right) - \bar{G}\left(\frac{j}{M}\right)\right].$$

Again, adding up and noting that $K(0) = 0$ yields

$$K(1) = \sum_{j=0}^{M-1} \left[K\left(\frac{j+1}{M}\right) - K\left(\frac{j}{M}\right) \right]$$

$$\leq \sum_{j=0}^{M-1} \frac{j+1}{M} \left[\bar{G}\left(\frac{j+1}{M}\right) - \bar{G}\left(\frac{j}{M}\right) \right],$$

establishing the claimed upper bound.

To complete the proof, note directly from the definitions that we can compute the difference between $K^{\max}(M)$ and $K^{\min}(M)$ as

$$K^{\max}(M) - K^{\min}(M) = \sum_{j=0}^{M-1} \frac{1}{M} \left[\bar{G}\left(\frac{j+1}{M}\right) - \bar{G}\left(\frac{j}{M}\right) \right]$$

$$= \frac{\bar{G}(1) - \bar{G}(0)}{M},$$

as claimed.

With the upper and lower limits converging, we can analyze the limit behavior of the upper bound. Note that

$$\sum_{j=0}^{M-1} \frac{j+1}{M} \left[\bar{G}\left(\frac{j+1}{M}\right) - \bar{G}\left(\frac{j}{M}\right) \right] = \bar{G}(1) - \frac{1}{M} \sum_{j=0}^{M-1} \bar{G}\left(\frac{j}{M}\right).$$

Taking the limit,

$$K(1) = \lim_{M \to \infty} \sum_{j=0}^{M-1} \frac{j+1}{M} \left[\bar{G}\left(\frac{j+1}{M}\right) - \bar{G}\left(\frac{j}{M}\right) \right]$$

$$= \bar{G}(1) - \lim_{M \to \infty} \frac{1}{M} \sum_{j=0}^{M-1} \bar{G}\left(\frac{j}{M}\right)$$

$$= \bar{G}(1) - \int_0^1 \bar{G}(\pi) d\pi$$

since $\bar{G}(\pi)$ is Riemann integrable as a monotone function, completing the proof.

6.4 Experimental Implementation

The recovery theorem states that the cost of attention for any problem A^π in the linear family can be computed by integrating a function that is identifiable off the SDSC for problems with lower incentives. CCLN introduce an experimental task to implement. They trivialize the identification of the true state by using a psychometric design. Each experimental task involves subjects being individually shown a rectangular array of polygons. Each shape is one of four regular polygons, seven- to ten-sided. The subject's task is to determine whether there are more seven- or nine-sided polygons. The eight- and ten-sided polygons serve as decoys. Their presence ensures that counting only one of the non-decoy shapes is never sufficient to determine the realized state. The location and rotation of the polygons as well as the total number of non-decoy shapes are generated randomly. Hence, no round carries information about any other round. In each round, the non-decoy shapes are equally likely to be more common, and subjects are told this in advance.

CCLN varied the difficulty level of the tasks between subjects by setting the difference in the number of non-decoy polygons. The difference in the numbers of the non-decoy polygons was set at 1, 2, 3, and 6, constituting variation in our treatment of difficulty. Each subject faced tasks of a fixed difficulty level only.

6.5 Linear Incentives

The payment scheme was designed with the recovery theorem in mind. Subjects who make a correct decision are rewarded with points that count toward the probability of winning a fixed final prize of $10. We vary the incentives according to a geometric scheme, and the probability points can take values of 0, 1, 2, 4, 8, 16, or 32. Overall, the maximum score is 200.

Subjects were not informed about their performance until the very end of the experiment, leaving them with probabilistic beliefs regarding the evolution of their score during the experiment. The effective incentives are thus set by the increments in the overall probability of winning since the subjects only know the increments but not the base in their score. To reward only attentive behavior, the probability of winning the final prize of $10 is determined by the formula (achieved final score $-$ 100)%. Subjects are informed of this.

Of value in practical terms is that the design is robust to moderate non-linearities in probability. For those who expect to perform significantly above chance but also far from perfectly, any such nonlinearities would be minor in standard formulations and smoothed out by averaging. The only note of caution is that anyone who believes they have made a mistake in a high-stakes case has a changed incentive since they may have to perform very well in the remaining trials to recover.

Finally, note how simple the implementation is from the subjects' viewpoints. As so often, their goal is to score as many experimental points as possible to improve their winnings. In this case, the incremental reward is in a metric that is precisely as called for in expected utility theory: the incremental probability of winning the good prize in a lottery between a good and a bad prize. Another advantage of the design is that it gets rid of risk aversion and portfolio effects when dollar winnings are local to a particular experimental run.

One innovation to make the outcome of the lottery credible is that CCLN let subjects stop the built-in clock of their computer and record the time up to millisecond precision. The last two digits of the stopped clock — which are impossible to control intentionally — provide a credible uniform distribution, which is then used to implement lotteries based on subjects' final scores. For instance, if a subject achieves a final score of 167 points, then the subject has a $(167 - 100)\% = 67\%$ chance of winning the final \$10 prize. This is implemented using the clock device. If the last two digits of the clock the subject stops upon completion is below 67, the subject wins the prize. Otherwise, they win nothing.

6.6 Experimental Results

CCLN estimate the incentivized psychometric curves across all difficulty levels jointly. For all levels of task complexity, subjects perform above chance even without external incentives. The difficulty of the task does have an impact on the non-incentivized performance, with the probability of correct discrimination decreasing in difficulty. For each difficulty level, higher incentive levels result in a higher probability of being correct with diminishing returns to incentives. One interesting finding is that while the slopes are similar across incentive levels, the intercepts are very different. How well attentionally demanding activities are performed in the absence of incentives is an important task-specific factor that our method uncovers.

In traditional psychometric experiments, the probability of correct discrimination is plotted against stimulus levels instead of incentive levels. In fact, in the majority of traditional psychometric experiments, subjects are not incentivized at all. The experimental design allows CCLN to plot the traditional "stimulus-based" psychometric curve by varying the difference between the number of non-decoy shapes. But the real value of the experiment is that it allows the estimation of the probability of a correct response as a function of both the incentive and difficulty levels. This therefore relates the economic and psychophysical approaches to explaining the probability of correct discrimination. The data reveal the precise trade-off, whereby increased task complexity can be compensated for by higher incentives. One can therefore plot these as iso-performance curves. In principle, analogous curves can be estimated for all psychometric tasks with a variety of axes.

A final feature of the approach is that the recovery theorem quantifies costs of attention purely from observed behavior without specifying potential inputs entering the cost function. An important question is how the recovered cost relates to psychological inputs that can be thought of as sources of attentional cost, e.g., time and neural activity. In particular, time may be an important common source of attention costs in distinct attentional tasks, as in the "mental labor theory" by Kool and Botvinik (2018). This is analogous to labor being an important input factor in many production processes. CCLN show that the computed cost correlates highly with measures of response time. There are very many obvious next steps in this form of hybrid between standard choice theory and psychometrics. I address some of them in Lecture 15.

6.7 Welfare Recovery

In this section, I show how to recover welfare without knowing either the utility function or the cost function. The key to this is to use a different class of decision problems. Rather than scaling incentives up and down, I follow Lu (2016) in scaling up and down the utility of an outside option. I show how to use the probability of choosing inside the set rather than choosing this outside option to recover welfare.

The ground rules in the case of welfare recovery are slightly different than in the case of cost recovery. The starting point is the same though: a finite set of states of the world $\omega \in \Omega$ and a fixed prior $\mu \in \Delta(\Omega)$. Again, there is an arbitrary finite choice set A with generic element $a \in A$. I will, however, want to work with prizes rather than utilities directly, so it is appropriate to reintroduce the prize space Z, together with the specification of what each action yields as a prize in each state, $z(a, \omega)$. The expected utility function $u : Z \to \mathbb{R}$ is, as always, known to the DM but remains unknown to the econometrician. Te domain of the cost function comprises Bayes' consistent posterior distributions $\mathcal{Q}(\mu)$. The cost function $K : \mathcal{Q}(\mu) \to \bar{\mathbb{R}}$, where $\bar{R}$ is the extended real line, is invariant to changes in the choice set. Inattention is assumed to be free to simplify derivations.

As in the case of cost recovery, the maintained assumption is that all SDSCs that are observed maximize net utility: the difference between prize-based expected utility and costs. My goal is to construct a class of decision problems such that, if SDSC is observed from all of these problems with the assumption that choices maximize net utility in a model with rational inattention, the net utility itself can be recovered without any separate understanding of either the utility function or the cost function. I conjecture that a combination of the method introduced here and the cost recovery above will allow both prize utilities and learning costs to be pinned down under weak regularity conditions.

The first step is to find good and bad prizes either inside the given set A or externally. The defining property of the good prize, which I label z_G, is that if we add an action a_G in which this is the prize in all states, then when the choice set is expanded to include it to $A \cup \{a_G\}$, the SDSCs show that a_G is chosen for sure in all states. The defining property of the bad prize, which I label z_B, is that when the choice set is expanded to include a bad action a_B offering this prize in all states to $A \cup \{a_B\}$, the SDSCs show that a_B is never chosen.

Note that it is to be expected that the best and worst prizes in set A itself will have this property since no action dominates them for sure. Of course, it need not work out that way, for example, if learning is free, in which case, other actions that yield either this prize or an indifferent one might equally well be chosen.

Following Lu (2016), a great deal more can be learned if we allow an additional class of mixture actions parameterized by $x \in (0, 1)$ as $a(x)$, with the definition that $a(x)$ offers in each state a lottery that assigns a probability of x to the good prize z_G and a probability of $1 - x$ to the bad prize z_B, independently of the actual state of the world. Note that the expected utility from any such lottery has no relation to the state of the world and is in that sense safe. Obviously, this covers the good and bad actions themselves if we add the endpoints $x = 0, 1$. This is precisely the class of decision problems for which I assume SDSC has been observed.

For any probability $x \in [0, 1]$, the econometrician is assumed to observe $\mathbf{P}^x$, the corresponding SDSC in the choice set $A \cup \{a(x)\}$. The observed probability of choosing within set A is denoted as $\mathbf{P}^x(A)$, with $\mathbf{P}^x(S)$ the corresponding probability of choosing the safe reservation option:

$$\mathbf{P}^x(S) = 1 - \mathbf{P}^x(A).$$

A simple observation is that, if the data set has a CIR, as we will assume, then $\mathbf{P}^x(S)$ is a non-decreasing function of x. To show this involves an application of NIAC, as might be expected. To the contrary, suppose that we can find $y > x$, with $\mathbf{P}^y(S) < \mathbf{P}^x(S)$. The claim now is that switching attention strategies strictly increases the sum of net utilities, which contradicts optimization.

The switch leaves choices within A for choice set $A \cup \{a(y)\}$ as they were in $A \cup \{a(x)\}$ and vice versa. Hence, the utilities of choices within set A are invariant to the switch. All that has changed is the utility from choosing outside A. In the claimed optimum, the sum is $y\mathbf{P}^y(S) + x\mathbf{P}^x(S)$, while with the switch, it is $y\mathbf{P}^x(S) + x\mathbf{P}^y(S)$. Given the assumption that $y > x$ and $\mathbf{P}^x(S) > \mathbf{P}^y(S)$,

$$y\mathbf{P}^x(S) + x\mathbf{P}^y(S) - y\mathbf{P}^y(S) - x\mathbf{P}^x(S) = (y - x)(\mathbf{P}^x(S) - \mathbf{P}^y(S)) > 0.$$

This improvement from a switch of attention strategies between the problems establishes the contradiction and with it that $\mathbf{P}^x(S)$ is indeed a non-decreasing function of x.

It is convenient to ensure that the probability of picking within A is interior to (0,1) for all $x \in (0, 1)$. Note that this is really WLOG. Using lotteries over these prizes, we may find ranges in which they are either picked for sure or rejected for sure. In such cases, we just replace the sure prizes with the lotteries that define the interior. With this, we can find the least attractive lottery between the best and the worst, at which the lottery is chosen for sure in the corresponding data and the best lottery such that it is never chosen and use these. So, let's forget this and treat it as if this was true of the good and bad prizes themselves so as not to waste effort and notation.

It is intuitive that we can learn a lot about unobservable utility, learning costs, and net utility by looking at the data sets $\mathbf{P}^x$. To establish this, it is important to define state-dependent probabilities separately for each original action $a \in A$ as $\mathbf{P}^x(a, \omega)$. Of course, these then add up to an unconditional probability of $\mathbf{P}^x(A)$.

What is the best recovery result we can hope for? Given $x \in [0, 1]$, we define the unobservables $G(x)$ and $K(x)$ as the levels of gross utility and cost in an optimal strategy (these exist by the hypothesis that observed is optimal). It is convenient to normalize to $G(1) = 1$ and $G(0) = 0$. The unobservable optimized net utility in decision problem $A(x)$ is then unique:

$$N(x) \equiv G(x) - K(x).$$

6.8   Convex Functions, Subdifferentials, and the FTC

The welfare result and other recovery results can be derived from a wonderful general version of the fundamental theorem of calculus: Rockafellar theorem 24.2.

Rockafellar Theorem 24.2. Let $h : \mathbb{R}_+ \longrightarrow \bar{\mathbb{R}}$ be a non-decreasing function with $h(0)$ finite. Let H be a closed convex function such that $H'_-(x) \leq h(x) \leq H'_+(x)$. Then,

$$H(x) = \int\limits_0^x h(t)dt + \alpha$$

for some $\alpha \in \mathbb{R}$.

Note that for a convex function to prove $H'_-(x) \leq h(x) \leq H'_+(x)$ involves a global proposition that the function lies above the supporting line at x with slope $h(x)$:

$$H(y) \geq H(x) + (y - x)h(x).$$

To apply this to the computation of net welfare, we need to find the corresponding functions H, h such that

$$H(y) \geq H(x) + (y - x)h(x).$$

So, what function can play the role of H? Whatever it is, we must be able to establish that it is a closed convex function and that it has $\mathbf{P}^x(S)$ as a sub-differential. In optimization theory, it tends to be value functions that can be shown to have shape properties. The obvious candidate is the optimized net utility function $N(x)$. It is standard that this is continuous and convex by simple feasibility arguments: In Rockafellar language, this is defined as closed and convex.

Note first that since the data from x is optimal, $K(x)$ is the difference between the corresponding gross EU and optimized net utility:

$$K(x) = x\mathbf{P}^x(S) + \sum_{a \in A} \sum_{\omega \in \Omega} u(a, \omega)\mathbf{P}^x(a, \omega) - N(x). \tag{49}$$

To show that $\mathbf{P}^x(S)$ is a subdifferential of N at x, pick any $y \in [0, 1]$ and compare it with the fixed $x \in [0, 1]$. In light of optimality, the evaluation of net expected utility with the optimal data from y is better than from the data picked with x:

$$N(y) = y\mathbf{P}^y(S) + \sum_{a \in A} \sum_{\omega \in \Omega} u(a, \omega)\mathbf{P}^y(a, \omega) - K(y)$$

$$\geq y\mathbf{P}^x(S) + \sum_{a \in A} \sum_{\omega \in \Omega} u(a, \omega)\mathbf{P}^x(a, \omega) - K(x).$$

Upon substitution, we conclude that

$$N(y) \geq (y - x)\mathbf{P}^x(S) + N(x).$$

Hence, indeed, $\mathbf{P}^x(S)$ is a subdifferential of N.

We can now apply Rockafellar theorem 24.2 to conclude that there exists $\alpha \in \mathbb{R}$ such that

$$N(x) \equiv \int_0^x \mathbf{P}^S(t)dt + \alpha.$$

We can pin down α by noting that $N(1) = 1$ since paying no attention and choosing the safe action with payoff 1 is optimal. Hence,

$$\alpha = 1 - \int_0^1 \mathbf{P}^S(t)dt = \int_0^1 \left[1 - \mathbf{P}^S(t)\right]dt = \int_0^1 \mathbf{P}^A(t)dt,$$

whereupon

$$N(x) \equiv \int_0^x \mathbf{P}^S(t)dt + \int_0^1 \mathbf{P}^A(t)dt$$

$$= \int_0^x \left[\mathbf{P}^S(t) + \mathbf{P}^A(t)\right]dt + \int_x^1 \mathbf{P}^A(t)dt = x + \int_x^1 \mathbf{P}^A(t)dt.$$

Hence,

$$N(0) = \int_0^1 \mathbf{P}^A(t)dt.$$

It is striking that we can compute the net utility directly using this equation. It is a welfare computation that makes no reference to the utility function. And it does not require the details of SDSC. It only requires the unconditional probability of choosing outside the set.

6.9   A Second and Simpler Recovery Method

There is in principle an easier and more direct method of recovering net utility. Observe the choice between A and each of the singleton choice sets containing the test functions only: $a(x)$. For a DM with a given utility function and a fixed, known learning cost, there will be a unique reservation level of x above which $a(x)$ is chosen and below which it is rejected in favor of choosing from the choice set. This will reveal the net utility directly.

Combining this direct elicitation with the indirect method above, we see that rational inattention theory has a very strong and restrictive implication: that recovery of welfare both ways should produce the same answer. I believe that conducting such experiments would be of great value. I can think of many ways by which the result might fail that would be insightful. Of course, it might also succeed. But the former is always more likely and, possibly, more interesting. Noting by how much it fails in different experimental circumstances may force us to model more richly. In fact, one of the main virtues of this method of approach is precisely to force the researcher's hand in terms of model enrichment, so hasten the day.

Menu choice data have an important decision-theoretic history. It was first formally conceptualized by Koopmans (1962), reflecting his stated belief that typical choices exclude certain options while leaving many others open (e.g., the choice of educational program, restaurant, etc.) The value of this data set was expanded upon by Kreps (1979), who used it to capture preference for flexibility. Following this, Dekel *et al.* (2001) and Gul and Pesendorfer (2001) showed how these data can be used to model self-control problems. The very deliberate field design by Toussaert (2018) implemented the model of Gul and Pesendorfer in the field, as did the survey work of Ameriks *et al.* (2008). One interesting aspect is that there are also identification problems in this data set. For example, De Oliveira *et al.* (2017) used it to characterize a general model of rational inattention. While the appropriate model might sometimes be clear from context, general methods for separately identifying these diverse theories may be of value. I suspect that it requires additional data engineering.

Lecture 7

Comparison of Revealed Experiments

As with the material on recovering rationalizing learning in Lecture 5, this lecture takes as its starting point the wonderful approach and results of Blackwell (1953) on ranking experiments by their information content. Given that it was not central to Lecture 5, I did not there note the third equivalent definition of one experiment being more informative than another, which is that it offers at least as high maximum utility function regardless of the particulars of the utility function. While Blackwell's characterization is definitive, it reveals that many experiments cannot be unequivocally ranked. This has given rise to a sub-literature whose goal is to find methods of comparing experiments that are less demanding than Blackwell's.

What I show in this lecture, following Caplin and Martin (2021), is that the revealed preference approach has a contribution to make in this regard. In the spirit of Blackwell, the econometrician will see data from two experiments that share a common structure (to be specified). They will identify this data as consistent with a BEU and use the NIAS constraints to identify all rationalizing utility functions. The natural question is whether the information that the data reveal about utilities is sufficient to rank revealed experiments that could not have been ranked using the Blackwell order. The answer Caplin and Martin provide is in the affirmative. There are revealed experiments that can be ranked due to the ability that the NIAS constraints provide to restrict the class of utility functions that need to be considered. It is actually stronger than that: We fully characterize revealed experiments that can be ranked using a simple orthogonality condition that can be readily checked.

I relate our approach to a modern literature on informational framing. Following Thaler and Sunnstein (2009), there is now a massive literature on using various different framings of one and the same decision problem to "nudge" DMs to change their choices. The open question is how one can confirm that such a nudge improved the quality of decision-making without imposing the nudger's utility function. If one wishes to do that, there must be some method for extracting the utility of the nudgee. That is precisely what the NIAS constraints accomplish, which is why this is such a fruitful combination of ideas.

One important point to note is that this lecture is based largely on the information content revealed in various experiments. It has nothing to say about how these experiments were arrived at or how costly they were. In applied settings, it focuses on what many mean by welfare, which is exclusively the quality of the final decision and not the process of arriving at it. So, costs are simply not going to be discussed. At the end of the lecture, I open the door to net welfare evaluation, but I will not close it. There are reasons to hope that a tight characterization will be available, but as yet, there is none.

7.1   Incompleteness of the Blackwell Order

A limitation of the Blackwell order of experiments introduced in Lecture 5 is that it is very much incomplete. One general observation illustrated in the following relates to convex geometry. The MPS characterization makes it clearly necessary that, in order to be more informative than another distribution, all posteriors that are possible in the latter must be contained in the convex hull of those that are possible for the former. The following example illustrates two experiments that cannot be ordered for this reason.

Example. Consider a two-equiprobable-state world, and let posterior distribution $\tilde{Q}$ specify $\tilde{Q}(0.8) = 0.25$ and $\tilde{Q}(0.4) = 0.75$. Conversely, let $\tilde{Q}'$ specify $\tilde{Q}'(0.6) = 0.75$ and $\tilde{Q}'(0.2) = 0.25$. Neither set of posteriors is contained in the convex hull of the other, so they are not Blackwell ranked. To establish this directly, one can create utility functions that rank either as strictly more valuable. There is a geometric method of doing this in cases

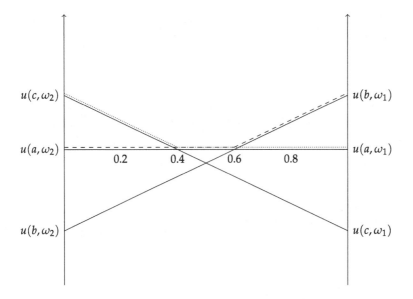

Figure 7.1   Necessity of nested convex hulls.

with two actions $\{a,b\}$ in one case and $\{a,c\}$ in the other. First, fix the common action to have a payoff of zero: $u(a,\omega_1) = u(a,\omega_2) = 0$. Define $u(b,\omega_1) = u(c,\omega_2) = 0.4$ and $u(b,\omega_2) = u(c,\omega_1) = -0.6$. Note, geometrically, that given choice set $\{a,b\}$, the only posterior with a strictly positive payoff is 0.8: Hence, $\tilde{Q}$ is strictly more valuable. Conversely, in set $\{a,c\}$, the only posterior with a strictly positive payoff is 0.2: Hence, $\tilde{Q}'$ is strictly more valuable.

Figure 7.1 illustrates this. As usual, the payoffs to the three actions in each state are indicated on the vertical axis and the probability of state 1 on the horizontal. The dashed line shows the utility of the optimal choice at all posteriors in choice set $\{a,b\}$. As noted, for choice set $\{a,b\}$, $\tilde{Q}$ is more valuable than $\tilde{Q}'$ since it includes one posterior at which there is a strictly positive payoff, while the payoff is zero at both posteriors that are possible according to $\tilde{Q}'$. Conversely, the dotted line shows the utility of the optimal choices at all posteriors in choice set $\{a,c\}$. In this case, $\tilde{Q}'$ is more valuable than $\tilde{Q}$ since it includes one posterior at which there is a strictly positive payoff, while the payoff is zero at both posteriors that are possible according to $\tilde{Q}$.

The converse is not true: Being contained in the convex hull is not sufficient for Blackwell ranking. A second simple example illustrates this.

Example. Let posterior distribution $\tilde{Q}''$ specify $\tilde{Q}''(1) = \tilde{Q}''(0) = 0.1$ and $\tilde{Q}''(0.5) = 0.8$. If the convex hull property is held, this would mean that this was more Blackwell informative than either $\tilde{Q}'$ or $\tilde{Q}''$. By way of contradiction, one can find utility functions that make $\tilde{Q}''$ less valuable than either. In fact, the simple tracking problem suffices since the value of $\tilde{Q}'$ is 0.8 while that of $\tilde{Q}''$ is 0.6. The issue is that one needs to think not just about possible posteriors but their likelihoods.

There has been much interest in somehow ranking experiments that are not Blackwell ordered. We now address that issue using the NIAS constraints that characterize Bayesian expected utility representations.

7.2 The NIAS Cone

In Lecture 5, we introduced the CIR and CCR utility cones for characterizing these representations. We now introduce the simpler conditions that characterize the NIAS utility cone comprising all utility functions that admit a BEU representation of the data. The NIAS conditions show this to be based on ruling out a set of changes in action choices as improving. The comparison of interests involves the following steps:

(1) We first define, for each m, the lottery associated with the actual observed data L^m by $L^m = (L_1^m, \ldots, L_K^m) \in \Delta(Z)$ so that for each prize z_k,

$$L_k^m = \sum_{\{a \in A^m, \omega \in \Omega | z(a,\omega) = z_k\}} \mathbf{P}^m(a, \omega).$$

(2) We now consider the set of actions that are chosen in the SDSC for data set $\mathbf{P}^m$: the set $A_{\mathbf{P}^m}$. We map this set to any **feasible** actions in set A^m according to $f^m : A_{\mathbf{P}^m} \longrightarrow A^m$.

(3) Given any pair (m, f^m), we define the corresponding SDSC on $a \in A^m$ as:

$$\mathbf{P}^{(m, f^m)}(a, \omega) \equiv \sum_{\{b \in A_{\mathbf{P}^m} | f(b) = a\}} \mathbf{P}^m(b, \omega).$$

This defines the data set corresponding to a set of holistic switches of actions within A^m. We define the lottery associated with the data set after all defined adjustments, $L^{(m,n,f)}$, so that for each prize z_k:

$$L_k^{(m,f^m)} = \sum_{\{a \in A^m, \omega \in \Omega | z(a,\omega) = z_k\}} \mathbf{P}^{(m,f^m)}(a,\omega).$$

(4) Define the difference in the lottery as between the chosen and counterfactual as $C^{(m,n,f)} \in \mathbb{R}^K$,

$$C_k^{(m,f^m)} = L_k^m - L_k^{(m,f^m)},$$

for $1 \leq k \leq K$.

(5) With all of these steps completed for a single specification (m, f^m), we repeat them for all such pairs. To simplify notation for this large set of counterfactual switches, we index all distinct triples (m, f^m) by $1 \leq i \leq I$ and define the corresponding lottery change as $C^i \equiv C^{(m(i), f^m(i))}$.

(6) As a final preparatory step, we think about positively weighted combinations of these vectors C^i. We call the convex cone defined by all such lottery changes the NIAC cone.

Definition 28: We call the convex cone formed by all C^i the **NIAS cone**:

$$\mathcal{C}^{NIAS} = \{C = \sum_{i=1}^I \alpha^i C^i \in \mathbb{R}^K | \alpha^i \in \mathbb{R}_+ \}.$$

The defining feature of a BEU representation is that each of the C^i reflects the choice of a particular feasible strategy over an alternative that could have been generated by the corresponding switch so that for the utility function to have such a representation is that staying with the chosen lottery cannot result in a reduction in expected utility. In fact according to Theorem 1, a **necessary and sufficient** condition for $u \in \mathcal{U}^{NIAS}$, the NIAS utility cone, is that the utility function has a non-negative dot product with all vectors C^i:

$$\sum_{k=1}^K u_k C_k^i \geq 0.$$

Given that the NIAS cone comprises only positively weighted combinations of C^i, this inequality extends to the entire cone. This gives rise to the key observation, which is essentially immediate in light of the above, that having a positive dot product with all vectors in the NIAS cone is equivalent to a utility function admitting a NIAS.

Proposition 4: *Utility function $u : Z \longrightarrow \mathbb{R}$ admits a BEU representation $u \in \mathcal{U}^{NIAS}$ if and only if*

$$\sum_{k=1}^{K} u_k C_k \geq 0$$

for all $C \in \mathcal{C}^{NIAC}$.

This reveals the set $\mathcal{U}^{NIAS}$ itself to be a convex cone. We, therefore, call it **the NIAS utility cone.**

7.3 Informational Frames and Comparison of Revealed Experiments

The big question in this lecture concerns how seeing SDSC for which rationalizing utility functions exist might allow us to provide welfare comparisons for otherwise unranked experiments. This part of the lecture contains large excerpts from Caplin and Martin (2021). We follow them first in laying out the question.

There are many field experiments designed to raise consumer welfare. In some cases, this is straightforward and credible, as when stopping over payment or choice of clearly dominated insurance contracts (Bhargava *et al.*, 2017). Yet, outside of these special cases, choice options have trade-offs, and in the presence of such trade-offs, even if an information frame changes behavior in the intended direction, that does not mean that welfare was improved. An information frame that draws attention to some aspect of a decision might inadvertently lead individuals to ignore other aspects of the decision which are more crucial, given their unobservable tastes and requirements.

We take the position of an observer who has seen SDSC from the same decision taken in two different presentational frames. We would like to see whether or not one is revealed to yield higher utility than the other. But we do not know the utility function or what is learned. These must be inferred from the data.

A first step before comparing utilities is to verify applicability of the Bayesian expected utility framework. What if we see two distinct SDSC data sets that correspond to different interior priors for the same pair of actions? Call these $\mathbf{P}^g$ and $\mathbf{P}^h$. Note that in this definition, we are interested in all utility functions that allow NIAS to be satisfied so that the vacuous one is included: This means that we drop the strictness clause. We call NIAS-F the framed version of NIAS.

Definition 29: Utility function u satisfies the **NIAS-F inequalities** with respect to $\mathbf{P}^f$ if, given $a, b \in A$,

$$\sum_{\omega \in \Omega} \mathbf{P}^f(a, \omega) u(z(a, \omega)) \geq \sum_{\omega \in \Omega} \mathbf{P}^f(a, \omega) u(z(b, \omega)),$$

for $f = g, h$.

We know that utility function u rationalizes data sets $\mathbf{P}^g$ and $\mathbf{P}^h$ with a BEU if and only if it satisfies NIAS-F. We have seen SDSC in two frames $f = g, h$, for which NIAS-F is satisfied. We want to know if there is a welfare ranking based on the theory that the frame did not *per se* change prize utility, the state space, or prior beliefs. Before turning to that, I illustrate the use of the Blackwell order when the revealed experiments $\mathbf{P}^g$ and $\mathbf{P}^h$ themselves are Blackwell ordered.

7.4 Revealed More Informative

The most obvious conditions to check for ranking valuations is the Blackwell order over the revealed experiments in the two distinct frames.

Definition 30: Frame g is *revealed Blackwell more informative* than frame h ($g \succsim_B h$) if the revealed experiment for frame h is a garbling of the revealed experiment for frame g.

Note that $g \succsim_B h$ implies that the revealed posteriors in frame h are in the convex hull of the revealed posteriors of frame g. Applying the results of Blackwell (1953), if the revealed experiment for frame h is a garbling of revealed experiment for frame g, then the value of information for the revealed experiment for frame g is higher for any utility function. Thus, if the revealed experiment for frame h is a garbling of the revealed experiment for frame g, then, clearly, the value of information is higher for frame g for every u that satisfies NIAS for $\mathbf{P}^g$ and $\mathbf{P}^h$.

This condition itself is of interest and not entirely intuitive given the subtleties of Bayes' rule. Consider the information frame of health-care plans. Imagine the choice between a low-premium, high-deductible healthcare plan ("Value PPO") and a high-premium, low-deductible plan ("Premium PPO"), and Value PPO is more cost-effective no matter an individual's health outcomes. Imagine that around half of the time (or for half of individuals), these plans are identical except for their costs, but Premium PPO is still chosen 20% of the time even though it is dominated.

There is evidence that consumers may have trouble understanding deductibles, so one possible solution is to provide plain-language descriptions of deductibles. When there is dominance, if the plain-language information frame of deductibles increases the probability that Value PPO is chosen from 80% to 90%, then this provides additional evidence that Value PPO is better and that the plain-language information frame is superior.

Imagine that the other half of the time, the company offers a version of Premium PPO that has better doctor availability but is otherwise the same. With normal information frame, Premium PPO is chosen more often when it has better doctor availability (80% of the time), but with the plain-language information frame, Value PPO is instead chosen more often (70% of the time). If we assume that Value PPO is still better even when it has worse doctor availability, it would appear again that plain-language information frame has benefited DMs by leading Value PPO to be chosen more often than Premium PPO.

In addition, a leading approach to behavioral welfare analysis is to ignore choices made under frames where DMs are "confused" (Bernheim and Rangel, 2009). In this example, one might conclude that choices made under the normal information frame were confused, so we should instead use choices made under the plain-language information frame to assess what is best for consumers. Clearly, this suggests that Value PPO is better, and so, the plain-language information frame has improved the welfare by increasing the fraction of the time it is chosen.

Taken together, it seems we have strong evidence that the Value PPO plan is always better and that the plain-language information frame leads to higher welfare. However, by leveraging variation in the underlying states (variation in the characteristics of Premium PPO) and choices under both frames, we can learn that individuals were better informed on average when taking actions under the plain-language information frame. This diagnosticity reveals that individuals received higher welfare.

To demonstrate this, we represent the corresponding data sets for normal information frame ($\mathbf{P}_N$) and plain-language information frame ($\mathbf{P}_{PL}$) as matrices, where the actions of choosing Premium PPO (a_P) or Value PPO (a_V) are given in the rows and the states of same doctor availability (ω_S) and better doctor availability (ω_B) are given in the columns:

$$\mathbf{P}_N = \begin{pmatrix} \overset{\omega_S}{\frac{10}{100}} & \overset{\omega_B}{\frac{40}{100}} \\ \frac{40}{100} & \frac{10}{100} \end{pmatrix} \begin{matrix} a_P \\ a_V \end{matrix} \quad \text{and} \quad \mathbf{P}_{PL} = \begin{pmatrix} \overset{\omega_S}{\frac{5}{100}} & \overset{\omega_B}{\frac{15}{100}} \\ \frac{45}{100} & \frac{35}{100} \end{pmatrix} \begin{matrix} a_P \\ a_V \end{matrix} .$$

This has revealed that there is a trade-off that individuals face between cost-effectiveness and doctor availability: Value PPO is preferred when plans have the same doctor availability, but Premium PPO is preferred when it has better doctor availability. Because of this trade-off, it is less clear if the plain-language information frame has improved decision-making.

To determine which information frame provides better information, we examine the revealed posteriors under each frame, which are the average beliefs when each action was taken. The revealed posteriors in frame N are

$$\gamma_N^{a_P} = \begin{pmatrix} \frac{10}{50} \\ \frac{40}{50} \end{pmatrix} \begin{matrix} \omega_S \\ \omega_B \end{matrix} = \begin{pmatrix} 20\% \\ 80\% \end{pmatrix} \begin{matrix} \omega_S \\ \omega_B \end{matrix} \quad \text{and} \quad \gamma_N^{a_V} = \begin{pmatrix} \frac{40}{50} \\ \frac{10}{50} \end{pmatrix} \begin{matrix} \omega_S \\ \omega_B \end{matrix} = \begin{pmatrix} 80\% \\ 20\% \end{pmatrix} \begin{matrix} \omega_S \\ \omega_B \end{matrix} ,$$

and the revealed posteriors in frame PL are

$$\gamma_{PL}^{a_P} = \begin{pmatrix} \frac{5}{20} \\ \frac{15}{20} \end{pmatrix} \begin{matrix} \omega_S \\ \omega_B \end{matrix} = \begin{pmatrix} 25\% \\ 75\% \end{pmatrix} \begin{matrix} \omega_S \\ \omega_B \end{matrix} \quad \text{and} \quad \gamma_{PL}^{a_V} = \begin{pmatrix} \frac{45}{80} \\ \frac{35}{80} \end{pmatrix} \begin{matrix} \omega_S \\ \omega_B \end{matrix} = \begin{pmatrix} 56.25\% \\ 43.75\% \end{pmatrix} \begin{matrix} \omega_S \\ \omega_B \end{matrix} .$$

These revealed posteriors reveal that, on average, individuals are better informed about the state when actions are taken in frame N.

What kind of utility function and signal structure could have produced this data and these revealed posteriors? Assume that the utility function is

$$u(a_P, \omega_S) = \frac{3}{2}u(a_V) = 2u(a_P, \omega_B),$$

so it is indifferent between choosing either plan if a fully uninformative signal is received. Now, imagine that no attention is paid and individuals choose randomly 40% of the time in each state with normal information frame. Also, imagine that the plain-language information frame reduces full inattention by 50% but makes the deductibles dimension more salient, so 60% of the time, individuals only pay attention the high-deductible dimension with the plain-language information frame. In combination with the utility of each outcome, this produces the data and revealed posteriors given above.

That said, it is not necessary to infer the utility function and information of DMs to determine which frame provides higher welfare. If there is higher diagnosticity (i.e., revealed posteriors show that individuals were better informed on average in one frame), then the conclusions about welfare are robust to any information structure and utility function that are consistent with the data.

7.5 Beyond Blackwell

How can we find non-Blackwell-ranked revealed experiments that can be welfare ranked due to the NIAS constraints required to rationalize the data? Recall that the Blackwell order is more demanding than needed because we do not need the revealed value of information to be higher for *any* utility function. The data themselves can rule out some utility functions, so we only want to consider *possible* utility functions given by the NIAS-F conditions.

Two examples that point in opposite directions highlight the challenge. Consider first the two-action a_1, a_2, two-state ω_1, ω_2 tracking problem with two prizes in which WLOG, we consider the solutions with $u(z_1) > u(z_2)$. Note that, in this case, there is a complete ordering based on the probability of getting the better prize. All that matters then is the arithmetic gap between the revealed posteriors. So, in this case, the Blackwell order can be completed. This is illustrated in Figure 7.2. In frame g, the revealed

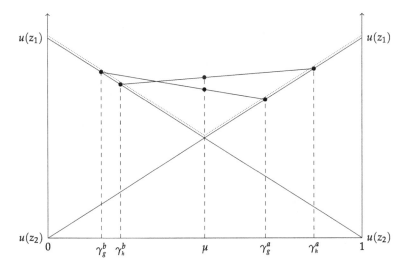

Figure 7.2 Welfare order without a Blackwell order for a two-prize case.

posteriors of state ω_1 are γ_g^a, γ_g^b, while in frame h, they are γ_h^a, γ_h^b. These are not Blackwell ordered since neither is in the convex hull of the other: $\gamma_h^a > \gamma_g^a > 0.5$ but $\gamma_g^b < \gamma_h^b < 0.5$. The value of each revealed experiment is defined by the height of the corresponding chord as it crosses the prior of 0.5. We see in this case that frame h has a higher value due to its greater height at this point. Geometrically, this is because the difference between the posteriors in g is higher, and in this simple two-prize case, that translates to a higher probability of winning the good prize. This is the general method of completing the Blackwell order in this simple case.

What happens when we make the smallest of changes to this example by adding a third prize in this simple two-equiprobable-state world? It turns out that this completely removes our ability to extend the Blackwell order. Figure 7.4 illustrates the general two-action, two-state case with one safe action offering prize z_s and one risky action offering prizes z_1 and z_2. In both frames g and h, the safe action (action b) is chosen at an interior-revealed posterior that is below 0.5 and the risky action (action a) at interior-revealed posterior above 0.5, as marked on the horizontal axis. Hence, in any non-trivial rationalization, z_2 is revealed strictly worse than z_1 and also strictly worse than z_s. Note that if either was an equality, then the other action would be weakly dominant and the revealed posterior

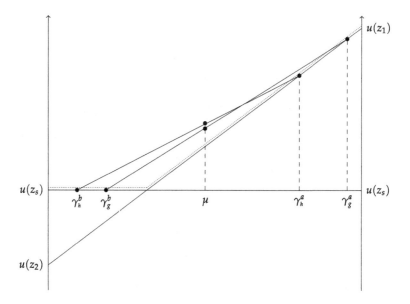

Figure 7.3   Frame h welfare dominates frame g.

associated with the other would be either 0 or 1, which we have assumed it is not. Hence, we have $u(z_1) > u(z_s) > u(z_2)$ as marked.

Note now that NIAS-F means there exists a "separating posterior probability" of state 1, $\gamma^E \in (0,1)$, such that all revealed posteriors associated with a lie on the right of it and all those for b lie on the other side, with at least one strictly not equal to γ^E. The issue is that this leaves a great deal of leeway for changing the ranking of frames. In Figure 7.3, frame g provides a higher expected utility (height of chord between revealed posteriors as it crosses the prior). Note that, in this case, the line between $(0, u(z_2))$ and $(1, u(z_1))$ that defines the expected payoff to action a at each posterior crosses $u(z_s)$ at a level significantly below the prior belief. In Figure 7.4, the difference is that this payoff line crosses $u(z_s)$ at a level significantly above the prior belief. In so doing, it reverses the ordering of the frames, with frame g providing higher expected utility than frame h.

To summarize, in cases with only two prizes, all frames are welfare ranked by the probability of the better prize. But if there are three prizes in the two-state, two-action world, then Blackwell and welfare are the same, as the above examples reveal. Is either of these general? If so, which? If not, how to make progress?

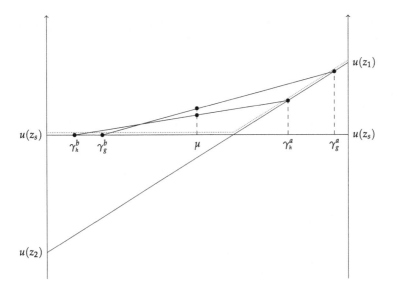

Figure 7.4   Frame g welfare dominates frame h.

7.6   Example

Before presenting the general logic, Caplin and Martin provide examples to illustrate that it is indeed possible to be welfare ordered but not Blackwell ordered. The first example is a tracking problem with distinct prizes associated with the distinct actions. Here is the matrix outlining the decision problem:

$$\begin{matrix} & \omega_1 & \omega_2 & \omega_3 & \\ & \begin{pmatrix} z_1 & z_B & z_B \\ z_B & z_2 & z_B \\ z_B & z_B & z_3 \end{pmatrix} & & & \begin{matrix} a_1 \\ a_2 \\ a_3 \end{matrix} \end{matrix} .$$

Here are the correspondingly organized framed data sets:

$$\mathbf{P}^g = \begin{pmatrix} \frac{20}{100} & 0 & 0 \\ 0 & \frac{22}{100} & \frac{18}{100} \\ 0 & \frac{18}{100} & \frac{22}{100} \end{pmatrix} \begin{matrix} a_1 \\ a_2 \\ a_3 \end{matrix} \quad \text{and} \quad \mathbf{P}^h = \begin{pmatrix} \frac{10}{100} & \frac{20}{100} & \frac{20}{100} \\ \frac{5}{100} & \frac{20}{100} & 0 \\ \frac{5}{100} & 0 & \frac{20}{100} \end{pmatrix} \begin{matrix} a_1 \\ a_2 \\ a_3 \end{matrix} .$$

What do these NIAS constraints imply? First, we normalize to $u(z_B) = 0$. The revealed value of the SDSC in frame g is

$$\frac{20}{100}u(z_0) + \frac{22}{100}u(z_1) + \frac{22}{100}u(z_2).$$

In frame g, it is

$$\frac{10}{100}u(z_0) + \frac{20}{100}u(z_1) + \frac{20}{100}u(z_2).$$

What this means is that if $u(z_1)$, $u(z_2)$, or $u(z_3)$ are all above zero, then frame f is revealed to yield higher welfare. This is in fact easy to show. For example, using the NIAS constraint for action a_1 chosen over action a_2 in frame g, we know that

$$\sum_{\omega \in \Omega} \mathbf{P}^f(a_1, \omega)u(z(a_1, \omega)) \geq \sum_{\omega \in \Omega} \mathbf{P}^f(a_1, \omega)u(z(a_2, \omega)),$$

$$\frac{20}{100}u(z_1) \geq \frac{20}{100}u(z_B) = 0.$$

What we need to show is that frames g and h are not Blackwell ordered. We use the convex hull result by observing that neither set of revealed posteriors contains the other. The revealed posteriors in frame g are

$$\gamma_{\mathbf{P}^g}^{a_1} = \begin{pmatrix} 1 \\ 0 \\ 0 \end{pmatrix} \begin{matrix} \omega_1 \\ \omega_2 \\ \omega_3 \end{matrix} \;,\; \gamma_{\mathbf{P}^g}^{a_2} = \begin{pmatrix} 0 \\ \frac{22}{40} \\ \frac{18}{40} \end{pmatrix} \begin{matrix} \omega_1 \\ \omega_2 \\ \omega_3 \end{matrix} \;,\; \text{and} \;\; \gamma_{\mathbf{P}^g}^{a_3} = \begin{pmatrix} 0 \\ \frac{18}{40} \\ \frac{22}{40} \end{pmatrix} \begin{matrix} \omega_1 \\ \omega_2 \\ \omega_3 \end{matrix} \;,$$

and the revealed posteriors in frame h are

$$\gamma_{\mathbf{P}^h}^{a_1} = \begin{pmatrix} \frac{10}{50} \\ \frac{20}{50} \\ \frac{20}{50} \end{pmatrix} \begin{matrix} \omega_1 \\ \omega_2 \\ \omega_3 \end{matrix} \;,\; \gamma_{\mathbf{P}^h}^{a_2} = \begin{pmatrix} \frac{5}{25} \\ \frac{20}{25} \\ 0 \end{pmatrix} \begin{matrix} \omega_1 \\ \omega_2 \\ \omega_3 \end{matrix} \;,\; \text{and} \;\; \gamma_{\mathbf{P}^h}^{a_3} = \begin{pmatrix} \frac{5}{25} \\ 0 \\ \frac{20}{25} \end{pmatrix} \begin{matrix} \omega_1 \\ \omega_2 \\ \omega_3 \end{matrix} \;.$$

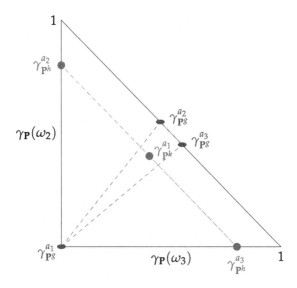

Figure 7.5 Frames g and h are not Blackwell ordered.

These are illustrated in Figure 7.5, in which the posteriors of all three states are illustrated in the Machina triangle with state 1 excluded.

7.7 Problems with Distinct Outcomes

With the NIAS constraints in a single-decision problem, much of the power comes from restrictions on prizes. That is why tracking problems are so simple. An interesting point is that seeing decisions in multiple frames may allow for utility restrictions even without any constraints on the prizes. To illustrate, we consider a common class of decision problems in which every action yields a distinct outcome in every state so that $z(a, \omega) \neq z(b, \nu)$ if $a \neq b$ or $\omega \neq \nu$.

Consider the three-action and three-state version of this tracking problem:

$$
\begin{array}{ccc}
\omega_1 & \omega_2 & \omega_3 \\
\end{array}
$$
$$
\begin{pmatrix}
z_{11} & z_{12} & z_{13} \\
z_{21} & z_{22} & z_{23} \\
z_{31} & z_{32} & z_{33}
\end{pmatrix}
\begin{array}{c}
a_1 \\
a_2 \\
a_3
\end{array} .
$$

One example of this is given by

$$
\mathbf{P}^g = \begin{array}{ccc} \omega_1 & \omega_2 & \omega_3 \end{array} \\
\begin{pmatrix} \frac{24}{72} & 0 & 0 \\ 0 & \frac{16}{72} & \frac{8}{72} \\ 0 & \frac{8}{72} & \frac{16}{72} \end{pmatrix} \begin{array}{c} a_1 \\ a_2 \\ a_3 \end{array}
\quad \text{and} \quad
\mathbf{P}^h = \begin{array}{ccc} \omega_1 & \omega_2 & \omega_3 \end{array} \\
\begin{pmatrix} \frac{12}{72} & \frac{6}{72} & \frac{6}{72} \\ \frac{6}{72} & \frac{5}{72} & \frac{13}{72} \\ \frac{6}{72} & \frac{13}{72} & \frac{5}{72} \end{pmatrix} \begin{array}{c} a_1 \\ a_2 \\ a_3 \end{array} .
$$

Like the tracking example, these distributions of actions and states will reveal that the DM prefers the outcome obtained when choosing action a_1 when the state is ω_1, prefers the outcomes obtained when choosing a_2 and a_3 in the other states and is perfectly informed when taking action a_1. Once again, it is as if for $\mathbf{P}^g$, the DM gets a signal realization that is perfectly informative of whether the state is ω_1, so knows to take action a_1 if the state is ω_1 and not to choose action a_1 otherwise.

However, unlike the tracking example, these $\mathbf{P}^g$ and $\mathbf{P}^h$ reveal that the utility obtained from taking actions a_2 and a_3 is the same in every state. This follows from the fact that the NIAS inequalities for a_2 chosen over a_3 and a_3 chosen over a_2 hold with equality for both $\mathbf{P}^g$ and $\mathbf{P}^h$, which is a consequence of Theorem 7, which states that an NIAS inequality is equal to zero if and only if that NIAS inequality can be expressed as a non-positive combination of other NIAS inequalities.

To illustrate the application, note that the NIAS inequality for a_2 chosen over a_3 for $\mathbf{P}^g$ is $\frac{16}{72}(u(a_2, \omega_2) - u(a_3, \omega_2)) + \frac{8}{72}(u(a_2, \omega_3) - u(a_3, \omega_3)) \geq 0$. Given that there are no common outcomes across states and actions in this decision problem, we shorten $u(z(a, \omega))$ to $u(a, \omega)$. The negative of this can be obtained by simply adding together the outcome lotteries from the NIAS inequalities for a_3 chosen over a_2 for $\mathbf{P}^g$, for a_2 chosen over a_3 for $\mathbf{P}^h$, and for a_3 chosen over a_2 for $\mathbf{P}^h$.

Given that the NIAS inequalities for a_2 chosen over a_3 and a_3 chosen over a_2 hold with equality for $\mathbf{P}^g$, the utility differences between a_2 and a_3 in ω_2 and the utility differences between a_2 and a_3 in ω_3 are both equal to 0 because those NIAS inequalities say that

$$
\frac{16}{72}(u(a_2, \omega_2) - u(a_3, \omega_2)) + \frac{8}{72}(u(a_2, \omega_3) - u(a_3, \omega_3)) = 0
$$

and

$$-\frac{8}{72}\left(u(a_2,\omega_2)-u(a_3,\omega_2)\right)-\frac{16}{72}\left(u(a_2,\omega_3)-u(a_3,\omega_3)\right)=0,$$

which is only possible if $u(a_2,\omega_2)-u(a_3,\omega_2)=0$ and $u(a_2,\omega_3)-u(a_3,\omega_3)=0$. Likewise, given that the NIAS inequalities for a_2 chosen over a_3 and a_3 chosen over a_2 hold with equality for $\mathbf{P}^g$, the utility difference between a_2 and a_3 in ω_1 is also equal to 0. Thus, the utility from taking a_2 is the same as the utility from taking a_3 in every state.

Given this, the value of information is higher for $\mathbf{P}^g$ if

$$\frac{12}{72}\left(u(a_1,\omega_1)-u(a_2,\omega_1)\right)$$

$$+\frac{6}{72}\left(u(a_2,\omega_2)-u(a_1,\omega_2)+u(a_2,\omega_3)-u(a_1,\omega_3)\right)\geq 0.$$

To show that this holds, we first note that $u(a_1,\omega_1)\geq u(a_2,\omega_1)$ (the DM preferring to take action a_1 in state ω_1) follows directly from the NIAS inequality for a_1 chosen over a_2 for $\mathbf{P}^g$. Second, because a_2 and a_3 give the same utility in every state, the NIAS inequalities for a_2 chosen over a_1 and a_3 chosen over a_1 for $\mathbf{P}^g$ yield

$$\frac{16}{72}\left(u(a_2,\omega_2)-u(a_1,\omega_2)\right)+\frac{8}{72}\left(u(a_2,\omega_3)-u(a_1,\omega_3)\right)\geq 0$$

and

$$\frac{8}{72}\left(u(a_2,\omega_2)-u(a_1,\omega_2)\right)+\frac{16}{72}\left(u(a_2,\omega_3)-u(a_1,\omega_3)\right)\geq 0.$$

Adding these together gives

$$u(a_2,\omega_2)-u(a_1,\omega_2)+u(a_2,\omega_3)-u(a_1,\omega_3)\geq 0.$$

With this, we conclude that $\mathbf{P}^g$ provides a higher value of information.

This example can also be generalized to any version of this problem with arbitrarily many actions and at least as many states as actions.

Construction of the NIAS cone and the NIAS utility cone suggests a geometric approach to ranking frames. The key step is to consider how the switch in frame impacted the lottery. Let $\vec{d}(g,h)$ be the $|Z|$-dimensional

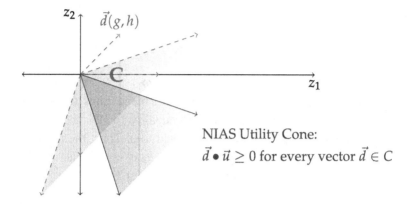

Figure 7.6   Frames *g* and *h* cannot be ranked.

vector that gives the outcome lottery gained from encountering $\mathbf{P}^g$ instead of $\mathbf{P}^h$ or, in other words, the additional probability of receiving each outcome from $\mathbf{P}^g$. For outcome z_m in Z, this is

$$\sum_{a \in A} \sum_{\omega \in \Omega} (\mathbf{P}^g(a, \omega) - \mathbf{P}^h(a, \omega)) \mathbf{1}_{\{z(a,\omega)=z\}}.$$

Intuitively, a welfare ranking in which $\mathbf{P}^g$ has unequivocally higher welfare than $\mathbf{P}^h$ is equivalent to $\vec{d}(g, h) \bullet \vec{u} \geq 0$, for all $\vec{u}$, in the NIAS utility cone. This is equivalent to $\vec{d}(g, h) \in C^{NIAS}$ because a vector is in C^{NIAS} if and only if it has a non-negative dot product with all $\vec{u}$ in the NIAS utility cone. Finally, because $\vec{d}(g, h)$ is in C^{NIAS} if and only if it is a non-negative weighted average of vectors in D, a necessary and sufficient condition for this welfare ranking corresponds to the outcome lottery gained from $\mathbf{P}^g$ being a non-negative weighted average of the outcome lotteries gained from not making wholesale switches from any action for either $\mathbf{P}^f$ or $\mathbf{P}^g$.

Returning to the example, $\mathbf{P}^h$ yields $(\frac{1}{2}, \frac{1}{6}, \frac{1}{3})$ and $\mathbf{P}^g$ yields $(\frac{1}{3}, 0, \frac{2}{3})$. Hence, $\vec{d}(g, h) = (\frac{1}{6}, \frac{1}{6}, -\frac{1}{3})$. We now add this to the plot of the NIAS cone and the NIAS utility cone in (z_1, z_2) space. Note geometrically, in Figure 7.6, that $\vec{d}(g, h)$ is not in D, so it does not have a positive dot product with the entire NIAS utility cone, so $\mathbf{P}^g$ and $\mathbf{P}^h$ are not welfare ranked. If it was in C^{NIAS}, then they would be ranked.

7.8　Technical Definitions

The main result given by Caplin and Martin (2021) makes the above intuition general in more general information-theoretic language. We start with the theoretical object. Given $u : Z \longrightarrow \mathbb{R}$ and any posterior-based experiment, Q^f is

$$V(u, Q^f) = \max_{P \in \Phi(Q^f)} \sum_{a \in A} \sum_{\omega \in \Omega} P(a, \omega) u(z(a, \omega)),$$

where $\Phi(Q^f)$ is the set of all distributions of actions and states feasible under Q^f (in that Q^f is informative enough for them to be taken). The function $V(u, Q^f)$ with the inattentive valuation subtracted is also known as the *value of information* for experiment Q^f given utility function u (Frankel and Kamenica, 2019).

We now introduce the SDSC $\mathbf{P}^f$. A Bayes' consistent distribution of posteriors Q^f is consistent with $\mathbf{P}^f$ given $u : Z \longrightarrow \mathbb{R}$ if $\mathbf{P}^f$ maximizes the expected utility among distributions of actions and states feasible under $Q^f \in \mathcal{Q}(\mu)$.

Definition 31: $\mathbf{P}^f$ is *consistent* with Q^f given $u : Z \longrightarrow \mathbb{R}$ if and only if

$$\mathbf{P}^f \in \arg \max_{P \in \Phi(Q^f)} \sum_{a \in A} \sum_{\omega \in \Omega} P(a, \omega) u(z(a, \omega)).$$

Thus, to allow the econometrician to rank the distributions of actions and states based on the value of information for consistent experiments, we formally define the relation $\succsim_W$ as

$$\mathbf{P}^g \succsim_W \mathbf{P}^h$$

if for every u,

$$V(u, Q^g) \geq V(u, Q^h),$$

for every Q^g consistent with $\mathbf{P}^g$ and every Q^h consistent with $\mathbf{P}^h$. Note that the above does not *per se* specify that the experiment is defined by the revealed experiment, as observed in the SDSC. It allows for any posterior-based experiment that can rationalize the data.

The value of information is defined by Frankel and Kamenica (2019) as the improvement over the inattentive choice. As given by Bernheim and

Rangel (2009), our welfare question concerns different presentations of one and the same decision problem, the value of the inattentive choice is the same in all frames. Hence, their value ranking is equivalent to their value of information ranking.

There are two features of the setting that help us in characterizing this relation. First, for a given u, every experiment Q^f consistent with $\mathbf{P}^f$ has the same value of information, which is the expected utility provided by $\mathbf{P}^f$:

$$V(u, Q^f) = \sum_{\omega \in \Omega} \sum_{a \in A} \mathbf{P}^f(a, \omega) u(z(a, \omega)).$$

This is a result we discussed earlier.

Second, we only need to consider those utility functions for which there exist experiments consistent with $\mathbf{P}^g$ and $\mathbf{P}^h$. Putting these together, $\mathbf{P}^g \succsim_W \mathbf{P}^h$ if and only if for all u, for which there are experiments consistent with $\mathbf{P}^g$ and $\mathbf{P}^h$,

$$\sum_{\omega \in \Omega} \sum_{a \in A} \mathbf{P}^g(a, \omega) u(z(a, \omega)) \geq \sum_{\omega \in \Omega} \sum_{a \in A} \mathbf{P}^h(a, \omega) u(z(a, \omega)).$$

The goal is to determine if and only if conditions under which one frame makes DMs have higher welfare than the other. Technically, we have a fixed decision problem (μ, A) and we have $\mathbf{P}^f(a, \omega) \in \mathcal{P}(\mu, A)$ for $f = g, h$ as data from which we generate revealed posterior-based strategies. We restrict our attention to cases in which there exists a utility function that rationalizes the data: As noted above, this involves imposing all NIAS constraints in both frames. We now pull these together.

Definition 32: Frame g is *revealed to be of higher welfare* than frame h ($g \succsim_W h$) if the revealed value of information is at least as high in frame g than in frame h for every utility function u that satisfies NIAS in any frame (NIAS-F).

Formally, $g \succsim_W h$ if

$$\sum_{a \in A} \sum_{\omega \in \Omega} \mathbf{P}^g(a, \omega) u(z(a, \omega)) \geq \sum_{a \in A} \sum_{\omega \in \Omega} \mathbf{P}^h(a, \omega) u(z(a, \omega)),$$

for every u such that for every $a, b \in A$,

$$\sum_{\omega \in \Omega} \mathbf{P}^g(a, \omega) u(z(a, \omega)) \geq \sum_{\omega \in \Omega} \mathbf{P}^g(a, \omega) u(z(b, \omega))$$

and

$$\sum_{\omega \in \Omega} \mathbf{P}^h(a, \omega) u(z(a, \omega)) \geq \sum_{\omega \in \Omega} \mathbf{P}^h(a, \omega) u(z(b, \omega)).$$

The goal of the research is to find a testable necessary and sufficient condition for welfare ranking. The main result by Caplin and Martin (2021) accomplishes this by formalizing the geometry of the NIAS cone and the NIAS utility cone.

Theorem: Welfare Ranking (Caplin and Martin, 2021): Given $\mathbf{P}^g$ and $\mathbf{P}^h$ that satisfy NIAS-F, $\mathbf{P}^g \succsim_V \mathbf{P}^h$ if and only if $\vec{d}(g, h) \in \mathcal{C}^{NIAS}$.

The proof of the theorem involves a direct application of Farkas lemma or, equivalently, the separating hyperplane theorem. In terms of the separating hyperplane, the normal vector of the hyperplane through the origin that separates a non-ranked lottery $\vec{d}(g, h)$ from $\mathcal{C}^{NIAS}$ is key to the construction.

7.9 Simple vs. Risky: Second Example

We consider a second simple decision problem that has a safe action:

$$\begin{array}{cc} \omega_1 & \omega_2 \\ \begin{pmatrix} z_1 & z_2 \\ z_3 & z_3 \end{pmatrix} & \begin{array}{c} a \\ b \end{array} \end{array}.$$

In this case, the SDSC in the two frames is as follows:

$$\mathbf{P}^g = \begin{array}{cc} \omega_1 & \omega_2 \\ \begin{pmatrix} .4 & .1 \\ .1 & .4 \end{pmatrix} & \begin{array}{c} a \\ b \end{array} \end{array} \quad \text{and} \quad \mathbf{P}^h = \begin{array}{cc} \omega_1 & \omega_2 \\ \begin{pmatrix} .15 & .05 \\ .35 & .45 \end{pmatrix} & \begin{array}{c} a \\ b \end{array} \end{array}.$$

The key to identifying the NIAS cone, as always, is to compute changes in the prize lottery that were revealed not optimal. Choosing a in $\mathbf{P}^g$ gets

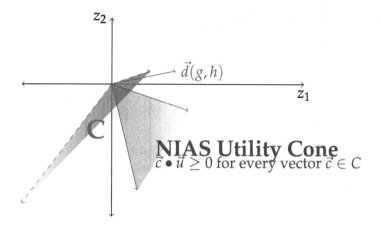

Figure 7.7   Frames g and h can be ranked.

z_1 and z_2 with unconditional probabilities .4 and .1. Choosing b gets z_3. Hence, sticking with a over b yields

$$\vec{d}^g(a,b) = (.4, .1, -.5).$$

Likewise, sticking with b over a in $\mathbf{P}^g$ gets z_3 rather than z_1 with unconditional probability .1 and z_2 with unconditional probability .4:

$$\vec{d}^g(b,a) = (-.1, -.4, .5).$$

Analogously,

$$\vec{d}^h(a,b) = (.15, .05, -.2),$$
$$\vec{d}^h(b,a) = (-.35, -.45, .8).$$

In this example, $\mathbf{P}^g$ yields $(.4, .1, .5)$ and $\mathbf{P}^h$ yields $(.15, .05, .8)$. Hence, $\vec{d}(g,h) = (.25, .05, -.3)$. As illustrated in Figure 7.7, $\vec{d}(g,h)$ is in D, so it has a positive dot product with the entire NIAS utility cone, so $\mathbf{P}^g$ and $\mathbf{P}^h$ are ranked by $\succsim_V$.

7.10   NIAS Equalities

As we have seen above, it is important to construct illuminating examples. In some of these examples, it is simplest if some of the NIAS inequalities hold with equality. I close the section by introducing an observation by

Caplin and Martin (2021) that is of help in constructing such examples: It characterizes precisely under what conditions any NIAS inequality must hold with equality.

A first point on generality: In the given examples to date, the NIAS utility cone is constructed based on observations from decision problems defined by a given prior and action set (μ, A) of a fixed state space. But all that the various data sets used in construction of this cone really need to share is a fixed set of prizes. The priors and even the state spaces can be different. What we are given then is a finite collection of SDSC, $\{\mathbf{P}^m\}_{m=1}^M$, with all actions yielding state-dependent prizes in fixed finite prize space Z. What we will need is that this entire collection have a CIR so that there is a fixed utility function over prizes that can rationalize them all. Note that there may be a very large number of NIAS constraints. For any one of the action sets, we need to consider all chosen actions and consider as the alternative any other feasible actions. I want simple notation for this collection, so they will be indexed by $1 \leq i \leq I$. The index will be associated with one of the action sets $a_i, b_i \in A^{m(i)}$, with a_i revealed chosen in the data. The NIAS inequality for choosing a_i rather than counterfactually switching wholesale to b_i is identified by $\vec{d}(a_i, b_i)$, the change in prize lottery induced by this switch. The corresponding NIAS constraint is

$$\vec{d}(a_i, b_i) \bullet \vec{u} \geq 0.$$

The next theorem precisely characterizes when those NIAS inequalities for any utility function that satisfies NIAS. It states that a set of NIAS inequalities must all hold as equalities for any such utility function if and only if there exist strictly positive weights under which their weighted sum is zero. It is a form of affine dependence with a sign constraint on the weights.

Theorem 11: *Consider a finite of set of NIAS inequalities $\vec{d}(a_i, b_i) \bullet \vec{u} \geq 0$, for $1 \leq i \leq I$, for which the corresponding NIAS cone is non-empty. A subset $1 \leq j \leq J$ of these hold as equalities:*

$$\vec{d}(a_j, b_j) \bullet \vec{u} = 0$$

if and only if there exist strictly positive weights $\lambda_j > 0$ such that

$$\sum_j \lambda_j \vec{d}(a_j, b_j) = 0.$$

Proof 11: To prove that existence of such weights is sufficient, set $j = 1$, normalize to $\lambda_1 = 1$, and note that if such weights exist,

$$\vec{d}(a_1, b_1) = -\sum_{j=2}^{J} \lambda_j \vec{d}(a_j, b_j).$$

Hence,

$$\vec{d}(a_1, b_1) \bullet \vec{u} = -\left[\sum_{j=2}^{J} \lambda_j \vec{d}(a_j, b_j)\right] \bullet \vec{u}$$

$$= -\sum_{j=2}^{J} \lambda_j \vec{d}(a_j, b_j) \bullet \vec{u}$$

$$\leq 0.$$

But since the NIAS constraint directly implies $\vec{d}(a_1, b_1) \bullet \vec{u} \geq 0$, equality follows. This is WLOG since the indexing of inequalities is arbitrary.

To show that existence of such weights is necessary, consider an NIAS inequality, WLOG $i = 1$, for which this is not true. A direct implication is that there cannot exist non-negative weights $\lambda_i \geq 0$ such that

$$-\vec{d}(a_1, b_1) = \sum_{i=2}^{I} \lambda_j \vec{d}(a_i, b_i).$$

By Farkas lemma, this implies the existence of $\vec{u} \in \mathbb{R}^K$ such that

$$-\vec{d}(a_1, b_1) \bullet \vec{u} < 0,$$

$$\vec{d}(a_i, b_i) \bullet \vec{u} \geq 0 \text{ for } 2 \leq i \leq I.$$

Reversing the sign of the first, we have identified a utility vector in the NIAS cone for which the first inequality holds strictly, completing the proof of necessity.

7.11   Welfare Ranking with Costs of Learning

At this stage we have the complete methods of recovering all utility functions that admit a CIR, and for each such utility function, we also have methods for identifying all rationalizing cost functions. This opens up the possibility of providing conditions for ranking revealed experiments by net welfare. This remains essentially uncharted water. I close the section by presenting a simple example in which precisely such a net welfare ranking is available. Interestingly, it was designed not to establish this result but simply to better understand the interplay of NIAS and NIAC. It was a surprise to find that it permitted an unequivocal net welfare ranking. In this lecture, the DM faces two frames, which we superscript g and h. Data are observed in two decision problems so that NIAC can have bite: We subscript the choice set in this case only. Note that this provides a meaning to a frame as something that can apply across decision problems: that might be something like "adding an index," highlighting price, etc.

To keep life simple, each decision problem is a two-action, two-equiprobable-state, and two-prize case. We also have two distinct safe options, b and c. The uncertain option is *ex ante* equally likely to give two distinct prizes:

$$
\begin{array}{cc}
\omega_1 & \omega_2 \\
\end{array}
$$
$$
\begin{pmatrix}
z_1^a & z_2^a \\
z^b & z^b \\
z^c & z^c
\end{pmatrix}
\begin{array}{c}
a \\
b \\
c
\end{array} .
$$

The two choice sets observed are $B = \{a, b\}$ and $C = \{a, c\}$. The SDSC data set in frame g is

$$\mathbf{P}_B^g(a,1) = \mathbf{P}_C^g(a,1) = \mathbf{P}_B^g(b,2) = \mathbf{P}_C^g(c,2) = 0.4,$$

$$\mathbf{P}_B^g(a,2) = \mathbf{P}_C^g(a,2) = \mathbf{P}_B^g(b,1) = \mathbf{P}_C^g(c,1) = 0.1.$$

The SDSC data in frame h is

$$\mathbf{P}_B^h(a,1) = \mathbf{P}_B^h(a,2) = 0.5,$$

$$\mathbf{P}_C^h(a,1) = \mathbf{P}_C^h(c,2) = 0.3,$$

$$\mathbf{P}_C^h(c,1) = \mathbf{P}_C^h(a,2) = 0.2.$$

Utility comparison hinges on six unknowns. First are the four unknown utilities, which are frame independent: u_1^a, u_2^a, u^b, u^c. Inattentive strategies are costless in both g and h. The attentive revealed experiment in g yields a 0.5 chance of posteriors $(0.8, 0.2)$ and $(0.2, 0.8)$: The unknown cost is $\bar{K}^g \geq 0$. The attentive revealed experiment in frame h in set C involves a 0.5 chance of posteriors $(0.6, 0.4)$ and $(0.4, 0.6)$: The unknown cost is $\bar{K}^h \geq 0$.

I first work out the implications of NIAS for frame g in set B (using the revealed posterior version). That for action a chosen over b at $(0.8, 0.2)$ yields

$$0.8u_1^a + 0.2u_2^a \geq u^b.$$

Action b chosen over a at $(0.2, 0.8)$ implies

$$u^b \geq 0.2u_1^a + 0.8u_2^a.$$

NIAS for frame g in set C is identical with u^b replaced by u^c. Hence, $u_1^a \geq u_2^a$ and

$$u^b, u^c \in [0.2u_1^a + 0.8u_2^a, 0.8u_1^a + 0.2u_2^a].$$

Hence, for not all to be indifferent, we need $u_1^a > u_2^a$. We can normalize to $u_1^a = 1$ and $u_2^a = 0$ so that

$$u^b, u^c \in [0.2, 0.8].$$

Is this consistent with NIAS for frame h?

Action a chosen over b in set B at inattentive strategy $(0.5, 0.5)$:

$$0.5 \geq u^b.$$

Action a chosen over c in set C at $(0.6, 0.4)$:

$$0.6 \geq u^c.$$

Action c chosen over a in set C at $(0.4, 0.6)$:

$$u^c \geq 0.4.$$

In combination, all NIAS conditions apply, provided $u_1^a = 1$, $u_2^a = 0$ and

$$u^b \in [0.2, 0.5],$$
$$u^c \in [0.4, 0.6].$$

Hence, there exists a (framed) BEU representation with these conditions satisfied.

It is intuitive that gross utility is higher in g than in h, given that in both cases, it results in a more Blackwell informative revealed experiment. To confirm, compare gross EU for B frame g as opposed to h:

$$EU_B^g = 0.4 + 0.5u^b \geq 0.5 = EU_B^h.$$

Likewise, for C,

$$EU_C^g = 0.4 + 0.5u^c > 0.3 + 0.5u^c = EU_C^h.$$

Hence, frame f yields at least as high gross expected utility as h in both cases. What of attention costs? Is there a CIR? What more does NIAC say?

Note that NIAC has no bite in frame g since the revealed experiments are the same. What about NIAC in frame h? The subtlety is the need to maximize at each possible counterfactual posterior. The switch of the inattentive strategy in B to C yields

$$\max[0.5, u^c].$$

With $u^c \in [0.4, 0.6]$, NIAS allows either to be higher. Considering the converse switch of the attentive strategy from C to B, note that at posterior $(0.6, 0.4)$, the NIAS constraints already tell us that a is better than b:

$$0.6 > u^b.$$

At posterior $(0.4, 0.6)$, the choice of b yields u^b, while the choice of a yields 0.4, interior to the set $u^b \in [0.2, 0.5]$ of NIAS consistent values. Maximized EU at this posterior is

$$\max[u^b, 0.4].$$

Each posterior is equally likely. Hence, the total EU is

$$0.3 + \max[.5u^b, 0.2].$$

The total EU from the switch is

$$0.3 + \max[.5u^b, 0.2] + \max[0.5, u^c].$$

The NIAC constraint is, therefore,

$$EU_B^h + EU_C^h = 0.8 + 0.5u^c \geq 0.3 + \max[.5u^b, 0.2] + \max[0.5, u^c].$$

Hence,

$$1 + u^c \geq \max[u^b, 0.4] + \max[1, 2u^c].$$

Four NIAS-consistent cases are relevant to the given maximum operators on the RHSs:

(1) $u^b, u^c \in [0.4, 0.5]$:

$$1 + u^c \geq u^b + 1 \Longrightarrow u^b \leq u^c.$$

(2) $u^b \in [0.4, 0.5]$, $u^c \in [0.5, 0.6]$:

$$1 + u^c \geq u^b + 2u^c \Longrightarrow u^b \leq 1 - u^c.$$

(3) $u^b \in [0.2, 0.4]$, $u^c \in [0.4, 0.5]$:

$$1 + u^c \geq 0.4 + 1 \Longrightarrow u^c \geq 0.4.$$

(4) $u^b \in [0.2, 0.4]$, $u^c \in [0.5, 0.6]$:

$$1 + u^c \geq 0.4 + 2u^c \Longrightarrow u^c \leq 0.6.$$

Note that the last two are already implied by NIAS. The first two are new. Combining them, we get

$$u^b \leq \min\{u^c, 1 - u^c\}.$$

Overall NIAC and NIAS are satisfied if $u_1^a = 1$, $u_2^a = 0$, $u^c \in [0.4, 0.6]$ and

$$u^b \in [0.2, \min\{u^c, 1 - u^c\}].$$

Given $u^c \in [0.4, 0.6]$, note that

$$\min\{u^c, 1 - u^c\} \in [0.4, 0.5],$$

implying indeed that NIAS is satisfied. The open question is how net utilities compare.

Note that the free inattentive strategy is always available in any frame. The fact that it was not used in frame g sets an upper bound on $\bar{K}^g$. The upper bound is tighter for the lower utility alternative b, in which a would have been optimal with inattention

$$EU_B^g - \bar{K}^g = 0.4 + 0.5u^b - \bar{K}^g \geq 0.5.$$

Hence,

$$\bar{K}^g \leq 0.5u^b - 0.1.$$

We now look to establish a lower bound on the cost $\bar{K}^h$ of the attentive strategy in set C. Note that it cannot be improving in frame h to switch the attentive strategy in C to set B and optimize from there. The inattentive strategy in B yields EU net of costs N_B^h of

$$N_B^h \equiv EU_B^h = 0.5.$$

With the attentive strategy in B, the optimal strategy depends on u^b. If $u^b \in [0.2, 0.4]$, it is optimal to pick a even at a worse posterior $(0.4, 0.6)$, so the total gross utility is still 0.5. This cannot be improving since $\bar{K}^h \geq 0$. If $u^b \in [0.4, \min\{u^c, 1 - u^c\}]$, it is optimal to pick b at $(0.4, 0.6)$, so the total gross utility is

$$0.3 + 0.5u^b.$$

Hence, the condition that inattention does not improve the constraint in frame h is

$$0.3 + 0.5u^b - \bar{K}^h \leq 0.5 \Longrightarrow \bar{K}^h \geq 0.5u^b - 0.2.$$

Overall, we have identified two inequalities on costs:

$$\bar{K}^g \leq 0.5u^b - 0.1,$$
$$\bar{K}^h \geq 0.5u^b - 0.2.$$

Subtraction yields

$$\bar{K}^g - \bar{K}^h \leq 0.1.$$

What do these tell us about net utility comparisons across frames? Compare net EU for B frame g as opposed to h:

$$N_B^g \equiv EU_B^g - \bar{K}^g = 0.4 + 0.5u^b - \bar{K}^g,$$
$$N_B^h = EU_B^h = 0.5.$$

Hence, $N_B^h \leq N_B^f$ if and only if

$$0.5 \leq 0.4 + 0.5u^b - \bar{K}^g,$$

or

$$\bar{K}^g \leq 0.5u^b - 0.1,$$

which is established.

Now, compute net *EU* for *C* frame *g* and *h*:

$$N_C^g = EU_C^f - \bar{K}^g = 0.4 + 0.5u^c - \bar{K}^g,$$

$$N_C^h = EU_C^h - \bar{K}^h = 0.3 + 0.5u^c - \bar{K}^h.$$

Hence, $N_C^h \leq N_C^g$ if and only if

$$0.3 + 0.5u^c - \bar{K}^h \leq 0.4 + 0.5u^c - \bar{K}^g,$$

or

$$\bar{K}^g - \bar{K}^h \leq 0.1,$$

which is established. We conclude that frame *g* welfare dominates frame *h* in both decision problems. Who knew?

Posterior-Separable Cost
Functions and Behavior

In this lecture, I introduce and analyze behavioral patterns associated with a large and important family of attention cost functions. Costs based on Shannon entropy introduced into economics by Sims opened the door. In this lecture, I introduce this cost function and indicate some of the many reasons why generalizations are being explored. In a nutshell, the model has properties that are often contradicted in data. With that in mind, I introduce some seemingly natural generalizations that share a key property of the Shannon model, which is posterior separability: Costs are additive in nature in a particular sense. These are now well studied due to their allowing for most observed empirical failings of the Shannon model.

The big open question relates to a comprehensive understanding of the behavioral properties that are associated with each model class. A narrow version of this question is whether there are particular behavioral features that define the Shannon model. It is known that Shannon entropy has many ideal features as a measure of information: Does this translate in an interesting way to behavior? But of course, the larger question concerns the behavioral characteristics of the broader classes that generalize the Shannon model. These are of considerable independent interest, in particular the uniformly posterior-separable and invariant posterior-separable classes.

In technical terms, this lecture is entirely drawn from the work of Caplin, Dean, and Leahy (2022a) (CDL henceforth in this lecture), from which it contains long excerpts. Throughout that paper, and correspondingly in this lecture, the utility function is treated as known. All the novelty lies in understanding the features of the cost function.

The characterization theorems in CDL are surprisingly clean. As part of the price for this, the data set required is particularly rich for technical reasons that will be outlined. I open the lecture by specifying the ideal data set that is used in the characterization theorems. It requires seeing rich SDSC for a limitless class of decision problems. Once the definitions are in place, the results are relatively simple to state. The proofs, however, are not simple. The interested reader will have little choice but either to try to create their own arguments or look at the online appendix to CDL that contains our proofs.

8.1   Some Enriched Definitions

CDL represent a massive step up in generality of treatment and therefore in the definition of decision problems and the corresponding data requirements. For that reason, CDL introduce some local notation that makes these additional enrichments simpler to specify. Here are some of the essential respects in which we amend the notation and definitions to allow for greater generality:

1. We let Ω denote the set of **conceivable** states of the world. In any given decision problem, only a finite number of these will be possible. For technical reasons, we assume that Ω is countably infinite.
2. CDL denote the known utility as $a(\omega)$ to economize on notation. Each action a is a function $a : \Omega \to \mathbb{R}$, in which $a(\omega)$ is the utility of action a in state ω. We will stick with that in this lecture to aid in reading that paper.
3. We let $\mathcal{A}$ denote the universe of potential actions. These allow for any conceivable real payoffs, $\mathcal{A} \equiv \{a : \Omega \to \mathbb{R}\}$.
4. As usual, a specific decision problem (μ, A) allows choice among a finite set of actions, $A \subset \mathcal{A}$, given the prior probability distribution μ over states in Ω. Throughout, we assume that the prior places positive probability on only a finite subset of states. With slight abuse of notation, we let $\Delta\Omega$ denote the set of probability distributions on Ω with finite support (omitting probability distributions with infinite support).

The assumptions on the data set are even more extreme. In the first place, SDSC is seen for all decision problems (μ, A). We let $\mathbf{P}^{(\mu, A)}$ specify the frequency that the agent chooses each action $a \in A$ in each state in support of μ. We use the notation $\mathbf{P}^{(\mu, A)}(a|\omega)$ for the conditional probability of observing action a in state ω in decision problem (μ, A) and $\mathbf{P}^{(\mu, A)}(a)$ for the unconditional probability of observing action a.

There is one more major conceptual change in the nature of the data that is needed. Much as in the case of classical revealed preference theory (Richter, 1966), the results are greatly simplified and global indifference ruled out if the ideal data set comprises **all** SDSC that a DM would willingly choose across all decision problems. Since the agent may be indifferent between multiple patterns of choice, this data set is a correspondence. Let $\mathbf{D}$ denote this correspondence. $\mathbf{D}^{(\mu, A)}$ is the set of observed SDSC functions $\mathbf{P}^{(\mu, A)}$ for the decision problem (μ, A).

8.2 Rational Inattention

The goal of the DM is to maximize expected utility net of attention costs. Given a decision problem (μ, A) and a feasible strategy $(Q, q) \in \Lambda(\mu, A)$, expected utility is computed in the standard manner:

$$G(Q, q|\mu, A) = \sum_{\gamma \in \text{supp } Q} \sum_{a \in A} Q(\gamma) q(a|\gamma) \left[\sum_{\omega \in \text{supp } \gamma} \gamma(\omega) a(\omega) \right],$$

where $\gamma(\omega)$ is the probability of state ω given the posterior γ.

As always, we assume that attention costs for strategy $(Q, q) \in \Lambda(\mu, A)$ depend only on the prior μ and the distribution of posteriors Q and not on the choice set A or the action probabilities q. The distinction from earlier lectures is that we explicitly allow for changes in possible states and beliefs over them. Hence, the domain of the cost function is far richer. It comprises all priors $\mu \in \Delta\Omega$ over any finite subset of the state space and all posterior distributions $Q \in \mathcal{Q}(\mu)$ consistent with that prior:

$$\mathcal{F} = \{(\mu, Q)|\mu \in \Delta\Omega, Q \in \mathcal{Q}(\mu)\}.$$

An **attention cost function** K maps the elements of $\mathcal{F}$ into the extended positive real line $K : \mathcal{F} \to [0, \infty]$. We normalize the cost of learning nothing to zero so that $K(\mu, Q) = 0$ whenever supp $Q = \{\mu\}$. Allowing $K(\mu, Q)$

to equal infinity for some Q allows for the possibility that some attention strategies in $\mathcal{Q}(\mu)$ are not chosen for any A. For example, there are interesting cases in which it is prohibitively costly to rule out *ex ante* possible states so that the DM will never choose posteriors on the boundary of $\Delta(\text{supp }\mu)$.

Given an attention cost function K, the value of a feasible strategy $(Q,q) \in \Lambda(\mu,A)$ is computed as always by subtracting the attention cost from expected utility:

$$V(Q,q|\mu,A,K) \equiv G(Q,q|\mu,A) - K(\mu,Q).$$

The value of an optimal strategy and the set of optimal strategies are defined in the natural manner as always using hats to denote the maximized value functions. While we write $\hat{V}$ as the supremum over all feasible strategies, the data set $\mathbf{D}$ assigns a choice to every decision problem. If K represents $\mathbf{D}$, meaning that the set of policies that maximize choice given K reproduce the data set $\mathbf{D}$, then $\hat{\Lambda}$ will never be empty, and there will always exist a policy that achieves the supremum:

$$\hat{V}(\mu,A|K) \equiv \sup_{(Q,q)\in\Lambda(\mu,A)} V(Q,q|\mu,A,K),$$

$$\hat{\Lambda}(\mu,A|K) \equiv \left\{ (Q,q) \in \Lambda(\mu,A) \,|\, V(Q,q|\mu,A,K) = \hat{V}(\mu,A|K) \right\}.$$

8.3 Representations

Given a decision problem (μ,A) and a strategy $(Q,q) \in \Lambda(\mu,A)$, recall that $P_{(Q,q)}$ is the theoretical counterpart to the data object $\mathbf{P}^{(\mu,A)}$. CDL add conditioning on the decision problem, given the richness of the data we are summarizing. Given $(Q,q) \in \Lambda(\mu,A)$, $P_{(\mu,A|Q,q)} \in \mathcal{P}(\mu,A)$ is defined by

$$P_{(\mu,A|Q,q)}(a,\omega) = \sum_{\gamma\in\text{supp }Q} q(a|\gamma)Q(\gamma)\gamma(\omega).$$

The CDL representation theorems are based on the equivalence of these two objects. They define K as representing $\mathbf{D}$ if the observed SDSC data set $\mathbf{D}$ comprises **all** SDSC data generated by the optimal policies of an expected utility maximizer facing the information cost function K.

Definition 33: The cost function K **represents** the data set **D** if, for all $(\mu, A) \in \Delta\Omega \times 2^{\mathcal{A}}$,

$$\mathbf{D}^{(\mu,A)} = \{P_{(\mu,A|Q,q)} | (Q,q) \in \hat{\Lambda}(\mu, A|K)\}.$$

Note that this data set is rich enough that the recovery theorem of the previous lecture implies that any such representation will be unique.

8.4 The Shannon Model

What will be of interest in the following are the versions of the representation theorem in which one can restrict attention to special classes of cost function. When we define such a class, we do so by looking for properties of the data that correspond to having a representation in that class: The naming will be obvious as we advance down the path.

The first key model whose behavioral properties are of particular interest is the model that is standard in large parts of the rational inattention literature following Sims. This is the cost function that is linear in the expected reduction in Shannon entropy between prior and posteriors. This function has many remarkable features, with the first such being identified in Shannon (1948). For the moment, we fix a finite set of states, $\bar{\Omega} \subset \Omega$, and consider a probability distribution with that support. Given a strictly positive distribution $p \in \Delta(\bar{\Omega})$ with a generic strictly positive belief $p(\omega) >> 0$, its entropy is measured as

$$H(p) = - \sum_{\omega \in \Omega} p(\omega) \ln p(\omega) > 0.$$

Note that the function is strictly positive on the interior of the simplex. It is filled in on any impossible state by the corresponding limit (L'Hospital):

$$\lim_{x \searrow 0} x \ln x = \lim_{x \searrow 0} \frac{\ln x}{\frac{1}{x}} = \lim_{x \searrow 0} \frac{\frac{1}{x}}{-\frac{1}{x^2}} = \lim_{x \searrow 0} -x = 0.$$

The function is very special as one can see with two states in which we use probability of state 1 as the argument of Shannon function:

$$H(p_1) \equiv -p_1 \ln p_1 - (1 - p_1) \ln(1 - p_1).$$

It is infinitely differentiable on $(0,1)$:

$$H'(p_1) = -\ln p_1 + \ln(1 - p_1) - 1 + 1 = \ln\left(\frac{1 - p_1}{p_1}\right),$$

$$H''(p_1) = -\frac{1}{1 - p_1} - \frac{1}{p_1} < 0.$$

Hence, it is strictly concave and symmetric around its maximum at 0.5:

$$H(0.5) = -\ln\frac{1}{2} = \ln 2,$$

which would be 1 if we used Shannon's real version with log base 2.

Note that, due to being pinned at zero on impossible states, disappearing states contribute zero to entropy. This has the unusual property that one can change the number of states and use this universal formula. In fact, we need not have introduced the support $\bar{\Omega} \subset \Omega$. This feature is not to be taken for granted. Many other functions that we introduce in the following have a fundamental dependence on the *ex ante* set of possible states in the functional form of costs. In a way, Shannon entropy also depends on the state space. This is related to a striking feature of the Shannon function, which is that the derivative is unbounded at end points:

$$\lim_{p_1 \searrow 0} \ln\left(\frac{1 - p_1}{p_1}\right) = \infty,$$

$$\lim_{p_1 \nearrow 1} \ln\left(\frac{1 - p_1}{p_1}\right) = -\infty.$$

This is unusual: Not many functions with infinite derivative at the boundary still heads to a bounded limit.

The Shannon cost function is defined by costs that are linear in the expected reduction in Shannon entropy between the prior and the posterior.

Definition 34: Given $\mu \in \Delta\Omega$ and any Bayes' consistent posteriors $Q \in \mathcal{Q}(\mu)$, a cost function is of the Shannon form if there exists $\kappa > 0$ such that

$$K(\mu, Q) = \kappa\left[\sum_{\gamma \in \text{supp } Q} -Q(\gamma)H(\gamma) + H(\mu)\right],$$

where the addition of the entropy of the prior serves only to normalize the cost of inattention to zero. Note that the signs here are very awkward.

The general idea is to take a function that is strictly convex in the posteriors and to compute costs as the difference between the average value of that function across posteriors and its value at the prior. By strict convexity, this makes it costly to learn. The awkwardness with the Shannon cost function is that, as defined, it is a strictly concave function that is **maximized** rather than minimized at the uniform prior. So, it needs to have its sign flipped to translate it into a strictly convex function. You may get signs wrong as often as I do, but probably not. Formulaically,

$$K(\mu, Q) = \kappa \Big[\sum_{\gamma \in \mathrm{supp}\, Q} Q(\gamma) \sum_{\omega \in \Omega} \gamma(\omega) \ln \gamma(\omega) - \sum_{\omega \in \Omega} \mu(\omega) \ln \mu(\omega) \Big].$$

Note that behaviorally, the unbounded marginal cost of learning for sure that a state is not possible means that this is never part of an optimal strategy. It is this fact that makes the set of *ex ante* possible states according to the prior important. All optimal learning strategies involve posteriors with the same support. This hides nicely in the apparently dimension-free definition.

8.5   Why Study Alternatives?

There are some arguments that costs are ideally of the Shannon variety. These are based on the amazingly special properties of this function. I do not think these *a priori* arguments hold water. Indeed, many forms of behavior have been identified that violate the implications of the Shannon model. To date, three specific violations have been addressed by replacing the Shannon cost function with other cost functions, almost all of which will be introduced in the following. Many more remain to be found. As indicated before, I think that getting more realistic about cost functions and inferring them from behavior is going to be a very important line of research for decades to come.

The first behavioral challenge to the Shannon model is a very strong form of behavioral symmetry it implies: Essentially, it has the property that the distribution of state-dependent payoffs is a sufficient statistic for behavior (this is made precise in the following). Yet, this is simply not so in many everyday decisions: Prices which are closer together are harder to distinguish than those which are far apart. By way of confirmation, Dean and

Neligh (2017) design an experiment that highlights precisely this failing of the Shannon model. A recent paper by Hébert and Woodford (2020) provides a family of uniformly posterior-separable cost functions that can accommodate the notion of perceptual distance. They propose a class of "neighborhood-based" cost functions. In order to construct these costs, the state space is divided into I "neighborhoods" $\Omega_1 \ldots \Omega_I$. A posterior is assigned a cost for each neighborhood based on some convex function of the distribution, conditional on being in that neighborhood. The total cost of the posterior is then the sum of costs across all neighborhoods. Hence, neighborhood-based cost functions allow for it to be more expensive to differentiate between some states than others: The cost of differentiating between two states depends on which neighborhoods they share. Hence, states that share more neighborhoods can be more costly to distinguish. Following Hébert and Woodford (2020) and Dean and Neligh (2017), consider a neighborhood-based cost function that does a good job of fitting the data from an experimental design in which perceptual distance plays a critical role in learning.

A second feature of the Shannon model, again associated with its strong invariance properties, is that behavior should be invariant to changes in prior beliefs that move probabilities between payoff-identical states. Woodford (2020) cites experimental evidence that challenges this implication. He discusses the experimental results of Shaw and Shaw (1977), in which a subject briefly sees a symbol which may appear at one of a number of locations on a screen. Their task is to accurately report the symbol. Since the location on the screen is payoff irrelevant, in the Shannon model, this should be irrelevant to the task performance. Yet, in practice, performance is superior at locations that occur more frequently. Caplin *et al.* (2017) show that a cost function based on Tsallis entropy (Tsallis, 1988) is sufficiently flexible to allow for this.

Third, the Shannon model makes precise predictions about the rate at which subjects improve their accuracy in response to improved incentives: Essentially, the observation of behavior in any given decision problem pins down the model's one free parameter and so behavior in any other decision problem. Caplin and Dean (2013) show in a simple two-state, two-action setup that agents are not responsive enough to changes in incentives: They do not pay enough attention at high rewards, given the attention paid at low rewards. Caplin and Dean (2013) and Dean and Neligh (2017) consider uniformly posterior-separable cost functions based on generalized entropy (Shorrocks, 1980). Dean and Neligh (2017) show that statistical tests on their experimental data favor a model with generalized entropy over the Shannon model.

8.6 Posterior-Separable Cost Functions

A far broader class of cost functions is additively separable across chosen posteriors. We call such cost functions posterior separable. This class includes most of the cost functions considered in the literature, including not only the Shannon model (Sims, 1998) but also expected Tsallis entropy (Caplin *et al.*, 2017), the neighborhood-based cost function given by Hébert and Woodford (2018), and the log-likelihood ratio cost function by Pomatto *et al.* (2018). Posterior separability is also generally assumed in the literature on Bayesian persuasion (Kamenica and Gentzkow, 2011). In this section, we formally define these cost functions and present several properties that will be useful in proving the representation theorems that follow.

8.6.1 *Definition*

Definition 35: An attention cost function K is **posterior separable** if, given $\mu \in \Delta\Omega$ and any Bayes' consistent posteriors $Q \in \mathcal{Q}(\mu)$,

$$K(\mu, Q) = \sum_{\gamma \in \text{supp } Q} Q(\gamma) T_\mu(\gamma),$$

for some convex function $T_\mu : \Delta(\text{supp } \mu) \to \bar{\mathbb{R}}$ such that $T_\mu(\gamma) \geq 0$ with $T_\mu(\mu) = 0$.

The essence of posterior separability is that the cost function is equal to the expectation of some function of the individual posteriors T_μ. In addition, the definition states that learning nothing is costless ($T_\mu(\mu) = 0$) and learning something is weakly costly ($T_\mu(\gamma) \geq 0$). The convexity of $T_\mu(\gamma)$ implies that the weak Blackwell property is satisfied. Technically, T_μ is a divergence extended to the boundary of the simplex.

Note that the convex function T_μ is allowed to depend in an arbitrary way on the prior. Different priors can lead to very different functions T_μ.

8.7 Posterior-Separable Representations

CDL (2022) start from a data set with a posterior-separable representation. There are a few prior steps in the CDL (2019) that deliver such a representation on top of NIAC. Denti (2022) provides an appealing characterization of PS for a finite data set with the standard assumption for that setting in which only one data set is seen. The starting point is the CD theorem about the existence of a CIR for $\{(A^m, \mathbf{P}^m)\}_{m=1}^M$ based on NIAC and NIAS. In this context, Denti shows that one other behavioral axiom implies that there is a posterior-separable representation. His main axiom for posterior separability strengthens NIAC by allowing reallocations of single revealed posteriors across decision problems. He refers to this as no improving posterior cycles, although his statement of it does not explicitly feature cycles or permutations. It asserts that the agent's total utility cannot be improved by reallocating single revealed posteriors. He also indicates why it is challenging to carry out the analysis when there are unbounded applications. So, this is somewhat unfinished business. While all ideas are common across CDL and Denti, the notation and the formalities are quite distinct. A full concordance would be desirable and will surely be available at some later point.

On a technical note, CDL make simplifying assumptions in the context of the representation results.

Regularity Assumption (CDL): *Let K be a posterior-separable cost function with*

$$K(\mu, Q) = \sum_{\gamma \in supp\, Q} Q(\gamma) T_\mu(\gamma).$$

We assume $T_\mu(\gamma)$ is strictly convex and continuous in γ and that $T_\mu(\gamma) < \infty$ on int $\Delta(supp\mu)$.

This regularity assumption adds strict convexity, continuity, and finiteness to the definition of a posterior-separable cost function. The assumption that $T_\mu(\gamma)$ is finite on the interior of the support of μ, together with the convexity of T_μ, ensures that all posteriors in the interior of the support of μ are optimal for some decision problem. Strict convexity simplifies the analysis by eliminating ties. Since T_μ is convex and finite valued, it is continuous on the interior of $\Delta(\text{supp } \mu)$. Assumption 1 adds that T_μ is continuous on the boundary. CDL show that this is without loss of generality, as this is implied by strict convexity.

Definition 36: A data set **D** has a **posterior-separable representation** if it is represented by a posterior-separable cost function that satisfies the regularity assumption.

From this point on, whenever we refer to a posterior-separable cost function, we assume that the additional restrictions of Assumption 1 hold unless otherwise stated.

8.8 Weakly Uniformly Posterior-Separable Cost Functions

The characterizations on which CDL focus involve specializing beyond posterior separability. Possibly, the most important such class comprises weakly uniformly posterior-separable cost functions. In the general posterior-separable model, if the prior μ changes, K can change in arbitrary ways. For a weakly uniformly posterior-separable representation, however, K can depend on μ only through its support: the set of possible states. A cost function K is weakly uniformly posterior separable if it is posterior separable and the strictly convex function T_μ depends only on the set of possible states. We label this definition "weak" uniform posterior separability because it is weaker than the definition introduced by Caplin *et al.* (2017). In that paper, we insist on a single function $T : \Delta\Omega \to \bar{\mathbb{R}}$ rather than a set of functions $T_{\bar{\Omega}}$ that depend on the support of the prior. The new definition greatly simplifies the analysis.

Definition 37: A posterior-separable cost function K is **weakly uniformly posterior separable** if for each finite subset $\bar{\Omega} \subset \Omega$, there exists a strictly convex function $T_{\bar{\Omega}} : \Delta(\bar{\Omega}) \to \bar{\mathbb{R}}$ such that, for all $\mu \in \Delta(\Omega)$ and $Q \in \mathcal{Q}(\mu)$,

$$K(\mu, Q) = \sum_{\gamma \in \text{supp } Q} Q(\gamma) T_{\text{supp } \mu}(\gamma) - T_{\text{supp } \mu}(\mu).$$

The defining characteristic of a weakly uniformly posterior-separable cost function is that it is additively separable in both the priors and the posterior. $T_{\text{supp}\,\mu}(\gamma)$ depends on μ only through the support of μ, not the value of μ itself. Allowing $T_{\text{supp}\,\mu}$ to depend on the support of μ allows us to handle cases in which the cost of setting $\gamma(\omega) = 0$ depends on whether or not $\mu(\omega)$ is zero. For example, it is costless to rule out *ex ante* impossible states but might be extremely costly to rule out *ex ante* possible ones. Subtracting off $T_{\text{supp}\,\mu}(\mu)$ is a normalization that ensures that it is costless not to learn anything. It has no effect on choice.

8.9   Invariant Cost Functions

Invariant cost functions impose two conditions on the costs of learning about states and about events (relatedly, see Hébert and La'O, 2019, who build on the work of Chentsov, 1982).

Both involve a fixed state space $\bar{\Omega} \subset \Omega$ of finite size and a partition $\{\bar{\Omega}_z\}_{z=1,\dots,Z}$ of $\bar{\Omega}$. Consider any prior $\mu \in \text{int}\,\Delta\bar{\Omega}$ and corresponding attention strategy $Q \in \mathcal{Q}(\mu)$. For each $\gamma \in \text{supp}\,Q$, construct γ' such that γ' assigns the same probability as γ to each subset $\bar{\Omega}_z$:

$$\gamma'(\bar{\Omega}_z) \equiv \sum_{\omega \in \bar{\Omega}_z} \gamma'(\omega) = \gamma(\bar{\Omega}_z) \equiv \sum_{\omega \in \bar{\Omega}_z} \gamma(\omega), \tag{50}$$

and within each subset $\bar{\Omega}_z$, the conditional probability of each state is equal to that of the prior:

$$\gamma'(\omega|\bar{\Omega}_z) = \mu(\omega|\bar{\Omega}_z). \tag{51}$$

Finally, let

$$Q'(\gamma') = Q(\gamma), \tag{52}$$

where γ is the posterior in Q used in the construction of γ'.

The first defining feature of invariance involves the sense in which Q' represents less learning than Q. When it comes to the question of whether or not a state is in one of the sets $\bar{\Omega}_z$, Q' assigns the same probabilities as Q, but when it comes to understanding the states within the subset $\bar{\Omega}_z$, Q' is no different than the prior. Q' captures the learning in Q about the partition but not the learning within the partition. It is therefore not unreasonable to assume that the attention strategy Q' is less costly:

$$K(\mu, Q) \geq K(\mu, Q'). \tag{53}$$

Versions of Equation (53) are often referred to as information monotonicity (see Amari, 2016, pp. 51–54). While intuitively appealing, this inequality is not without content. CDL show this in a decision problem with three states, $\bar{\Omega} = \{\omega_1, \omega_2, \omega_3\}$. Consider a partition into two sets, $\bar{\Omega}_1 = \{\omega_1, \omega_2\}$ and $\bar{\Omega}_2 = \{\omega_3\}$. Suppose that the prior is uniform, and consider two attention strategies: Q comprises the posteriors $\gamma_1 = (2/3, 1/3, 0)$ and $\gamma_2 = (0, 1/3, 2/3)$ with equal probability (where the ith element of the vector denotes the probability of state ω_i), while Q' comprises $\gamma_1' = (1/2, 1/2, 0)$ and $\gamma_2' = (1/6, 1/6, 2/3)$. Note that the two attention strategies agree on the probability of the partition: $\gamma_1(\bar{\Omega}_1) = \gamma_1'(\bar{\Omega}_1)$ and $\gamma_2(\bar{\Omega}_1) = \gamma_2'(\bar{\Omega}_1)$. Also, γ_1' and γ_2' are uniformly conditional on $\bar{\Omega}_1$. Monotonicity would therefore imply that Q' is less costly than Q. Suppose, however, that ω_1 is very easy to distinguish from ω_3 and that ω_2 is very difficult to distinguish from ω_3. In this case, it is entirely possible that Q is the less costly attention strategy. Monotonicity rules out this sort of asymmetry.

The second defining feature of invariance relates to any alternative prior $\bar{\mu}$ which assigns the same probabilities as the original prior μ to each subset $\bar{\Omega}_z$ in the partition:

$$\bar{\mu}(\bar{\Omega}_z) = \mu(\bar{\Omega}_z).$$

For each $\gamma \in \text{supp } Q$, construct $\bar{\gamma}$ as we did γ'. For each $\bar{\Omega}_z$, set

$$\bar{\gamma}(\bar{\Omega}_z) = \gamma(\bar{\Omega}_z),$$

and for each $\omega \in \bar{\Omega}_z$, set

$$\bar{\gamma}(\omega | \bar{\Omega}_z) = \bar{\mu}(\omega | \bar{\Omega}_z).$$

Finally, let $\bar{Q}(\bar{\gamma}) = Q(\gamma)$. There is a sense in which Q' and $\bar{Q}$ represent the same amount of learning. The posterior distributions over the partition $\{\bar{\Omega}_z\}$ are the same for each learning strategy, and in each case, the conditional distribution over states within the partition is equal to the prior. In each case, the same information is learned about the partition and nothing else. An invariant cost function imposes equal costs on the two strategies:

$$K(\mu, Q') = K(\bar{\mu}, \bar{Q}).$$

We now define an invariant cost function formally. Before doing so, it is useful to define the operation that took us from Q to Q' and $\bar{Q}$. Given Q, let Q_μ denote the attention strategy defined by the operations (50), (51), and (52) so that $Q' = Q_\mu$ and $\bar{Q} = Q_{\bar{\mu}}$.

Definition 38: A cost function K is **invariant** if, for all finite sets of states $\bar{\Omega} \subset \Omega$, all partitions of $\bar{\Omega}$, all pairs of priors μ, and μ' that place equal probability on each partition subset and all feasible strategies $Q \in \mathcal{Q}(\mu)$,

$$K(\mu, Q) \geq K(\mu, Q_\mu)$$

and

$$K(\mu, Q_\mu) = K(\bar{\mu}, Q_{\bar{\mu}}).$$

A cost function is **invariant posterior separable** if it is both invariant and posterior separable.

CDL give examples to show that information monotonicity is a very different concept from the Blackwell order. They show that the two information structures Q and Q' above are monotonic but not Blackwell ordered. They likewise show that it is possible to find two distributions of posteriors that are Blackwell ordered but not monotonic.

8.10   LIP and UPS Representations

The first key behavioral question relates to the additional conditions on behavior that all form a uniformly posterior-separable representation. Understanding this derives from what is perhaps the most telling property of the entire posterior-separable class: that the corresponding rational inattention problems can be solved with Lagrangian methods. In formalizing this, because both the cost function and expected utility are additively separable in the posteriors, we can rewrite the value of any given strategy

(Q,q), collecting terms specific to each chosen posterior and each action associated with that posterior:

$$V(Q,q|\mu,A,K) = \sum_{\gamma \in \text{supp } Q} \sum_{a \in A} Q(\gamma)q(a|\gamma) \left[\sum_{\omega \in \text{supp } \gamma} \gamma(\omega)a(\omega) - T_\mu(\gamma) \right].$$

Whenever $q(a|\gamma) > 0$, the term in brackets is the **net utility** of action a and posterior γ:

$$N_\mu^a(\gamma) \equiv \sum_{\omega \in \text{supp } \gamma} \gamma(\omega)a(\omega) - T_\mu(\gamma).$$

Note that since $T_\mu(\gamma)$ depends on μ, so does $N_\mu^a(\gamma)$.

Writing the maximization problem in terms of net utilities allows a simple geometric interpretation of the solution. Maximizing the value function is equivalent to maximizing a Bayes' consistent weighted average of net utilities. Net utilities are concave since net utility is the difference between expected utility, which is linear in the probabilities, and the cost of information, which is convex. These curves differ in the utility that they assign to each state and action. Any finite set of posteriors that include the prior in their convex hull are feasible. The optimal action at each posterior provides the highest net utility. This is identified as the upper envelope of all net utility functions.

The value of choosing any set of posteriors can be identified geometrically as the height of the hyperplanes joining the points on the upper envelope of net utility curves as it passes over the prior. To find the maximal such height geometrically is to find the highest such point above the prior. In technical terms, the entire operation revolves around construction of the concavified net utility function, defined as the minimal concave function that majorizes all net utilities (Rockafellar, 1970). In standard cases, the highest chord lies on the line tangent to the lower epigraph at the prior. The optimal posteriors are the points at which this tangent plane meets the net utilities. All other net utilities lie (weakly) below this tangent plane.

It is credible that this geometric intuition is general. We can always find the optimal posteriors by considering the hyperplane tangent to the lower epigraph at the prior and finding where this supporting hyperplane meets the net utilities. Suppose that the support of the prior μ has J distinct states and label these states ω_j for $j = \{1,\ldots,J\}$. Given an optimal posterior $\hat{\gamma}$, we can write the supporting hyperplane as the set of potential net utility levels N such that

$$N = N_\mu^a(\hat{\gamma}) + \sum_{j=1}^{J-1} \theta_j(\gamma(\omega_j) - \hat{\gamma}(\omega_j)),$$

where the Lagrange multipliers θ_j for $j = 1, \ldots, J-1$ capture the change in net utility as the posterior $\gamma(\omega_j)$ is raised at the expense of reducing $\gamma(\omega_J)$. Note that which optimal posterior is used in this construction does not matter as all combinations of optimal posteriors $\hat{\gamma}$ and their corresponding net utility levels $N_\mu^a(\hat{\gamma})$ lie on this plane. Net utilities for all other posteriors lie weakly below the plane, that is, $N_\mu^a(\gamma) \le N_\mu^a(\hat{\gamma}) + \sum_{j=1}^{J-1} \theta_j(\gamma(\omega_j) - \hat{\gamma}(\omega_j))$. This result is summarized in the following theorem. All results are proved in the online appendix to CDL (2021).

Lagrangean Lemma (CDL): *Given a posterior-separable cost function K and decision problem (μ, A) with dimension $J = |supp\ \mu|$, $(Q, q) \in \hat{\Lambda}(\mu, A|K)$ if and only if there exists $\theta \in \mathbb{R}^{J-1}$ such that, given $\gamma \in supp\ Q$ and $a \in A$ with $q(a|\gamma) > 0$,*

$$N_\mu^{a'}(\gamma') - \sum_{j=1}^{J-1} \theta(j)\gamma'(j) \le N_\mu^a(\gamma) - \sum_{j=1}^{J-1} \theta(j)\gamma(j),$$

for all $\gamma' \in supp\ \mu$ and $a' \in A$.

In analytic terms, our results rely heavily on this lemma, which show that the model can be solved by identifying the tangent to the concavified net utility function. This approach has been widely used most notably in the area of Bayesian persuasion (Kamenica and Gentzkow, 2011).

To understand the behavioral implications of weak uniform posterior separability, note that so long as the support of μ remains unchanged, μ enters additively into the cost function so that changes in μ do not affect the relative cost of any posterior. The only role that the prior plays is to determine what posteriors are consistent with Bayes' rule. This has strong implications for the structure of optimal policies. If K is weakly uniformly posterior separable, then changes in μ shift net utility curves up or down by the same amount. With two actions and a prior with revealed posteriors $\hat{\gamma}^a$ and $\hat{\gamma}^b$, these remain optimal so long as they are still feasible, and they are feasible so long as the prior lies in the open interval $(\hat{\gamma}^a, \hat{\gamma}^b)$. So, if a data set has a uniformly posterior-separable representation and $\hat{\gamma}^a$ and $\hat{\gamma}^b$ are revealed posteriors for the problem (μ, A), they must also be observed in any problem (μ', A) in which $\mu' \in (\hat{\gamma}^a, \hat{\gamma}^b)$. We call this property *locally invariant posteriors.* Importantly, this property is not only necessary but also sufficient for a data set with a posterior-separable representation to have a weakly uniformly posterior-separable representation.

Axiom 1 (CDL): Locally Invariant Posteriors: *Consider any decision problem (μ, A) and SDSC data $\mathbf{P}^{(\mu, A)} \in \mathbf{D}^{(\mu, A)}$ with revealed strategy $(\mathbf{Q}, \bar{\mathbf{q}})$ such that $\bar{\mathbf{q}}$ is a deterministic action choice function. Consider (Q', q') with $\sum\limits_{\gamma \in supp\, Q'} \gamma Q'(\gamma) = \mu'$. If supp $Q' \subset supp$ $\mathbf{Q}$, supp $\mu' = supp$ μ, and $q'(\gamma) = \bar{\mathbf{q}}(\gamma)$ for all $\gamma \in supp$ Q', then $P_{(Q', q')} \in \mathbf{D}^{(\mu', A)}$.*

The axiom states that if an attention strategy $\mathbf{Q}$ is observed for the decision problem (μ, A), then the posteriors in $\mathbf{Q}$ remain optimal for (μ', A), where μ' lies in the convex hull of supp $\mathbf{Q}$.

The first theorem in CDL states that a data set with a posterior-separable representation has a weakly uniformly posterior-separable representation if and only if it satisfies locally invariant posteriors (Axiom 1). The proof is involved but straightforward.

Theorem 1 (CDL): UPS Representation: *A data set $\mathbf{D}$ with a posterior-separable representation has a weakly uniformly posterior-separable representation if and only if it satisfies locally invariant posteriors.*

8.11   Only Payoffs Matter and IPS Representations

We say that a data set $\mathbf{D}$ has an **invariant posterior-separable representation** if it can be represented by an invariant posterior-separable cost function. Behaviorally, what might be expected of an invariant cost function? Consider a decision problem (μ, A) in which two states ω_1 and ω_2 are redundant in the sense that for all $a \in A$, we have $a(\omega_1) = a(\omega_2)$. In this case, the expected utility of any deterministic policy (Q, q) depends only on the sum $\gamma(\omega_1) + \gamma(\omega_2)$ for each $\gamma \in$ supp Q, as the payoffs in these states are identical for all actions. The cost of attention, however, depends individually on $\gamma(\omega_1)$ and $\gamma(\omega_2)$. With an invariant cost function, however, it will always be cheaper to choose $\gamma(\omega_1)$ and $\gamma(\omega_2)$ so that the conditional probability of ω_1 given the event $\{\omega_1, \omega_2\}$ is equal to the prior probability of ω_1 conditional on $\{\omega_1, \omega_2\}$. It follows immediately that $\gamma(\omega_1)$ and $\gamma(\omega_2)$ are proportionate to $\mu(\omega_1)$ and $\mu(\omega_2)$ so that

$$\frac{\gamma(\omega_1)}{\mu(\omega_1)} = \frac{\gamma(\omega_2)}{\mu(\omega_2)}.$$

Note that our strictly convex cost function will imply that in an optimal strategy, each action is chosen at only one posterior: γ^a for action a. Hence, $q(a|\gamma^a) > 0$, and Bayes' rule states that

$$P(a|\omega_1) = \frac{\gamma^a(\omega_1)P(a)}{\mu(\omega_1)} = \frac{\gamma^a(\omega_2)P(a)}{\mu(\omega_2)} = P(a|\omega_2).$$

Invariance therefore implies that the frequency with which each action is chosen is equalized across states, which provide the same payoff to all actions. The two states ω_1 and ω_2 may, WLOG, be considered a single state. The "states" that matter for choice are not the states ω but the partition of the state space defined by the payoffs.

"Only payoffs matter" captures this idea that the true economically relevant states are determined by the payoffs to actions. Given a set of actions A, let $\overrightarrow{A} = \{a_1, \ldots, a_n\}$ define an ordered labeling of the actions. Note that this labeling is arbitrary. The expected utility only depends on the payoffs to actions, and the information costs depend only on posterior beliefs. Neither depends on the labeling of actions. It follows permuting $\overrightarrow{A}$ does not affect behavior.

Given a labeling $\overrightarrow{A} = \{a_1, \ldots, a_n\}$, define the payoff profile $\overrightarrow{A}(\omega)$ in state ω as the vector $(a_1(\omega), \ldots, a_n(\omega)) \in \mathbb{R}^n$. We say that two decision problems (μ_1, A^1) and (μ_2, A^2) are **payoff equivalent** if there exist labeling $\overrightarrow{A}_1$ and $\overrightarrow{A}_2$ such that $\mu_1\{\omega|\overrightarrow{A}_1(\omega) = f\} = \mu_2\{\omega|\overrightarrow{A}_2(\omega) = f\}$ for all observed payoff vectors $f \in \mathbb{R}^n$. Payoff-equivalent decision problems assign the probability to each payoff profile. They differ only in the mapping between these payoffs and the states that generate them. The labeling orders the actions so that the ith action in $\overrightarrow{A}_1$ has the same distribution of payoffs as the ith action in $\overrightarrow{A}_2$. Note that given the fixed length of the vector f, two payoff-equivalent decision problems must have the same number of actions. Given this notion of payoff equivalence, we can define what it means for behavior to depend only on payoffs. Consider two payoff-equivalent decision problems (μ_1, A^1) and (μ_2, A^2) and associated labelings

$\overrightarrow{A}_1$ and $\overrightarrow{A}_2$ such that $\mu_1\{\omega \in \Omega | \overrightarrow{A}_1(\omega) = f\} = \mu_2\{\omega \in \Omega | \overrightarrow{A}_2(\omega) = f\}$. Suppose that we have SDSC data for both decision problems. For behavior to depend only on payoffs, it must be the case that the probability of choosing the ith action from $\overrightarrow{A}_1$ must be the same as the probability of choosing the ith action from $\overrightarrow{A}_2$ across states with the identical payoff profiles. This implies that the probability of choosing an action a from $\overrightarrow{A}_1$ must be equal across states with the same profile of payoffs, as we can match any two states in which $\overrightarrow{A}_1(\omega) = f$ to a single state in which $\overrightarrow{A}_1(\omega) = f$.

Axiom 2 (CDL): Only Payoffs Matter: *Given any two payoff-equivalent decision problems* (μ_1, A^1) and (μ_2, A^2) and associated labelings $\overrightarrow{A}_1$ and $\overrightarrow{A}_2$ such that $\mu_1\{\omega \in \Omega | \overrightarrow{A}_1(\omega) = f\} = \mu_2\{\omega \in \Omega | \overrightarrow{A}_2(\omega) = f\}$, $\mathbf{P}^{(\mu_1, A^1)} \in \mathbf{D}^{(\mu_1, A^1)}$ *if and only if there exists* $\mathbf{P}^{(\mu_2, A^2)} \in \mathbf{D}^{(\mu_2, A^2)}$ *such that*

$$\mathbf{P}^{(\mu_2, A^2)}(a_1^{(i)} | \omega_2) = \mathbf{P}^{(\mu_1, A^1)}(a_2^{(i)} | \omega_1),$$

where given $a_1^{(i)} \in \overrightarrow{A}_1$ and $a_2^{(i)} \in \overrightarrow{A}_2$ such that $a_1^{(i)}, a_2^{(i)}$ are each the ith element in their respective labelings and $\omega_1 \in \text{supp } \mu_1$ and $\omega_2 \in \text{supp } \mu_2$ are such that $\overrightarrow{A}_1(\omega_1) = \overrightarrow{A}_2(\omega_2)$.

"Only payoffs matter" is a very powerful behavioral axiom. Theorem 2 establishes that it takes us from a data set with a posterior-separable representation to one with an invariant posterior-separable representation. A data set $\mathbf{D}$ with a posterior-separable representation has an invariant posterior-separable representation if and only if it satisfies the axiom. In the process of establishing this, CDL show that "only payoffs matter" implies behavior is symmetric in the sense that rearranging or renaming the states has no effect on choice. It also implies that the frequency of choice is equalized across all states that share the same payoff profile. The proof is difficult. The proof involves two steps. The first step is to show that "only payoffs matter" is identical to another axiom that we call "invariance under compression." "Invariance under compression" is similar to "only payoffs matter," except that it applies to a fixed set of states and a fixed set of actions. "Only payoffs matter," on the other hand, applies to all payoff-equivalent decision problems. It is then relatively straightforward to show that invariance implies "invariance under compression." Showing that "invariance under compression" implies invariance, however, is a bit more involved.

Theorem 2 (CDL): IPS Representation: *A data set* **D** *with a posterior-separable representation has an invariant posterior-separable representation if and only if it satisfies "only payoffs matter."*

8.12   Shannon Cost Functions and Representations

We say that data set **D** has a Shannon representation if it can be represented by $K^{\kappa S}$ for $\kappa > 0$. CDL's last theorem states that the Shannon cost function is the unique invariant and uniformly posterior-separable cost function. That the Shannon cost function is invariant and uniformly posterior separable is easy to establish. The complication is in showing that these properties define the Shannon cost function. The hard part of the proof is showing that $T_{\text{supp}\,\mu}(\gamma)$ is differentiable in γ, which allows us to use results from information geometry. The key insights are, first, that payoff equivalence allows for the construction of decision problems in which the chosen posteriors are proportionate to the prior and, second, that the Lagrangian Lemma relates the subdifferential of $T_{\text{supp}\,\mu}(\gamma)$ at these chosen posteriors.

Theorem 3 (CDL): Shannon Characterization: *The Shannon cost function is unique in that it is invariant and weakly uniformly posterior separable.*

A direct corollary characterizes those data sets with PS representations that have Shannon representations.

Corollary (CDL): Shannon Representation: *A data set* **D** *with a posterior-separable representation has a Shannon representation if and only if it satisfies both locally invariant posteriors (Axiom 1) and "only payoffs matter" (Axiom 2).*

8.13   Literature

Uniformly posterior-separable models were introduced by Caplin and Dean (2013), while Caplin *et al.* (2017) introduced the broader category of posterior-separable cost functions. Uniformly posterior-separable models have been studied in part because there are settings in which locally invariant posteriors are intuitively reasonable. For example, this behavioral axiom underlies the drift-diffusion model, which has proven popular in psychology (Ratcliff and McKoon, 2008) and economics (Fehr and Rangel, 2011). According to the basic version of this model, an agent gathers information to resolve prior uncertainty over two *ex ante* possible states and acts only when posterior beliefs reach some threshold values. Since the thresholds do not change as the agent learns, the same posteriors are used for any prior that lies between the posteriors. Recent works by Morris and Strack (2019), Hébert and Woodford (2019), and Bloedel and Zhong (2020) provide a related perspective on why uniformly posterior-separable cost functions may be of interest. These model costly information processing with essentially unrestricted flow costs of incremental updating from any given posterior. They link static uniformly posterior-separable models and continuous time models of optimal stopping. This enhances interest both in the broad class and in those functions that capture particular respects in which the Shannon model may be unrealistic in application.

There are also well-motivated cost functions in the literature that are posterior separable but not uniformly posterior separable, such as the log-likelihood ratio cost function given by Pomatto *et al.* (2018). Yet, the economic research in this area remains in its infancy. To date, most of the literature has focused on uniformly posterior-separable costs and failings of payoff equivalence. While there is as yet little direct research demonstrating failings of locally invariant posteriors, we believe that this will change as cost functions become more widely studied. As these violations are noted, posterior-separable cost functions will provide an attractive combination of tractability and flexibility.

Csaba (2021) introduces invariant cost functions that are not posterior separable and that allow for general attentional elasticities of learning with respect to incentives. They can be solved explicitly using a version of the standard Blahut–Arimoto algorithm.

8.14   A Few Reflections

The results above follow about 10 years of research effort. This started with Mark Dean and I sharing theorists' standard skepticism about the Shannon cost function as somewhat arbitrary seeming and having particular properties that clearly do not apply in many situations. The generalization to UPS functions and properties, such as locally invariant posteriors, occupied our early work on this. Jointly with John Leahy, we became very curious about why the Shannon model appeared to give such relatively tractable and qualitatively sensible conclusions about where to focus our attention, as illustrated by Matejka and McKay (2015), Caplin *et al.* (2019), and Mackowiak *et al.* (2021). We were aware of the various remarkable characterizations of Shannon entropy itself, starting with that of Shannon himself. It was natural for us to pursue behavioral properties in light of this being the predominant thrust of our research interest.

One clear feature of the Shannon cost function is its apparent disregard for anything but probabilities over possible action payoffs. We came up with various versions of this property: A look at the working paper version will show that we were then using an axiom called "invariance under compression," which is less all-encompassing than our final axiom of payoff equivalence. That the Shannon model has the property is clear once its solution is internalized.

As all those who struggle forward with this form of logic know, the characterization process involves finding obvious necessary conditions, identifying cases that they do not cover, adding more such conditions, and hoping that this process has an interesting stopping point. We operated in this spirit for a while but increasingly found dependence on the probabilistic structure of payoffs alone to be lurking in the background. At some point, we arrived at the conjecture that adding some such behavioral axiom alone would characterize the Shannon cost function within the UPS class.

Personally, I swung from believing it must be true to believing it to be entirely fantastical. To generate disbelief, consider the following thought experiment. The UPS class is massively large: It allows for the entire universe of convex functions of posteriors, $T(\gamma)$. The Shannon class is a one-parameter family with a linear scaling factor $\kappa > 0$. If costs are of this form, a single observation of attentive choice pins down this parameter.

What the above theorems demonstrate is that, starting from the UPS class, and imposing the seemingly sensible condition that the stochastic pattern in action payoffs is all that matters for learning, one can conclude that this single observation of attentive behavior, by pinning down the value of κ, is enough to predict behavior in any decision problem whatsoever. It seemed to me then, as now, to be a crazy thought. A full five years was spent expecting to find counterexamples. At the end of the process, we know that none will be found. To round off the intellectual journey, I am hugely more respectful of the Shannon model at this point than I was before. Lectures 9–11, which will be spent working with the model, are not wasted.

Part 2

THE SHANNON MODEL OF RATIONAL INATTENTION

Lecture 9

Solving the Shannon Model

9.1 Two New Domains of Choice

As is now standard, a decision problem involves a finite set of states of the world $\omega \in \Omega$ (this finite set is fixed going forward), prior beliefs $\mu \in \Delta(\Omega)$, and a finite set of actions $a \in A$. We specify the DM's known (to them) utility as $u(a, \omega)$ as part of the decision problem since we are not particularly interested in the prize space in the world of optimization. I outline two different approaches to solving the Shannon model. One method is associated with picking an SDSC strategy, the other picking actions and a corresponding Bayes' consistent distribution of posteriors associated with each chosen action. But even the latter is best formulated in a slightly different manner.

9.1.1 *Action probabilities and posteriors*

The first reformulation of the rational inattention problem involves the domain of action choice probabilities and associated posteriors. This rests on first noting a clear feature of optimization in all posterior-separable functions (strictly convex form), which is that it is never optimal to choose a given action at two distinct posteriors: Averaging appropriately across distinct posteriors at which a given action is chosen strictly lowers costs while leaving expected utility unchanged. With this, we can define an alternative version of the strategy space, which is to pick combinations of unconditional action probabilities and associated posteriors averaging back to the prior. Note that I will not do anything interesting with this strategy space, so I do not want to introduce any new notation. I just write such a strategy as a pair $(\vec{P}, \vec{\gamma})$ specifying action probabilities $P(a)$ and posteriors γ^a of chosen actions. The Shannon cost function is then

$$K_\kappa^S(\vec{P}, \vec{\gamma}) \equiv \kappa \left[\sum_{a \in A} P(a) \sum_{\omega \in \Omega} \gamma^a(\omega) \ln \gamma^a(\omega) - \sum_{\omega \in \Omega} \mu(\omega) \ln \mu(\omega) \right],$$

filled in for any impossible states by the limit value of zero:

$$\lim_{x \searrow 0} x \ln x = \lim_{x \searrow 0} \frac{\ln x}{\frac{1}{x}} = \lim_{x \searrow 0} \frac{\frac{1}{x}}{-\frac{1}{x^2}} = \lim_{x \searrow 0} -x = 0.$$

It is also clear that we can associate gross utility with any such strategy as

$$G(\vec{P}, \vec{\gamma}) = \sum_{a \in \text{supp } \vec{P}} \sum_{\omega \in \Omega} P(a) \gamma^a(\omega) u(a, \omega),$$

essentially completing the formulation of the RI problem as that of maximizing the difference $G(\vec{P}, \vec{\gamma}) - K_\kappa^S(\vec{P}, \vec{\gamma})$ across feasible strategies.

9.1.2   *The SDSC approach*

There is an entirely different and at least equally well-studied method of expressing the Shannon cost function based on the "mutual information" between actions and states. With the linear scaling factor $\kappa > 0$,

$$\kappa I(a, \omega) = \kappa \sum_{\omega \in \Omega} \sum_{a \in A} P(a, \omega) \ln \left[\frac{P(a, \omega)}{P(a) \mu(\omega)} \right].$$

To see that this and the posterior-based formulation represent equivalent expressions for the cost, we can ignore the constant $\kappa > 0$ and establish that the posterior-based expression for the expected entropy of the posteriors less that of the prior is precisely the mutual information

$$\sum_{a \in A} P(a) \sum_{\omega \in \Omega} \gamma^a(\omega) \ln \gamma^a(\omega) - \sum_{\omega \in \Omega} \mu(\omega) \ln \mu(\omega)$$

$$= \sum_{\omega \in \Omega} \sum_{a \in A} P(\omega|a) P(a) \ln P(\omega|a) - \sum_{\omega \in \Omega} \left[\sum_{a \in A} P(\omega|a) P(a) \right] \ln \mu(\omega)$$

$$= \sum_{\omega \in \Omega} \sum_{a \in A} P(\omega|a) P(a) \ln \left[\frac{P(\omega|a) P(a)}{P(a) \mu(\omega)} \right]$$

$$= \sum_{\omega \in \Omega} \sum_{a \in A} P(a, \omega) \ln \left[\frac{P(a, \omega)}{P(a) \mu(\omega)} \right] = I(a, \omega).$$

The mutual information $I(a, \omega)$ can also be rewritten in terms of SDSC as

$$\sum_{\omega \in \Omega} \sum_{a \in A} P(a, \omega) \ln \left[\frac{P(a, \omega)}{P(a) \mu(\omega)} \right]$$

$$= \sum_{\omega \in \Omega} \sum_{a \in A} P(a|\omega) \mu(\omega) \ln \left[\frac{P(a|\omega) \mu(\omega)}{P(a) \mu(\omega)} \right]$$

$$= \sum_{\omega \in \Omega} \sum_{a \in A} P(a|\omega) \mu(\omega) \ln P(a|\omega) - \sum_{a \in A} \left[\sum_{\omega \in \Omega} P(a|\omega) \mu(\omega) \right] \ln P(a)$$

$$= \sum_{\omega \in \Omega} \mu(\omega) \left[\sum_{a \in A} P(a|\omega) \ln P(a|\omega) \right] - \sum_{a \in A} P(a) \ln P(a),$$

where $P(a|\omega)$ denotes the probability of choosing action a in state ω.

This suggests another domain of choice on which to specify the rational inattention problem. The domain is the set of all Bayes' consistent SDSC strategies:

$$\mathcal{P}(\mu, A) = \{ P \in \Delta(A \times \Omega) | \Sigma_{a \in A} P(a, \omega) = \mu(\omega) \text{ for all } \omega \in \Omega \}.$$

The costs are then computed as above, noting that conditional probabilities are implied:

$$P(a|\omega) = \frac{P(a, \omega)}{\mu(\omega)}.$$

The value of any such strategy can be computed directly as

$$V(P) = \sum_{(a, \omega) \in A \times \Omega} u(a, \omega) P(a, \omega).$$

Note what a simple optimization problem this is comparatively: For example, the domain is a compact convex set. Given this and the fact that the objective is continuous, existence of an optimum is guaranteed.

9.2 The SDSC-Based Solution

Matejka and McKay (2015) introduce the SDSC-based solution (see also Cover and Thomas, 1999, and Mattsson and Weibull, 2002). The key result is that an optimal policy must satisfy a logit-like condition for all chosen actions. Define

$$z(a, \omega) \equiv \exp\left\{ \frac{u(a, \omega)}{\kappa} \right\},$$

$$Z^P(\omega) \equiv \sum_{b \in A} P(b) z(b, \omega).$$

The first SDSC optimality condition (due to Matejka and McKay, 2015) is that for all chosen actions (those with $P(a) > 0$)

$$P(a|\omega) = \frac{P(a) z(a, \omega)}{Z^P(\omega)}.$$

For necessary and sufficient conditions, we have to go one small step further and think about what actions might be unchosen. We first define the set of actions which are chosen with a positive probability as the *consideration set*:

$$B(P) = \{ a \in A | P(a) > 0 \}.$$

Using this definition, we can provide necessary and sufficient conditions for P to be a solution to the rational inattention problem. This only requires solving for the unconditional probabilities of the options $P(a)$ as the SDSCs $P(a|\omega)$ are completely determined by these unconditional probabilities and the MM conditions above. The proofs illustrate the amazing algebra of the Shannon model. Going forward, I call these the SDSC-based optimality conditions.

Theorem: SDSC Optimality Conditions (Matejka and McKay): *The policy $P \in \mathcal{P}(\mu.A)$ is optimal if and only if*

$$\sum_{\omega \in \Omega} \frac{z(a, \omega) \mu(\omega)}{Z^P(\omega)} \leq 1,$$

for all $a \in A$, with equality if $a \in B(P)$, and if for all such actions,

$$P(a|\omega) = \frac{P(a) z(a, \omega)}{Z^P(\omega)},$$

for all $\omega \in \Omega$.

Do not underestimate the power, simplicity, or intricacy of this solution: Appreciation grows only through worked examples. The exchangeable model of strategic interactions in school matching in Lecture 11 puts its full power on full display. Intuitively, the conditions assert that the optimal policy "twists" the choice probabilities toward states in which the payoffs are high. It can be well described in terms of actions selected being good enough once one bears in mind some notion of how easy or difficult it is to get rewards in a given state. If most actions pay off poorly in a given state, an action can be chosen simply due to its ability to raise normalized utility in that state. The value of this normalized utility in turn is a function of the choice probabilities, so this is something of a balancing act. It is worth keeping this perspective in mind when solving the model.

9.3 The Posterior-Based Solution

The second method of solution to the Shannon model derives from the posterior-based approach. Note that given $P \in \mathcal{P}(\mu, A)$, we can identify a unique corresponding strategy $(\vec{P}, \vec{\gamma})$ by computing the corresponding unconditional choice probabilities and posteriors:

$$P(a) = \sum_{\omega \in \Omega} P(a, \omega) \mu(\omega),$$

$$\gamma^a(\omega) = \frac{P(a, \omega)}{P(a)}.$$

We can rewrite the necessary and sufficient conditions of the SDSC-based optimality conditions in terms of these objects. Going forward, I call these the posterior-based optimality conditions (Caplin and Dean, 2013; Caplin *et al.*, 2019).

Theorem: Posterior-Based Optimality Conditions (Caplin and Dean):
Given decision problem (μ, A), policy $(\vec{P}, \vec{\gamma})$ is optimal if and only if:

(1) **Invariant Likelihood Ratio (ILR) Equations for Chosen Options**:
Given $a, b \in B(\vec{P})$ and $\omega \in \Omega$,

$$\frac{\gamma^a(\omega)}{z(a, \omega)} = \frac{\gamma^b(\omega)}{z(b, \omega)}.$$

(2) **Likelihood Ratio Inequalities for Unchosen Options**: Given $a \in B(\vec{P})$ and $c \in A \backslash B(\vec{P})$,

$$\sum_{\omega \in \Omega} \left[\frac{\gamma^a(\omega)}{z(a, \omega)} \right] z(c, \omega) \leq 1.$$

Caplin and Dean (2013) established this using Lagrangean logic directly. Caplin *et al.* (2019) showed that it follows immediately from the SDSC-based necessary and sufficient conditions that, for $a \in B(\vec{P})$,

$$\frac{\gamma^a(\omega)}{z(a, \omega)} = \frac{\mu(\omega)}{\sum_{b \in A} P(b) z(b, \omega)}.$$

The SDSC necessary and sufficient conditions then become

$$\frac{\gamma^a(\omega)}{z(a, \omega)} = \frac{\gamma^b(\omega)}{z(b, \omega)}$$

when options a and b are chosen and

$$\sum_{\omega \in \Omega} z(c, \omega) \frac{\gamma^a(\omega)}{z(a, \omega)} \leq 1$$

when option a is chosen and option c is not.

An important role of the posterior-based solution is to make clear the locally invariant posteriors property. Optimal strategies for changes in the prior that remain in the convex hull of the posteriors chosen at a different prior are trivial: They reweigh the optimal posteriors to generate the new prior. This is a general feature of posterior-separable models, as noted in Lecture 8. It is very useful in practice. For example, in two-action cases with both actions chosen, there is one and only one pair of optimal posteriors defined by the ILR conditions when options a and b are chosen since if the posteriors are chosen for any strictly positive unconditional probabilities, then we know that they satisfy the required ILR condition:

$$\frac{\gamma^a(\omega)}{z(a, \omega)} = \frac{\gamma^b(\omega)}{z(b, \omega)},$$

which remains satisfied for any other strictly positive unconditional probabilities. This is of value in finding simple methods of solving the model as we will illustrate.

It is of value at times to impose conditions for uniqueness of the optimal strategy. Caplin and Dean (2013) establish that affine independence of the normalized payoff vectors $\{z(a) \in \mathbb{R}^\Omega | a \in A\}$ ensures the uniqueness of the optimal strategy. Affine independence is as follows:

$$\sum_{a \in A} \alpha(a) z(a, \omega) = 0 \implies \beta \equiv 0.$$

Since linear independence implies affine independence, it too is sufficient. Note that this really stems from the concavification picture, and its implication is that no linear segments of the concavified net utility function are touched on their interiors by net utility functions.

9.4 Safe vs. Risky: The SDSC-Based Conditions

A particular model illustrates an interesting interplay of the SDSC-based and the posterior-based solution methods. It involves a safe action (e.g., as when there is an outside option in search). I first derive the SDSC solution. There are two states, $\Omega = \{\omega_1, \omega_2\}$. The prior probability of states is μ_i with $\mu_1 \in (0,1)$. There are two actions: a risky action r and a safe action s, $A = \{r, s\}$. Attention costs are of the Shannon form with parameter $\kappa > 0$. To fully specify, we assume that the risky action has higher utility in state ω_1 and the safe action in state ω_2. We normalize the payoff of the safe action to 0. Hence,

$$u(r, \omega_1) = u_H > 0,$$
$$-u(r, \omega_2) = u_L < 0,$$
$$u(s, \omega_2) = u(s, \omega_2) = 0.$$

We now follow the MM formulas and correspondingly transform utilities:

$$z(r, \omega_1) = z_H \equiv \exp\{u_H / \kappa\} > 1,$$
$$z(r, \omega_2) = z_L \equiv \exp\{u_L / \kappa\} < 1,$$
$$z(s, \omega_1) = z(s, \omega_2) = 1.$$

We first consider solutions in which both actions are chosen. Here, the MM conditions assert that there is a solution with unconditional probability of the risky action interior, $P(r) \in (0,1)$, if and only if

$$\sum_{i=1,2} \frac{z(r,\omega_i)\mu(\omega_i)}{Z^P(\omega_i)} = \sum_{i=1,2} \frac{z(s,\omega_i)\mu(\omega_i)}{Z^P(\omega_i)} = 1,$$

where

$$Z^P(\omega_1) = P(r)z_H + 1 - P(r),$$

$$Z^P(\omega_2) = P(r)z_L + 1 - P(r).$$

This requires equality of the sums for the distinct actions: Note that it simplifies to define this condition by the prior of state 1, which we write without subscript as $\mu_1 = \mu$ and $\mu_2 = 1 - \mu$. Hence, the equality condition is

$$\frac{\mu z_H}{P(r)z_H + 1 - P(r)} + \frac{(1-\mu)z_L}{P(r)z_L + 1 - P(r)} = \frac{\mu}{P(r)z_H + 1 - P(r)}$$

$$+ \frac{(1-\mu)}{P(r)z_L + 1 - P(r)}.$$

Hence,

$$\frac{\mu[z_H - 1]}{P(r)z_H + 1 - P(r)} = \frac{(1-\mu)[1 - z_L]}{P(r)z_L + 1 - P(r)}.$$

We end up with a closed-form solution for $P(r) \in (0,1)$, which simplifies to

$$P(r) = \frac{\mu z_H - 1 + z_L - \mu z_L}{(1 - z_L)(z_H - 1)} = \frac{\mu(z_H - z_L) - (1 - z_L)}{(1 - z_L)(z_H - 1)}.$$

Note that the denominator is always strictly positive. So, for $P(r) > 0$, we need to check that the numerator is also strictly positive:

$$\mu > \frac{1 - z_L}{z_H - z_L}.$$

This is not universal. In effect, we are pursuing guess and verify, and the verification fails if this condition fails. Likewise, for $P(r) < 1$, we need that

$$\mu < \frac{z_H(1 - z_L)}{z_H - z_L}.$$

We now need to solve the full model starting with priors for which both actions are chosen. So, we pick $\mu \in \left(\frac{1 - z_L}{z_H - z_L}, \frac{z_H(1 - z_L)}{z_H - z_L} \right)$ and note that by the

SDSC conditions, the corresponding conditional probabilities are

$$P(r|\omega_1) = \frac{P(r)z_H}{P(r)(z_H - 1) + 1},$$

$$P(s|\omega_1) = \frac{1 - P(r)}{P(r)(z_H - 1) + 1},$$

$$P(r|\omega_2) = \frac{P(r)z_L}{P(r)(z_L - 1) + 1},$$

$$P(s|\omega_2) = \frac{1 - P(r)}{P(r)(z_L - 1) + 1}.$$

Given the closed-form solutions for $P(r)$, we arrive at the formulae for the conditional probabilities. For example,

$$P(r|\omega_1) = \frac{[\mu(z_H - z_L) - (1 - z_L)]z_H}{\mu(z_H - z_L)(z_H - 1)}.$$

Multiplying by the prior of each state gives us the full optimal strategy $P(a, \omega)$.

For priors outside this range, we know that there is no solution with both chosen with a strictly positive probability. Again, we can use the necessary and sufficient conditions to guess and verify. We first look for solutions corresponding to the corner in which $P(r) = 0$. In this case, note that $Z^P(\omega) = z(s, w)$ so that

$$\sum_{i=1,2} \frac{z(s, \omega_i)\mu(\omega_i)}{Z^P(\omega_i)} = \sum_{i=1,2} \mu(\omega_i) = 1.$$

The condition for optimality is that the corresponding sum for action r is no higher than 1:

$$\sum_{i=1,2} \frac{z(r, \omega_i)\mu(\omega_i)}{z(s, \omega_i)} = z_H\mu + z_L[1 - \mu] \le 1,$$

or equivalently,

$$\mu \le \frac{1 - z_L}{z_H - z_L}.$$

This is reasonable. If state ω_1 is unlikely, the risky action may not be worth picking.

To close, we look for the converse solution in which $P(r) = 1$. Again, the satisfaction of the necessary and sufficient conditions comes down entirely to ensuring that the key sum for the unchosen action is no higher than 1:

$$\sum_{i=1,2} \frac{z(s, \omega_i)\mu(\omega_i)}{z(r, \omega_i)} = \frac{\mu(\omega_1)}{z_H} + \frac{1 - \mu(\omega_1)}{z_L} \leq 1,$$

or equivalently,

$$\mu z_L + (1 - \mu)z_H \leq z_H z_L,$$

or

$$\mu \geq \frac{z_H - z_H z_L}{z_H - z_L} = \frac{z_H(1 - z_L)}{z_H - z_L}.$$

Again, this seems reasonable: If state ω_1 is likely enough, the safe action may not be chosen at all.

9.5   Safe vs. Risky: The Posterior-Based Approach

In the SDSC solution, the impact of the prior on the optimal strategy looks intricate. Yet, this is not so as revealed by the Lagrangean geometry in the previous lecture and the implied property of locally invariant posteriors. We consider a simple case with $z_H = 2$ and $z_L = \frac{1}{2}$ so that

$$P(r) = \frac{\frac{3}{2}\mu - \frac{1}{2}}{\frac{1}{2}} = 3\mu - 1.$$

To see the implied structure, consider any interior prior in which the optimal strategy involves picking both actions. We can now compute the corresponding posteriors of state ω_1 associated with picking the risky and safe actions, γ^r and γ^s, respectively, as

$$\gamma^r = \frac{P(r, \omega_1)}{P(r)} = \frac{P(r|\omega_1)\mu}{P(r)},$$

$$\gamma^s = \frac{P(s|\omega_1)\mu}{P(s)}.$$

Algebraically, with $z_H = 2$ and $z_L = \frac{1}{2}$, the SDSC-based optimality conditions give

$$P(r|\omega_1) = \frac{P(r)z(r,\omega_1)}{P(r)z(r,\omega_1) + (1 - P(r))z(s,\omega_1)} = \frac{2P(r)}{1 + P(r)}.$$

Hence,

$$\gamma^r = \frac{2\mu}{1 + P(r)} = \frac{2}{3}.$$

Likewise,

$$\gamma^s = \frac{P(s|\omega_1)\mu}{P(s)} = \frac{\mu}{1 + P(r)} = \frac{1}{3}.$$

The form of invariance in the posteriors associated with chosen actions as the prior changes is precisely what LIP implies.

I now give two examples of solution strategies based on knowledge that LIP holds. The first involves solving for the prior that results in both actions being chosen with equal probability. Note that if ever actions define a consideration set, then there exists a prior such that these actions are taken with any unconditional probabilities: This is clear from the convex geometry of the concavified net utility function in the posterior-separable model. Equiprobable is particularly simple. One then finds the corresponding posteriors and hence the prior that generates this solution. One can then solve for all priors in the convex hull of the identified posteriors.

In our simple case with $z_H = 2$ and $z_L = \frac{1}{2}$, we look for the posteriors and the prior that results in optimally choosing $\bar{P}(r) = \bar{P}(s) = 0.5$. By the necessary and sufficient conditions in SDSC strategies, this requires

$$\bar{P}(r|\omega_1) = \frac{0.5z(r,\omega_1)}{0.5z(r,\omega_1) + 0.5z(s,\omega_1)} = \frac{2}{3} = \frac{0.5z(s,\omega_2)}{0.5z(r,\omega_2) + 0.5z(s,\omega_2)} = \bar{P}(s|\omega_2),$$

$$\bar{P}(r|\omega_2) = \frac{0.5z(r,\omega_2)}{0.5z(r,\omega_2) + 0.5z(s,\omega_2)} = \frac{1}{3} = \frac{0.5z(s,\omega_1)}{0.5z(r,\omega_1) + 0.5z(s,\omega_1)} = \bar{P}(s|\omega_1).$$

To solve for the prior of state ω_1 that generates these choices, $\bar{\mu}$, it must validate $\bar{P}(r) = 0.5$:

$$\bar{\mu}\bar{P}(r|1) + (1 - \bar{\mu})\bar{P}(r|2) = \frac{1}{2}.$$

Hence,

$$\frac{2}{3}\bar{\mu} + \frac{1}{3}(1-\bar{\mu}) = \frac{1}{2} \iff \bar{\mu} = 0.5.$$

Outside this range has already been solved. This can obviously be repeated for general values of z_H, z_L.

LIP and the SDSC solution combine to produce a particularly simple method of solving all two-action problems as we now illustrate. It begins by specifying the conditions for choosing only one of the actions. In the general case, this can be derived from either approach directly. For the safe only to be chosen, it is necessary and sufficient that

$$\mu \leq \frac{1 - z_L}{z_H - z_L}.$$

For the risky only to be chosen, it is necessary and sufficient that

$$\mu \geq \frac{z_H - z_H z_L}{z_H - z_L} = \frac{z_H(1 - z_L)}{z_H - z_L}.$$

Now, the posterior-separable geometry suggests that the full solution for priors between these upper and lower bounds involves correspondingly mixing the two boundary posteriors:

$$\bar{\gamma}^r = 2\bar{P}(r, \omega_1) = \frac{z_H(1 - z_L)}{(z_H - z_L)},$$

$$\bar{\gamma}^s = 2\bar{P}(s, \omega_1) = \frac{1 - z_L}{(z_H - z_L)}$$

so that for all $\mu \in \left(\frac{1-z_L}{z_H-z_L}, \frac{z_H-z_H z_L}{z_H-z_L}\right)$, the unconditional probability $P(r)$ mixes these to satisfy Bayesian consistency, as defined immediately above. The easiest method of solving is then to identify the unique prior $\mu_{P(r)} \in \left(\frac{1-z_L}{z_H-z_L}, \frac{z_H(1-z_L)}{z_H-z_L}\right)$ that makes the risky action optimally chosen with any interior probability $P(r) \in (0,1)$. This is, transparently,

$$\mu_{P(r)} = \frac{[1 + P(r)(z_H - 1)(1 - z_L)]}{z_H - z_L}.$$

This can be inverted to give the unconditional probability for any given prior $\mu \in \left(\frac{1-z_L}{z_H-z_L}, \frac{z_H(1-z_L)}{z_H-z_L}\right)$ precisely as was derived in the SDSC version:

$$P(r) = \frac{\mu(z_H - z_L) - (1 - z_L)}{(1 - z_L)(z_H - 1)}.$$

9.6 Choosing Among Options with IID Priors

I show now in an i.i.d case that the results are remarkably clean. In fact, I will show in Lecture 11 that a far richer case is correspondingly simple, but introducing this now serves to clarify the nature of the state space and the power of the SDSC characterization. Note that with the Shannon model, payoff sufficiency implies that one can specify states of the world by the distribution of payoffs. I consider the simplest case of two possible prizes $V = \{u_H, u_L\}$, with the high value being a good option, $u_H > u_L = 0$. The prior specifies the probability $p \in (0,1)$ that utility is high for each option.

As always, solving the Shannon model starts with normalization:

$$z_H = \exp^{\left(\frac{u_H}{\kappa}\right)} > 1 = \exp^{\left(\frac{u_L}{\kappa}\right)}.$$

Note that there is a simple way of summarizing the state space in this two-payoff world as comprising the indices of the alternatives $H \subset \{1,\ldots,M\}$ of actions with high payoffs:

$$z(a_m, H) = \begin{cases} z_H & \text{if } m \in H, \\ 1 & \text{if } m \notin H. \end{cases}$$

It is natural to conjecture that the symmetry of the prior will give rise to uniform unconditional probabilities of choosing each option. In fact, we will prove that there is always a unique optimal strategy of that nature in a far larger class of symmetric decision problems in Lecture 11. For now, we pursue just such an optimal strategy. Note that with uniformity, we can work out the corresponding denominators in all SDSC conditions as the unconditional average z values:

$$\overline{Z}(H) = \sum_m \frac{z(a_m, H)}{M} = \frac{z_H |H| + (M - |H|)}{M} = \frac{M + (z_H - 1)|H|}{M}.$$

From this, we solve for conditionals from the MM conditions:

$$P(a_m | H) = \begin{cases} \frac{z_H}{M\overline{Z}(H)} = \frac{z_H}{M + (z_H - 1)|H|} & \text{if } m \in H, \\ \frac{1}{M\overline{Z}(H)} = \frac{1}{M + (z_H - 1)|H|} & \text{if } m \notin H. \end{cases}$$

All we need are the unconditional state probabilities, and we are done. Given the binomial, these are immediate:

$$\mu(H) = p^{|H|}(1 - p)^{M - |H|},$$

and the unconditional probabilities are

$$P(a_m, H) = \begin{cases} \frac{z_H p^{|H|}(1-p)^{M-|H|}}{M + (z_H - 1)|H|} & \text{for } m \in H, \\ \frac{p^{|H|}(1-p)^{M-|H|}}{M + (z_H - 1)|H|} & \text{if } m \notin H. \end{cases}$$

I work this example forward in low dimensions both to clarify what it implies and to show how formulae simplify due to the mysterious simplicity of Shannon entropy. I show, in particular, how relevant economic characterizations of mistakes and their implications are identified. The notation in the example is strictly local.

With $M = 2$, there are four states, $H \in \{\{1,2\}, \{1\}, \{2\}, \emptyset\}$, with the prior:

$$\mu(\{1,2\}) = p^2,$$
$$\mu(\{1\}) = \mu(\{2\}) = p(1 - p),$$
$$\mu(\emptyset) = (1 - p)^2.$$

For $\overline{Z}(H)$, we get

$$\overline{Z}(\{1,2\}) = \frac{2z_H}{2} = z_H,$$
$$\overline{Z}(\{1\}) = \overline{Z}(\{2\}) = \frac{z_H + 1}{2},$$
$$\overline{Z}(\emptyset) = \frac{2}{2} = 1.$$

We can then derive the conditional probabilities from the SDSC-based optimality conditions as

$$P(a_1|\{1,2\}) = \frac{\frac{z_H}{2}}{z_H} = \frac{1}{2} = P(a_2|\{1,2\}),$$

$$P(a_1|\{1\}) = \frac{\frac{z_H}{2}}{\frac{z_H+1}{2}} = \frac{z_H}{z_H+1} = P(a_2|\{2\}),$$

$$P(a_1|\{2\}) = \frac{\frac{1}{2}}{\frac{z_H+1}{2}} = \frac{1}{z_H+1} = P(a_2|\{1\}),$$

$$P(a_1|\emptyset) = \frac{\frac{1}{2}}{1} = \frac{1}{2} = P(a_2|\emptyset).$$

Hence, the full SDSC solution is

$$P(a_1,\{1,2\}) = P(a_1|\{1,2\})\mu(\{1,2\}) = \frac{p^2}{2} = P(a_2,\{1,2\}),$$

$$P(a_1,\{1\}) = P(a_1|\{1\})\mu(\{1\}) = \frac{p(1-p)z_H}{z_H+1} = P(a_2,\{2\}),$$

$$P(a_1,\{2\}) = P(a_1|\{2\})\mu(\{2\}) = \frac{p(1-p)}{z_H+1} = P(a_2,\{1\}),$$

$$P(a_1,\emptyset) = P(a_1|\emptyset)\mu(\emptyset) = \frac{(1-p)^2}{2} = P(a_2,\emptyset).$$

The real power of this simple solution is that it allows us to summarize how well the DM does in closed form. The posteriors over states $\gamma^m(H)$ for actions a_m are

$$\gamma^1(\{1,2\}) = \frac{P(a_1,\{1,2\})}{P(a_1)} = p^2 = \gamma^2(\{1,2\}),$$

$$\gamma^1(\{1\}) = \frac{P(a_1,\{1\})}{P(a_1)} = \frac{2p(1-p)z_H}{z_H+1} = \gamma^2(\{2\}),$$

$$\gamma^1(\{2\}) = \frac{P(a_1,\{2\})}{P(a_1)} = \frac{2p(1-p)}{z_H+1} = \gamma^2(\{1\}),$$

$$\gamma^1(\emptyset) = \frac{P(a_1,\emptyset)}{P(a_1)} = (1-p)^2 = \gamma^2(\emptyset).$$

The probability of a high payoff (win or W) in each state in the optimal strategy $W(H)$, with $H = \{1,2\}$, can be computed as

$$W(\{1,2\}) = P(a_1|\{1,2\}) + P(a_2|\{1,2\}) = 1.$$

With $H = \{1\}$ or $H = \{2\}$ it is

$$W(\{1\}) = P(a_1|\{1\}) = \frac{z_H}{z_H + 1} = P(a_2|\{2\}) = W(\{2\}).$$

Obviously,

$$W(\emptyset) = 0.$$

The unconditional probability of winning is found by reweighting these conditionals with prior to arrive at

$$E[W] = p^2 + \frac{2z_H p(1-p)}{z_H + 1}.$$

Gross expected utility is, therefore,

$$E[U] = \left[p^2 + \frac{2z_H p(1-p)}{z_H + 1} \right] u_H$$

$$= \left[p^2 + \frac{2z_H p(1-p)}{z_H + 1} \right] \kappa \ln z_H$$

since $z_H = \exp\{\frac{u_H}{\kappa}\}$.

Perhaps, the most telling is that we can produce closed-form expressions for the entropy costs from the SDSC-based expression for $\left[\frac{K^s(\mu, P)}{\kappa} \right]$. Specializing to two-equiprobable choices and using general notation for the prior, we get

$$\sum_H \mu(H) \left[\sum_{a_m \in A} P(a_m|H) \ln P(a_m|H) \right] - \sum_{a_m \in A} P(a_m) \ln P(a_m).$$

In our two-action symmetric case, we get

$$\sum_{a_m \in A} P(a_m) \ln P(a_m) = \ln \frac{1}{2}.$$

For conditional probabilities, we have

$$P(a_1|\{1,2\}) = P(a_2|\{1,2\}) = P(a_1|\emptyset) = P(a_2|\emptyset) = \frac{1}{2},$$

$$P(a_1|\{1\}) = P(a_2|\{2\}) = \frac{z_H}{z_H + 1},$$

$$P(a_1|\{2\}) = P(a_2|\{1\}) = \frac{1}{z_H + 1}.$$

Hence,

$$\frac{K^s(\mu, P)}{\kappa} = 2\sum_H \mu(H)P(a_1|H)\ln P(a_1|H) - \ln\frac{1}{2},$$

where

$$\sum_H \mu(H)P(a_1|H)\ln P(a_1|H).$$

This can be evaluated as

$$p(1-p)\left[\frac{z_H}{z_H+1}\ln\frac{z_H}{z_H+1} + \frac{1}{z_H+1}\ln\frac{1}{z_H+1}\right]$$

$$+ \left[p^2 + (1-p)^2\right]\frac{1}{2}\ln\frac{1}{2}.$$

Hence,

$$\frac{K^s(\mu, P)}{\kappa} = 2p(1-p)\left[\frac{z_H}{z_H+1}\ln\frac{z_H}{z_H+1} + \frac{1}{z_H+1}\ln\frac{1}{z_H+1}\right]$$

$$+ \ln\frac{1}{2}\left[p^2 + (1-p)^2 - 1\right]$$

$$= 2p(1-p)\left[\frac{z_H}{z_H+1}\ln\frac{z_H}{z_H+1} + \frac{1}{z_H+1}\ln\frac{1}{z_H+1} - \ln\frac{1}{2}\right]$$

$$= 2p(1-p)\left[\frac{z_H}{z_H+1}\ln\frac{2z_H}{z_H+1} + \frac{1}{z_H+1}\ln\frac{2}{z_H+1}\right]$$

$$= 2p(1-p)\left[\frac{z_H}{z_H+1}\ln z_H + \ln\frac{2}{z_H+1}\right].$$

The net utility is correspondingly simple:

$$N(2|p,z_H) \equiv G(2|p,z_H) - K^s(\mu, P)$$

$$= \left[p^2 + \frac{2z_H p(1-p)}{z_H+1}\right]\kappa\ln z_H$$

$$- 2\kappa p(1-p)\left[\frac{z_H}{z_H+1}\ln z_H + \ln\frac{2}{z_H+1}\right]$$

$$= \kappa\left[p^2\ln z_H - 2\kappa p(1-p)\ln\frac{2}{z_H+1}\right].$$

To illustrate, with $p = 0.5$, $z_H = 2$, and $\kappa = 1$, in which case we get the "winning" probabilities $W(\{1,2\}) = 1$, $W(\emptyset) = 0$, and

$$W(\{1\}) = P(a_1 | \{1\}) = \frac{2}{3} = P(a_2 | \{2\}) = W(\{2\}).$$

Hence, the overall probability of getting a good option is

$$E[W] = p^2 + \frac{2z_H p(1-p)}{z_H + 1}$$

$$= p^2 + \frac{4p(1-p)}{3} = \frac{1}{4} + \frac{1}{3} = \frac{7}{12}.$$

Gross expected utility is, therefore,

$$E[U] = \left[p^2 + \frac{2z_H p(1-p)}{z_H + 1} \right] \kappa \ln z_H$$

$$= \frac{7}{12} \ln 2 \approx 0.404335855.$$

The costs are

$$K^s(\mu, P) = 2p(1-p) \left[\frac{z_H}{z_H + 1} \ln z_H + \ln \frac{2}{z_H + 1} \right]$$

$$= \frac{1}{2} \left[\frac{2}{3} \ln 2 + \ln \frac{2}{3} \right] = \frac{1}{2} \left[\frac{2}{3} \left[\ln 2 + \ln \frac{2}{3} \right] + \frac{1}{3} \ln \frac{2}{3} \right]$$

$$= \frac{1}{2} \left[\frac{2}{3} \ln \frac{4}{3} + \frac{1}{3} \ln \frac{2}{3} \right] \approx 0.0283.$$

Hence,

$$N = \frac{7}{12} \ln 2 - 0.0283 \approx 0.376.$$

Confirming indirectly,

$$N = \kappa \ln z_H p^2 - 2\kappa p(1-p) \ln \frac{2}{z_H + 1}$$

$$= \frac{\ln 2}{4} - \frac{1}{2} \ln \frac{2}{3} \approx 0.376.$$

What happens as we expand the number of options with $p = 0.5$, $z_H = 2$, and $\kappa = 1$? For conditional probabilities, the substitution in the corresponding formulae with three options yields

$$P(a_m | \{1,2,3\}) = P(a_m | \emptyset) = \frac{1}{3} \text{ for } m = 1,2,3,$$

$$P(a_{1,2} | \{1,2\}) = P(a_{1,3} | \{1\}) = P(a_{2,3} | \{2\}) = \frac{2}{5},$$

$$P(a_3 | \{1,2\}) = P(a_2 | \{1\}) = P(a_1 | \{2\}) = \frac{1}{5},$$

$$P(a_1 | \{1\}) = P(a_2 | \{2\}) = P(a_3 | \{3\}) = \frac{1}{2},$$

$$P(a_{2,3} | \{1\}) = P(a_{1,3} | \{2\}) = P(a_{1,2} | \{3\}) = \frac{1}{4}.$$

One can compute the winning probability as

$$E[W] = p^3 + \frac{3 * 4p^2(1-p)}{5} + \frac{3 * p(1-p)^2}{2}.$$

Hence for $p = \frac{1}{2}$,

$$E[W] = \frac{1}{8} + \frac{12}{40} + \frac{3}{16}$$

$$= \frac{10 + 24 + 15}{80} = \frac{49}{80}.$$

In this three good-case, equiprobable-case entropy, cost is

$$K^s(\mu, P) = \frac{1}{8} \left[\sum_{\omega \in \Omega} \sum_{a_m \in A} P(a_m | \omega) \ln P(a_m | \omega) \right] - \ln \frac{1}{3}.$$

By symmetry, one can just work with action a_m:

$$\sum_{\omega \in \Omega} P(a_m | \omega) \ln P(a_m | \omega) = \frac{2}{3} \ln \frac{1}{3} + \frac{4}{5} \ln \frac{2}{5} + \frac{1}{5} \ln \frac{1}{5} + \frac{1}{2} \ln \frac{1}{2} + \frac{1}{2} \ln \frac{1}{4}.$$

Hence,

$$K^s(\mu, P) = \frac{3}{8} \left[\frac{2}{3} \ln \frac{1}{3} + \frac{4}{5} \ln \frac{2}{5} + \frac{1}{5} \ln \frac{1}{5} + \frac{1}{2} \ln \frac{1}{2} + \frac{1}{2} \ln \frac{1}{4} \right] - \ln \frac{1}{3}$$

$$= \frac{3}{8} \left[\frac{4}{5} \ln \frac{2}{5} + \frac{1}{5} \ln \frac{1}{5} + \frac{1}{2} \ln \frac{1}{2} + \frac{1}{2} \ln \frac{1}{4} \right] + \frac{3}{4} \ln 3$$

$$= \frac{3}{8} \left[\frac{4}{5} \ln \frac{6}{5} + \frac{1}{5} \ln \frac{3}{5} + \frac{1}{2} \ln \frac{3}{2} + \frac{1}{2} \ln \frac{3}{4} \right] \approx 0.0385.$$

Comparing the cases 2 and 3 options, note that the probability of getting a good prize increases:

$$\frac{49}{80} = \frac{147}{240} > \frac{140}{240} = \frac{7}{12}.$$

The net utilities are correspondingly ordered:

$$\frac{49}{80} \ln 2 - 0.0385 \approx 0.386,$$

$$\frac{7}{12} \ln 2 - 0.0283 \approx 0.376.$$

What happens as one further expands the number of available options? One valuable observation in this i.i.d case is that the prior over the proportion of good options converges in the limit to match the probability that each option is good. In the case with $p = 0.5$, in the limit, 50% of the available options are good almost always. Upon more algebraic manipulation, one can derive very simple limit formulae for all market statistics in a quite general case. Rather than display that now, I wait until Lecture 11 before digging more into the magical properties of the Shannon model with symmetry. The key observations therein are that the simplicity extends to a far larger class than the i.i.d. class, that it applies to a large class of symmetric decision problems, and that these decision problems can be embedded in strategic settings in which there are significant asymmetries.

9.7 Rationally Inattentive Nash Equilibrium

This section presents a closing note on the emerging literature on equilibria in games where multiple agents face costs of information acquisition. Spurlino (2022) provides an approach to solving for equilibria that takes advantage of the SDSC-based optimality conditions: State-dependent action utilities yield best responses in SDSC, and thus, there is a direct map from one agent's SDSC strategy to their opponent's SDSC strategy. An equilibrium, then, is a fixed point in this mapping. One issue for standard approaches to existence is that there is often a trivial no learning equilibria in which no learning occurs and all agents choose some action with certainty. The problem in such settings is to determine the non-trivial equilibrium. Spurlino reformulates the fixed-point problem to a more tractable problem of searching for a fixed point in a mapping from the unconditional choice probabilities into the unconditional choice probabilities. As an illustration, suppose there are only two actions, accept or reject. The SDSC optimality conditions of Matejka and McKay translate the unconditional choice probabilities into optimal SDSC strategies. This makes it possible to express the optimal SDSC of either agent based on the unconditional entry probabilities of all agents. These conditional probabilities, weighted by priors, then yield a new unconditional choice probability for that agent. Repeating the exercise for both agents yields a system that maps the unconditional choice probabilities into unconditional choice probabilities and is numerically and graphically simple to solve for an interior fixed point in which entry is possible but not certain.

I will return to strategic matters in the next two lectures. Lecture 11 focuses on matching markets. In that setting, an entirely different strategy works. Again, it takes strong advantage of the SDSC-based optimality conditions of Matejka and McKay (2015). The idea in that case is to generalize the simplicity of the i.i.d. structure and identify conditions under which symmetric strategies define the Nash equilibria. The form of the symmetry is quite particular to the rational inattention model, as will be seen.

Lecture 10

Optimal Consideration Sets and the Invariant Likelihood Ratio Hyperplanes

Caplin *et al.* (2019) focus on the fact that many options are unchosen. In this section, I analyze this in a few special cases and introduce the ILR hyperplanes, a general-purpose analytic structure for mapping from prior beliefs in a given decision problem to the structure of the consideration set and optimal unconditional choice probabilities. There is much more to be done with these hyperplanes, both computationally and in terms of economic analysis. A few openings and pointers are provided. I open by providing a very standard model of type I and type II errors that illustrates the value of understanding the conditions under which inattentive choice is optimal. I then present two examples from CDL, in both of which the key issue is to identify the optimal consideration set. The ILR hyperplanes are then introduced and discussed. The lecture closes by pointing toward dynamics, in particular to the work of Miao and Xing (2020), which is posterior based and applies to the broad class of uniformly posterior-separable cost functions.

10.1 Type I and Type II Errors

Consider now the standard (e.g., Kamenica–Gentzkow) trial model with two states, innocent and guilty, and two verdicts, acquit and convict:

$$\Omega = \{G, I\} \text{ and } V = \{C, A\}.$$

An error of type 1 occurs when an innocent party is found guilty and of type 2 when a guilty party is found innocent. There are four utility levels:

$$u(C,I) = -L_1,$$

$$u(A,G) = -L_2,$$

$$u(C,G) = u(A,I) = 0,$$

where $L_1 > 0$ is the loss from a type 1 error and $L_2 > 0$ is the loss from a type 2 error. The cost function for learning is of the RI of Shannon form with linear scaling factor $\kappa > 0$. Hence, we know that the solution is based on the exponential transform of payoffs, and

$$z(C,I) = \exp\left\{\frac{-L_1}{\kappa}\right\} \equiv z_1 \in (0,1),$$

$$z(A,G) = \exp\left\{\frac{-L_2}{\kappa}\right\} \equiv z_2 \in (0,1),$$

$$z(C,G) = z(A,I) = e^0 = 1.$$

We now apply the simplest solution method above based on the extreme behaviors of convict for sure and acquit for sure. In this example, we specify priors and posteriors in terms of how likely is the state of guilty so that the prior is $\overline{\mu}_G$. Let's now work out the conditions for it to be optimal to acquit for sure, $P(A) = 1$. To reiterate the general conditions,

$$\sum_{\omega \in \Omega} \frac{z(a,\omega)\mu(\omega)}{Z^P(\omega)} \leq 1,$$

for all $a \in A$, with equality if $a \in B(P)$. For the corner solution corresponding to $P(A) = 1$, note that $Z^P(\omega) = z(A,\omega)$ so that, as usual, the condition

$$\sum_{\omega = I,G} \frac{z(A,\omega)\mu(\omega)}{Z^P(\omega)} = 1$$

is trivially satisfied. Therefore, all that needs to be checked is the single inequality that the corresponding sum for action C of conviction is no higher than 1:

$$\frac{\mu(G)z(C,G)}{z(A,G)} + \frac{(1-\mu(G))z(C,I)}{z(A,I)} = \frac{\mu(G)}{z_2} + (1-\mu(G))z_1 \leq 1,$$

or equivalently,

$$\mu(G) \leq \frac{z_2 - z_1 z_2}{1 - z_1 z_2} \equiv m.$$

Note that the RHS, which we denote as m, is strictly between zero and one, given that $z_1, z_2 \in (0,1)$, and therefore, there are indeed priors of guilt low enough to acquit for sure. This is also pretty sensible in comparative static terms since it is decreasing in z_1: A smaller loss for false conviction pushes z_1 up to 1 and makes the numerator shrink to zero for any fixed z_2, making it optimal to acquit only for very low prior probabilities of guilt. Vice versa, this threshold is increasing in z_2: A smaller loss from acquitting when guilty pushes z_2 up to 1 and makes the numerator approach the denominator for any fixed z_1, making it optimal to acquit for sure unless there is a very high probability of guilt.

We now look for the converse solution in which it is optimal to convict for sure, $P(C) = 1$. As we have seen, this comes down to checking a single inequality related to the value of the unchosen action not being excessive:

$$\frac{\mu(G)z(A,G)}{z(C,G)} + \frac{(1-\mu(G))z(A,I)}{z(C,I)} = \mu(G)z_2 + \frac{1-\mu(G)}{z_1} \leq 1,$$

or equivalently,

$$\mu(G) \geq \frac{1-z_1}{1-z_1 z_2} \equiv M.$$

Again, the RHS, which we denote as M, is strictly between zero and one, given that $z_1, z_2 \in (0,1)$, and therefore, there are indeed priors of guilt high enough to convict for sure. Note also that $M > m$ since they only differ in the numerator in which M is strictly large.

Note that by the ILR conditions, we can use corner solutions to solve the model for all priors. For $\mu_G \in (m,M)$, define the unconditional probability of conviction $\hat{P}(C)$ to mix the invariant posteriors over guilt $\overline{P}(G|A) = m$

and $\overline{P}(G|C) = M$ to satisfy Bayesian consistency:

$$\mu_G = \overline{P}(G|C)\hat{P}(C) + \overline{P}(G|A)\left[1 - \hat{P}(C)\right]$$
$$= M\hat{P}(C) + m\left[1 - \hat{P}(C)\right].$$

Hence,

$$\hat{P}(C) = \frac{\mu_G - m}{M - m},$$
$$\hat{P}(A) = \frac{M - \mu_G}{M - m}.$$

Of course, this produces the probabilities of type 1 (convicting the innocent) and type 2 (acquitting the guilty) errors in case learning, in fact, to occur:

$$E_1 = P(I,C) = \frac{(1-M)(\mu_G - m)}{M - m}$$

$$= \left[\frac{z_1(1-z_2)}{1 - z_1 z_2}\right] \frac{(\mu_G - m)}{\left[\frac{1-z_1}{1-z_1 z_2} - \frac{z_2(1-z_1)}{1-z_1 z_2}\right]}$$

$$= \left[\frac{z_1(1-z_2)}{1 - z_1 - z_2(1-z_1)}\right](\mu_G - m)$$

$$= \frac{z_1}{1 - z_1}(\mu_G - m).$$

Likewise, the optimal probability E_2 for type II errors is

$$E_2 = P(G,A) = \frac{m(M - \mu_G)}{M - m}$$

$$= \frac{\frac{z_2(1-z_1)}{1-z_1 z_2}(M - \mu_G)}{\left[\frac{1-z_1}{1-z_1 z_2} - \frac{z_2(1-z_1)}{1-z_1 z_2}\right]}$$

$$= \frac{z_2(1-z_1)(M - \mu_G)}{(1-z_1)(1-z_2)}$$

$$= \frac{z_2}{1 - z_2}(M - \mu_G).$$

10.2 Independent Valuations

CDL consider settings they call independent. The consumer is faced with the choice of M possible actions: $A = \{a_1, \ldots, a_M\}$. Let $X \subset \mathbb{R}$ be the (finite) set of possible utility levels for all actions. We define the state space as $\Omega = X^M$. A typical state is therefore a vector of realized utilities for each possible action:

$$\omega = \begin{pmatrix} \omega_1 \\ \omega_2 \\ \vdots \\ \omega_M \end{pmatrix},$$

where $\omega_i \in X$, for all $a_i \in A$. The utility of a state/action pair is then given by

$$u(a_i, \omega) = \omega_i.$$

The assumption of independence implies that there exist probability distributions $\mu_1, \ldots, \mu_M \in \Delta(X)$ such that, for every $\omega \in \Omega$,

$$\mu(\omega) = \Pi_{i=1}^M \mu_i(\omega_i).$$

The optimal approach to information acquisition in such an independent consumption problem includes a cutoff strategy determining a consideration set of alternatives about which the consumer will learn and from which they will make their eventual choice. CDL establish that the cutoff is in terms of the expectation of the normalized utilities $z(a, \omega) \equiv \exp(u(a, \omega)/\kappa)$ evaluated at prior beliefs. Technically, there exists $c \in \mathbb{R}$ such that, for any $a_i \in A$, $P(a_i) > 0$ if and only if

$$Ez(a_i, \omega) = \sum_{\omega \in \Omega} z(a_i, \omega)\mu(\omega) = \sum_{\omega \in \Omega} \exp(\omega_i/\kappa)\mu_i(\omega_i) > c$$

and $P(a_i) = 0$ otherwise.

This result can be applied to study links between risk aversion and portfolio choice. CDL consider two actions with the same *ex ante* expected payoffs, a safe action that pays its expected value in every state and a risky one whose payoff varies across states. They use this to show that the risky action will be more valuable since the DM can tailor their information strategy in such a way that they take this action in high-valuation states and avoid this action in low-valuation states. This explains the convex transformation of the payoffs: Variance is valuable in a learning environment. Recall that payoffs are in utility terms, so risk aversion does not play a role. This also explains the role of information cost. As κ rises, information becomes more costly so that the ability to tailor choice to the state diminishes. As κ approaches infinity, $Ez(a_i, \omega)/Ez(a_j, \omega)$ approaches $Eu(a_i, \omega)/Eu(a_j, \omega)$, and the choice is based on *ex ante* expected payoffs. As κ approaches zero, information becomes free, and the best action is chosen in each state. An action remains unchosen only if it is not maximal in any state. In this case, $Ez(a_i, \omega)/Ez(a_j, \omega)$ approaches infinity for all j if and only if a_i is chosen.

In the independent consumption problem, the ordering of actions is far from obvious without applying the necessary and sufficient conditions. CDL show that the nature of the consideration set can change in surprising and non-monotonic ways with the cost of attention.

10.3   Asymmetric Prior Tracking Problem

CDL consider a consumer faced with a range of possible goods identified as set $A = \{a_1, \ldots, a_J\}$. One of these options is good. The others are bad. The utilities of the good and bad options are u_G and u_B, respectively, with $u_G > u_B$. The DM has a prior in which the available options are good. The state space is to be the same as the action space $\Omega = A$, with the interpretation that state ω_i is the state in which option i is of high quality and all others are of low quality. Thus,

$$u(a_i, \omega_j) = u_G \text{ if } i = j,$$

$$= u_B \text{ otherwise.}$$

$\mu(\omega_i)$ is therefore the prior probability that option a_i yields the good prize. We order states according to the perceived likelihood

$$\mu_i \equiv \mu(\omega_i) \geq \mu(\omega_{i+1}) \equiv \mu_{i+1}.$$

The DM can expend attentional effort to gain a better understanding of where the prize is located. The cost of improved understanding is defined by the Shannon model with parameter $\kappa > 0$. It is convenient to transform parameters by defining $\delta > 0$ as follows:

$$z(a_i, j) = \begin{cases} \exp\left(\frac{u_H}{\kappa}\right) \equiv (1+\delta) & \text{if } i = j, \\ \exp\left(\frac{u_L}{\kappa}\right) = 1 & \text{if } i \neq j. \end{cases}$$

CDL provide a full characterization of the solution. I restate it here.

Theorem: CDL. *If* $\mu_J > \frac{1}{J+\delta}$, *define* $\hat{K} = J$. *If* $\mu_J < \frac{1}{J+\delta}$, *then define* $\hat{K} < J$ *as the unique integer such that*

$$\mu_{\hat{K}} > \frac{\sum_{k=1}^{\hat{K}} \mu_k}{\hat{K} + \delta} \geq \mu_{\hat{K}+1}.$$

Then, the optimal attention strategy involves

$$P(a_i) = \frac{(\hat{K}+\delta)\mu_i - \sum_{k=1}^{\hat{K}} \mu_k}{\delta \sum_{k=1}^{\hat{K}} \mu_k} > 0$$

for $i \leq \hat{K}$, *with* $P(a_i) = 0$ *for* $i > \hat{K}$.

It is of interest to see how the ILR conditions play out in this solution. To that end, we compute the posteriors. Note that for $a_i \in B$, the posteriors satisfy

$$\gamma^i(\omega_j) = \frac{z(a_{i,}, \omega_j)\mu_j}{\sum_{k=1}^{K} P(a_k)z(a_k, \omega_j)}.$$

Hence, for $j = i$,

$$\gamma^i(\omega_i) = \frac{x(1+\delta)\mu_i}{\sum_{k=1}^{K} P(a_k)z(a_k, \omega_j)} = \frac{x(1+\delta)\mu_i}{x(1+\delta P(a_i))} = (1+\delta)\rho_i = \frac{(1+\delta)\sum_k \mu_k}{K+\delta}.$$

Moreover, for $j \neq i$ and $j < \hat{K}$,

$$\gamma^i(\omega_j) = \frac{x\mu_j}{\sum_{k=1}^{K} P(a_k)z(a_k, \omega_j)} = \frac{x\mu_j}{x(1+\delta P(a_i))} = \rho_i = \frac{\sum_k \mu_k}{K+\delta}.$$

Finally, for $j > \hat{K}$,

$$\gamma^i(\omega_j) = \frac{x\mu j}{\sum_{k=1}^{K} P(a_k)z(a_k, \omega_j)} = \frac{x\mu_i}{x} = \mu_j.$$

What this means is that the posteriors associated with all chosen options $a_i \leq \hat{K}$ take the same form:

$$
\gamma_j^i = \begin{cases} \frac{(1+\delta)\sum_{k=1}^{\hat{K}}\mu_k}{\hat{K}+\delta} \text{ for } i=j, \\ \frac{\sum_{k=1}^{K}\mu_k}{\hat{K}+\delta} \text{ for } i \neq j \text{ and } j \leq \hat{K}, \\ \mu_j \text{ for } j > \hat{K}. \end{cases}
$$

The common posterior of each chosen action being good is striking and in fact clear from the ILR conditions applied. These ILR ratios are indeed equalized among all chosen actions $1 \leq i \leq \hat{K}$. For any unchosen action $i' > \hat{K}$, we can compute the relevant sum relative to chosen action 1 and thereby validate the ILR inequalities:

$$
\sum_{k \leq \hat{K}} \left[\frac{\gamma_k^1}{z(1,k)} \right] z(i',k) = \frac{\gamma_1^1}{1+\delta} + 1 - \gamma_1^1 < 1.
$$

10.4   The ILR Hyperplanes

One feature that makes the Shannon model difficult to solve is the necessity of finding sets of posteriors that average to the prior. CDL show that the converse problem of finding priors associated with any given consideration set is somewhat simpler to characterize. They show how the ILR conditions partition $\Delta(\Omega)$ into sets of priors. The heart of the analysis is to define a set of ILR hyperplanes:

$$
f(x;a,b) = \sum_{\omega \in \Omega} \left[\frac{z(b,\omega)}{z(a,\omega)} \right] x(\omega),
$$

where $x \in \mathbb{R}^{|\Omega|}$ and $a,b \in A$, and to consider the equation

$$
f(x;a,b) = 1.
$$

This equation defines a plane of dimension $|\Omega| - 1$ in $\mathbb{R}^{|\Omega|}$ which divides $\mathbb{R}^{|\Omega|}$ into two sets: one in which $f(x;a,b) > 1$ and another in which $f(x;a,b) < 1$. If both a and b are chosen, the ILR conditions, $\frac{\gamma^a(\omega)}{z(a,\omega)} = \frac{\gamma^b(\omega)}{z(b,\omega)}$, imply that

$$f(\gamma^a;a,b) = \sum_{\omega \in \Omega} \left[\frac{z(b,\omega)}{z(a,\omega)}\right] \gamma^a(\omega) = \sum_{\omega \in \Omega} \gamma^b(\omega) = 1.$$

Hence, $f(\gamma^a;a,b) = 1$ implicitly defines the set of possible posteriors γ^a for action a such that both action a and action b are chosen with positive probability. Moreover, according to the likelihood ratio inequalities for unchosen options, the set of γ^a such that $f(\gamma^a;a,b) \leq 1$ represent the set of possible posteriors for action a such that a is chosen and b cannot be chosen.

CDL show how the inequalities partition $\Delta(\Omega)$ into priors which support different consideration sets. They use a simple tracking problem to illustrate with only three goods, $A = \{a_1, a_2, a_3\}$. As always, the utilities of the good and bad options are u_G and u_B, respectively, with $u_G > u_B$. For illustrative purposes, we set the utility and Shannon cost parameters such that $z_G = 2$ and $z_B = 1$. What we leave unspecified is the prior belief about which is good, just as in the asymmetric tracking problem above.

To understand the ILR hyperplanes, consider action a_1 and its possible joint choice with action a_2. The corresponding ILR hyperplane specifies

$$f(x;a_1,a_2) = \sum_{\omega \in \Omega} \left[\frac{z(a_2,\omega)}{z(a_1,\omega)}\right] x(\omega)$$

$$= \frac{1}{2}x_1 + 2x_2 + x_3 = 1.$$

For both actions a_1 and a_2 to be chosen, the posterior beliefs must lie on this line by the ILR conditions. The ILR inequalities reveal, as indicated, that if this is satisfied as the strict inequality

$$\frac{1}{2}x_1 + 2x_2 + x_3 < 1,$$

then the choice of action a_1 precludes the choice of action a_2.

It is striking that one can look at a posterior for one of the chosen actions and that this alone can rule out the choice of an alternative action by using the inequality aspect of the ILR conditions. The idea is that the state in which action a_2 dominates has to be sufficiently likely relative to that at which a_1 dominates to justify the choice of a_2. The probability of a_3 is irrelevant since the two actions pay off equally. While this is in some sense intuitive, the linear structure is not. It is just valid.

What beliefs lie on the ILR hyperplane defining where a_1 is chosen with a_2? It passes through prior $(0,0,1)$ that puts all weight on state ω_3. It also passes through prior $\left(\frac{2}{3},\frac{1}{3},0\right)$. It is linear in between.

One can likewise work out the ILR hyperplane in which a_1 is chosen with a_3:

$$\frac{1}{2}x_1 + x_2 + 2x_3 = 1.$$

This passes through priors $(0,1,0)$ and $\left(\frac{2}{3},0,\frac{1}{3}\right)$.

How does this allow us to identify consideration sets? As a step in that direction, we identify posteriors of action a_1 consistent with all actions being chosen. It is immediate from the ILR equations that this is defined by the point of the corresponding lines $f(x;a_1,a_3) = 1$ and $f(x;a_1,a_2) = 1$. Algebraically, this is the point $\left(\frac{1}{5},\frac{2}{5},\frac{2}{5}\right)$.

Before going further, it is clear that a geometric approach may be helpful. Figure 10.1 illustrates all ILR hyperplanes and uses them to construct the consideration sets. The solid lines $\overline{\omega_2 H}$ and $\overline{\omega_3 D}$ show $f(x;a_1,a_3) = 1$ and $f(x;a_1,a_2) = 1$, respectively, and their intersection pins down $\hat{\gamma}^{a_1} = \left(\frac{1}{5},\frac{2}{5},\frac{2}{5}\right)$ at point **A**. Included are analogous ILR hyperplanes for the other actions.

The figure by CDL reveals precisely how to partition the simplex into priors $S(B)$ that correspond to all possible consideration sets $B \neq \oslash \subset A$.

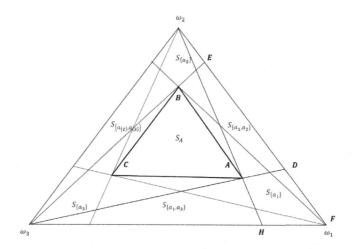

Figure 10.1   ILR hyperplanes.

Consider first $S(A)$, the priors at which all actions are chosen. By a reasoning entirely symmetric to that for action a_1, there are unique posteriors for the other actions at which they can be chosen along with both others. These are marked at the intersection of the corresponding hyperplanes as $\hat{\gamma}^{a_2} = \left(\frac{2}{5}, \frac{1}{5}, \frac{2}{5}\right)$ and $\hat{\gamma}^{a_3} = \left(\frac{2}{5}, \frac{2}{5}, \frac{1}{5}\right)$, respectively. S_A corresponds to the interior of the convex hull of these three points, which is the interior of the triangle $\overline{ABC}$ in the figure. Note that every point in $\overline{ABC}$ is equal to the average of the points $\mathbf{A}$, $\mathbf{B}$, and $\mathbf{C}$ with strictly positive weights. These weights are the action probabilities $P(a)$ from the optimal strategy. On the boundary of $\overline{ABC}$, some action probability falls to zero and the consideration set shrinks.

Now, consider $S_{\{a_1,a_2\}}$. To identify this, we look for beliefs for which $f(x; a_1, a_2) = 1$ and $f(x; a_1, a_3) \leq 1$. This corresponds to the line segment $\overline{AD}$ in the figure. The ILR conditions map $\overline{AD}$ to the line segment $\overline{BE}$ via the function $\hat{\gamma}_{a_2}\left(\Gamma^{a_1}_{\{a_1,a_2\}}\right)$. $S_{\{a_1,a_2\}}$ includes all points that lie between these two line segments but not the line segments themselves. This includes points along $\overline{AB}$ which lie on the boundary of S_A, meaning that $S_{\{a_1,a_2\}}$ is equal to the trapezoid $\overline{ADEB}$ excluding the line segments $\overline{AD}$ and $\overline{BE}$. We can construct $S_{\{a_1,a_3\}}$ and $S_{\{a_2,a_3\}}$ in a similar manner. $S_{\{a_1\}}$ is the set of points at which $f(x; a_1, a_2) \leq 1$ and $f(x; a_1, a_3) \leq 1$. This is the trapezoid $\overline{ADFH}$. Similar constructions apply for $S_{\{a_2\}}$ and $S_{\{a_3\}}$.

It is also of note that one can precisely pin down all action probabilities in the figure, even those in which there are multiple methods of weighting the posteriors to recover the prior. One can solve at the boundaries of the region where there is a unique convex combination that reproduces the prior. In the interior, one relies on the ILR conditions surviving under convex combinations.

CDL present the general corresponding method of identifying consideration sets from the ILR hyperplanes. Given a non-empty subset $B \subseteq A$, define $S_B \subseteq \Delta(\Omega)$ as the set of priors for which B is the consideration set. Note that this set may be empty if B is not the consideration set for any prior. CDL show how our understanding of the sets of posteriors that are associated with a given consideration set allows us to characterize the corresponding priors as the set of all convex combinations. The statement involves a convexification operation that is somewhat subtle to specify. The first step is to choose $a \in B$ and to define $\Gamma_B^{\bar{a}}$ as the set of posteriors for action $\bar{a}$ which are consistent with the consideration set B:

$$\Gamma_B^{\bar{a}} = \{x \in \Delta(\Omega) \,|\, f(x;\bar{a},b) \leq 1 \text{ for all } b \in A \backslash \bar{a} \text{ with equality for } b \in B \backslash \bar{a}\}.$$

The second step is to select $\hat{\gamma}_{\bar{a}} \in \Gamma_B^{\bar{a}}$ and then use the ILR conditions to generate $\hat{\gamma}_b(\hat{\gamma}_{\bar{a}})$ for all $b \in B$ as follows:

$$\hat{\gamma}_b(\omega) = \frac{z(b,\omega)}{z(\bar{a},\omega)}\hat{\gamma}_{\bar{a}}(\omega).$$

For $b = \bar{a}$, this is simply the identity mapping. The key result is that for B to be the consideration set, μ must lie in the interior of the convex hull of $\hat{\gamma}_b(\hat{\gamma}_{\bar{a}})$ for some $\hat{\gamma}_{\bar{a}} \in \Gamma_B^{\bar{a}}$.

Theorem: CDL. *Given $\mu \in \Delta(\Omega)$, B is the consideration set for the decision problem (μ, A) if and only if, given $\bar{a} \in B$,*

$$\mu \in S_B = \cup_{\hat{\gamma}_{\bar{a}} \in \Gamma_B^{\bar{a}}} int\{conv\{\hat{\gamma}_b(\hat{\gamma}_{\bar{a}})|b \in B\}.$$

CDL note that the convexification operation is essential. One might be tempted to associate the set of priors for which B is the consideration set with the set of μ such that $f(\mu;a,b) \geq 1$ for all $a,b \in B$. These conditions, however, are neither necessary nor sufficient. That $f(\mu;a,b) \geq 1$ is not sufficient can be seen from the figure: For all priors μ in the triangle $\overline{\text{ABG}}$, we have $f(\mu;a,b) \geq 1$ for all $a,b \in A$, but a_3 is not in the consideration set. In their appendix, CDL identify a case in which necessity fails: $f(\mu;a,b) < 1$ and both a and b lie in the consideration set. What matters is not the location of the prior but the location of the posteriors that average to the prior.

CDL highlight several features of this construction. First, we can find the set of posteriors consistent with $\bar{a} \in B$ merely by looking at the set of posteriors that satisfy a system of linear equations and inequalities. Second, knowing one chosen posterior is sufficient to construct all of the posteriors and the action probabilities. For a given $\hat{\gamma}_{\bar{a}}$, the ILR inequalities determine B, the ILR conditions determine the other posteriors, and Bayes' rule determines the values of $P(a)$ given μ.

Note that the construction illustrates that the conditions under which all actions are taken are very strict. If there are as many actions as states and since the normalized payoffs are linearly independent, Γ_A^q can only contain one posterior. This posterior determines the others through the ILR conditions, which then determines the set of priors consistent with all actions being chosen. Any other priors will leave some action unchosen. Moreover, this set shrinks toward the uniform distribution as the payoffs to all become more similar.

There are interesting paths forward algorithmically. In the example above, for any consideration set that is possible, one can identify priors such that unconditional probabilities are equal for all activities within a consideration set. For example, to find $\triangle ABC$, we start with a belief such that all three actions are chosen with equal probabilities. In this particular case, it is obvious, but the procedure is general. One can construct the convex hull of the resulting action-specific posteriors and note that they apply to all priors in their convex hull. An analogous procedure works for all possible consideration sets. Identifying which subsets are in fact possible consideration sets is an interesting challenge.

10.5 Strategic Applications

The analysis of strategic interactions and how they impact consideration sets is at the earliest stage. Ghosh (2022) starts on this path by considering a strategic communication problem inspired by the difficulties that have plagued governments during the COVID-19 pandemic. She considers a planner who wants to convey the right course of action to the public concerning appropriate measures to take. But the public understands that the planner would like to promote behavior that forces recipients to internalize negative externalities (e.g., don't wear a mask when masks are scarce, do wear a mask otherwise). What makes the case interesting is that the planner is also struggling with scientific ignorance. The fact that they have a clear credibility problem then feeds back in interesting ways not only on what is communicated but the progress of scientific knowledge itself.

What Ghosh shows is that much of the interesting action of the planner involves providing information to guide the consideration set of private agents, which form the basis for further costly private learning. Instead of strategically manipulating the action of the agent, the planner chooses to manipulate the consideration set of the agent. This is particularly relevant in a setup where agents also have access to information but learning is costly. As indicated, a key impact is on what the planner knows. An important aspect of strategic communication is its effect on the planner's learning policy. If the communication problem involves acquiring scientific knowledge, such as the appropriate public health behavior during a pandemic or the most effective environmental policy, the resulting limits in scientific knowledge can have severe welfare implications.

10.6   Dynamics and Value Functions

Dynamic rational inattention problems, as given by Sims (2003), have often been analyzed and solved in the linear–quadratic–Gaussian framework; see, for instance, Mackowiak *et al.* (2021) and references therein. Recently, there have also been advances in analyzing dynamic rational inattention problems in a framework with discrete action and state spaces. Steiner *et al.* (2017) use the SDSC approach of Matejka and McKay (2015). They reformulate this dynamic problem as a control problem with an observable state, reducing the dynamic problem to a sequence of interrelated static problems without relying on value functions or dynamic programming.

Miao and Xing (2020) analyze the same problem, building on the posterior-based approach instead and proposing a framework to solve general classes of dynamic, discrete-choice RI problems with minimal assumptions. They reduce the dynamic problem to a collection of static problems using the Bellman equation. They propose a solution method that can be applied to problems within the broad class of uniformly posterior-separable cost functions. In this framework, they characterize Markovian solutions and provide an efficient forward–backward procedure based on the Arimoto–Blahut (sic) algorithm to numerically compute the solution. A benefit of this approach is that it also allows for corner solutions, a common feature of rational inattention problems that drive the endogenous formation of consideration sets. For a subclass of cost functions, including the Shannon entropy case, they provide a tractable characterization of the problem that gives necessary and sufficient conditions for optimality. Finally, Miao and Xing apply the framework to explain several economic phenomena, including status quo bias, confirmation bias, and belief polarization.

Lecture 11

Equilibrium, Exchangeability, and Symmetry

This section opens with two simple models of how rational inattention plays out in market settings. The first makes one simple point: In models with free entry, equilibrium conditions can be used to pin down beliefs about market composition. For that purpose, it is particularly useful to use the posterior-based formulation of optimal strategies, which show many features of the solution to survive variation in prior beliefs, aiding in equilibrium analysis. The second example is dynamic and makes a distinct point: Past market outcomes reveal information that causes priors to be updated. Social learning from market outcomes may, in some cases, be less onerous than private learning. This points to the direction of dynamics. Again, knowing how to solve the model for all priors is of particular value.

After illustrating each of these phenomena, I introduce an approach to identifying rationally inattentive equilibria that rests on the remarkable symmetry properties of the Shannon model that have been hinted at before. The Shannon model and a broader class of symmetric cost functions turn out to be highly complementary with prior beliefs that likewise have symmetry properties: These are the exchangeable distributions made famous by the deep work of de Finetti and introduced to most of us by Kreps (1978). Work on this is jointly done with Stefan Bucher (Bucher and Caplin, 2021). In a nutshell, what our work suggests is that exchangeability is to rational inattention theory as i.i.d. is to search theory. Since i.i.d is a very special case of exchangeability, the advantage here is with rational inattention theory.

When thinking about this verbally, one might imagine that a method based on exchangeability is of value only in symmetric games. Symmetry in, symmetry out. But this is not the case. One can solve games with rich asymmetries using methods that one might expect to work only in symmetric cases. The case that we use to illustrate this involves school matching. In the market we consider, students are all very different in terms of how desirable they are to schools. We impose only one-sided symmetry: Schools are *ex ante* indistinguishable to students. This turns out to be enough for us to solve for an equilibrium that has many symmetry properties. The strategic learning is sophisticated: Lower-ranked studies face entirely different incentives to learn than do higher-ranked students, so they learn differently and correspondingly achieve matches of very different quality. Yet, the solution to the entire model can be identified by solving a relatively simple set of symmetric individual rational inattention problems. All formulae are shockingly simple, reflecting the remarkable properties of Shannon entropy. The general approach to symmetry that we develop may have other applications.

11.1   A Market Setting with Endogenous Prior

Recall the solution to the simple model with one safe and one risky option from Lecture 9. We limit attention to the interior solutions. Given prior

$$\mu \in \left(\frac{1-z_L}{z_H - z_L}, \frac{z_H(1-z_L)}{z_H - z_L} \right),$$

$$P(r) = \frac{\mu(z_H - z_L) - (1 - z_L)}{(1 - z_L)(z_H - 1)}.$$

This can be used as a module in a model of search and matching markets. There are *ex ante* homogenous workers and firms. Firms post job offers at fixed costs. Workers direct search toward an observable job offer type at a fixed cost. Searching workers match with firms with some probability that depends on the mass of searchers and vacancy postings. The key assumption is that, while wages are visible, it is difficult for workers who get a job offer to know exactly all utility-relevant characteristics on offer. Uncertainty can be reduced to some extent before accepting via costly attention. Once on the job, experience quickly resolves all remaining uncertainty. Jobs separate when the worker quits or after exogenous separation shock.

To illustrate the mechanism and the endogeneity of the prior, consider an essentially static version of the model. Firms are risk-neutral, expected-profit maximizers. They post jobs at fixed cost. All jobs posted get one applicant. Firms have a choice as to whether to make the job good or bad (*G* or *B*, respectively) for the worker. It is cheaper (for simplicity, half as cheap) to make the job bad. The worker will learn with Shannon costs, and this will yield acceptance probabilities of $P(A|G)$ and $P(A|B)$. The zero expected profit condition for each type implies that the good job must be twice as likely to be accepted:

$$P(A|G) = 2P(A|B).$$

All else is in the searcher's optimization. As usual, define $z(\omega) = \exp\left(\frac{u(\omega)}{\kappa}\right)$ so that

$$z(G) > z(\varnothing) = 1 > z(B).$$

In this case, the conditional probabilities for $\omega \in \{G, B\}$ satisfy

$$P(A|\omega) = \frac{P(A)z(\omega)}{P(A)z(\omega) + [1 - P(A)]}.$$

We can combine the above with $P(A|G) = 2P(A|B)$ to solve $P(A)$ and identify conditions for interior solution $P(A) \in (0,1)$:

$$\frac{P(A)z(G)}{P(A)z(G) + [1 - P(A)]} = \frac{2P(A)z(B)}{P(A)z(B) + [1 - P(A)]}.$$

Hence,

$$z(G)\left[P(A)z(B) + [1 - P(A)]\right] = 2z(B)\left[P(A)z(G) + [1 - P(A)]\right]$$

or

$$P(A) = \frac{z(G) - 2z(B)}{z(G)z(B) + z(G) - 2z(B)} \in (0,1),$$

provided $z(G) > 2z(B)$.

To solve for the unconditional probabilities based on a prior over job types on the part of the workers defined by $\mu(G) \in (0,1)$, the prior probability of any job match being good. What one does first is work out a choice probability weighted average value of each state. For example, in the good state,

$$Z_P(G) \equiv P(A)z(G) + [1 - P(A)] = \frac{z(G)\left[z(G) - 2z(B)\right] + z(G)z(B)}{z(G)z(B) + z(G) - 2z(B)}$$

$$= \frac{z(G)\left[z(G) - z(B)\right]}{z(G)z(B) + z(G) - 2z(B)}.$$

In the bad state,

$$Z_P(B) \equiv P(A)z(B) + [1 - P(A)] = \frac{z(B)\left[z(G) - 2z(B)\right] + z(G)z(B)}{z(G)z(B) + z(G) - 2z(B)}$$

$$= \frac{z(B)\left[z(G) - z(B)\right]}{z(G)z(B) + z(G) - 2z(B)} = \left[\frac{z(B)}{z(G)}\right] Z_P(G).$$

The RI conditions for both actions chosen relate to the corresponding prior weighted averages associated, respectively, with accept and reject:

$$\frac{\mu(G)z(G)}{Z_P(G)} + \frac{(1 - \mu(G))z(B)}{Z_P(B)} = \frac{\mu(G)}{Z_P(G)} + \frac{1 - \mu(G)}{Z_P(B)} = 1.$$

This solves for $\mu(G)$: Using reject (second condition) after multiplication by $Z_P(G)$, we have

$$\mu(G) + \frac{z(G)\left[1 - \mu(G)\right]}{z(B)} = Z_P(G)$$

or

$$\mu(G) = \left[\frac{z(B)}{z(G) - z(B)}\right]\left[\frac{z(G)}{z(B)} - Z_P(G)\right]$$

$$= \left[\frac{z(B)}{z(G) - z(B)}\right]\left[\frac{z(G)}{z(B)} - \frac{z(G)\left[z(G) - z(B)\right]}{z(G)z(B) + z(G) - 2z(B)}\right]$$

$$= \frac{z(G)}{z(G) - z(B)} - \frac{z(B)z(G)}{z(G)z(B) + z(G) - 2z(B)}.$$

This simple static framework can be built into a dynamic macroeconomic model of job transitions, search frictions, and unemployment.

11.2 Social Learning Application

I now outline a market-level application of consideration set logic from Caplin *et al.* (2015). The idea is to marry relatively inexpensive social learning from market data with costly private learning about preferences and to look at market implications. The conceptual change is to link prior beliefs with observed market shares. The key assumption is that agents enter a market not knowing their "type." They use data on past market shares, assumed freely available, to provide information on what they might like. They can also engage in costly private learning. The intricacy is that market share is a reflection of beliefs as well as actual tastes, so inference is subtle. As usual, the Shannon model is greatly simplifying.

The simplest illustration involves a market version of the simple asymmetric tracking problem. Time is discrete and indexed by $t \in \{0, 1, \dots\}$. There is a fixed finite set of options $i \in A = \{1, \dots, N_A\}$. Each period, a continuum of agents is born and make once-off choices from A. There are a finite number of distinct preference types $\omega \in \Omega = \{1, \dots, N_\Omega\}$. The underlying utility function is $u : \Omega \times A \to \mathbb{R}$. Let $g^* \in \Delta(\Omega)$ be the time-invariant density of preference types and $g^*(\omega)$ the share of type ω agents.

Newborn agents are born with common prior G over potential population distribution. G is a probability measure over distributions in $\Delta(\Omega)$. We suppose it has continuous density and define $\Gamma^0 \equiv \mathrm{supp}(G) \subseteq \Delta(\Omega)$, $g^* \in \mathrm{int}(\Gamma^0)$. Social learning involves the observation of past market shares and also costly private learning. In combination, these lead to type-specific demands: $P(i, \omega | \mu)$. We normalize the measure of types to 1.

We solve the model from period 0 onward. Given Γ_0, the prior beliefs of those in this cohort are

$$\mu_0(\omega) = \int_{g \in \Gamma_0} g(\omega) dG.$$

Given μ_0, each agent type solves the optimal learning problem generating type-dependent stochastic choice data over options $P(i, \omega | \mu_0)$. Given

$P(i, \omega | \mu_0)$, the market shares are

$$M(i|\mu, g^*) = \sum_{\omega \in \Omega} g^*(\omega) P(i, \omega | \mu).$$

Agents in period 1 observe period 0 market shares and eliminate all beliefs in support of Γ_0 that are inconsistent with them. Hence,

$$\Gamma_1 = \left\{ g \in \Gamma_0 \,\middle|\, \sum_{\omega \in \Omega} g(\omega) P(i, \omega | \mu_0) = M(i | \mu_0, g^*) \qquad \forall i \in A \right\}.$$

Note that $g^* \in \Gamma_0$ for all t.

This process iterates recursively: Given Γ_t, period t proceeds in a manner similar to period t. Learning involves keeping densities that "work" and rejecting the rest. All $g \in \Gamma_t$ were elements of Γ_t and hence generate the same market shares in period t as g^*. It follows that $g \in \Gamma_{t+1}$ if $g \in \Gamma_t$, and for all $i \in A$,

$$\sum_{\omega \in \Omega} [g(\omega) - g^*(\omega)] P(i, \omega | \mu_t) = 0.$$

This orthogonality condition defines a plane in $R^{|\Omega|}$.

Γ_0 is a full-dimensional (given interiority of true population distribution) subset of the $N_\Omega - 1$-dimensional simplex in R^{N_Ω}. Γ^{t+1} is equal to the intersection of Γ^t and at most N_A such hyperplanes. Each additional orthogonality condition either reduces the dimension of Γ^{t+1} relative to Γ^t or not. If not, $\Gamma^{t+1} = \bar{\Gamma}$. If $\bar{\Gamma} = g^*$, then learning is complete.

We provide the simplest illustrative example using the simple properties of the Shannon cost function. The example involves N options and N types and a single best option for each type: Act i is best for type i, and there are binary payoffs, good or bad. Specifically,

$$\exp(u(i, j)/\kappa) = \begin{cases} 2 & \text{if } i = j, \\ 1 & \text{if } i \neq j. \end{cases}$$

Options differ in prior probabilities for generation zero. To give a simple example,

$$(\bar{\mu}_1, \bar{\mu}_2, \bar{\mu}_3, \bar{\mu}_4, \bar{\mu}_5, \ldots) = (0.1, 0.09, 0.08, 0.07, 0.06, \ldots).$$

Suppose that all options are originally chosen. If that is the case, then the initial market shares are defined by the prior. But we know that with this prior, the optimal solution involves choices of the most preferred goods only of the first four types with no other actions chosen. These then are the long-run market shares with the correct prior. But the social outcome has unattractive features. Market share differences multiply up underlying popularity differences:

$$(\mathbf{P}^1, \mathbf{P}^2, \mathbf{P}^3, \mathbf{P}^4) = \left(\frac{16}{34}, \frac{11}{34}, \frac{6}{34}, \frac{1}{34}\right).$$

We have *ex post* heterogeneous tastes, but we also have a well-defined welfare criterion, as each agent solves the same maximization problem. Note also that there is a welfare disparity benefiting the majority:

$$\left(0.64, \frac{22}{45}, \frac{12}{40}, \frac{2}{35}\right).$$

Goods favored by types 5 and higher are never chosen. We never learn the true probability of these types. Note that behavior is consistent with 50% of the population preferring good 5, in fact.

If initial beliefs are biased against some items, they will not initially be chosen even if in reality they would be liked by a great many. As in standard social learning models, this makes experimentation socially valuable. Expanding the choice set can only make agents better off. This suggests "handicapping" policies that give a boost to seemingly unpopular choices.

One possible application of the broad method is to consider the informational advantage of an outside observer in understanding preferences. There are interesting cases in which individuals belong to groups with different tastes which they may or may not be fully aware of. An agent with access to market data has advantages in this setting. It can potentially collect more information: The government, Google, Amazon, etc., are in just such a position. Ideally, it would fully see type-dependent choice and thereby infer the entire preference ordering. Choice probabilities are "twisted" by preferences: This makes market shares by type informative about preferences. In the steady state

$$M(i, \omega | \mu) = \frac{M(i | \mu) \exp(u(\omega, i)/\kappa)}{\sum_{j \in A} M(j | \mu) \exp(u(\omega, j)/\kappa)}.$$

Hence,

$$\frac{u(\omega, i) - u(\omega, j)}{\kappa} = \log\left(\frac{M(i, \omega)}{M(j, \omega)} \middle/ \frac{M(i)}{M(j)}\right).$$

The idea that an agent is able to observe type-specific demands can play a major welfare-enhancing role in practice ("people like you"). How to develop this research idea is open.

The framework has clear and, I believe, important applications to recent political dynamics. There are some subgroups that might not have known how large they were until there was some form of revelation on social media. Much in the world that is going wrong might be blamed on this.

11.3 Symmetric Decision Problems

Rational inattention models can be solved for a large class of symmetric cost functions, including, in particular, the Shannon model. In this section, I introduce the abstract treatment of symmetry due to Bucher and Caplin (2021) and apply it to school matching. While the symmetry definition applies more generally, I restrict attention to solving the Shannon model since this is such a central and simple case. In fact, the solution in such cases is dramatically simple: The unweighted logit formula of Matejka and McKay (2015).

Bucher and Caplin define symmetry for general decision problems (μ, A, u) consisting of a prior $\mu \in \Delta(\Omega)$ over a finite state space Ω, a choice set A, and a utility function $u : A \times \Omega \to \mathbb{R}$.

Definition 39: Define the partition $\{\Omega_k\}_{1 \leq k \leq K}$ of the state space, with $\omega, \omega' \in \Omega_k \subseteq \Omega$ for some k if and only if there exists a bijection $\alpha_{\omega\omega'} : A \to A$ such that

$$u(a, \omega) = u(\alpha_{\omega\omega'}(a), \omega') \qquad \forall a \in A.$$

A decision problem (μ, A, u) is **symmetric** if, for any k,

$$\mu(\omega) = \mu(\omega') \quad \forall \omega, \omega' \in \Omega_k$$

and, for any $a, b \in A$ and k, there exists a bijection $\pi_{ab} : \Omega_k \to \Omega_k$ such that

$$u(a, \omega) = u(b, \pi_{ab}(\omega)) \quad \forall \omega \in \Omega_k.$$

This definition states that, within each subset Ω_k of the partition, each state is equally likely and the utilities of each pair of actions and each pair of states are permutations of each other. The subtle part of this definition is the third clause concerning the bijection between states within any element of the partition linking an arbitrary pair of actions. This formalizes the intuitive idea that no element of the partition *per se* favors any action over any other action. For this reason, one might call it action payoff equivalence within any element of the partition.

The critical simplification is that symmetry of a decision problem ensures that the corresponding rational inattention problem has a particularly simple solution. In this case, it is SDSC strategies that are most convenient to work with:

$$P \in \mathcal{P}(\mu, A) \equiv \left\{ P \in \Delta(A \times \Omega) \mid \sum_{a \in A} P(a, \omega) = \mu(\omega) \forall \omega \in \Omega \right\}.$$

The general rational inattention problem with Shannon mutual information costs is given by

$$\max_{P \in \mathcal{P}(\mu, A)} \sum_{a \in A} \sum_{\omega \in \Omega} P(a, \omega) u(a, \omega) - K(\kappa, P).$$

We add notation for action-specific posterior beliefs:

$$\gamma^a(\omega) \equiv \frac{P(a, \omega)}{\sum_{v \in \Omega} P(a, v)}$$

and write the cost function as

$$K(\kappa, P) \equiv \kappa \sum_{a \in A} [H(\mu) - H(\gamma^a)] \sum_{\omega \in \Omega} P(a, \omega),$$

with the Shannon entropy $H(p) = -\sum_{\omega \in \Omega} p(\omega) \ln(p(\omega))$.

Bucher and Caplin focus on strategies reflecting the decision problem's symmetry.

Definition 40: A strategy $P \in \mathcal{P}(\mu, A)$ is symmetric if, for all $a, b \in A$,

$$\sum_{\omega \in \Omega} P(a, \omega) = \sum_{\omega \in \Omega} P(b, \omega).$$

The main symmetry result is that there is a unique symmetric solution to symmetric rational inattention problems that involve conditional choice probabilities of the (undistorted) multinomial logit form. The proof is worthwhile since symmetry is going to be important in rational inattention modeling.

Theorem 12: *If a decision problem (μ, A, u) is symmetric, then the unique symmetric solution of the rational inattention problem satisfies*

$$P(a|\omega) \equiv \frac{P(a,\omega)}{\mu(\omega)} = \frac{z(a,\omega)}{\sum_{c \in A} z(c,\omega)} \qquad \forall a \in A, \omega \in \Omega,$$

where $z(a,\omega) \equiv \exp(u(a,\omega)/\kappa)$.

Proof 12: First, note that, given $\omega, \omega' \in \Omega_k$ for some $1 \leq k \leq K$, by Definition 39, there exists a bijection $\alpha_{\omega\omega'} : A \to A$ satisfying equation 39 so that $u(c,\omega) = u(\alpha_{\omega\omega'}(c), \omega')$, for all $c \in A$. It follows that

$$Z(\omega) \equiv \sum_{c \in A} z(c,\omega) = \sum_{c \in A} z(\alpha_{\omega\omega'}(c), \omega') = Z(\omega') \quad \forall \omega, \omega' \in \Omega_k,$$

where the last equality follows from the fact that $\alpha_{\omega\omega'}$ is a permutation. Note moreover that, given any $a, b \in A$ and $1 \leq k \leq K$, by Definition 39, there exists a bijection $\pi_{ab} : \Omega_k \to \Omega_k$ such that $u(a,\omega) = u(b, \pi_{ab}(\omega))$, for all $\omega \in \Omega_k$, from which it follows that

$$\sum_{\omega \in \Omega_k} z(a,\omega) = \sum_{\omega \in \Omega_k} z(b, \pi_{ab}(\omega)) = \sum_{\omega \in \Omega_k} z(b,\omega) \quad \forall a, b \in A,$$

where the last equality follows from the fact that π_{ab} is a permutation. For all $\omega, \omega' \in \Omega_k$, given some $1 \leq k \leq K$, it is the case that $\mu(\omega) = \mu(\omega') =: \mu_k$ by Definition 39 and $Z(\omega) = Z(\omega') =: Z_k$ so that

$$\sum_{\omega \in \Omega_k} \mu(\omega) \frac{z(a,\omega)}{Z(\omega)} = \frac{\mu_k}{Z_k} \sum_{\omega \in \Omega_k} z(a,\omega) = \frac{\mu_k}{Z_k} \sum_{\omega \in \Omega_k} z(b,\omega)$$

$$= \sum_{\omega \in \Omega_k} \mu(\omega) \frac{z(b,\omega)}{Z(\omega)} \quad \forall a, b \in A.$$

This implies, for any $a, b \in A$, that

$$\sum_{\omega \in \Omega} \frac{z(a, \omega)}{Z(\omega)} \mu(\omega) = \sum_{k=1}^{K} \sum_{\omega \in \Omega_k} \frac{z(a, \omega)}{Z(\omega)} \mu(\omega) = \sum_{k=1}^{K} \sum_{\omega \in \Omega_k} \frac{z(b, \omega)}{Z(\omega)} \mu(\omega)$$

$$= \sum_{\omega \in \Omega} \frac{z(b, \omega)}{Z(\omega)} \mu(\omega)$$

and thus

$$\sum_{\omega \in \Omega} \frac{z(a, \omega)}{Z(\omega)} \mu(\omega) = 1/|A| \qquad \forall a \in A.$$

For any symmetric strategy satisfying $\sum_{\omega \in \Omega} P(c, \omega) = 1/|A|$ for all $c \in A$, it is thus the case that

$$\sum_{\omega \in \Omega} \frac{z(a, \omega) \mu(\omega)}{\sum_{c \in A} z(c, \omega) \sum_{\omega \in \Omega} P(c, \omega)} = |A| \sum_{\omega \in \Omega} \frac{z(a, \omega)}{Z(\omega)} \mu(\omega) = 1 \quad \forall a \in A,$$

so by the SDSC necessary and sufficient conditions for optimality, the conditional choice probabilities of equation in the statement of the theorem identify the unique symmetric solution.

Note that one can define other cost functions that are symmetric and for which an equivalent result on symmetric equilibria exists. Interesting examples are symmetric UPS, for example, in CDL using other entropies, and the classes introduced by Csaba (2021) that are invariant. These, in particular, may play the role of CES to the Shannon's Cobb–Douglas.

11.4 School Matching

Taken directly from Bucher and Caplin, I introduce a model of school matching that is highly asymmetric on one side and yet to which the symmetry result applies. A finite number $N = c \cdot M$ of students $i \in I = \{1, \ldots, N\}$ is matched with schools $x \in X$ in a finite set of cardinality $|X| = M$, each of capacity $c \in \mathbb{N}$, using the deferred acceptance (DA) algorithm. Each student i submits a rank-order list $l^i \in A^i$ to the matching mechanism, a permutation of schools with $l^i(m) \in X$ indicating the school listed at position m.

The asymmetry that we introduce is stark. We assume that it is common knowledge that all schools submit the same list to the matching mechanism, according to which students are ranked in strict order given by their index i (so that student 1 is top ranked and thus has the highest priority). This unanimous ranking of students could reflect their scores on a standardized admissions test, for example, or the random outcome of a single tie-breaking rule. When submitting list l^i, student i is matched with school $\vec{x}^i_{DA}(l^i, \vec{l}^{-i}) \in X$, which is the deterministic matching resulting from DA when the lists submitted by all other students are $\vec{l}^{-i} \in \vec{A}^{-i} \equiv \times_{j \neq i} A^j$. The utility student i derives from being matched with a school $x \in X$ is determined by their type $\theta^i \in \Theta^i \equiv V^M$, a vector of length M whose elements — denoted by θ^i_x — are the type's valuations of each school $x \in X$, which are in the finite set $V \subset \mathbb{R}$ of possible utility levels. The notation θ^i_x implies an ordering of the elements in X, which is arbitrary and assumed where convenient for brevity. Students' types θ^i are drawn independently of each other from their priors $\mu^i \in \Delta(\Theta^i)$. Let $\vec{\Theta}^{-i} \equiv \times_{j \neq i} \Theta^j$. Students do not know their types *ex ante*; rather, they can resolve some of the uncertainty about their own (but not others') types (i.e., about their valuation of schools) by acquiring a costly signal before submitting their list. They choose an arbitrary (finite) information structure before observing a signal realization and submitting a rank-order list. The cost of an information structure is linear in its expected reduction of Shannon entropy.

Note that the switch in name and symbol from state ω to type θ is for ease of communication with the target audience.

11.5 Exchangeable Prior Beliefs

In order to apply an approach that is based on symmetry to a problem in which the students are so different from the viewpoint of schools, we impose strong symmetry on the other side of the market. Specifically, we assume that each student's prior belief about their valuation of schools is exchangeable. By definition, this means that for any permutation $\alpha : X \to X$ of schools,

$$\mu^i\left(\theta^i_1, \ldots, \theta^i_M\right) = \mu^i\left(\theta^i_{\alpha(1)}, \ldots, \theta^i_{\alpha(M)}\right).$$

Exchangeability requires that all permutations of the elements of θ^i are equiprobable. Note that the priors can be heterogeneous, so long as they are all exchangeable.

As research on strategic rational inattention takes off, it will bring about renewed interest in exchangeability. Importantly, the class is closed under a set of operations, some of which are highly relevant to strategic situations.

The most well-studied closure property involves mixtures. Given $\mu, \mu' \in \Delta(\Theta)$ and $\lambda \in (0,1)$, define the corresponding **mixture distribution** $\eta^{(\mu,\mu',\lambda)} \in \Delta(\Theta)$ by

$$\eta^{(\mu,\mu',\lambda)} = \lambda \mu(\theta) + (1 - \lambda)\mu'(\theta).$$

Note that if $\mu, \mu' \in \Delta(\Theta)$ are exchangeable, so is $\eta^{(\mu,\mu',\lambda)}$ since invariance under permutation survives under mixtures. De Finetti's theorem states that in the limit as M grows, the only exchangeable distributions are mixtures of i.i.d distributions. It is a very sophisticated result, as will become clear. The reason for this is based on how very large the class of exchangeable distributions is for any fixed finite M.

In the school setting, two other features of exchangeability are important. First, it is preserved in the remaining capacities of schools while independence cannot be. Second, it survives essentially arbitrary Bayesian updating: A signal about a student's valuation of one school can carry information about their valuation of other schools. In models of costly sequential search, this type of updating becomes intractable quickly. For example, it can imply that there is no reservation strategy: Observing a school of high utility can imply that utilities are generally high and justify further search, while observing a school of low utility can imply the converse. An example is presented in the following in discussing hybrid models, allowing for both search and rational inattention.

There are many other perspectives on exchangeable distributions that may be of value. One method of generating them is to specify probabilities on the non-decreasing sequences and use invariance under permutation to fill in the rest. In fact, one can do this in reverse order. The key is to count equivalent permutations and assign non-negative numbers to non-decreasing such that the resulting sum is 1. If payoffs to distinct actions are always different, invariance under permutation is satisfied iff the sum of probabilities to non-decreasing is $\frac{1}{M!}$. This can be used to specify the full counting operation. For example, if one only assigns probabilities to the unit vectors, the only way to satisfy exchangeability is to assign each probability $\frac{1}{J}$. At the other extreme is if one assigns probability 1 to a set of values, all of which are distinct.

Note that the above works directly with the set of possible utilities. An alternative approach is to specify correlations before specifying valuations, which might be called a macro state measure of characterizing exchangeability. A natural conjecture is that the exchangeable class is characterized by complete freedom in specifying feasible values and how often each is found in the joint distribution.

11.6 Nash Equilibrium in SDSC Strategies

Bucher and Caplin characterize the symmetric equilibrium of the general model. The game between students who acquire costly information structures before submitting a rank-order list can be expressed equivalently as a game in stochastic choice strategies. This game consists of each student i choosing a stochastic choice strategy $P^i \in \mathcal{P}(\mu^i, A^i)$ so as to maximize, given others' strategies $\vec{P}^{-i} \equiv (P^1, \ldots, P^{i-1}, P^{i+1}, \ldots, P^N)$, where $P^j \in \mathcal{P}(\mu^j, A^j)$, for all $j \neq i$, and expected utility

$$U^i(P^i, \vec{P}^{-i}) = \sum_{(l^i, \vec{l}^{-i}) \in A^i \times \vec{A}^{-i}} \sum_{(\theta^i, \vec{\theta}^{-i}) \in \Theta^i \times \vec{\Theta}^{-i}} P^i(l^i, \theta^i) \vec{P}^{-i}(\vec{l}^{-i}, \vec{\theta}^{-i}) \theta^i_{\vec{x}^i(l^i, \vec{l}^{-i})}$$

net of information costs $K(\kappa^i, P^i)$. Note that $\vec{P}^{-i}(\vec{l}^{-i}, \vec{\theta}^{-i}) = \prod_{j \neq i} P^j(l^j, \theta^j)$ since students' types are independent, as are their simultaneous list submissions.

This formulation of student i's rational inattention problem gives rise to the following equilibrium: $\vec{P}^* = (P^{1*}, \ldots, P^{N*}) \in \times_{i \in I} \mathcal{P}(\mu^i, A^i)$ is a Nash equilibrium if, for all $i \in I$,

$$U^i(P^{i*}, \vec{P}^{-i*}) - K(\kappa^i, P^{i*}) \geq U^i(P^i, \vec{P}^{-i*}) - K(\kappa^i, P^i) \text{ for all } P^i \in \mathcal{P}(\mu^i, A^i).$$

It is symmetric if every strategy P^{i*} is symmetric according to Definition 40.

Bucher and Caplin focus on equilibria in symmetric strategies that reflect the fact that schools are *ex ante* identical under each student's prior belief. The central challenge in identifying the equilibrium is to characterize the strategic uncertainty that each student faces. This is rendered feasible by the observation that if others' strategies are symmetric, then a student's problem is symmetric in the sense of Definition 39 and thus has a unique symmetric solution itself by Theorem 8.

11.7 Anonymous Mechanisms and Symmetric Equilibria

It is important to note that the symmetry-based approach applies broadly. In particular, it rests on the fruitful joining between exchangeability of prior beliefs with matching mechanisms that have anonymity properties, which are ubiquitous: The names of the schools and of the applicants are *per se* irrelevant. In our setting, suppressing notation for the school side of the market, a matching mechanism $\vec{x}$ is a vector-valued function $\vec{x} : \times_{i \in I} A^i \to X^N$ such that, for all $x \in X$ and $l^1, \ldots, l^N \in \times_{i \in I} A^i$,

$$\sum_{i \in I} \mathbf{1}\{\vec{x}^i(l^1, \ldots, l^N) = x\} \le c,$$

where $\vec{x}^i(l^1, \ldots, l^N) \in X$ denotes the school $x \in X$ with which student $i \in I$ is matched when the submitted lists are $l^1, \ldots, l^N$. We define, loosely following Ehlers (2008), a class of mechanisms that are invariant to renaming of schools.

Definition 41: Given any $l^i \in A^i$ and any permutation $\alpha : X \to X$ of schools, let l^i_α be the list such that

$$l^i_\alpha(m) = \alpha(l^i(m)) \quad m = 1, \ldots, M.$$

A matching mechanism $\vec{x}$ is **anonymous** if, for any permutation $\alpha : X \to X$,

$$\vec{x}^i(l^i_\alpha, \vec{l}^{-i}_\alpha) = \alpha(\vec{x}^i(l^i, \vec{l}^{-i})),$$

for all $i \in I$, $l^i \in A^i$, and $\vec{l}^{-i} \in \vec{A}^{-i}$.

What we show is that exchangeability of student priors and anonymity of the matching mechanism combine to produce a very simple structure in which list order is the only determinant of the probability of any given student matching with any given school. To state the result formally, we define student i's probability, given $\vec{P}^{-i}$, of being matched with school $x \in X$ when submitting list $l^i \in A^i$ as

$$\pi^i(x|l^i, \vec{P}^{-i}) \equiv \sum_{\vec{l}^{-i} \in \vec{A}^{-i}} \sum_{\vec{\theta}^{-i} \in \vec{\Theta}^{-i}} \vec{P}^{-i}(\vec{l}^{-i}, \vec{\theta}^{-i}) \mathbf{1}\left\{\vec{x}^i(l^i, \vec{l}^{-i}) = x\right\}.$$

Theorem: List-Position Sufficiency (Bucher and Caplin). *If, for any $i \in I$, P^j is symmetric for all $j \neq i$ in the sense of Definition 40, then for any anonymous matching mechanism $\vec{x}$, there exists, for all $i \in I$, $h^i \in \Delta(\{1, \ldots, M\})$ such that*

$$\pi^i(l^i(m)|l^i, \vec{P}^{-i}) = h^i(m),$$

for all $l^i \in A^i$ and all $m \in \{1, \ldots, M\}$.

List-position sufficiency rests on students' symmetric information which they acquire endogenously in light of their exchangeable priors. Given others' strategies $\vec{P}^{-i}$, student i's expected utility of submitting rank-order list $l^i \in A^i$, when their true type is $\theta^i \in \Theta^i$, is

$$u^i(l^i, \theta^i) = \sum_{x \in X} \pi^i(x|l^i, \vec{P}^{-i})\theta_x^i = \sum_{m=1}^{M} \pi^i(l^i(m)|l^i, \vec{P}^{-i})\theta_{l^i(m)}^i.$$

The distribution h^i of random variable m thus captures the entire strategic uncertainty under the matching mechanism. List-position sufficiency implies that the student's problem is symmetric, provided that their prior is exchangeable.

Theorem: (Bucher and Caplin). *If, for any $i \in I$, P^j is symmetric for all $j \neq i$ in the sense of Definition 40, then for any anonymous matching mechanism $\vec{x}$, there exists, for all $i \in I$, $h^i \in \Delta(\{1, \ldots, M\})$ such that*

$$\pi^i(l^i(m)|l^i, \vec{P}^{-i}) = h^i(m),$$

for all $l^i \in A^i$ and all $m \in \{1, \ldots, M\}$.

Theorem: (Bucher and Caplin). *The problem of student i with choice set $A = A^i$, an exchangeable prior $\mu^i \in \Delta(\Theta^i)$ over state space $\Omega = \Theta^i$, and utility*

$$u^i(l^i, \theta^i) = \sum_{m=1}^{M} h^i(m)\theta_{l^i(m)}^i$$

is symmetric.

Together, these results imply that, for a wide class of matching mechanisms, there is a unique symmetric equilibrium since each student has a unique symmetric best response to others' symmetric equilibrium strategies.

11.8   A Simple Example

I illustrate how to solve the model with the Deferred Acceptance Algorithm (DA) used for matching in an example taken directly from Bucher and Caplin (2021). This example demonstrates how each student's symmetric solution results in lower-ranked students' problems being symmetric so that symmetry is inherited. This implies that, in equilibrium, each student is unconditionally equally likely to match with any of the schools, which will permit a combinatoric answer to the question of how likely each school is to be available for ensuing students.

The example involves three students $i \in \{1, 2, 3\}$ who are to be matched by the Deferred Acceptance Algorithm with three schools $x \in \{a, b, c\}$ of unit capacity. Each student values schools as either good or bad, receiving utility $u_G > 0$ from matching with a good school and $u_B = 0$ from a bad one. For simplicity, we assume that all students face the same marginal cost κ of information. Since the schools unanimously rank the students in order of their index, the matching resulting from DA is characterized by serial dictatorship so that each student is matched with the first school on their submitted rank-order list that has not been assigned to a higher-ranking student. We first solve for the Nash equilibrium of the resulting game between students whose strategies consist of type-dependent stochastic choice data. The solution permits us to analyze key features of the equilibrium: what each student learns and what type of mistakes they make, inequities in the gross and net welfare they attain, and the potential for cost-reducing policies to reduce inequity. Bucher and Caplin generalize these analyses to arbitrary numbers of schools and students, general utilities, and heterogeneous information costs.

Each student's equilibrium strategy will reflect the three-stage lottery they face: First, they face **signal uncertainty** about the outcome of their chosen information structure. Second, the matching outcome resulting from a submitted list is stochastic due to the uncertainty about other students' submissions. We will refer to this as **strategic uncertainty**. Note that while DA's strategy-proofness implies that strategic uncertainty does not affect a student's list-submission strategy, it can affect their information-acquisition strategy. What is worth learning for a given student depends on how likely they are to be matched with each school on their submitted list. Characterizing this distribution is combinatorically challenging even in the simplest of cases, which would be compounded when relaxing independence across students, as observing a signal would permit inference about what others likely learn and thus schools' availability. Assuming that students' types are drawn independently of each other allows us to abstract from this complication, as students have no way of learning — directly or indirectly — about others' types. Third, students' endogenously imperfect information results in remaining **value uncertainty** about the utility they obtain from the school with which they are matched. In equilibrium, each student bears these types of uncertainty in mind when choosing the extent of the effort they put into understanding schools. Solving the model thus requires us to identify each student's probability, in equilibrium, of being matched with each school on their list. This will further allow us to specify each student's probability distribution as a function of their rank and their prior valuation of schools over the set of feasible rank-order list submissions as well as their posterior beliefs when submitting each possible list.

There are eight states of the world defined by the quality in sequential order of schools a, b, and c. Since each student i has an exchangeable prior μ^i, prior probabilities are a function only of the cardinality of the set of good schools:

$$\mu^i(GGB) = \mu^i(GBG) = \mu^i(BGG) =: \mu^i(2) \geq 0,$$

$$\mu^i(GBB) = \mu^i(BGB) = \mu^i(BBG) =: \mu^i(1) \geq 0.$$

We define $\mu^i(GGG) =: \mu^i(3)$ and $\mu^i(BBB) =: \mu^i(0)$ accordingly. The only additional restriction that exchangeability imposes apart from non-negativity is that $\mu^i(3) + 3\mu^i(2) + 3\mu^i(1) + \mu^i(0) = 1$. A student's expected utility of submitting a rank-order list depends on their type θ^i but also on their rank i. Since, by serial dictatorship, student 1 receives their first-listed school with certainty, their utility of submitting list l^1 is given by

$$u^1(l^1, \theta^1) = \theta^1_{l^1(1)}$$

when their type is θ^1. *Ex ante*, student 1 thus only faces the **signal uncertainty** associated with the random realization from their chosen signal

Table 11.1 Type-conditional choice probabilities $P^{1*}(l^1|\theta^1)$ of student 1, where $P^{1*}(a,*,*|\theta^1)$ is the probability of submitting **each** list that ranks school a first, i.e., (a,b,c) and (a,c,b).

$l^1\backslash\theta^1$	GGG	GGB	GBG	BGG	GBB	BGB	BBG	BBB
$(a,*,*)$	$\frac{z}{6z}$	$\frac{z}{4z+2}$	$\frac{z}{4z+2}$	$\frac{1}{4z+2}$	$\frac{z}{2z+4}$	$\frac{1}{2z+4}$	$\frac{1}{2z+4}$	$\frac{1}{6}$
$(b,*,*)$	$\frac{z}{6z}$	$\frac{z}{4z+2}$	$\frac{1}{4z+2}$	$\frac{z}{4z+2}$	$\frac{1}{2z+4}$	$\frac{z}{2z+4}$	$\frac{1}{2z+4}$	$\frac{1}{6}$
$(c,*,*)$	$\frac{z}{6z}$	$\frac{1}{4z+2}$	$\frac{z}{4z+2}$	$\frac{z}{4z+2}$	$\frac{1}{2z+4}$	$\frac{1}{2z+4}$	$\frac{z}{2z+4}$	$\frac{1}{6}$

structure and the **value uncertainty** referring to the remaining uncertainty in the resulting posterior about their valuation $\theta^1_{l^1(1)}$ of their top-listed school. Their learning problem is therefore a standard rational inattention problem which is symmetric, as specified in Definition 39.

The optimal symmetric strategy follows directly from the standard rationally inattentive solution and is given in full in Table 11.1, where we define $z \equiv \exp(u_G/\kappa)$. Given the strong symmetry properties of the solution, we can effectively summarize all choice probabilities focusing on states in which the good schools are earlier in the alphabet than bad schools: If there is one good school, it is school a, and if there are two, they are a and b. For each state, we show the solution for a subset of rank-order lists which are "representative" for other lists that give rise to the same sequence of good and bad schools. The choice probabilities are given in Table 11.1.

The solution has many noteworthy features. First, note that for student 1, only the quality of the top-ranked school matters for the probability with which a list is submitted. Second, $z \equiv \exp(u_G/\kappa)$ is a sufficient statistic for the extent to which the utility of picking a good school and costs of identifying such a school impact choice probabilities, as has been understood since Matejka and McKay (2015). Third, the simple way of understanding these probabilities in all cases is to note that the numerator reflects the transformed utility of the particular list submitted, while the denominator reflects the corresponding value added up across all lists. What this means is that the fewer such schools, the higher the likelihood of identifying a particular school as good: With $z = 2$, for example, there is a 50% probability of listing the good school first if exactly one school is good. If exactly two schools are good, each of these is 40% likely to be top ranked.

Most strikingly, these conditional probabilities apply regardless of the structure of the prior, provided it is exchangeable. The same formulae thus characterize conditional choice probabilities regardless of what learning about one school might imply about the probability of the other schools being good. This contrasts profoundly with models of sequential search, in which the realized utilities of early schools can create all kinds of intricacies in the subsequent search patterns, making conditional choice probabilities in the optimal strategy strongly path dependent and far from invariant to the structure of the prior. Finally, note that the **un**conditional choice probabilities of student 1 are uniform, so *ex ante*, they are equally likely to be matched with any of the three schools. This is critical for student 2 since whichever school student 1 is matched with will not be available to them. Having chosen an information structure given their prior belief μ^2, student 2 faces uncertainty about the realization of the signal and the posterior belief γ^2 it induces. Given their posterior belief, they submit a utility-maximizing rank-order list l^2 to the mechanism, which results in an outcome that is stochastic as it depends on the submission of student 1. There is remaining uncertainty about their valuation of their matched school.

In addition to value and signal uncertainty, all students other than student 1 also face **strategic uncertainty** about the outcome resulting from the list they submit. Consider student 2. First, nature draws a signal from the information structure chosen by the student, which results in a posterior belief $\gamma^2 \in \Delta(\Theta^2)$ about their type θ^2, under which they will submit a utility-maximizing rank-order list l^2. Second, the student faces strategic uncertainty about the outcome resulting from their submitted list. Third, there is value uncertainty remaining about the utility of their realized outcome. By choosing an information structure, the student determines how much value uncertainty will be remaining. Note that the choice of information structure is implicit in our formulation, as is now standard in the literature. Since their types are independent, student 2 cannot infer anything about the type of student 1 from what they learn about their own type. From the perspective of student 2, each of the three schools is thus equally likely to still be available, hence they will be matched with their top-ranked schools with a probability of $2/3$ and their second-ranked schools with a probability of $1/3$. For student 2, the resulting expected utility of submitting a list l^2 when their true type is θ^2 is thus

$$u^2(l^2, \theta^2) = \frac{2}{3}\theta^2_{l^2(1)} + \frac{1}{3}\theta^2_{l^2(2)}.$$

The strategic uncertainty about which of the schools on their list student 2 is matched with affects their learning incentives, which is reflected in their type-conditional choice probabilities. Student 2's optimal strategy has the same qualitative features and essentially the same simplicity and separability properties as those of student 1. Again, $z \equiv \exp(u_G/\kappa)$ is a sufficient statistic for the impact of learning costs as well as the utility differential between schools on patterns of mistakes. As was the case for student 1, student 2 is more likely to submit better lists for higher values of z. The conditional probabilities again apply regardless of the structure of the prior, and the unconditional choice probabilities of student 2 are also uniform, so *ex ante* they are equally likely to be matched with any of the three schools. The solution has one more striking feature related to strategic uncertainty. Student 2 is less likely than student 1 to submit a good list because their learning incentive is diluted by the strategic uncertainty, which is reflected in the exponents of z. The formulae reveal in a precise and simple manner how the strategic uncertainty impacts what is learned. If only the first school on a list is good, z is raised to the power of $2/3$ to reflect the fact that the first school is received with this probability. If only the second school on a list is good, the exponent $1/3$ reflects the fact that the second school is received with this probability. If both are good, z has an exponent of 1 since student 2 will find themselves at a good school regardless of how the strategic uncertainty resolves. Finally, the exponent is zero when the first two are both bad. As for student 1, the numerator can be seen as the value of the list in question, while the denominator is the total value of all lists in the given state, which depends only on the number of good schools in that state. As we will see, these findings apply equally in the general case. Finally, note that there is an even stronger form of symmetry here, as identifying the one good school gives rise to the same conditional probabilities (after canceling) as identifying the one bad school.

Since whichever schools students 1 and 2 match with will not, by serial dictatorship, be available to student 3, their submission is inconsequential, so they optimally acquire no information and are indifferent between lists.

11.9   Value Uncertainty in Students' Posterior Beliefs

Beyond specifying students' type-conditional choices, solving the model analytically allows Bucher and Caplin to analyze the form and likelihood of the mistakes each student makes. This is revealed by their posterior beliefs: $P^{i*}(\theta^i|l^i) \equiv P^{i*}(l^i, \theta^i)/\sum_{\theta \in \Theta^i} P^{i*}(l^i, \theta)$. Students' posterior beliefs exhibit a strong form of symmetry: They depend only on the order of good and bad schools in the submitted list but not on the schools' identities. Due to this symmetry, the nature of students' posteriors is best summarized through the value uncertainty, which is captured by the probability

$$P^i(m) \equiv \sum_{\theta^i \in \Theta^i} P^{i*}(\theta^i|l^i) \mathbf{1}\left\{\theta^i_{l^i(m)} = u_G\right\}$$

that the mth-listed school on any list l^i submitted by student i is a school whose valuation is good under their true type. This probability is independent of l^i due to the posteriors' symmetry.

In the three-school example, student 1 does not face any strategic uncertainty, and their value uncertainty is standard as in any individual rational inattention model. The probability that the top-listed school (the only possible outcome) is good for student 1 is

$$P^1(1) = \mu^1(3) + 3\mu^1(2)\frac{2z}{2z+1} + 3\mu^1(1)\frac{z}{z+2},$$

which is increasing in z. For student 3, the strategic uncertainty is maximal, as they face a $1/3$ probability of matching with any of the schools regardless of their submission. Student 3 thus will not learn anything, so their value uncertainty will be defined by the prior irrespective of information costs:

$$P^3(1) = P^3(2) = P^3(3) = \mu^3(3) + 2\mu^3(2) + \mu^3(1) =: P^3.$$

More interesting are the mistakes made by student 2 who faces non-trivial strategic uncertainty (unlike student 1) and non-trivial signal uncertainty (unlike student 3) and thus resembles the generic student in our general model. The nature of the mistakes depends on how the strategic uncertainty resolves: When being matched with the first school on their list, the probability of that school being good is

$$P^2(1) = \mu^2(3) + 3\mu^2(2)\frac{z+z^{\frac{2}{3}}}{z+z^{\frac{2}{3}}+z^{\frac{1}{3}}} + 3\mu^2(1)\frac{z^{\frac{2}{3}}}{z^{\frac{2}{3}}+z^{\frac{1}{3}}+1},$$

which is increasing in z, as was the case for student 1 above. The pattern of mistakes is more interesting if the strategic uncertainty results in student 2 being matched with their second-listed school, whose probability of being good is

$$P^2(2) = \mu^2(3) + 3\mu^2(2)\frac{z+z^{\frac{1}{3}}}{z+z^{\frac{2}{3}}+z^{\frac{1}{3}}} + 3\mu^2(1)\frac{z^{\frac{1}{3}}}{z^{\frac{2}{3}}+z^{\frac{1}{3}}+1}.$$

Note that this is increasing in z if and only if $\mu^2(2) > \mu^2(1)$ so that the pattern of mistakes depends on the structure of the prior. In a tracking problem, in which exactly one of the schools is good (so that $\mu^2(1) = 1/3 > 0 = \mu^2(2)$), for example, this probability decreases when information costs are reduced, as the student is increasingly successful in identifying the one good school and ranking it first ("cherry picking"). Conversely, if $\mu^2(2) = 1/3$ so that there is exactly one bad school ("lemon dropping"), this probability increases as information costs are reduced. This is because the student will be more successful in identifying the one bad school and ranking it last.

11.10 Equilibrium Characterization

Given students' symmetric equilibrium strategies, Bucher and Caplin find combinatoric expressions for each student's probability of being matched by the Deferred Acceptance Algorithm with each school on their list, which fully characterizes the strategic uncertainty they face. This permits us to describe the unique symmetric equilibrium analytically. It is only at this last stage that the rationally inattentive cost function comes into play — most of the intricacy relates to the inescapable strategic uncertainty. In addition to the abstract results based on symmetry, the theorem rests on intricate combinatoric analysis. The challenge in generalizing it is entirely combinatoric. It is hard to find insightful methods of counting for mechanisms other than DA.

Nash Equilibrium (Bucher and Caplin). *Given an anonymous mechanism, $(P^{1*}, \ldots, P^{N*})$ is a symmetric Nash equilibrium if and only if, for all $i \in I$,*

$$P^{i*}(l^i \mid \theta^i) \equiv \frac{P^{i*}(l^i, \theta^i)}{\mu^i(\theta^i)} = \frac{z^i(l^i, \theta^i)}{Z^i(\theta^i)} \quad \forall l^i \in A^i, \theta^i \in \Theta^i,$$

where

$$z^i\left(l^i, \theta^i\right) = \exp\left(\frac{1}{\kappa^i} \sum_{m=1}^{M} h^i(m) \theta^i_{l^i(m)}\right)$$

and

$$Z^i(\theta^i) = \sum_{l' \in A^i} z^i(l', \theta^i).$$

Under DA,

$$h^i_{DA}(m) = \sum_{\vec{k} \in \mathbb{N}^{c+1}} \binom{M-m}{k_0 + 1 - m} \bigg/ \binom{M}{k_0} \cdot f^{i-1}(\vec{k}),$$

where the probability mass functions f^n over a random vector $\vec{k} = (k_0, k_1, \ldots, k_c)$ are defined recursively as

$$f^0\left(\vec{k}\right) = \mathbf{1}\{k_c = M, k_r = 0 \forall r \neq c\},$$

$$f^{n+1}\left(\vec{k}\right) = \sum_{r=1}^{c} \frac{k_r + 1}{M - k_0 + 1\{r = 1\}} f^n\left(\vec{k} + \vec{e}_r - \vec{e}_{r-1}\right),$$

with $\vec{e}_r$ being the unit vector of length $c+1$ such that $(\vec{e}_r)_\rho = \mathbf{1}\{\rho = r\}$ for $\rho = 0, \ldots, c$ and where $f^n(\vec{k}) = 0$ unless $k_r \in \{0, \ldots, M\}$ for all r and $\sum_{r=0}^{c} k_r = M$.

It is hard to express how absurdly simple this solution is given the intricacy of the strategic information acquisition challenge each student faces. The Shannon form takes this one level further providing extremely simple formulae for all interesting information-theoretic structures.

11.11 Equilibrium Value of Information and Net Welfare

Our characterization of the symmetric equilibrium shows that the powerful separability properties of the solution found in the three-school example are fully general. Each student's optimal strategy has the same qualitative features and essentially the same simplicity as in that special case. The conditional probability of any list in any state can be computed as a ratio between a transformed payoff to that list in that state and the sum of the correspondingly transformed payoffs in that state across all lists. The novel feature of this formula relates to the strategic uncertainty it captures in a student's probability $h^i(m)$ of receiving the mth-listed school on any list, which determines the expected utility of the **stochastic** outcome resulting from an action in a given state. Note that this is different from standard rational inattention models in that the learnable state does not resolve all of the uncertainty: The DM can only reduce value uncertainty but not strategic uncertainty. The probability of choosing any list is then obtained by the usual transformation of dividing the expected utility of that list by the cost parameter κ^i and exponentiating, divided by the sum across all lists of that expression. It is hard to imagine a simpler formula that takes into account in a flexible manner all strategic considerations.

Note finally that the prior is separable just as in the three-school case. Variations in the prior change the pattern of behavior without in any way changing the conditional choice probabilities in each state. Of course, the prior does impact posterior beliefs and hence welfare, which we now discuss. One can solve for equilibrium posterior beliefs as

$$P^{i*}(\theta^i|l^i) = \mu^i(\theta^i) \frac{z^i(l^i, \theta^i)}{Z^i(\theta^i)/(M!)}$$

when submitting any list $l^i \in A^i$. The posterior distorts the prior in a systematic and continuous manner: The prior probability $\mu^i(\theta^i)$ of any state is divided by this state's average value across all lists, $Z^i(\theta^i)/(M!)$, and then multiplied by the state's value $z^i(l^i, \theta^i)$ when submitting a given list l^i. This implies that states giving higher-than-average utility for a list are more likely under a student's posterior belief when submitting that list than they are under the student's prior. Bucher and Caplin show that this allows full analysis of the nature of the mistakes each student makes.

With regard to welfare, student i attains the equilibrium gross utility $U^{i*}(\kappa^i, \mu^i) \equiv U^i(P^{i*}, \vec{P}^{-i*})$ given by

$$U^{i*}(\kappa^i, \mu^i) = \sum_{m=1}^{M} h^i(m) U^{i*}(\kappa^i, \mu^i|m)$$

$$= \kappa^i \sum_{\theta^i \in \Theta^i} \mu^i(\theta^i) \frac{\sum_{l^i \in A^i} z^i(l^i, \theta^i) \ln z^i(l^i, \theta^i)}{Z^i(\theta^i)}.$$

Student i attains the net utility $N^{i*}(\kappa^i, \mu^i) \equiv U^{i*}(\kappa^i, \mu^i) - K^{i*}(\kappa^i, \mu^i)$ given by

$$N^{i*}(\kappa^i, \mu^i) = \kappa^i \sum_{\theta^i \in \Theta^i} \mu^i(\theta^i) \ln \left(\frac{Z^i(\theta^i)}{M!} \right).$$

I would not have been able even to imagine such a simple formula for net utility before starting the analysis.

11.12 Inequity in the Boston Mechanism

Chen and He (2021) have observed that the immediate acceptance (IA) algorithm or Boston mechanism may incentivize more equitable information acquisition than DA. In the three-student example, for example, it would give rise to strategic uncertainty captured by the probability mass function

$$h_B^1 = (1, 0, 0),$$

$$h_B^2 = \left(\frac{6}{9}, \frac{2}{9}, \frac{1}{9} \right),$$

$$h_B^3 = \left(\frac{4}{9}, \frac{5}{18}, \frac{5}{18} \right).$$

Student 2 still has a two-thirds chance of being matched with their first pick, which is the case unless that school is also the first pick of student 1. If student 2 does not receive their first choice, they are no longer guaranteed to be matched with their second choice; however, they will miss out on their second choice if it is the first choice of student 3, which is the case with a probability of $1/3$. Student 2 thus has a lower incentive to resolve their preference under IA than they did under DA. Student 3, on the other hand, now has a positive value of information. They will be matched with their first choice if it is neither the first choice of student 1 nor of student 2, which is the case with a probability of $4/9$. In this example, it is thus more equitable in incentivizing information acquisition.

It is reasonable to conjecture that some such result holds somewhat more generally. The barrier is combinatoric.

11.13 Sequential Search

Modeling students as rationally inattentive, with learning costs that are linear in the expected reduction in Shannon entropy between their prior and posterior beliefs, gives rise to equilibrium strategies that reflect the strategic learning incentives in a remarkably compact and simple form. The central analytic challenge, irrespective of learning costs, is solving for the strategic uncertainty. It is thus natural to conjecture that many of the qualitative features of the equilibrium are robust to changes in the cost function.

Most significant perhaps is to consider qualitatively different costs, such as those that characterize standard models of sequential search. While the Shannon cost function is uniformly posterior separable and as such can be micro-founded based on continuous incremental learning and optimal stopping, sequential search is a more appropriate description for situations in which agents incur fixed costs to perfectly learn their valuation of a school (e.g., through a campus visit). The most realistic cases may be of hybrid form, with both fixed and flow costs.

Bucher and Caplin revisit the three-school example and show that its key conclusions are indeed robust to replacing the Shannon cost function with optimal sequential search. Recall that the example involves three schools of unit capacity and three students whose valuation of schools is either good or bad, yielding utility $u_G > 0$ or $u_B = 0$, respectively. For example, one of the central findings is that lower-ranked students are affected disproportionately by information costs. While the precise shape depends on parameters, the broad qualitative features of relative welfare remain intact in this example. First, the relative welfare falls faster for student 2 as search costs rise above zero. Second, it is always (weakly) higher for student 1 than for student 2. It is this second property which implies that no search is optimal for student 2 at a lower cutoff than for student 1.

Note that sequential search gives rise to piece-wise linear functions, while the Shannon case is smooth. This reflects the different nature of the two information cost functions. In sequential search, students pay a fixed cost to fully reveal their valuation of a school. This results in strategies that vary discontinuously with search costs, which would make the equilibrium analysis beyond this example challenging. Shannon information costs, in contrast, make it easier to analyze the resulting equilibrium even for relatively general cases.

11.14   Hybrid Models of Search and Rational Inattention

As noted above, exchangeable distributions are closed under certain forms of updating. As one example, this allows one to develop hybrid models of sequential search and rational inattention, allowing for options to be searched at a certain fixed cost with full resolution of uncertainty as in standard sequential search, otherwise learned about in the style of RI.

By way of illustration, consider the working example with three schools and three students and an exchangeable prior:

$$\mu(GGB) = \mu(GBG) = \mu(BGG) =: \mu(2) \geq 0,$$
$$\mu(GBB) = \mu(BGB) = \mu(BBG) =: \mu(1) \geq 0.$$

We define $\mu(GGG) =: \mu(3) \geq 0$ and $\mu(BBB) =: \mu(0) \geq 0$ with $\mu(3) + 3\mu(2) + 3\mu(1) + \mu(0) = 1$.

How does updating work if one of these items is searched at some fixed search cost $C > 0$? What is the updated distribution over the remaining two schools b and c if a is good? First, one computes the *ex ante* probability that this school (any school due to exchangeability) is good: Define this $\bar{\mu}(G|\varnothing)$ as conditioning on no information:

$$\bar{\mu}(G|\varnothing) = \mu(GGG) + \mu(GGB) + \mu(GBG) + \mu(GBB)$$
$$= \mu(3) + 2\mu(2) + \mu(1).$$

The conditionals over the remaining two are implied: We write this as $\mu'(**|G)$ since it really is the same whichever of a, b, and c was searched:

$$\mu'(GG|G) = \frac{\mu(3)}{\bar{\mu}(G|\varnothing)} \equiv \mu'(2|G),$$

$$\mu'(GB|G) = \mu'(BG|G)\frac{\mu(2)}{\bar{\mu}(G|\varnothing)} \equiv \mu'(1|G),$$

$$\mu'(BB|G) = \frac{\mu(1)}{\bar{\mu}(G|\varnothing)} \equiv \mu'(0|G).$$

The key point is that this distribution is itself exchangeable over the two remaining options. This would also be true if the first were to be low. Updating under sequential search preserves exchangeability. Given observations of the values of some K of the M available actions, one can update arbitrarily on the remaining. In fact, it seems reasonable to imagine that one can update to any exchangeable distribution over the remaining $M - K$ options. This is the reason why search models do not fit well with exchangeability. The optimal strategy can be an extremely intricate function of what has been seen so far along the search path. What the above indicates is that hybrid models may be workable, provided the search costs are high enough that the number of such searches is optimally kept low. This seems reasonable in cases in which learning in the standard style of search so as to effectively resolve all uncertainty involves a physical visit.

11.15   What Class of Games Can be Analogously Solved?

The larger question that the approach of Bucher and Caplin opens up concerns the reach of the symmetry assumption. A general result would identify the richest class of games for which symmetric strategies of some subset of players, themselves heterogenous, meeting with anonymous strategies of a separate set of players, give rise to strategic learning environments that can be solved analogously based on symmetry properties.

There are some obvious paths to generalization. For example, certain externalities can be handled in matching markets. Crowding disutility just impacts the nature of the lottery over prizes and, in that sense, impacts incentives without impacting symmetry. At the same time, one can deal with purely exogenous symmetric stochastic capacity. In the case of school matching, this allows uncertainty to survive even as the number of schools grows in our model. The most important change is to soften the symmetry assumption.

Stefan Bucher and I are currently working on a generalization to tiered markets, which are characterized by a partial order on options on the other side of the matching market, with symmetry only within those that are in the same equivalence class in the vertical order. In essence, this allows for a hybrid of vertical and horizontal differentiation in a world of costly learning.

There is no reason to limit our attention to matching markets *per se*. Provided one set of players has strong enough symmetry properties and the strategically relevant others have appropriate anonymity properties, an analogous symmetry result should be available. It is also clear that that the symmetry result applies to a broader class of cost functions. It is likely that in symmetric cases, there are other models that solve formulaically. In particular, there may be some form of CES function that applies to symmetry: The functions introduced by Csaba (2021) are strong candidates. Identifying the most tractable such class is a very worthwhile topic of research.

Part 3

APPLICATIONS

The remaining lectures represent a major break in perspective. They translate the modeling framework introduced above directly into the heart of applied social science and also open up other methods of error measurement. Each lecture is concerned with a different set of scientific issues. To help orient readers, I open each lecture by providing a high-level overview of what is to follow.

Key questions in terms of application concern how widespread is availability of SDSC and what substitutes might be available when this ideal data are not available. This is best discussed once I have covered some concrete cases. For now, two comments are in order. First, there is much discretion in defining the state of the world, and this can be used to expand the reach of the corresponding analytic methods. Second, there are important correlates of mistakes that can be linked to it by highly plausible models. The very last topic in Lecture 16 relates to a judicial application, and I use that as a launchpad for the broader discussion with which this portion of the lecture notes concludes.

Lecture 12

Modeling Machine Learning

This lecture applies the methods of Parts 1 and 2 to model, better understand, and better apply machine learning methods in decision-making. All of the work is jointly conducted with Daniel Martin and Philip Marx and much is taken directly from Caplin *et al.* (2022b). Algorithms are the most important "decision makers" in the modern world today and will become ever increasingly so. They predict if a driving route has a low expected travel time, an eye scan shows physical damage, a manufactured product has a defect, a house for sale is a likely match, internet activity is a security threat, an email is spam, and so on. Virtually all industries, jobs, and consumer experiences have been impacted in some way by the rapid rise in automation brought about by this technology. Economically important applications of machine learning include what ads to serve, what content to show, what coupons to provide, facial recognition, translation, voice assist, credit scoring and loan decisions, medical decisions, product recommendations, driving routes, spam filters, fraud detection, and so on.

What exactly do we mean by saying that a machine is a DM? Technically, it is precisely what we mean in the case of human decision-making. There is a set of feasible actions specified in the program. In the case of classification tasks, these comprise labels, for example, assigning one of a set of possible labels to an image that may or may not represent a cancerous cell. The labels are typically not categorical and definitive but rather reflect some form of "confidence." The actions are commonly referred to as "predictions." In many cases, these take the same form as probabilities: numbers between 0 and 1 that add to 1. The question of whether or not they literally be interpreted as probabilistic labels is one that has occupied the literature (under the name of "calibration") and is one to which we will return.

The question we address is how one might rationalize and explain the pattern in the mistakes that machine learning algorithms make. The increasing amount and richness of data combined with deep learning techniques is leading to improved algorithmic prediction across an ever-growing range of economic problems. Given their importance, it is surprising how little work has been done to understand the nature of algorithmic predictions. As the scope of algorithmic prediction increases, the importance of understanding **why** algorithms make certain predictions increases as well. However, even if an analyst knows all of the code behind an ML algorithm, it is nearly impossible to fully grasp its inner workings, which has made algorithmic prediction a form of "black box." This opacity has only increased, as training protocols have become more complex, the number of parameters has exploded, and algorithms have become more and more nested. The pattern of errors algorithms make is of great and ever-growing social importance, e.g., if it appears to discriminate against particular groups. Providing the full code or even the precise sequence of mathematical operations is not valuable in this regard. Our understanding of the most recent machine learning algorithms is obscured by stochastic choice among local solutions to non-convex problems and is confounded by nested training protocols and model architectures involving a large number of parameters. Even if an analyst knows all of the code behind such an algorithm, it is essentially impossible to fully grasp its inner workings.

Because a complete **as is** understanding of modern machine learning algorithms is increasingly out of reach, a natural question is whether there exist parsimonious **as if** representations of opaque machine learners that can reasonably approximate their behavior. This is in the same spirit as a long literature in economics, psychology, and neuroscience that aims to generate parsimonious representations that reasonably approximate the behavior generated by the black box of human cognition. There are those, including some economists, who are convinced that algorithmic outputs are fully understandable and that there is no role for "as if" modeling. I have two comments. First, easier said than done. What they call "as is" is itself "as if" resting on a different set of ideal objects.

The lecture proceeds as follows. I begin by laying foundations and making clear the high potential of the methods of the first part of the book for understanding machine learning. I then formalize the analogy and introduce **signal-based representations** (SBRs), the machine learning equivalent of Bayesian expected utility representations and the corresponding analog of the NIAS test. Section 12.6 returns to the broader issue of calibration of machine learning algorithms when incentives are proper in the sense that the algorithm is incentivized by the loss function to provide scores that reflect implicit beliefs, which remains much debated. I then cover feasibility-based machine learning which are entirely analogous and have the same technical form as the CCRs of Lecture 5. This is followed by defining and characterizing cost-based machine learning and making precise the analogy with CIRs and the NIAC conditions. I close the lecture by providing an extensive discussion of **proper scoring rules**, which incentivize truthful revelation of subjective probabilities by any agent maximizing expected score. These loss functions play a key role in modern machine learning in defining the loss function that algorithms minimize (Carvalho, 2010). There is one finding in this section which is surprising, at least to me. It concerns a precise analogy between proper scoring rules and rationally inattentive decision problems. While proper scoring rules were developed only to elicit beliefs once learning was complete, there are reasons to believe that, in practice, they do something entirely different. They shape information processing. This is directly implied by the characterization of strictly proper scoring rules by Gneiting and Raftery (2007), which builds on the insights of De Finetti (1965) and Savage (1971). **Their characterization implies that any strictly proper scoring rule provides a strict incentive to learn more.** This works in the reverse direction also. **Any method of incentivizing an expected score maximizing agent (e.g., an algorithm trained to minimize expected losses) to learn more is associated with a specific proper scoring rule.** What this means in practice is that one should not expect different proper scoring rules to **reveal** fixed beliefs but rather to incentivize different forms of learning.

Rather than being a defect, this is a great virtue in machine learning. It means that one can, in principle, tailor the objective of the machine to focus on those aspects of learning that matter most in application. It is understood that proper scoring rules also incentivize calibration, whereby subjective and objective probabilities align. In fact, the punishment for miscalibration is also highly flexible and distinct between proper scoring rules and is another important design feature. I discuss ongoing research with Daniel Martin and Philip Marx on how the incentives implicit in proper scoring rules can be designed to optimize an underlying objective function, for example, for policy purposes. Both classification accuracy and calibration may feature in such larger social objective functions.

12.1   Why the SDSC-Based Methods of the Book Apply?

That the first application of the theoretical material in Parts 1 and 2 is to machine learning is perhaps unexpected. But technically, there is good reason for this. The analogy between human and machine learning is powerful. Good as they may be at, for example, classification tasks, algorithms are not perfect, and the pattern of errors they make is important to understand. The method that is used in designing algorithms for a particular use case involves identifying patterns in the errors in a "test set." **This pattern comes precisely in the form of SDSC data**. The analyst knows true classifications and assesses the performance of the algorithm by the pattern in the mistakes it makes. The optimal algorithm in a particular use best balances the importance of different types of error according to a loss function that is specified in algorithmic design.

A second important distinction between applications to human and to machine learning relates to the objective function. In the case of human DMs, we have to infer the utility function: not knowing this is essentially the central identification problem in part 1. By contrast, **in the case of machine learning, the loss function is specified**. In fact, a key design feature in an algorithm is the precise specification of the loss function it is seeking to minimize. This is hardly a problem. In fact, it is a virtue. It allows a crisp focus on inferring the information-theoretic constructs an algorithm produces without having then to consider how this interacts with possible utility-based explanations. In the case of the algorithm, the loss function is explicit and known.

The fact that one can program the loss function gives rise to a third key difference. Just as the key to the recovery of costs is variation in the decision problem, we propose that the best way to understand what algorithms are doing involves **varying the loss function. This is trivial for machines since all one has to do is correspondingly tweak the loss function.** A final advantage of the algorithmic setting is that human decisions contain strong and possibly immutable deviations from the precise constraints imposed by models of optimal learning. While humans are surely constrained by learning costs, the idea that they are optimally balancing costs and benefits remains controversial. There may be largely immutable human biases of the form studied in behavioral economics. For example, a human may learn poorly in practice because they update in a biased manner, possibly for self-protective reasons. The value of diagnosing such a problem is limited if it is largely hardwired. In the case of algorithms, the diagnostic approach is clearly of value. It is far harder to argue that machines have immutable biases, such as overconfidence, that may give rise to behavior that contradicts the standard model of information-constrained optimal choice on which the modeling and measurement approach of these lectures is founded. Only a very poor data scientist would refuse to change the code out of psychological defensiveness, and if they did, they might find themselves out of a job. Changing the human code is far more challenging and problematic.

With these points of perspective in mind, Caplin *et al.* (2022b) build a model of machine learning that exactly mirrors how human learners are often modeled in economics, psychology, and neuroscience and how we have modeled them throughout: as DMs who engage in signal gathering, belief formation, and choice. Specifically, we assume that when facing a test set of observations, a machine learner engages in a two-stage decision process: First, it optimally chooses a signal structure, and second, it chooses actions that minimize expected losses, given the posterior beliefs generated by signal realizations. In our theoretical model, the essential impact of varying the loss function is that it varies the machine's incentives for making different predictions.

The definitions of explainability that we employ derive entirely from continuing this analogy. The models of machine learning that we characterize are defined by the nature of the constraints on the algorithm's ability to perfectly match the training data that derive from computational constraints. In one model, we translate this technically into unknown but fixed constraints on the feasible set of models that the algorithm compares for this purpose. We call explanations of this form **feasibility based**. They precisely mirror the CCRs of Lecture 5. Our second model allows models that are searched among to vary with the loss function. In our second model, the algorithm adjusts its learning in response to additional, unobservable costs of learning. These are not the monetary costs incurred in running the algorithm, instead they reflect the intrinsic difficulty the algorithm has in learning the true outcome given its training procedures and the available training data. Technically, this second explanation maps precisely to CIRs. For obvious reasons, we call it **cost based**. So strong is the analogy that the entire analytic apparatus of earlier lectures can be transferred to the algorithmic setting upon suitably transforming objects. What this allows us to do is to get new diagnostic conditions for algorithms. Feasibility-based machine learning requires that what the algorithm learns with one learning cost function is preferred to what it learns under alternative functions since the alternative information structures are also feasible and thus could have been chosen. Cost-based learning makes a related prediction but net of additional, if unobservable, costs of learning.

In addition to presenting a structure for explaining what an algorithm does, this allows us to provide diagnostic tests that are of potential value in identifying limitations of the algorithm. If they are not satisfied, the algorithm fails to achieve optimality in specific and interesting ways that may call for changes. Moreover, if the algorithm can be explained by an "as if" cost function, one can use the methods of the book to recover all such "explanations" for algorithms that have a cost-based explanation.

12.2   Instances, Outcomes, and Loss Functions

I now introduce the formalization of algorithmic data from the work of Caplin *et al.* (2022b) There is a **test set**, X, that is used to evaluate algorithms, and a generic element, x, of this set is called an **instance** (e.g., an image, a patient record). There is also a finite set of **outcomes** Y (e.g., types of image, range of diagnoses) and a deterministic map between instances and outcomes given by $f : X \to Y$ that is called the **ground truth**. The overall distribution of outcomes in the test set is given by $\mu \in \Delta(Y)$. Note that we rename states from $\omega \in \Omega$ to $y \in Y$ to be closer to the machine language literature.

In our running application, the set of instances X is over 100,000 chest X-ray images, the set of possible outcomes $Y = \{0, 1\}$ is an indicator for the presence of pneumonia, and the ground truth is the actual outcome (pneumonia or not) corresponding to each image. As is standard when evaluating algorithms, we assume that this ground truth is correct, but our approach could be extended to include uncertainty about the ground truth.

An algorithm is a procedure that makes **predictions** about the outcome for instances in the test set. The set of possible predictions A has generic element a (i.e., a "confidence score" about an outcome, the outcome itself, groups of outcomes, etc.). This generic set A can accommodate an array of possibilities. For example, many classification algorithms output a numeric **confidence score** for each instance and possible outcome. Our framework also accommodates situations where the analyst only has data on predicted outcomes or wishes to model the scoring algorithm jointly with a downstream classification rule.

An important input to an algorithm is the **loss function** $L : A \times Y \to \mathbb{R}$, which indicates the value of a prediction given the outcome. For example, a popular loss function for binary cases with two predictions and two actions is mean squared error (MSE):

$$L(a, y) = (a - y)^2.$$

What this says is that when $y = 0$, the loss is zero only if $a = 0$ and increases the further away the prediction is from this true state. Correspondingly, when $y = 1$, the loss is zero only if $a = 1$ and increases the further away it is from this true state. It is also standard in binary cases to reweight the loss function to make losses higher or lower for a particular outcome. For example, to give more weight to squared errors when $y = 1$, the loss function might be $.4(a - 0)^2$ when $y = 0$ and $.6(a - 1)^2$ when $y = 1$. This is often done when one outcome is less common or with the hope of achieving some external objective in which the possible mistakes are of different significance.

By squaring the difference in both cases, the quadratic loss function imposes ever-increasing marginal cost on higher errors. An alternative loss function that is less responsive on the margin to increased error is absolute error, $L(a, y) = |a - y|$. A third and particularly important class of loss function with binary outcomes is β-weighted cross-entropy. As noted above,

the asymmetric class weight is used to increase the weight that the algorithm places on mistakes when instances are in the minority class:

$$L^\beta(a,y) = -\beta y \log(a) - (1-\beta)(1-y)\log(1-a). \tag{54}$$

There is often a consensus about which loss function is best to use for a
given algorithm and prediction problem. For example, it is standard practice to use cross-entropy when training deep learning neural nets to predict
the class to which an instance belongs. In what follows, the loss function
will play the role that has been played by the specification of prize $z(a, \omega)$,
which, in combination with the expected utility function, precisely pins
down $u(a, \omega)$, the analog of $L(a,y)$.

12.3   The Trained Model and SDSC

It is striking how tightly the objects above are related to those to the Blackwell model introduced in Part 1 of these lectures. There are a few changes.
On the trivial side, we have relabeled states of the world as types of the
data, Ω to Y. Almost equally nominal is the change from a utility function
that specifies how well each action does in each state to a loss function
based on how bad is each misprediction. With a sign flip, this is essentially
the same. This raises the question of whether or not the rest of the apparatus that we have introduced above has valid analogs in the algorithmic
setting. In the remainder of the section, this question is answered in the
affirmative.

The most important observation is how precisely the data that are routinely produced in judging the performance of algorithms matches our theoretical ideal of SDSC. Given loss function L, an algorithm generates a
trained model $g^L : X \rightarrow A$. The econometrician or data scientist knows
ground truth in the test data (e.g., the actual map from $f : X \rightarrow Y$ from
instances to outcomes) and thereby sees patterns in the mistakes made by
the DM (in this case, the algorithm). The performance of the trained model
is assessed on how well its predictions align with actual outcomes, as specified by the ground truth. As is standard practice in the machine learning
literature, we study algorithmic predictions over a test sample that is independently drawn from the same population as the data on which the algorithm is trained. Because the characteristics of instances can vary widely

for a particular outcome, performance is typically evaluated on how well it performs on aggregate for each outcome.

Formally, aggregate level performance for each outcome is summarized by **performance data** $\mathbf{P}^L : A \times Y \to [0,1]$, which is the joint distribution of predictions and outcomes for the trained model in a test data set:

$$\mathbf{P}^L(a,y) = \frac{|\{x \in X \,|\, g^L(x) = a \,\&\, f(x) = y\}|}{|X|}.$$

For stochastic algorithms that can generate different predictions for the same input, we take g^L to be an average prediction for each instance across trained models, which is called an **ensemble** model. Note that technically our approach can be applied to any set X, but since algorithmic performance is typically evaluated on a holdout or **test set** of instances, a natural interpretation of X is that it is the test set.

Because X is finite, $supp(P_A^L)$ is also finite. An adjustment is needed if the action space is sufficiently rich (say, the continuous unit interval) that each action is observed only once because this makes all probabilities in the performance data either 0 or 1. In such cases, our approach can instead be applied to bins of actions, with binning achieved, for example, by rounding real numbers or aggregating them into empirical quantiles. Such binning introduces its own fine points that are not central to our theoretical approach, so we do not introduce these additional formalities in our framework.

12.4 Variation in the Loss Function

The point of departure from standard ML methods is that we adopt the decision-theoretic approach of these lectures, in which the key is variation in the action set for a fixed prior. In the case of algorithms, this translates to variation in the loss function. That means our data set will provide rich information on how changes in the loss function impact what is implicitly learned by the algorithm. The issue of dealing with the match between the loss function and the performance data has not been central to machine learning, but it is central to our approach. Formally, we study how this performance data vary across a set of loss functions $\mathcal{L}$. For both realism and simplicity, we assume that for all $L \in \mathcal{L}$, the support of $\mathbf{P}^L$ over A, denoted $supp(\mathbf{P}_A^L)$, is finite.

A common class of loss functions with binary outcomes is the β-weighted cross entropy. The asymmetric class weight is used to increase the weight that the algorithm places on mistakes when instances are in the minority class:

$$L^{\beta}(a,y) = -\beta y \log(a) - (1-\beta)(1-y)\log(1-a). \qquad (55)$$

Under the weighted cross-entropy loss with binary outcomes (55), loss calibration takes a unique closed form as a function of revealed posterior probabilities. In the binary case, the posterior probabilities are also summarized by the scalar probability that the outcome is $y = 1$. We adopt this scalar posterior in the following observation for convenience.

Observation 1: Consider the weighted cross-entropy loss (55). For any weight $\beta \in (0,1)$ and all posterior probabilities $\gamma \in supp(Q)$ that the outcome is one, the unique loss-calibrated confidence score is given by

$$\alpha^{\beta}(\gamma) = \frac{\beta\gamma}{1 - \beta - \gamma + 2\beta\gamma}. \qquad (56)$$

In the case of unweighted cross-entropy loss ($\beta = 0.5$), the loss-calibrated scoring function (56) collapses to an (unconditionally) **calibrated** scoring function, $\alpha^{0.5}(\gamma) = \gamma$. Thus, as is well known, unweighted cross-entropy is a **proper** loss function, which incentivizes truthful revelation of beliefs.

12.5   Signal-Based Representations

We now present the information-theoretic foundations of the learning models we consider, their testable implications and positive evidence of these foundations in our empirical application. We follow the Blackwell model of experimentation, signal processing, and choice. We model the algorithm as an optimizing agent that (i) starts with a prior $\mu \in \Delta(Y)$ over outcomes, (ii) gets signals that provide information about the outcome, (iii) forms posterior beliefs $\gamma \in \Delta(Y)$ via Bayesian updating, and (iv) chooses predictions based on these posteriors to minimize expected losses. As before, we define $\mathcal{Q}$ as those distributions of posteriors with finite support that satisfy Bayes' rule. We change the name of the mixed strategy $q : supp(Q) \to \Delta(A)$ to fit the application by calling it a **prediction function**. For a given loss function L and distribution of posteriors $Q \in \mathcal{Q}$, the set of optimal prediction functions $\hat{q}(L,Q)$ are those that minimize total losses:

$$\sum_{\gamma \in supp(Q)} Q(\gamma) \sum_{a \in A} q(a|\gamma) \sum_{y \in Y} \gamma(y) L(a,y).$$

As is by now standard, any pair (Q,q) produces a joint distribution of predictions and outcomes given by $P_{(Q,q)} : A \times Y \to [0,1]$, where

$$P_{(Q,q)}(a,y) \equiv \sum_{\gamma \in supp(Q)} Q(\gamma) q(a|\gamma) \gamma(y).$$

With these elements in place we can define the foundation of our subsequent learning models.

Definition 42: For a given loss function L, $\mathbf{P}^L$ has a **signal-based representation** (SBR) if there exists prior $\mu \in \Delta(Y)$, a Bayes' consistent distribution of posteriors $Q \in \mathcal{Q}$, and a prediction function $q : supp(Q) \to \Delta(A)$ such that:

(1) The prior is correct: $\mu(y) = \sum_{a \in supp(P_A^L)} \mathbf{P}^L(a,y)$.
(2) Predictions are optimal at all possible posteriors: $q \in \hat{q}(L,Q)$.
(3) Predictions are generated by the model: $\mathbf{P}^L(a,y) = P_{(Q,q)}(a,y)$.

If $\mathbf{P}^L$ has an SBR, then it is **as if** the algorithm makes predictions to minimize the loss function, given the Bayesian posterior beliefs induced by its statistical experiment.

The NIAS inequalities introduced in Lecture 2 have a straightforward translation to this setting. To fit the new setting, we call this **loss calibration,** It requires that switching wholesale from any prediction a to any alternative prediction a' would never strictly reduce losses.

Definition 43 (Loss Calibration): Performance data $\mathbf{P}^L$ is **loss calibrated** to loss function L if a wholesale switch of predictions does not reduce losses according to L:

$$a \in \underset{a' \in \mathbb{R}^n}{\arg\min} \sum_{y \in Y} \mathbf{P}^L(a,y) L(a',y) \text{ for all } a \in supp(P_A^L). \quad (57)$$

Any algorithm that fails this condition makes predictions that are not suitable for the loss function and that are thus inconsistent with an SBR and

Bayesian expected loss minimization.[1] We summarize the characterization in the following result.

Proposition 5 (Testing SBR): *For a given loss function L, performance data* $\mathbf{P}^L$ *has an SBR if and only if it is loss calibrated to L.*

To illustrate this diagnostic condition in a simple and stark way, consider a setting with binary outcomes $Y = \{0,1\}$, binary predictions $a = \{0,1\}$, and absolute error (i.e., the proportion of mistakes) as the loss function. In this case, the loss function can be represented by the following matrix:

$$L = \begin{pmatrix} \overset{y=0}{0} & \overset{y=1}{1} \\ 1 & 0 \end{pmatrix} \begin{matrix} a=0 \\ a=1 \end{matrix}.$$

An algorithm that produces the following performance data would not be loss calibrated:

$$\mathbf{P}^L = \begin{pmatrix} \overset{y=0}{0.25} & \overset{y=1}{0.4} \\ 0.25 & 0.1 \end{pmatrix} \begin{matrix} a=0 \\ a=1 \end{matrix}.$$

In other words, this algorithm makes a prediction of $a = 0$ and a prediction of $a = 1$ equally often when the outcome is $y = 0$ but makes a prediction $a = 0$ more often when the outcome is $y = 1$. Note that the data set is balanced: The prior over outcomes is uniform.

This algorithm is not loss calibrated because a wholesale switch to predicting $a = 1$ when the algorithm predicted $a = 0$ would lower losses (reducing losses by 0.15). In addition, a wholesale switch to predicting $a = 0$ when the algorithm predicted $a = 1$ would also lower losses by 0.15.

---

[1] Nevertheless, this is easy to rectify. Whenever this loss function is input into the algorithm, a single line of code at the end of the computer program making a wholesale switch to predicting a whenever it would have predicted a' would make this algorithm loss calibrated for this loss function.

12.6 Calibration in Machine Learning: Theory and Practice

Given any proper loss functions that induce truthful reporting of beliefs, loss calibration coincides with calibration: Each score should equal the true probability of the instance given that score. This form of calibration is an important and much-studied property in machine learning (and beyond). Predictions should correctly reflect uncertainty.

While there is no inherent tension between the aims of accuracy and calibration in our "as-if" model of a machine, the relationship is more nuanced in the "as-is" theory and practice of machine learning. This is due to machine learning's extrapolative nature: A machine learns a model from a training sample of data in order to predict new instances outside the training sample. Furthermore, the training sample is often small relative to the potential complexity of the model.[2] The machine must therefore balance the competing aims of capturing the essential features of the training data (not underfitting), while remaining are generalizable to new instances (not overfitting). Theoretically, this problem of optimal out-of-sample learning from limited data can be cast as an optimal trade-off between bias and variance, respectively, how far predictions depart systematically from truth and how much predictions depend on the idiosyncrasies of the training data.

An optimal resolution of the bias–variance trade-off often involves introducing bias into the predictive model in order to reduce variance.[3] Introducing bias may also introduce miscalibration, e.g., in the case of lasso or ridge regressions that penalize coefficient size and thereby generate **underconfident** models whose predictions are biased toward the overall mean, i.e., shrinkage bias. Formally, miscalibration implies bias but bias does not imply miscalibration. A simple example of bias without miscalibration is extreme shrinkage bias: a constant prediction of the average training outcome, regardless of features. At the other extreme, miscalibration

---

[2]For example, in our application, a data set of 112,120 images is used to train and evaluate an ensemble of neural networks, each of which has 6,968,206 learnable parameters (Rajpurkar *et al.*, 2018).

[3]This is arguably the main distinction of machine learning relative to the regression-based methods traditionally employed in economics to address questions of causal inference.

may also arise from high variance, for example in the case of **overconfident** models whose out-of-sample confidence scores are biased toward the extremes due to overfitting of the training data. Since the machine aims to balance the competing objectives of reducing bias and variance, calibration and its relationship to accuracy are ultimately empirical questions.

Deep convolutional neural networks have been shown to suffer from miscalibration, specifically overconfidence, with the severity of miscalibration increasing in model size (Guo *et al.*, 2017). Yet, more recent findings paint a different picture. In particular, Minderer *et al.*, 2021 conduct a comprehensive comparison of 180 image classification models and find that the most accurate current models are not only well calibrated compared to earlier models but also that their calibration is more robust to distributions that differ from training.

12.7   Feasibility-Based Machine Learning

An SBR leaves open the question of how a machine learning algorithm arrives at its signal structure, that is, what (and why) the machine learns based on its incentives. We now propose and characterize two nested alternatives: choosing among a set of feasible signal structures or choosing among signal structures of different costs.

Our first model class assumes the algorithm chooses among a set of feasible signal structures to best match the incentives provided by the loss function. This precisely matches the search for a CCR in Lecture 5. As there, we define a feasible set of experiments, $\mathcal{Q}^* \subset \mathcal{Q}$. This feasible set depends only on the algorithm's capability and is not specific to the loss function provided. We define the algorithm's strategy space Λ to include both Q and q:

$$\Lambda = \{(Q,q)|Q \in \mathcal{Q}, q : supp(Q) \to \Delta(A)\}.$$

For a given loss function L and feasible set $\mathcal{Q}^*$, the set of optimal strategies $\tilde{\Lambda}(L, \mathcal{Q}^*)$ is

$$\tilde{\Lambda}(L, \mathcal{Q}^*) \equiv \underset{(Q,q)\in\Lambda, Q\in\mathcal{Q}^*}{\arg\inf} \sum_{\gamma\in supp(Q)} Q(\gamma) \sum_{a\in A} q(a|\gamma) \sum_{y\in Y} \gamma(y)L(a,y).$$

With this, we can define all performance data sets that are consistent with optimality for a given feasible set Q^* as

$$\tilde{P}(L, Q^*) \equiv \{P_{(Q,q)} | (Q,q) \in \tilde{\Lambda}(L, Q^*)\}.$$

Feasibility-based machine learning requires that there exist a feasible set Q^* such that the performance data produced by an algorithm are optimal given that feasible set for all $L \in \mathcal{L}$.

Definition 44: An algorithm is consistent with **feasibility-based machine learning** if there exists a feasible set $Q^* \subset Q$ such that $\mathbf{P}^L \in \tilde{P}(L, Q^*)$ for all $L \in \mathcal{L}$.

12.8 Cost-Based Machine Learning

Our second model class mimics the logic of a CIR. It assumes that the algorithm chooses among signal structures of different costs. To formalize this, we define a learning cost function, $K : Q \to \mathbb{R}$, and denote the set of all possible learning cost functions as $\mathcal{K}$. An algorithm's learning cost function depends only on its capabilities and is not specific to the loss function provided. Note that we do not imbue this function with meaning at this stage beyond its possible role in rationalizing algorithmic performance.

Given loss function $L \in \mathcal{L}$ and learning cost function $K \in \mathcal{K}$, the **resource-adjusted loss** $\hat{L}$ of strategy (Q,q) is

$$\hat{L}((Q,q)|L,K) \equiv \sum_{\gamma \in supp(Q)} Q(\gamma) \sum_{a \in A} q(a|\gamma) \sum_{y \in Y} \gamma(y) L(a,y) + K(Q).$$

The corresponding set of optimal strategies $\hat{\Lambda}(L,K)$ is then defined as

$$\hat{\Lambda}(L,K) \equiv \underset{(Q,q) \in \Lambda}{\arg\inf} \ \hat{L}((Q,q)|L,K).$$

This optimization problem formalizes the way in which the algorithm trades off losses with learning costs. Given any $L \in \mathcal{L}$, the set of all performance data sets that are consistent with optimality for a given learning cost function $K \in \mathcal{K}$ is

$$\hat{P}(L,K) \equiv \{P_{(Q,q)} | (Q,q) \in \hat{\Lambda}(L,K)\}.$$

Definition 45: An algorithm is consistent with **cost-based machine learning** if there exists a learning cost function $K \in \mathcal{K}$ such that $\mathbf{P}^L \in \hat{P}(L,K)$ for all $L \in \mathcal{L}$.

The second (cost-based) learning model generalizes the first (feasibility-based) model because a feasible set of posterior distributions Q^* is equivalently specified as a learning cost function K^* for which the cost is zero for every feasible posterior distribution $Q \in Q^*$ and infinite otherwise.

As noted before, this algorithm is not strongly loss adapted because a wholesale switch to the prediction data $\mathbf{P}^1$ when the loss function is L^2 would produce lower losses (by 0.08). This algorithm is also not loss adapted because adding a wholesale switch to the prediction data $\mathbf{P}^2$ when the loss function is L^1 would not offset this decrease in losses, as it would increase losses by less.

12.9   Testing the Models

Given the precise analogy of a feasibility-based machine learning with a CCR and of cost-based with a CIR, we are in position to apply the characterizations from Part 1 to identify the testable implications of these models of machine learning. In order to simplify the characterizations, we restrict consideration to data sets with an SBR representation (or its empirically verifiable counterpart, loss calibration). Because indexing will be useful in what follows, we will take as given a finite set of M loss functions, indexed by $1 \leq m \leq M$. For notational simplicity, we denote the performance data set from training the algorithm with the mth loss function as $P^m = P^{L^m}$. Our characterization of feasibility-based learning is precisely as in Lecture 5. The key idea is to ensure that losses cannot be lowered by counterfactually switching to the predictions from training with a different loss function. All such comparisons are visible in the **cross-loss matrix** G, with generic element G^{mn} in row m and column n that specifies the minimized expected losses when the loss function is L^m, and the performance data is P^n:

$$G^{mn} \equiv \sum_{a \in supp(P_A^n)} \min_{a' \in A} \sum_{y \in Y} L^m(a', y) P^n(a, y).$$

The operation on the RHS takes any prediction $a \in supp(P_A^n)$, picks some alternative prediction $a' \in A$ to replace it wholesale, computes the corresponding expected losses for L^m, and minimizes.

Note that even when an algorithm is loss calibrated (Definition 43), the computation of the G matrix typically involves recalibrating confidence scores across loss functions since the scores that are optimal for one loss function may be suboptimal for another. For example, this is the case in our application as we vary the weights in weighted cross-entropy loss (55).

Observation 2: Consider weighted cross-entropy loss (55), and suppose the algorithm is loss calibrated across weights $\beta_m \in (0,1)$, where $1 \leq m \leq M$. For simplicity of notation, denote the loss-calibrated scoring rule (56) by $\alpha_m = \alpha^{\beta_m}$. Then, cross-losses in row m and column n are minimized at every action by the recalibration rule

$$\alpha_m(\alpha_n^{-1}(a)) \in \arg\min_{a' \in A} \sum_{y \in Y} L^m(a', y) P^n(a, y). \tag{58}$$

The recalibration formula is the composite function $\alpha_m \circ \alpha_n^{-1}$ that recovers posteriors from P^n and scores them according to L^m. Unless weights are equal $\beta_m = \beta_n$ or confidence scores are extremal $a \in \{0,1\}$, this implies non-trivial recalibration, $\alpha_m(\alpha_n^{-1}(a)) \neq a$.

A feasibility-based machine learning representation requires that no switch of recalibrated performance data can lower losses. To formalize, define the $M \times M$ **direct loss difference matrix** D_0 by

$$D_0^{mn} \equiv G^{mn} - G^{mm}. \tag{59}$$

An algorithm with an SBR is **strongly loss adapted** if for all $1 \leq m, n \leq M$,

$$D_0^{mn} \geq 0.$$

Together with loss calibration, the results of Lecture 5 show that an algorithm being strongly loss adapted is necessary and sufficient for feasibility-based machine learning. To apply these results, one maps utility maximization to loss minimization and action sets to loss functions.

To illustrate strongly loss-adapted diagnostic condition, we expand our running example to include a second absolute error loss function (L^2) that punishes errors more when the outcome is $y = 1$:

$$L^1 = \begin{pmatrix} y=0 & y=1 \\ 0 & 1 \\ 1 & 0 \end{pmatrix} \begin{matrix} a=0 \\ a=1 \end{matrix} \quad \text{and} \quad L^2 = \begin{pmatrix} y=0 & y=1 \\ 0 & 1.2 \\ 0.8 & 0 \end{pmatrix} \begin{matrix} a=0 \\ a=1 \end{matrix}.$$

Suppose the algorithm produces the performance data $\mathbf{P}^1$ and $\mathbf{P}^2$:

$$\mathbf{P}^1 = \begin{pmatrix} \overset{y=0}{0.25} & \overset{y=1}{0.1} \\ 0.25 & 0.4 \end{pmatrix} \begin{matrix} a=0 \\ a=1 \end{matrix} \quad \text{and} \quad \mathbf{P}^2 = \begin{pmatrix} \overset{y=0}{0.3} & \overset{y=1}{0.2} \\ 0.2 & 0.3 \end{pmatrix} \begin{matrix} a=0 \\ a=1 \end{matrix}.$$

Both data sets are loss calibrated. To confirm, note that in neither case can switching to any of the three feasible alternatives strictly reduce losses. However, the data are not strongly loss adapted because a wholesale switch to the performance data $\mathbf{P}^1$ (in which there a fewer mispredictions when the outcome is $y = 1$) when the loss function is L^2 would produce lower losses (by 0.08). To see this, note that misclassification when the outcome is $y = 1$ would fall to a fraction of all observations from 20% to 10% with a loss reduction of 0.12 as a result, while misclassification when the outcome is $y = 0$ would rise to a fraction of all observations from 20% to 25%, with a resulting absolute loss increase of 0.04, netting out to a loss reduction of 0.08.

The corresponding characterization of cost-based learning is in Lecture 3. Recalling that $H(m,n)$ comprises all sequences of indices $\vec{h} = (h(1), h(2), \ldots, h(J(\vec{h})))$ in which the first $J(\vec{h}) - 1$ entries are distinct, the **indirect loss difference matrix** computes the minimized summed loss differences on such paths:

$$D^{mn} \equiv \min_{\{\vec{h} \in H(m,n)\}} \sum_{j=1}^{J(\vec{h})-1} D_0^{j(j+1)}. \tag{60}$$

By direct analogy with the NIAC conditions, we know that an algorithm with an SBR has a cost-based explanation if and only if no cycle of switches can lower losses, which we call **loss adapted**. Formally, an algorithm with an SBR is **loss adapted** if for all $1 \le m \le M$,

$$D^{mm} \ge 0.$$

Recall that this matrix can be computed in polynomial time by applying the Floyd–Warshall algorithm to the complete weighted directed graph with weight D_0^{mn} on the directed edge from node $1 \le m \le M$ to node $1 \le n \le M$.

The preceding discussion of empirical content of the learning models is summarized in the following result.

Proposition 6 (Testing Models of Machine Learning): *An algorithm with an SBR has a feasibility-based representation if and only if it is strongly loss adapted. An algorithm with an SBR has a cost-based representation if and only if it is loss adapted.*

Lecture 4 shows how to identify all **qualifying costs of revealed learning** $\{K^m\}_{m=1}^M$ that rationalize the observed performance data according to cost-based machine learning in that costs are minimized by choosing data set P^m at cost K^m when the loss function is L^m:

$$D_0^{mm} + K^m \leq D_0^{mn} + K^n, \tag{61}$$

for all $1 \leq m, n \leq M$. For present purposes, key observations are that, normalizing to $K^M = 0$, qualifying learning costs $\{K^m\}_{m=1}^M$ define a convex polyhedron in $\mathbb{R}^{M-1}$ with the sign-inverted Mth row $(-D^{M1}, \ldots, -D^{M(M-1)})$ and the Mth column $(D^{1M}, \ldots, D^{(M-1)M})$ as a subset of the extreme points. Furthermore, an average difference $\bar{K}$ across normalizations is potentially appealing as a representative learning cost because it is "central," qualifying, and easy to compute.

To illustrate cost recovery, consider a loss-calibrated algorithm for which we specify the corresponding T matrix directly as

$$
\begin{array}{ccc}
\mathbf{P}^1 & \mathbf{P}^2 & \mathbf{P}^3
\end{array}
$$
$$
G = \begin{pmatrix} 3 & 1 & 10 \\ 5 & 2 & 5 \\ 10 & 1 & 3 \end{pmatrix} \begin{array}{c} L^1 \\ L^2. \\ L^3 \end{array}
$$

Writing out the D matrix, we get

$$
\begin{array}{ccc}
\mathbf{P}^1 & \mathbf{P}^2 & \mathbf{P}^3
\end{array}
$$
$$
D = \begin{pmatrix} 0 & -2 & 1 \\ 3 & 0 & 3 \\ 1 & -2 & 0 \end{pmatrix} \begin{array}{c} L^1 \\ L^2. \\ L^3 \end{array}
$$

The only elements of D that reflect lowering losses through indirect paths are D^{13} and D^{31}:

$$D^{13} = G^{12} - G^{11} + G^{23} - G^{22} = 1,$$
$$D^{31} = G^{32} - G^{33} + G^{21} - G^{22} = 1.$$

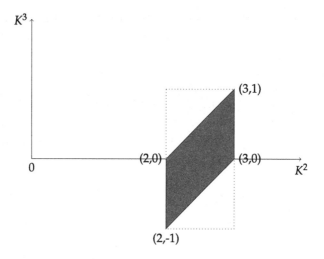

Figure 12.1   Learning cost polyhedron.

The zeros on the diagonal and the positive sums of off-diagonal pairs reveal this to be loss adapted. The theorem also implies directly that $(-1, 2)$ and $(1,3)$ are extreme points of the cost polyhedron normalized to $K^3 = 0$. The entire normalized polyhedron involves also the upper and lower bounds on $K^1 - K^2$:

$$K^1 - K^2 \leq D^{12} = -2,$$
$$K^2 - K^1 \leq D^{21} = 3.$$

This is marked in Figure 12.1.

12.10   Application

The empirical implementation in CMM involves changing the machine's incentives for making different predictions by varying class weights. We find that predictions are consistent with cost-based learning but not feasibility-based learning. This arises because of a common preference for information structures chosen across class weights, which violates feasibility-based learning but can be rationalized with recourse to additional structural costs of learning inherent to the algorithm. In addition, we recover sharp bounds on the structural cost parameters and construct a "representative" learning cost for the algorithm. These bounds and representative costs suggest that by placing relatively lower weights on pneumonia instances, the algorithm incurs higher learning costs, which is sensible given that doing so places relatively higher weights on non-pneumonia instances, which are far more common. One reason for looking for explanations of the form we do is to recover something stable that survives comparative statics, much as in inverse reinforcement learning. Going forward, one research goal will be to see if this form of cost recovery does indeed help to understand counterfactual algorithmic performance for different loss functions. Investigating this is part of a long research road ahead of us.

CMM evaluate and estimate these models using CheXNeXt, an influential deep learning convolutional neural network for predicting thoracic diseases from chest X-ray images (Rajpurkar *et al.*, 2018). We vary the algorithm's loss function by varying its class weights, which dictate the relative value a loss function places on correct and incorrect predictions across different class labels. Rajpurkar *et al.* (2018) follow standard practice in using class weights to increase the value that the algorithm places on mistakes made for observations in the underrepresented class, which is important given that only 1.3% of chest X-rays are, in fact, labeled with pneumonia. In our implementation, we isolate the task of pneumonia detection and train the algorithm across various β-weighted cross-entropy loss functions:

$$L^{\beta}(a,y) = -\beta y \log(a) - (1-\beta)(1-y)\log(1-a), \qquad (62)$$

specifically $\beta = 0.7, 0.9, 0.99$. The class weight used in the analysis of rajpurkar2017chexnet is approximately 0.99 because the probability of positive pneumonia cases in the data set is 0.0127. We employ ensemble (model-averaging) methods to isolate the substantive effects of what the machine learns from random noise inherent to the stochastic training procedure.

The first finding is that confidence scores are loss calibrated, as in (56), across various weights β in weighted cross-entropy loss (55). This includes unconditional calibration for unweighted cross-entropy loss ($\beta = 0.5$), which is a proper loss function. Going beyond this, they estimate the cross-loss and indirect loss-difference matrices G and D. Given the strong evidence of loss calibration, the intermediate step is to compute the D_0 matrix by directly applying the recalibration formula (58) to recover optimal confidence scores across weights. This analytical mapping circumvents the need to bin data to recover posterior beliefs, avoiding the finite sample issues associated therewith.[4] Values in each matrix are normalized by a constant preceding the matrix for improved legibility:

$$G = 0.01 \begin{array}{ccc} P^{0.7} & P^{0.9} & P^{0.99} \\ \begin{pmatrix} 3.750 & 3.752 & 3.762 \\ 3.349 & 3.352 & 3.362 \\ 1.365 & 1.366 & 1.370 \end{pmatrix} & \begin{array}{c} L^{0.7} \\ L^{0.9} \\ L^{0.99} \end{array} \end{array},$$

$$D = 0.1^5 \begin{array}{ccc} P^{0.7} & P^{0.9} & P^{0.99} \\ \begin{pmatrix} 0 & 2.548 & 12.467 \\ -2.529 & 0 & 9.938 \\ -6.993 & -4.463 & 0 \end{pmatrix} & \begin{array}{c} L^{0.7} \\ L^{0.9} \\ L^{0.99} \end{array} \end{array}.$$

CMM develop a statistical confirmation that the D_0 matrix is not strongly loss adapted so there is no feasibility-based explanation of the data. Further inspection of D_0 reveals a systematic reason for why we reject the null hypothesis: Loss functions have a common preference for the experiments revealed by lower β. They then observe that, since D has a main diagonal of zero, the algorithmic data are consistent with cost-based learning:

$$\mathcal{H}_0 : D^{mm} = 0 \quad \text{for all } 1 \leq m \leq M.$$

Intuitively, even though all loss functions are minimized (among revealed experiments) under lower-β experiments, the gains from switching experiments are lower for higher-β loss functions.

Because the data are consistent with cost-based learning, CMM also recover all qualifying costs. Given that the value of revealed experiments is decreasing in the β of the weighted loss function, the costs of the

---

[4]Note, however, that the evidence of loss calibration still involved binning the data into deciles.

revealed experiments must also be decreasing in β in order to rationalize the observed choices. These bounds and representative costs suggest that by placing relatively lower weights on pneumonia instances, the algorithm incurs higher learning costs, which is sensible given that doing so places relatively higher weights on non-pneumonia instances, which are far more common. CMM conclude by noting that the test has high power: Any reordering of revealed experiments would have resulted in a point-wise rejection of pair-wise loss adaptedness and, therefore, also of full loss adaptedness.

12.11 Characterization of Proper Scoring Rules

The research team is actively engaged in the next steps. For example, our approach implies that the standard approach to ranking algorithms in simple binary cases based on the receiver operating curve (ROC) should not be applied to the actual scores but rather based on the scores optimal according to the loss function after loss recalibration. There are also obvious applications to counterfactual analysis and the understanding of what makes particular forms of learning more or less costly for an algorithm. If an algorithm has an SBR, a feasibility-based representation, or a cost-based representation, it will respond in lawful and predictable ways to variation in its loss function. Varying the loss function and applying our methods should allow the analyst to better pinpoint and potentially manipulate what is learned.

The extent to which one can one shape learning to achieve important end goals by manipulating the loss function depends critically on how rich is the class of loss functions. Particularly important are **proper** loss functions which provide an incentive to report probabilistic beliefs accurately, all of which are calibrated if our model applies. As in the case of cross-weighted entropy, these themselves can be reweighted should an application so suggest and their predictions inverted to reveal corresponding posterior beliefs.

Fortunately, much is already known about proper scoring rules, which are defined as the converse of proper loss functions, in that the assumed goal is to maximize rather than minimize expected score. In relating to this very large literature, it is best to switch to the maximizing perspective before introducing the wonderful characterization of proper scoring rules that incentivize accurate reporting of beliefs due essentially to Savage (1971), with the complete formulation by Gneiting and Raftery (2006).

A few formal definitions are of value. Suppose that there are N possible states of the world, identified by the index $1 \leq n \leq N$. The action set is the set of stated beliefs $p \in \Delta^{N-1}$, the $N-1$ dimensional probability simplex. For each such stated belief, a scoring function is specified that defines the score associated with each state n realizing. So, a scoring rule can be regarded as comprising a set of N functions of the stated belief, $S_n(p)$.

Definition 46: A scoring rule is proper if the expected reward from truthful reporting is at least as high as that of any other report:

$$\sum_n q_n S_n(q) \geq \sum_n q_n S_n(p), \tag{63}$$

for all $q, p \in \Delta^{N-1}$. It is strictly proper if the inequality is strict whenever $p \neq q$.

The LHS of equation (64) is the expected score of reporting q when believing q, while the RHS is the expected score of reporting p when believing q.

To illustrate, consider the two-state (binary) case in which the report and reward scheme depend only on the reported and actual probabilities of state 1 r_1, p_1 as $S_1(r_1, (1 - r_1))$ and $S_2(r_1, 1 - r_1)$, respectively, so that the expected reward is

$$\bar{S}(r_1|p_1) = p_1 S_1(r_1, 1 - r_1) + (1 - p_1)S_1(r_1, 1 - r_1).$$

The two best known such proper scoring rules are the quadratic and the logarithmic, both of which were introduced above in the case of losses and play a large role in machine learning in that form. A standard formal specification of the quadratic scoring rule for maximization rather than minimization is as follows:

$$S_1^Q(r_1, 1 - r_1) = 2r_1 - r_1^2 - (1 - r_1)^2,$$
$$S_2^Q(r_1, 1 - r_1) = 2(1 - r_1) - r_1^2 - (1 - r_1)^2.$$

To see that this is proper, note that the expected value $\bar{S}^Q$ satisfies

$$\bar{S}^Q(r_1|p_1) = p_1[2r_1 - r_1^2 - (1 - r_1)^2] + (1 - p_1)[2(1 - r_1) - r_1^2 - (1 - r_1)^2]$$
$$= 4r_1 p_1 - 2r_1 - 2p_1 + 2 + 1 - r_1^2 - (1 - r_1)^2.$$

Taking the derivative w.r.t r_1 and setting to zero reveals that the unique solution is $r_1 = p_1$. Note also that the second derivative at this point is strictly negative, so this is a strict maximum verifying properness.

The logarithmic scoring rule is defined by

$$S_1^L(r_1, 1 - r_1) = \ln r_1,$$
$$S_2^L(r_1, 1 - r_1) = \ln(1 - r_1).$$

The expected reward satisfies

$$\bar{S}^L(r_1|p_1) = p_1 \ln r_1 + (1 - p_1)\ln(1 - r_1).$$

Taking the derivative w.r.t r_1 and setting to zero again reveals that the unique solution is $r_1 = p_1$, and with the second derivative at this point is negative, this is a strict maximum again verifying properness.

Proper scoring rules were introduced initially by Brier (1950) for weather forecasting to incentivize accurate revelation of probabilistic beliefs. They are now routinely used in experimental economics (Nyarko and Schotter, 2002; Schotter and Trevino, 2014; Armantier and Treich, 2013). Proper scoring rules are now ubiquitous in machine learning (see Carvalho, 2016). There are many studies of the different forms of such rule and the grounds on which one might choose between them. These have generally been somewhat aesthetic in nature. This form of discussion was already familiar to Savage:

> It would therefore seem important to study in what respects one scoring rule is better than another. But this question has thus far proved surprisingly unproductive. Its elusiveness is brought out by the consideration than an ideal subject responds to all proper scoring rules, including those involving extremely small payments, in exactly the same way. Therefore, any criteria for distinguishing among scoring rules must arise out of departures of actual subjects from the ideal. (Savage, 1971, p. 798)

With due respect to Savage, this argument holds only under strong assumptions. It requires both that learning is independent of the scoring rule and that DMs are perfectly calibrated. Neither of these is universally valid. In this lecture, I address the issue for the case of machine learning and, in the next, for the case of human learning.

12.12   Proper Scoring Rules Incentivize Learning

In the machine learning context, the most basic issue is that scoring rules differentially impact the incentive to learn. These scoring rules do not incentivize reporting of current beliefs. Rather, they incentivize additional learning. It is easiest to see this by applying the general characterization of proper scoring rules by Gneiting and Raftery (2007). Their approach is based entirely on convex analysis and the characterization of convex functions in terms of subdifferentials by Rockafellar (1971).

The key computation is to define expected reward as a function of the truthful report $r_1 = p_1$. Take first the quadratic case

$$\bar{S}^Q(p_1|p_1) = 4p_1^2 - 2p_1 + 2.$$

This is strictly positive so that this function is strictly convex. Its slope increases from 2 at $p_1 = 0$ to 6 at $p_1 = 1$. Now, take the logarithmic case,

$$\bar{S}^L(p_1|p_1) = p_1 \ln p_1 + (1 - p_1) \ln (1 - p_1).$$

This is nothing but the negative of Shannon entropy, so famously convex.

The fact that these are both strictly convex functions of beliefs is the beginning and end of why they constitute proper scoring rules. Take any proper convex function of beliefs $G : \Delta^{N-1} \longrightarrow \mathbb{R}$ and identify subdifferentials $g_q : \Delta^{N-1} \longrightarrow \mathbb{R}$ at all points $q \in \Delta^{N-1}$. The subdifferential is a linear function that is, at least, locally a supporting hyperplane to the epigraph of the function. By definition, a function is strictly convex if and only if all subdifferentials lie everywhere below the function G and strictly below expect at the point that defines it. The beautiful proof that one can define a corresponding proper scoring rule is entirely geometric (see Gneiting and Raftery, 2007, Figure 1). What one does is to identify the value of this linear functional at the nth unit vector e_n as $g_q(e_n)$ and set this to be the score given probabilistic answer q if that given answer is correct:

$$S_n(q) = g_q(e_n). \tag{64}$$

Strict properness of this scoring rule for any strictly convex function G is directly implied by the fact that all subdifferentials lie strictly below that function except at the point of definition. This is not only sufficient but necessary for the scoring rule to be strictly proper.

A reward function that is a strictly convex function of beliefs is not a neutral method of revealing beliefs. In fact, just such strictly convex reward functions for different posterior motivate learning in the model of rational inattention in Parts 1 and 2 of the book. **Hence, each proper scoring rule provides a different incentive for the DM to learn.** Conversely, any decision problem in which learning is incentivized can be mapped directly to a proper scoring rule defined by precisely the same incentive to learn. The lack of discussion of this issue in the literature is striking. While designed only to elicit honesty, these rules by their structure incentivize learning. Each convex function of posteriors has rich properties beyond merely being proper. They specify precisely how much more valuable it is to know more based on the *G* function. Strict convexity of this expected reward is equivalent to the statement that it is always strictly better to know more. Precisely how much is tightly modulated by the precise shape of this function. One can design proper multiple-choice tests that essentially provide arbitrary convex incentives for better understanding the truth.

Note that the above applies directly to machine learning because the loss function is the ultimate incentive driving the machine's strategy. Things are more intricate in the case of human learning in which there may be an ultimate reward that makes the grade *per se* of less importance, as discussed briefly in the following lecture.

12.13   Proper Scoring Rules and Calibration

In addition to defining the incentive to learn, each proper scoring rule specifies precisely how damaging it is to have an incorrect probabilistic belief: This is related to the distance between the function evaluated at true belief q as opposed to alternative belief p as in the term

$$D(p,q) \equiv \sum_n q_n S_n(q) - \sum_n q_n S_n(p).$$

In standard well-behaved cases, this is a Bregman divergence. Again, this can be manipulated by design of the scoring rule. This means that one can design penalties for poorly calibrated algorithms that fail to match subjective beliefs with objective probabilities.

There is an interesting modeling challenge associated with how what the machine learns responds to altered incentives for calibration. As Savage argues, there is always an incentive to be well calibrated with any proper scoring rule. Moreover, the theory of rational inattention, while making no direct reference to calibration, is implicitly based on the assumption that the DM knows their actual posterior belief and uses this calibrated posterior in choosing among actions. The idea that altering the punishment for different forms of miscalibration would change learning is, therefore, beyond the reach of the theory in current form.

Lecture 13

Teaching, Testing, and Learning

In this lecture, I outline applications of the ideas and methods of the book to teaching and testing protocols for humans rather than for machines. I pick up where the last lecture left off, with the use of proper scoring rules to better understand and to impact learning. Both de Finetti (1965) and Savage (1971) proposed the use of just such scoring rules in multiple-choice tests. To date, this approach has found traction only within decision analysis, where it appears to have proven its worth (Bickel, 2010). I outline some of the powerful arguments in favor of broader experimentation and implementation.

The reason for pursuing research on testing, teaching, and learning is analogous to the reasons for applying the methods of the book to machine learning. All of the elements put in place in earlier lectures are of clear relevance. Costs of learning are central: A key role of teaching is surely to lower these costs for as yet unrealized future decision problems. Incentives for students to learn depend on the course grading scheme and also on how these grades are translated into final rewards, for example, in the labor market. So, the teaching and testing processes impact student decisions on the deployment of attention, as in rational inattention theory. On the other side of the ledger, for a teacher to have a clear view of how best to teach requires them to monitor what is being learned during the teaching process. The data that are derived in many tests used to gauge progress of students toward their goal is SDSC data. The teacher presumably knows the correct answer to questions posed and is judging students' abilities to identify this "state of the world," as reflected by their choice of answer.

That is precisely what SDSC measures. Inference from the results of the test involves statistical analysis of the resulting SDSC.

This lecture is entirely forward-looking. It provides motivation for and lays out a research agenda designed to improve the quality of teaching, testing, and learning. All of the proposals involve pursuing in depth the methods of the book and build on their application to machine learning. The research path involves developing formal models of testing protocols and their interaction with learning as well as complementary evidence in lab and field. The ultimate goal is to promote implementation of methods that are found to be of particular value. The lecture is structured as follows:

1. I open by laying out the basic proposals of De Finetti (1965) and Savage (1971) concerning the use of proper scoring rules in multiple-choice tests. By providing a richer set of responses than do standard such tests, they allow richer information to be gleaned than do standard all-or-nothing tests. Richer inference presumably allows subsequent teaching to be improved and provides better information to all who wish to gauge student skill levels.

2. I outline the case for further experimentation on testing protocols in real classroom settings. The only example that has been formally written up and is widely available is that of Bickel (2010), who details the use of proper scoring rules in decision analysis. The basic findings are positive: As expected, much more is revealed than would have been in a standard multiple-choice test. Each class that is taught provides a natural opportunity for further such experimentation. As teachers, we design the tests we give and can implement ideas first in less important settings (e.g., an informal quiz) before moving to wider implementation. To be effective, research on implementation will need to be centrally organized and results widely disseminated.

3. A key to the possible value of proper scoring rules in the teaching process is the information they reveal on students' degree of **calibration**. This reflects their accuracy in understanding their level of uncertainty. This is well studied in machine learning, as outlined in the previous lecture: If an image of an animal that is either a dog or a cat is predicted to be 0.9 dog, does that translate to a 90% chance objectively? An analogous question can be asked in a multiple-choice test in which one

allows probabilistic answers. Strictly proper scoring rules **incentivize** calibration: An individual who expresses great confidence in an answer that is wrong scores lower than an individual who assigns highest probability to the same wrong answer yet is less confident that it is correct. Just such cases were identified by Bickel (2010). In a medical setting, Currie and MacLeod (2017) show that physicians not only have diverse operating skills but also different apparent awareness of the appropriate medical course, given their skills. Hence, **calibration is important in the field.** It needs to be studied its own right and will grow ever more important due to its critical role in human–computer interactions. Successful such interactions in decision-making require both human and machine to be well calibrated so that rules for one overriding a suggested decision of the other are appropriate.

4. **Is calibration itself a learnable skill?** I introduce Savage's view that a key virtue of proper scoring rules is precisely to get students comfortable with, and skilled in, gauging their degree of uncertainty. This is an area about which we know next to nothing. I know of no systematic exploration of the extent that Savage is correct in viewing calibration as learnable.

5. Given how many important open questions there are in the area of teaching, testing, and learning, I outline a holistic research program interacting experimental design with theoretical innovation. There are numerous interesting modeling challenges that interact with experimental advance: For example, if it is found experimentally that calibration is a learnable skill, it will point to next generation models of rational inattention with an explicit role for lack of awareness.

6. Powerful as it might be, the analogy between human and machine learning is far from complete. The application to human learning suggests the need to take into account of sophisticated aspects of the process of learning that psychologists are studying at depth, with the recent engagement of economists, which have as yet no clear machine learning counterpart. The burgeoning literature on metacognition is innovating in the design of measurements to elicit the degree of awareness of own knowledge and of costs of learning (Summerfield and Yeung, 2012; Enke and Graeber, 2019). Another important literature relates to instinctual errors that appear to require costly cognitive control to override. How precisely

this form of error can be separated from more standard forms of error induced by sheer complexity is important from the viewpoint of teaching, which in itself a subject of ongoing research.

7. I close the lecture by considering human learning on a variety of different time scales. Just as there are short-, medium-, and long-run costs of production in the Marshallian vision of firm behavior, so there are for psychological costs that determine error propensities. Starting in the very short run, there is the process of arriving at the answer to a question. Here, insights derive from process measurements, such as decision times, deriving from the psychological tradition. At the other end of the scale are life-cycle patterns: from skill development in the early years, through learning by doing in the working years, all the way to cognitive decline in the later years. This highlights the vast range of cognitive factors that come into play in the process of learning and unlearning skills, with important consequences for the structure of decision-making mistakes.

13.1 Proper Scoring in Multiple-Choice Tests

The previous lecture made the case for modeling machine learning using methods that originate in the study of human learning. There are equally strong arguments for applying methods to understand machine learning to improve our understanding of human learning. A particularly salient example involves the design of multiple-choice tests. A standard such test involves the student picking one option and being scored on how many answers are correct. The obvious question is why we do not allow richer answers, analogous to the "predictions" that are the output of machine learning. Why not allow probabilistic answers indicating how likely the respondent believes each answer to be correct? Why is this standard practice in the context of machine learning but not of human learning?

I am far from the first to suggest the value of richer scoring rules. In fact it was interest in just this possibility that prompted de Finetti (1965) and Savage (1971) to study proper scoring rules in the first place. They explicitly proposed allowing probabilistic answers indicating how likely the respondent believed each answer to be correct. They noted that standard multiple-choice tests are very uninformative about the student's state of knowledge. They pointed out how much more the teacher might understand about the sources of misunderstanding if answers were of this form. Their argument was based, in large part, on the rich information about student comprehension that proper scoring rules can reveal:

> Proper scoring rules hold forth promise as more sophisticated ways of administering multiple-choice tests in certain educational situations. The student is invited not merely to choose one item (or possibly none) but to show in some way how his opinion is distributed over the items, subject to a proper scoring rule or a rough facsimile thereof. (Savage, 1971, p. 800)

To illustrate the point, note that a probabilistic answer is likely to be more Blackwell informative than a standard 0–1 answer in almost any model of student motivation. Taking the simplest case of a risk-neutral test taker aiming to maximize expected grade, providing the more likely correct answer garbles private information and makes student ranking far cruder and less informative. This lower information operates on two levels. First, the student is less able to accurately reflect their understanding in the response. Second, by lowering the signal-to-noise ratio, standard tests make the results of the test less informative for all users. As a direct result, teachers get far less information with which to diagnose the limits of student comprehension and to identify any confusion for which they themselves might be responsible. The lower signal quality is also important to all later users of the information that the score conveys, for example in relation to further education or later employment.

13.2 Educational Experimenters Needed

There is an early psychological literature on probabilistic scoring of multiple-choice tests (Ben-Simon *et al.*, 1997), but a much broader consideration of proper scoring rules and other changes in test design is warranted. Likely, there are those who will claim that common proper scoring rules are "too complex." One can even imagine jokes about the course that students would need to understand them. My own experience teaching suggests exactly the opposite. If there are clear rules about how to earn a grade, students follow them in fine detail. Grades are so profoundly important that how they are earned, which varies course by course, is job number 1 to explain. If proper scoring rules of a few well-tested forms were to be introduced and used in multiple settings, students would understand them intimately. Online resources would explain them engagingly. All that is required is a will and an appropriate research effort. That such research would be undertaken was certainly Savage's hope. The above quote on the information content of proper scoring rules continues precisely with a call for experimentation:

> Though requiring more student time per item, these methods should result in more discrimination per item than ordinary multiple-choice tests, with a possible net gain. Also they seem to open a wealth of opportunities for the educational experimenter. (Savage, 1971, p. 800)

Fortunately, there is one field in which proper scoring rules have found traction: decision analysis. Experiences using these methods are outlined by Bickel (2010). His paper indicates a number of important respects in which the rules reveal rich information about what is understood. For example, there are answers that many would have got correct if forced to pick one response but about which there was high uncertainty, calling for the topic to be revisited.

13.3   Calibration is a Key Skill

As standardly conceived, skills relate to the quality of performance in a given task. Tests are designed primarily to assess those skills. This focus is to a large extent understandable: We would like those who design skyscrapers to have the technical expertise to judge the impact of subtle changes in where they are building on the stability of the resulting design. In this regard, the fact that proper scoring rules incentivize calibration, matching of subjective with objective probabilities, may appear to be of second-order importance. To the contrary, I believe that calibration is a critical skill, often as important as task performance, and will only grow more so over time.

In a clear demonstration of why calibration matters in practice, Currie and MacLeod (2017) use standard administrative data to study C-sections to identify doctors whose decision-making is significantly worse than the norm using detailed information about health conditions. They examine both the quality of decision-making and the quality of execution of those decisions. This is an important distinction. To be aware of what operation is best to perform requires a form of calibration, while to be able to perform successfully is a task skill. So, improved calibration is, in many cases of human decision-making, just as important as the underlying task skill itself.

Looking forward, calibration is likely to be ever more important as human–machine interactions come to dominate decision-making. Optimizing these interactions in various decision-making procedures is already a major area of research. Calibration is of the essence for the appropriate coordination of such interactions. Both human and machine need accurate information on the quality of the others' predictions if they are to work in tandem and arrive at a high-quality final decision. This is increasingly essential in almost all decisions of import. For example in many of the important areas of decision-making, such as medical diagnoses, a human expert gets the final word after receiving multiple machine-generated predictions. Awareness on the part of the human DM of their actual abilities in comparison with those of their algorithmic advisers is critical to reducing mistakes. We will want the human DM to understand whether they actually have information that can improve on the algorithm's decisions, and hence override them, and when they do not. This calls as much for calibration as it does for task skills.

There is a larger research gap that these considerations suggest. There are no broad modeling approaches in place that allow us to capture the breadth and depth of interactions between human and machine learning that dominate the modern world. In addition to needing to study methods of improving decision-making quality through appropriately structuring "teams" of humans and machines arriving at a final decision of consequence, we have failed to note that the prevalence of human–machine interactions renders archaic the time-honored distinction in economics between consumption and production. The services that each of us derive from one and the same purchase are entirely different, depending on how well we are able to master the necessary technology. The costs of learning impact the level of effective consumption from given spending. This is a modern version of the distinction that Aguiar and Hurst (2005) introduced between spending and consumption in comparing the pre-retirement period with the post-retirement one.

13.4   Is Calibration a Learnable Skill?

There are many studies of calibration that indicate various behavioral issues, such as overconfidence (Moore and Healy, 2008). Yet, we know very little of a systematic nature about how well calibrated are human DMs when answering properly incentivized test questions in an exam. Bickel (2010) finds that calibration varies across subjects. Averaging across students in his courses, he found that answers were approximately calibrated. Across the student body as a whole, the answer 0.75 corresponded approximately to a proportion of 0.75 of corresponding answers being correct. Yet, he noted large individual differences in how well calibrated his students were. There were students who did not approach the maximum degree of certainty, yet earned some of the highest marks because they assessed their more limited state of knowledge well. Conversely, there were students who expressed great confidence in answers being correct and were therefore penalized heavily because too high a proportion of such answers were wrong.

Given that not all appear perfectly calibrated, there is a natural follow-up question. We need to investigate the extent to which differences in precisely how different scoring rules incentivize calibration impacts how calibrated students learn to be. One might expect students who were heavily punished in their grade for their overconfidence to learn to temper their judgement in the direction of realism. Reinforcement learning alone should accomplish this. Savage himself was strongly of the opinion that calibration is not only crucial but itself a learnable skill when making the case for investigating the use of proper scoring rules:

> Above all, the educational advantage of training people, possibly beginning in early childhood-to assay the strengths of their own opinions and to meet risk with judgment seems inestimable. The usual tests and the language habits of our culture tend to promote confusion between certainty and belief. They encourage both the vice of acting and speaking as though we were certain when we are only fairly sure and that of acting and speaking as though the opinions we do have were worthless when they are not very strong. (Savage, 1971, p. 800)

There is one arena in which there is already evidence suggesting that awareness of cognitive constraints is a learned skill. In baseball and basketball, filming of games means that there is essentially 50–50 vision in hindsight. Making accurate calls is of clear payoff relevance since umpires and referees are judged and ultimately rewarded based on reviews of their performance. Archsmith *et al.* (2021) exploit high-frequency data on the accuracy of umpires' calls in Major League Baseball. They also develop a model of the importance of each call based on pivotality (e.g., the chance that a mistake would significantly change the balance of play). They find many patterns consistent with high awareness of cognitive constraints and rational inattention, for example that umpires make fewer mistakes in higher-stakes decisions. They also observe a pattern of increased mistakes after important decisions and find evidence of anticipatory shepherding of resources. They show that an expectation of higher stakes in upcoming decisions leads to more errors in current decisions, consistent with forward-looking behavior by umpires aware of attention scarcity, particularly for experienced umpires. While many of these findings are spiritually in line with classical production theory, the roles of tiredness *per se* and the impact of expectations represent a particularly human aspect of the theory.

13.5 Calibration and Metacognition

The issue of how well people understand the actual degree of objective uncertainty associated with their choices is part of a broader issue of awareness of cognitive limits and cognitive costs. Recent findings suggest that this form of awareness is limited. Bronchetti *et al.* (2020) conduct a number of experiments demonstrating that the impact of interventions, such as reminders, on learning are not well understood. Interestingly the same appears to apply to environmental factors and distractions that are surely common in the workplace, yet whose role appears not to be well understood. Mani *et al.* (2013) argue that poverty affects income-earning capacity through a variety of channels that deplete attentional resources and negatively impact job performance. In support, Kaur *et al.* (2021) paid poor subjects a piece rate for completing a repetitive yet intricate attention-demanding task. They found that workers who were paid earlier were better able to complete these tasks and consequently earned higher incomes. They note the value that mid-day breaks have in terms of raising productivity, yet failure of workers to take, and firms to provide, such breaks. Other poverty-related factors that have been found to affect attentional constraints and income are sleep deprivation, exposure to high levels of air pollution, and exposure to high levels of noise pollution.

In her recently completed PhD, Salcher (2022) examines to what extent workers are aware of factors affecting their productivity and invest in their productivity, using the case of interruptions which shift workers' attention away from the task at hand. In an online experiment, each participant works on a representative real-work task with and without interruptions, where interruptions are incoming emails requiring a short but immediate response. Following this, Salcher measures subjects' beliefs about their work performance by allowing a choice of payment scheme, finding widespread unawareness both of the overall quality of their performance and the impact of the interruptions. Belief elicitation confirms high levels of misunderstanding.

Looking forward, there would be great value in joining the study of calibration with literatures on metacognition in psychology and, increasingly, in economics, which involve entirely different research methods (Yeung and Summerfield, 2012; Enke and Graeber, 2019). A prominent such method involves enriching the domain of choice and offering choice of tasks in which higher attentional complexity is rewarded by higher levels of possible payout. For example, one might offer one option that is informationally simple, yet offers little reward and a second that is more challenging, yet offers high reward. Experiments along these precise lines have been conducted by Avoyan and Romagnoli (2019), Carvalho and Silverman (2019), and Oprea (2020).

13.6 A Research Agenda

The above makes a number of points in favor of experimentation with proper scoring rules in educational settings. I now sketch a recently initiated research path, jointly with John Leahy, designed to address key challenges of modeling and measurement:

1. Fixing learning as independent of the scoring rule, as has traditionally been assumed, what precisely is the difference in information between different testing protocols? To model this, one needs to specify both

the objective of the test taker and the underlying structure of knowledge. For example, a risk-averse test taker has an incentive to diversify answers if there is an uncertain common component that determines the answer to more than one question. Standard proper scoring rules cannot get around this, but variations on the theme (e.g., probabilities over sets of answers) might.

2. In the case of machine learning, there is no gap between the scoring rule and the loss function. For that reason, any change in the loss function gives rise to a corresponding change in the incentive to learn. This simple equation is not appropriate in the case of human learning. The grading scheme determines numerical scores. But on top of this, there is a complex value function defined on what can be inferred about human skills from the results of the test. This too needs to be modeled. For later use post education, the quality of the signal that the education provides is critical.

3. As noted above, important factors in the value function may be not only skills but also awareness and metacognition, depending on later employment options. These are certainly impacted by the scoring rule and may feature in the value function. Hence, the degree to which they are learnable needs to be measured and modeled. The question of whether calibration is a learnable skill is essentially empirical, and experimental designs are critical.

4. There are deep modeling challenges. Rational inattention theory in its current form is, at least implicitly, based on well-calibrated beliefs. How might one model poor calibration and its response to incentives if uncovered? What does it take to model a situation in which changes in the punishment for miscalibration result in corresponding changes in the actual degree of calibration? The most obvious change conceptually is to take account of the difficulty in learning the map between subjective signals and properly calibrated posteriors. Formally, one would need to amend the domain of the cost function accordingly. This advance will be important if patterns in miscalibration are responsive to incentives, as they may well be. One interesting conceptual barrier that needs to be overcome concerns how to formulate learning incentives and recover learning costs for a DM who is deluded. To take an extreme case, if an individual learns nothing but believes they know everything, they

have no incentive to learn more. Observing their choices, one would see mistakes being made left and right. The DM's revealed posteriors would display their actual ignorance, but they would subjectively be fully informed. It may be effectively impossible to identify learning costs in such cases. Practically, that may not matter: One would infer that their costs of learning were infinite, and so they would appear. For most purposes, objective trumps subjective. We want to work in buildings that are stable, not those that reflect false confidence of architects, builders, and building inspectors. As to why one might wish anyway to moderate false confidence, history has 1,000 examples.

5. The dynamics of learning costs need to be measured and modeled. One can view a large part of education through the learning-by-doing lens, as designed to reduce the costs of learning and aid in later decision-making. When skills have to be learned, one would like to measure the extent that mistakes are reduced over time and relate it to a broader vision of what doors to further learning are thereby opened.

13.7   Instinctual Errors and Costly Control

Not all errors have the same psychological source. In many tests, the barrier to a correct answer is that the student lacks appropriate knowledge. But there are errors that derive from very different sources, such as some form of interference, in which the respondent has an automatic instinct on the correct answer and finds it hard to exert the control needed to take the question in and respond more appropriately. The paradigm control tasks in psychology are Stroop tasks, as when the subject is asked to identify the color in which a word (itself specifying a color) is written but finds it hard to control the trained instinct to read the word instead. The universal finding is that far fewer mistakes are made in "congruent" trials, in which word and color are the same, than in "incongruent" trials, in which they differ.

There is a massive psychological literature on this form of error and the "cognitive control" it takes to give the correct answer. The expected value of control theory by Shenhav *et al.* (2013) proposes that an agent determines the optimal amount of control by maximizing the net value of control, that is, the expected utility of implementing a control signal with a given intensity u minus an intrinsic cost that scales with the intensity of the signal. Intuitively, psychologists define cognitive control as a collection of mechanisms that enables us to adapt information processing in service of current task goals. In principle, this covers both standard efforts to learn hard material and the effort to "unlearn" an instinctual behavior. Moving forward, such separation seems important. Our capacity to exert control over maladapted instincts is believed to be crucial for accomplishing complex tasks and is related to various real-life outcomes, such as work success and good health. Yet, numerous factors can constrain our capacity to exert control, including its efficacy and cost. Individual differences in these factors, and the resulting capacity for control, have been theorized to predict performance outside the laboratory (Musslick *et al.*, 2019).

In actual tasks that require discrimination, mistakes may be driven by either pure lack of knowledge or failures of cognitive control. We do not have well-articulated theoretical and experimental methodologies as yet for separately identifying these in practice. Early-stage research, jointly conducted by Stefan Bucher, Laura Bustamente, Ivan Grahek, Ham Huang, Sebastian Mussick, and Jennifer Trueblood, is aimed at improving discrimination in this regard and separately identifying the costs of overriding an instinctual response, as opposed to the costs of absorbing a complex environment. As a first step, we are designing and implementing an experiment to assess the effect of incentives by applying the linear family of experiments of Lecture 6, in which precisely the same control challenge is faced at varying incentive levels that linearly scale up and down the reward. A next step involves variation in the prior. It is known that performance in incongruent trials is generally better when they are more frequent. In the limit in which all trials are incongruent, the algorithm of always saying the opposite of the color would probably take hold and make performance good if repeated often enough. Could one identify a natural prior biased in favor of congruence for evolutionary reasons? Of course, that is not to minimize the phenomenon in ecological terms. In naturalistic settings, mistakes will be made precisely because subjects do not understand that they are in anything but the standard environment, so they follow their instinctual response despite the resulting behavior being apparently mistaken (to a fully informed outside observer, such as an econometrician).

13.8   Short-, Medium-, and Long-Run Dynamics

One possible method of separating out distinct forms of mistakes involves process measurement. For example, one can infer much about learning from decision times. These have a distinguished history of psychometric study and are increasingly becoming subjects of research in economics. The speed–accuracy trade-off is particularly pertinent. From a theoretical perspective, an obvious starting point involves emerging models of optimal stopping with costs of learning, as done by Hebert and Woodford (2019, 2020), Morris and Strack (2019), and Bloedel and Zhang (2020). Another theoretical tradition is the drift-diffusion model of psychology (Ratcliff and McKoon, 2008), variants of which are increasingly making their way into economics (see Fehr and Rangel, 2011; Krajbich and Rangel, 2011; Fudenberg *et al.*, 2018).

A non-standard implication of the drift-diffusion model is prevarication: that choice among options that are of similar utility take a long time. Alós-Ferrer *et al.* (2021) develop a complete model along these lines. A reasonable conjecture is that interacting time to decide with choice process data may allow for the separate identification of classical models of costly learning and models with prevarication. Choice process data capture provisional choices during the search process and can be generated experimentally. The smoking gun for the prevarication effect might be a prolonged period of rapid switching between options in the time shortly before finalizing selection. Other promising avenues for future research involve the ongoing efforts of both economists and psychologists to develop decision-theoretic models of visual attention, such as the works of Krajbich and Rangel (2011), Fehr and Rangel (2011), and Callaway *et al.* (2021). As might be expected, these ongoing developments involve increased collaboration between economists and psychologists, who have studied visual behavior at great depth (Carrasco, 2011).

Learning costs operate on all time scales. Caplin *et al.* (2020) make clear the analogy between the costs of learning and production functions and the cost curves in the theory of the firm. I believe that this analogy is strong enough that all aspects of production theory will have valid counterparts in the science of mistakes. In particular, the distinction between short-, medium-, and long-run is important to bear in mind. This lecture has implicitly dealt with the early period of formal training in educational settings. The ensuing lectures focus attention on decisions that take place after the standard educational process ends. In the middle years, learning by doing continues in many settings. In the later years, biology takes over once again, not to our advantage. Each phase introduces entirely new challenges for modeling and measurement.

Lecture 14

Management Skills and Productive Efficiency

We don't stop making mistakes when we leave school. We just stop measuring them. The few cases alluded to above, such as sporting calls, are exceptional in this respect because ideal SDSC is available. While there is value in finding other settings in which this is true, at least to a first approximation, there is also value in developing entirely different research strategies in bringing the science of mistakes to the field. My focus in this lecture is on development and deployment in the field of cognitive instruments. Many mistakes can be seen as reflecting cognitive skills that are required, for example, to make a correct sporting call or identify the appropriate medical procedure and implement that procedure effectively. This suggests a psychometric approach of developing cognitive skill measures that predict particular mistakes and implementing them in field settings. If one identifies differences in skill using cognitive instruments and finds that these differences are strongly correlated with clearly related bad outcomes in the field, it strengthens the plausibility of a causal channel running from cognitive skill to behavioral mistakes.

A particularly well-developed short instrument relevant to economic decision-making is the three-question financial skill instrument developed by Lusardi and Mitchell (200). The process of developing this instrument and a wide variety of applications are summarized by Lusardi and Mitchell (2014). Their first question measures the capacity to do a simple compound interest calculation. The second question measures the understanding of inflation, again in the context of a simple financial decision.

The third question investigates the knowledge of equity markets in general and the idea of risk diversification. This short instrument has been shown to have a strong association with what looks like poor financial performance and financial mistakes. A particularly strong link has been established with clear errors in valuing annuities (Brown *et al.*, 2017). In the psychological literature, another great success is the cognitive reflection task of Shane Frederick (Frederick, 2005), which poses a battery of only three questions, in which the instinctive and considered answers are different and which has been deployed in many settings to great effect. This is clearly related to cognitive control, the study of which was introduced in the previous lecture. A third leading case is the work of Weidmann and Deming (2021) on team skills. They design an experimental protocol in which they elicit individual productivity in a variety of tasks, as well as putting individuals together in productive teams. By deliberately varying team membership, they are able to differentiate an individual's between-task skills and their contributions to team productivity. A psychometric instrument related to the ability to put oneself in others' shoes factors importantly in the individual's teamwork, not their individual productivity.

This lecture introduces ongoing research with David Deming, Soren Leth-Petersen, and Ben Weidmann, which further develops these methods of skill elicitation and applies them to study management skills and their links with productive efficiency and business performance. Our angle of attack involves formulating an information-theoretic model linking management skill to productivity. Recent research has indicated the profound role that "good management" plays in improving productive efficiency. Likewise, it is well documented that changes in management can have large impacts on measured efficiency. The goal of our research is to develop a cognitive instrument to elicit management skills and to field a short version of this instrument thereby to assess in administrative data the impact on past and future performances. I outline the research path forward noting that a key will be scientific flexibility. It cannot really be otherwise: This research path itself necessitates a great deal of learning by doing:

1. In the first research stage, we have built a rational inattention model that captures the idea of Welch (1970) concerning the "allocative skills" of management.

2. We are developing and implementing experimental protocols, ranging from the abstract to the realistic, to measure allocative skill using experimentally generated SDSC.
3. The third stage of this research, which is in the planning phases, involves the development of corresponding short survey instruments capable of being fielded in a variety of real-world contexts.
4. The fourth stage is to combine these survey instruments with additional survey questions directly related to management experience and to link with sources of administrative data. The research team is focusing, in particular, on fielding instruments in the Danish population registries. The direct link with the registries allows us to access individual histories, to use the entire Danish population as a sample frame for random sampling, to identify key aspects of sample selection, and also to gauge the accuracy of factual responses (Kreiner *et al.*, 2014). This will enable us to direct the survey instrument appropriately, to know relevant details of respondents' histories and those of any businesses they manage, and to track their future outcomes (Andersen and Leth-Petersen, 2021).
5. The final research stage will involve empirical analysis of the cognitively enriched registry data. In addition to exploring the role of these instruments in understanding the patterns of manager and business performances, we will explore their value in understanding income dynamics even for those who are not officially managers. We are all managers of the ultimate scarce resource: our time.

14.1 Management Skills and Productivity

In recent years, applied microeconomists have taken an increased interest in factors that determine differences in productivity across factories and firms and on how these differences come about. An increasingly important strand of this literature focuses on the role of good management (Bertrand and Schoar, 2003; Lazear *et al.*, 2015; Bloom *et al.*, 2012). Syverson (2011) finds a factor-of-two difference in total factor productivity between the 10th and 90th percentile firms in the same country. Bartel *et al.* provide granular analyses of productivity changes to separate forces at work.

One possible method of gaining insight involves conducting case studies. Certainly these are necessary and insightful, but they require huge depth of knowledge and are highly particular. Each productive unit is different, as is each management team. A study in depth of any one such case requires a massive investment of time and energy. The data may be very hard to gather. The classification and quantification of inputs require great judgement. Management is not easy to define and not static. So, there are deep challenges in gathering data to accurately measure inefficiency, let alone to pinpoint sources of it in managerial decision-making. For the foreseeable future, indirect methods of measurement are likely to be important. The joint research program that this lecture details is of this nature. Feasibility of measurement plays a major role in the research design, as will be clear.

14.2   X-Efficiency and Errors

Variations in productive efficiency are not a new discovery. A voluminous literature in production management analyzes differences in productive efficiency in many different domains. In setting after setting, it is noted that essentially the same measured inputs produce very different levels of output in different productive units. There are literally thousands of papers that document and drill down into the apparent differences in productivity. The vast majority of these studies of inefficiency are to be found outside the economic literature, in fields such as operations management. This is a little ironic since the tools that are in most widespread use, in particular data envelope analysis, originated in the works of Debreu (1951) and Farrell (1957).

Given the long history of research in the area, one might expect determinants of the "errors" that result in poor use of resources to be reflected in the economic models of production. Yet, this is far from the case. The theory of production has not fully embraced the imperfect information revolution that has swept the rest of economics. With notable exceptions (such as in the work of Jovanovic and Nyarko, 1994), information-theoretic constructs play a second-order role in the theory of production. Production functions are typically still written in a reduced-form manner as mappings from a set of inputs to a set of outputs. There may be many different underlying methods of deploying the inputs, but for each of these, the corresponding outputs are assumed to be known, and what is in the end observed in the data reflects an optimal use of the underlying scarce resources. Efficiency is assumed.

An early objector to the standard deterministic production function methodology was Harvey Liebenstein (1966), who treated "wasteful behavior" as an important economic construct. He provided a valuable qualitative discussion illustrating how multifaceted such behavior was. However, he did not introduce corresponding quantitatively oriented modeling frameworks. Rather, he baptized waste as reflecting "X-Efficiency." This made him vulnerable to scientific critique, and George Stigler provided just that. What makes Stigler's point of view particularly interesting is that he provided hints on the appropriate path forward as involving better modeling of mistakes:

> Waste is error within the framework of modern economic analysis, and it will not become a useful concept until we have a theory of error. (Stigler, 1976, p. 216)

In his later comments supportive of Liebenstein, Frantz agrees that errors are important but is less concerned with the need to develop a corresponding theory:

> Leibenstein assumed that individuals are at least capable of making, *ex ante* and *ex post*, avoidable errors....The reasons for making avoidable errors include laziness, and inappropriate conventions and habitual ways of doing things. (Frantz, 2013)

With the advent of rational inattention theory, we now have a powerful theory of error, allowing us belatedly to pick up on Stigler's suggestion in modeling apparent differences in productivity.

14.3 A Simple Model of Allocative Skill

The idea that we build on is that of Welch (1970) on the importance of managerial skill or allocative ability. When information is abundant and attention is scarce, the ability to process information strategically — choosing what to focus on and what to ignore — is critically important. While good management has many facets, a key appears to be precisely the ability to solve complex allocation problems. Good management requires good resource allocation. Resources are physical things but also managers' and others' time, attention, and effort. What should be done? Who should do it? In what order? So, it seems that what is needed is a way to include productive and allocative human capital together in a single framework.

Adding allocative skill to a production framework requires a significant conceptual change. Standard production functions involve a mechanical mapping of inputs to outputs as specified by a fixed production function. What is needed is an information-theoretic formulation of production in which the amount of output produced by a fixed set of inputs depends on how well DMs understand the true nature of their productive opportunities. This brings us right back to the central point of these lectures, which is the need in setting after setting to think about mistakes, the role of learning in helping to avoid them, and the costs that prevent complete learning. In essence, the idea is to capture managerial and allocative skills as defining of a learning cost function. Those with high such costs will manage poorly, and those with low such costs will manage well. A very basic such model is now sketched. It enriches the human capital model by including productive and allocative human capital together in a single framework.

In our model, managers assign workers to jobs, and information about worker productivity is costly to acquire. The model is deliberately abstract about the reasons why productivity is imperfectly observed. One possibility is that the manager must invest time and effort to observe a worker's true productivity (through communication, monitoring, etc.). Another possibility is that productivity itself depends on a state of the world that is *ex ante* unknown but that managers can choose to acquire costly signals about before making an allocation. Following the rational inattention literature, managers endogenously choose to acquire signals about worker productivity. They must deploy their scarce attention over workers and jobs, acquiring information that will maximize the value of output net of learning costs. Their choice of information structure depends on prior beliefs, the strength of their incentives, the production function that maps job performance to output, and their costs of learning (which define allocative skill). Since managers condition their actions only on the signals they receive, learning and allocation decisions are interdependent.

Our starting point is the task literature that has been pioneered by Autor *et al.* (2003) and Acemoglu and Autor (2011). Technically, a task is a unit of work activity that produces output. A skill is a worker's stock of capabilities for performing various tasks. Workers apply their skills to tasks in exchange for wages. A production function F is given that maps the inputs of a number of different tasks $1 \leq n \leq N$ into measured output. The task levels can each be measured as real numbers $x_n \geq 0$ so that the production function is a mapping,

$$F : \mathbb{R}_+^N \longrightarrow \mathbb{R},$$

that is weakly increasing in all arguments. A finite labor force L is available to work on the tasks and produce output. In the simplest of cases, in which each task is to be filled by one and only one worker, the work force itself comprises N members. These are arbitrarily indexed by $1 \leq n \leq N$ and with $L = \{1, \ldots, N\}$, with the interpretation as a worker defined by context.

Not all workers are equally productive in all tasks. There is a finite set $X \subset \mathbb{R}_+^N$ of possible such **productivity types** $\vec{x}^\tau = (x_1^\tau, \ldots, x_N^\tau)$ for $1 \leq \tau \leq T$:

$$X = \{\vec{x}^\tau = (x_1^\tau, \ldots, x_N^\tau) \in \mathbb{R}_+^N | 1 \leq \tau \leq T\}.$$

A type mapping, $\omega : \{1, \ldots, N\} \longrightarrow \{1, \ldots, T\}^N$ with $\omega(n) \in \{1, \ldots, T\}$, specifies the productivity types of all workers. In essence, this is the unknown state of the world that has to be learned. As is standard, we define Ω to be the set of such states:

$$\Omega = \{\omega : \{1, \ldots, N\} \longrightarrow \{1, \ldots, T\}^N\}.$$

The action space in our simple version of an assignment problem is a one-to-one and onto function $a : \{1, \ldots, N\} \longrightarrow \{1, \ldots, N\}$, with $a(n) \in \{1, \ldots, N\}$ the task to which worker n is assigned. We let A be the set of such assignments:

$$A = \{a : \{1, \ldots, N\} \longrightarrow \{1, \ldots, N\}\}.$$

We define the inverse function $a^{-1}(m) \in \{1, \ldots, N\}$ as the worker assigned to task m.

With this formalism in place, we can directly compute the level of output for any allocation of workers $a \in A$ in any state $\omega \in \Omega$, which we write as $u(a, \omega)$:

$$u(a, \omega) \equiv F\left(x_1^{\omega(a^{-1}(1))}, \ldots, x_N^{\omega(a^{-1}(N))}\right).$$

This is an expected utility function given the subjective uncertainty.

A standard allocation problem is to assign workers to tasks in the manner that is maximally productive. In a world without uncertainty, what we have just described has been well studied. Abstractly, it is a version of the Koopmans and Beckmann (1957) assignment problem, in which the goal is to assign factories that are differentially impacted by their geographic locations in a manner that maximizes a standardized measure of total output. This is a model of greatest importance in operations research and is strongly related to rational inattention theory.

In the current context, a model of this form without any uncertainty would give little room for skill in internalizing the likely productivity of available resources in an uncertain world and deploying them effectively. This is precisely what our model focuses on. We consider a manager who has to make a series of allocation decisions, in each of which the appropriate allocation may be different. In each case, they get to observe relevant information about the optimal allocation. Their allocative skill precisely relates to how well they process this information, as revealed in the extent that they do or do not achieve the factually optimal allocation. We now introduce the corresponding formalism which assumes that a high ability manager deploys resources well according by being good at learning about worker productivity. All differences in the model derive from differences in the ability to internalize information effectively rather than pure mathematical competence. In practice, the same skills that make it possible to internalize the relative productivity of different workers may also be of value in solving the resulting optimization problem, but that is not something that our model can capture at this stage.

In technical terms, we consider a setting in which there is uncertainty concerning the type mapping that characterizes the labor force L. As noted above, the state of the world is the actual mapping $\omega : \{1, \ldots, N\} \longrightarrow \{1, \ldots, T\}^N$, with Ω the set of such functions and with $\omega(n) \in X$ the productivity type of worker n. The prior $\mu \in \Delta(\Omega)$ specifies beliefs about workers' possible types. The model that we work with involves rational inattention, so can be precisely specified, as in Lecture 3. At each posterior belief $\gamma \in \Delta(\Omega)$, the DM solves the allocation problem. The reason that allocation errors are made in the model is that learning is costly according to a cost function $K(\mu, Q)$ on Bayes' consistent distributions $Q \in \mathcal{Q}(\mu)$.

To make the ideas concrete, I present a simple illustrative example that involves symmetry of the form introduced by Bucher and Caplin (2021), as detailed in Lecture 11. While obviously special, this case is of particular interest because it represents the idea of starting out, knowing nothing to differentiate a set of workers so that all that ends up being known is derived from observation rather than from prior beliefs. This simple starting point aids also in the experimental implementation that is outlined after the model section.

One simplifying assumption is symmetry. As in Lecture 11, the technical translation of this is to assume that the prior is exchangeable: For any bijection $\alpha : L \to L$ of workers,

$$\mu\left(\omega(1),\ldots,\omega(N)\right) = \mu\left(\omega(\alpha(1)),\ldots,\omega(\alpha(N))\right).$$

What this means is that we consider an allocation problem involving workers whose skills are initially seen as equivalent based, for example, on similar credentials, but whose particular skills can be identified by a good manager based on observations that are made prior to deciding on the actual assignment.

The second assumption is made to exhibit simple formulae characterizing the model solution. Specifically, we follow Bucher and Caplin (2021) and work with the Shannon cost function with parameter $\kappa > 0$. The first step is to transform state-dependent utilities $u(a,\omega)$ according to the Matejka–Mckay formula:

$$z(a,\omega) \equiv \exp\frac{u(a,\omega)}{\kappa}.$$

The second step is to add these up on a state-by-state basis:

$$Z(\omega) \equiv \sum_{a \in A} z(a,\omega).$$

The model solution is then fully specified by the state-dependent choice probabilities:

$$P(a|\omega) \equiv \frac{z(a,\omega)}{Z(\omega)}.$$

Among many other striking features of the solution, note that the form of the optimal policy in terms of $P(a|\omega)$ is entirely unaffected by this specification of the prior. Of course, the actual information content of signals is greatly affected. These are reflected in the corresponding posterior beliefs associated with the choice of each allocation. By Bayes' rule, the posterior belief of any given state in either allocation, $\gamma^a(\omega)$, is

$$\gamma^a(\omega) \equiv \frac{P(a|\omega)\mu(\omega)}{P(a)} = \frac{z(a,\omega)\mu(\omega) * N!}{Z(\omega)}$$

since all $N!$ allocations are equiprobable. This closed-form solution allows rich comparative statics concerning, in particular, the impact of allocative skill, parameterized by κ, on output, worker income, and costs of learning. The solution is generically unique. It also exhibits the ILR property of the optimal solution. The relative likelihoods of any two allocations a and b is determined by the ratio of their normalized payoffs:

$$\frac{\gamma^a(\omega)}{\gamma^b(\omega)} = \frac{z(a,\omega)}{z(b,\omega)}.$$

Indeed, one can characterize the solution using these conditions and setting all allocations as unconditionally equally likely to be chosen.

A further specialization illustrates how subtle and rich this simple solution is. Consider two workers and two tasks, $i = 1,2$. Workers are good or bad at each task, with productivity x_G if good and x_B if bad, with $x_G > x_B \geq 0$. Suppose further that the probabilities of being good are task specific. The prior will effectively be defined by these task-specific probabilities. The state will be the actual tasks at which the each of the workers is good. The reward in terms of output to getting good workers in both tasks can be defined as $F(2)$, which is defined by the production function with both tasks performed at level x_G when we consider production functions that are symmetric in tasks. The reward when one is good is $F(1)$, which is defined by the production function with one task performed at level x_G and the other at level x_B. When neither is good output is $F(0)$, which is defined by the production function with both tasks performed at level x_B. The solution of the model involves exponentiating these divided by the attention case as $z(j) \equiv \exp\frac{F(j)}{\kappa}$ and then working out what each assignment does in the given state and having the sum of these in the denominator.

Pursuing this one level further, the conditional probabilities combine the features of the production function with the realized worker productivities in an intelligent and subtle fashion, as is characteristic of the Shannon model. There are seven distinct types of state:

1. There is one state in which both workers are good at both tasks. In this case, the sum in the denominator is $2z(2)$. This means that the two assignments are equiprobable.
2. There are four states in which one worker is good at both tasks, the other at one. In this case, the denominator is $z(2) + z(1)$. The probability of the better assignment is therefore $\frac{z(2)}{z(2)+z(1)}$.
3. There are two states in which one worker is good at both tasks and the other at none. In this case, the denominator is $2z(1)$ and again assignments are equiprobable.
4. There are two states in which both are good at precisely one task, and these tasks are distinct. Now, the sum is $z(2) + z(0)$. The probability of the good assignment is the ratio $\frac{z(2)}{z(2)+z(0)}$.
5. There are two states in which both are good at precisely one task, and these tasks are the same. Now, the sum is $2z(1)$ so that both assignments are equiprobable.
6. There are four states in which one worker is good at one task and the other at none. Now, the sum is $z(1) + z(0)$. The probability of the good assignment is the ratio $\frac{z(1)}{z(1)+z(0)}$.
7. There is one state in which both workers are good at neither task. In this case, the sum in the denominator is $2z(0)$. This means that the two assignments are equiprobable.

The exchangeability of the prior implies that all states within each of the above classes are equiprobable. Other than that, it imposes no restrictions. So, the general model allows for any seven type-dependent probabilities that add up to 1 when one takes account of how many states there are of each type. This is a far-reaching generalization of the i.i.d. case. While $P(a|\omega)$ is unaffected by this specification of the prior, the posterior beliefs $\gamma^a(\omega)$ are directly affected:

$$\gamma^a(\omega) \equiv \frac{P(a|\omega)\mu(\omega)}{P(a)} = \frac{2z(a,\omega)\mu(\omega)}{Z(\omega)},$$

reflecting the fact that both allocations are equiprobable.

A particularly tight connection with rational inattention theory arises when changing the production function while leaving the attentional challenge invariant. For example, one can present precisely the same data on individual productivities and create very different attentional incentives if the production function is sensitive to minimum productivity, average productivity, and maximal productivity, which can be varied by changing parameter in a CES production function. What one precisely can be inferred about about learning costs by applying the NIAC conditions is of great interest. There are also a number of interesting econometric issues involved in assessing individual differences from incomplete data. These lie ahead. Another interesting set of analytic issues relate to the value of invariance properties of the cost function, which will apply beyond the Shannon case. The invariant cost functions of Csaba (2021) would appear to have much to offer in this respect. There may also be a great deal learned by less parametric methods that rely on symmetry and posterior separability properties alone.

14.4   Experimental Implementation

We are developing a multi-modal approach to operationalizing our model of allocative skill. Our first step, which is ongoing, involves the development and testing of a protocol to measure allocative skill using experimentally generated SDSC. Participants are presented with information about the productivity of a set of "workers" in a corresponding number of distinct tasks. Their experimental task involves assigning the workers to tasks to maximize a measure of total output. There is no *ex ante* information distinguishing workers so that the symmetry conditions of the model apply.

If the subjects could take in and hold on to all details of the productivities they are shown, they would know precisely the state of the world and, with it, the payoff to each allocation of workers to tasks. This full information optimal assignment is made difficult only by the excessive mental load of attempting to solve the problem optimally. To do well in the task involves both understanding the principle of comparative advantage (if there is a best worker, they cannot be assigned to all tasks) and focusing on the economic challenge of optimally assigning these scarce resources that have multiple uses.

The goal of the experiment is to recover individual costs of attention. We vary the incentives, the number of workers and tasks, the complexity of workers' absolute and comparative advantages over one another and the payoffs for different tasks. In so doing, we can make the allocation problem range from trivial to nearly impossible. In each case, we map the experimental manipulations back to the model objects and identify key parameters which relate to learning costs. We use both non-parametric methods based on NIAS and NIAC and more parametric methods based on particularly well-understood cost functions, such as the Shannon cost function, as detailed directly above.

The experiment and the model are deliberately stark. This is to allow in future for many variations on the theme. For example, we can provide some *ex ante* information on the workers to change prior beliefs and see how this impacts learning. We can allow for differences in worker pay. We can change the production function so that the important features to learn vary. We can allow many workers to be assigned to the same activity. This will also allow us to model team production by introducing variants in which some workers work particularly well or badly together for either idiosyncratic reasons or because one or more of the individuals are particularly good at working in teams. Overall, our stark design is intended to serve as a template for broader investigation of decision-making skills in economic settings.

14.5 Next Steps

There are three ongoing next steps all of which will build the ultimate data set for analyzing management skills. The fourth and final research stage will involve analyzing the resulting data and identifying general factors to stimulate further modeling and measurement:

1. The experimental measure of allocative skills is deliberately stark and tightly tied to a simple rational inattention model. In a sense, it is a hybrid of a general intelligence test and a specific economic challenge related to the basic idea of scarce resources. The key to its value for the purposes of investigating performance of a manager is that the skills it gauges above and beyond standard measures of intelligence are critical in actual management tasks. We are aware that this does not come guaranteed. Before launching an instrument in the Danish population registry, we are designing and will shortly field a more free-form management task to act as a test bed for the stark allocation game design. This "Trello" task involves a more free-form set of allocation decisions with a far larger possibility space. At heart, the issue remains one of how to allocate resources. However, the options are richer, including,

in particular, the manager having to decide when to join in a work task and when instead to monitor their "work force" to identify how to assign them to future tasks. There is likely to be some iteration as we design simple allocation tasks that are particularly informative about productivity differences in the Trello task. Performance in that task may also suggest other decision-making skills that are important, such as a realistic assessment of own abilities.

2. The next key phase, also conducted first in experimental contexts, involves the development and validation of a corresponding survey instrument for later deployment in the field. The idea is to take a few of the experimental designs that are particularly of value in identifying management skills and to design short, experimentally validated survey instruments that are capable of being implemented in a form that is suitable for the Danish registries. Here, brevity is of the essence. The lead examples that light the path in this respect are the cognitive reflection task of Frederick (2005), the financial literacy battery of Lusardi and Mitchell (2008, 2014), and the social skills battery of Weidmann and Deming (2021).

3. In fielding cognitive instruments in the Danish registries, we will need to add direct questions relating to management experience. Many of those to whom we will field the survey will themselves be *ex ante* identifiable as managers of small businesses. For these, we will pose a few additional questions to dig into their experiences and decision-making styles. We are also designing instruments to fill in the gap between official job titles and actual job responsibilities. There are many whose job includes a large management aspect, yet who are not so titled, and questions will be posed to identify such individuals.

4. The final research stage will involve empirical analysis of the cognitively enriched registry data. In addition to focusing on the value added by the cognitive instruments in understanding the patterns of manager and business performance in the registries, we will explore the value of these instruments more broadly in understanding income dynamics even for those who are not officially managers. After all, we each manage our own time, and being good at that is a skill that may turn out to be of great importance beyond management *per se.*

Lecture 15

Decision-Making Skills, Job Transitions, and Income

Decision-making skills matter in all phases of life. While being a manager of a fixed group of workers is a particularly salient example of this, there is no realm of behavior in which such skills are irrelevant. In this lecture, I focus on a particularly important set of decisions that are known to have massive impact on lifetime income: decisions on whether and how to search for jobs, including when to quit, what to do in the face of an impending layoff, when to take time out of the labor force and retool, and when to retire. These transitions are important events that appear to have a large effect on income dynamics over the life cycle. When, why, and how such transitions are made is much studied in administrative data. However, the facts alone are not rich enough to determine whether or not there were significant gaps in knowledge and/or illusions that rationalized erroneous decisions. Decision quality is as much about what was **not** known as what was and about actions that were **not** taken as much as those that were. In this lecture, I outline research in which measurements are enriched to distinguish between those who make successful labor market transitions and those who do not, thereby to gain insight into the role that decision-making skills play in lifetime income.

I begin the lecture by outlining the broad hypothesis of Deming (2021) that abstract decision-making skills are of growing importance in determining lifetime income. His hypothesis is very broad-based and relates not only to job transitions but also to learning and earning on the job. It is part of his broader research designed to identify the skills that are rewarded in the workforce. It is clear that education is important for earnings. Yet, we know little about the skills that are needed to survive and thrive in the work force of the future. It is in this respect that he argues that more abstract "higher level" skills need to be better modeled and, measured, and understood. Of course, this connects with the previous lecture since the long-term goal is to ensure that we educate students in skills relevant to their well-being, financial and otherwise, in their later lives once their formal education is complete.

Earned income over the life cycle is hardly a new area of economic research. To the contrary, understanding patterns in earned income is one of the most important and central areas of study and joins applied microeconomics with macroeconomics. Given the centrality of life-cycle earnings in economic research, a massive effort has been dedicated to gaining access to the administrative data that record actual dynamic patterns of earnings for entire populations. In this lecture, I outline research that requires not only complete data on earnings over the life cycle but additional forms of data engineered to increase the understanding of decision quality. To motivate these additional measurements, I open with the very highest level of overview of some key facts about income dynamics that have been revealed from administrative data and the hints these data provide about possible areas to explore, which might be revealing of relevant decision-making skills. Specifically, research identifies widespread heterogeneity in patterns of income growth both in a particular job and in switching between jobs. Particularly of note are the diverse experiences of those who are out of the labor force, with some quickly returning to work and others searching for a long time. Another important differentiator relates to job-to-job transitions, with some successfully transitioning up the job ladder by moving from job to job and with others making fewer moves with less apparent success.

Necessary as it is to have rich administrative data of actual patterns in lifetime income, it is not sufficient. While it is clear that there are diverse experiences within a given job and in job transitions, there is very little direct evidence on why this is so and the extent to which it might be a result of clear differences in **task skills** rather than identifiable differences in **decision-making skills**. Is it largely that better workers have better outcomes in all job phases than worse workers, or is a significant portion determined by differential abilities of similarly skilled workers in recognizing and taking advantage of potential opportunities?

What forms of data enrichment are needed to better identify the role of workers' decision-making skills? In these lectures, the focus is on the introducing methods of identifying workers' abilities to take in and effectively process the information that is required to successfully navigate the labor market. Identifying opportunities to advance within a job, and job switches that might open important new opportunities, is a particularly salient case in point. The best studied transition in this regard is job search among unemployed workers. Survey research on unemployed workers' patterns of search, in particular Mueller *et al.* (2021), suggests that the beliefs of unemployed workers about their chances of finding a job are surprisingly little impacted by past failure to do so. There are those who remain unemployed due to an apparently false belief that continued search will soon land them a relatively high-paying job.

The key to the ability of Mueller *et al.* (2021) to identify possible decision-making mistakes is that they gather panel data on the beliefs and decision-making strategies that guide searchers' decisions. Central to this is the elicitation of reservation wages: the level of earnings that would be acceptable to currently searching unemployed workers. The higher the reservation wage, the harder it is to leave unemployment. Gathering the dynamic pattern of reservation wages allows the assessment of whether those who fail to find employment flexibly lower their reservation wage in the face of negative experience.

There is a broader moral of this research process. It is key to gather data on beliefs and their evolution in the face of experience in order to gain traction in separating out an unfortunate run of bad luck from a poor decision-making strategy. Gathering such a panel and integrating it into rich administrative data is therefore a necessary step forward. Ideally, this data will relate not only to job search among the unemployed but to decisions on job market transitions by the broader workforce. The goal will be to understand what workers believe about their job options, the informational basis for these beliefs, how these relate to underlying realities, and their ability to act effectively to take advantage of the opportunities that they perceive.

The first step in the research process involves measuring beliefs in a suitably rich manner in the context of suitably rich administrative data. Precisely to that end, I outline ongoing work in the Danish registry that richly measures contingent beliefs relevant to labor market outcomes and the path of lifetime income. The Copenhagen Life Panel (CLP), a new panel implemented in the Danish population registries, is designed, in large part, to deepen our understanding of the subjective forces at work in job transitions. It measures beliefs about possible future job transitions and how they might impact income dynamics. While still in the early stages, the research to date, jointly conducted with Victoria Gregory, Soren Leth-Petersen, Eungik Lee, and Johan Saeverud, reveals great heterogeneity in beliefs and also reveals the powerful links between beliefs and behavior (Caplin *et al.*, 2023b). Those who believe that their incomes would rise little if they stay in the current job but would rise significantly if they were to quit not only believe that they are more likely to quit but also do just that. Yet, not all who believe that they would benefit from a move do so, suggesting possibly substantial individual differences in effective decision-making.

In addition to studying income dynamics during the main career phase, I outline planned research on the "retirement" phase. The transition into retirement is a fascinating period with plenty of scope for decision-making errors. Survey evidence (Ameriks *et al.*, 2020a) shows that many older individuals would work longer, especially if schedules were flexible. Even those who are long retired have strong willingness to work, especially in a job with a flexible schedule. Following up on that, our survey research in Denmark has revealed a rather sudden drop off in beliefs about how easy it would be to find a job post retirement. Those who have not yet retired are more optimistic about the chances of reemployment. Is this an illusion to which well-informed DMs are less susceptible?

In addition to introducing the CLP that covers the evolution of beliefs about wage dynamics and its interaction with job transitions, I outline research in the planning phases to develop and field cognitive instruments to measure key decision-making skills that have potentially discrete and important roles in determining observed patterns of lifetime income. Building on the importance of job transitions, a first target is to drill down into the aspects of **search skill**: noticing threats (e.g., possible future firing), identifying opportunities (higher-paying jobs to move to), searching effectively among these opportunities, and adapting appropriately to feedback from experience. Fielding cognitive instruments in the Danish registry offers us the opportunity not only to view jobs from the side of workers but also from the side of firms. That some firms are better to move to than others is now clear. Do those with high measured search skills do a better job selecting high-paying opportunities? Other important issues relate to broad-based allocative skills, **planning abilities**, and the degree of **calibration and realism**. Are there significant individual differences in how well tied to reality are the beliefs that different individuals hold? Is there a simple cognitive instrument that might identify such differences? I provide only thumbnail sketches since this research is in the earliest of planning phases.

15.1 The Deming Hypothesis

The motivation for interest in decision-making skills is our lack of granular understanding of what it is about being educated that is of value in the work force. This is explicitly ignored in the reduced-form workhorse model of modern labor economics, the human capital model. In this model, firms take capital and labor as inputs into a production function and direct these factors toward their most productive use. A classical production function has capital and labor. Human capital identifies a type of capital. More education means higher such capital, which leads to higher income. This is in effect a physical interpretation of labor as effectively operating machines robotically. This is particularly inappropriate as robots take over more and more routine jobs. A model in which earnings do not depend on the ability to make good decisions is not a good basis for a granular understanding of the skills that individuals accumulate in the educational process that are of particular value. A more granular understanding of what aspects of work are complementary with technological revolutions of the era of algorithms is therefore of highest importance.

Deming (2021) hypothesizes that as routine jobs are being replaced by machines, the remaining tasks are increasingly open ended, requiring workers to make decisions and to adapt to unforeseen circumstances. Automation of routine tasks causes skill upgrading and an increased emphasis on worker flexibility and problem-solving. In the benchmark human capital model, jobs are fully scripted in advance with no decisions necessary. In that case, only productive human capital matters. However, when workers make decisions, the possibility space quickly becomes large, and decision-making skills are of the essence. It is this kind of flexible problem-solving skill that Deming labels decision-making skills.

Intuitively, it is surely correct that the skills that are hardest to replace are those that operate at a high level of abstraction in terms of flexibly responding to unique circumstances. Again, abstractly, it is clear that this idea connects with learning costs, a point that Deming himself noted in suggesting a link between decision-making skills and costs of learning. It is this meeting of the minds that led to our research teams joining forces.

In introducing his thesis on the importance of decision-making skills, Deming uses a mix of different forms of evidence, including paths of earnings over the life cycle. He models decision-making skills as taking longer to accumulate in high variance, non-routine jobs. His findings indeed suggest that life-cycle wage growth in decision-intensive occupations has increased over time, and it has increased relatively more for highly skilled workers. While this and other evidence are suggestive, differential patterns in lifetime income growth across professions may largely reflect differences in how long it takes to accumulate the specific skills that earn higher pay over time rather than general decision-making skills. The challenge is broader. The most important data sets in labor economics and macroeconomics more generally are administrative. In the case of earned income, these data provide massive insight into patterns of life-cycle income. An important set of findings relate to heterogeneous patterns of income growth in a given job. To some extent, this is due to differences in worker skill, to some extent match quality, and to some extent firm quality *per se* (Gregory, 2020). Rich as the findings are, the role of decision quality is hard to parse. What the data cannot reveal is what role that the worker's own decision-making skill plays into income growth. Perhaps, the allocative skill measure implemented for management will have a role, after all one's work day is a fixed resource in need of being allocated properly, but that is not the most direct link one can imagine.

15.2 Job Transitions and Income Dynamics

To advance our understanding of the link between decision-making skills and income, it is important to identify particular decision-making nodes at which these skills might play a critical role. Job transitions are a prime candidate, given what we know from administrative data about their critical role in determining patterns in lifetime income. Job transitions can involve quitting to move up the job ladder, quitting to take time out of the labor force, retiring from the career job, and being fired. Given the importance of job transitions in life-cycle income, they are widely studied. Topel and Ward (1992) find quitting is closely related to wage growth in the early years of workers' careers, which shows the role of job transitions in upside income risk. Layoffs also play a key role in life-cycle earnings risk. Jacobson *et al.* (1993) and Von Wachter *et al.* (2009) show that earning losses from mass layoffs are highly persistent and greater for older people, with many remaining out of the labor force for a significant time after such a layoff. Carrington (1993) finds the effect to be heterogeneous across gender, tenure, industry, and location. Guvenen *et al.* (2015) show that the higher-order moments in income risk are notably different in job switchers compared to job stayers.

Estimates of the impact of job transitions need to be understood in the life-cycle context. Regarding job transition dynamics, key findings are that there are particularly frequent job changes during the first 10 years of working life, with worker mobility staying at a perhaps surprisingly high average level even for older workers (Topel and Ward, 1992). When younger people quit their current job, they frequently increase their earnings, as if moving up the job ladder. On the flip side, Jacobson *et al.* (1993) showed greater earnings losses upon job loss for older employees. Chan and Huff Stevens (1999) show that reemployment rates are lower in higher age groups. The job search literature provides mechanisms that might underlie the effects of age and tenure on the impact of job transitions. Menzio *et al.* (2016) develop a directed search model that adds the heterogeneity in workers' ages and years of experience in directed search model to show the life-cycle patterns. Bagger *et al.* (2014) develop a random search model with human capital accumulation that rationalizes the higher wage growth for the younger workers.

15.3   Beliefs, Updating, and Reservation Wages

The above patterns indicate the profound importance of better understanding job switches. But they do not have much to say directly about why some move up the job ladder and others do not, why some are unemployed for a long time after losing a job and others are not, etc. These clear limits of administrative data have given rise to a rapidly increasing body of research that buttresses administrative data with additional survey-based measures of beliefs and strategies.

Best developed in this regard is research on the process of search among unemployed workers. In all models of search, choices depend on what searchers believe their options are from not accepting a particular opening. Hence, there is a body of research on these beliefs and how well-founded they might be among unemployed job searchers. A key finding is high heterogeneity, as identified by Hendren (2017), Conlon *et al.* (2018), and Mueller *et al.* (2021). Conlon *et al.* (2018) use a new nationally representative panel data set on individuals' labor market expectations and realizations. They find that, while expectations about future job offers are highly predictive of actual outcomes, deviations of *ex post* realizations from *ex ante* expectations are often sizable.

Mueller *et al.* (2021) design panel data on unemployed job seekers' perceptions about their employment prospects together with actual labor market transitions. They use both the Federal Reserve Bank of New York Survey of Consumer Expectations and the Survey of Unemployed Workers in New Jersey, which cover a large sample of unemployment insurance recipients. They find that perceived job-finding probabilities significantly and strongly predict actual job finding at the individual level. But there is great heterogeneity. Some get reemployed almost immediately, while others enter long-term unemployment. Broadly, exiting unemployment is more and more unlikely as the spell stretches. They find that job seekers with a high underlying job-finding rate tend to be over-pessimistic, whereas job seekers with a low job-finding rate are over-optimistic. Since illusions about job-finding probabilities impact the reservation wage, the over-optimistic beliefs of the long-term unemployed themselves contribute to the observed decline in job-finding rates. As a result, the long-term unemployed substantially overestimate their probability of finding a job.

15.4   The Copenhagen Life Panel and Job Transitions

The impact of possibly incorrect beliefs about reservation search serves to highlight the importance of research on subjective beliefs. As the case of search makes clear, expectations drive behavior and these are essentially subjective. Having a panel of beliefs and outcomes allows the investigation of how beliefs arise that might give rise to important decision-making mistakes over the economic life cycle not only in the case of search but more broadly. In particular, such a research design is of value not only for unemployed workers but for all aspects and forms of possible job transition, given the key role that the administrative data reveal these to have in lifetime income. Understanding how beliefs about the impact of possible job transitions and related decisions are formed is a priority if we are to understand mistakes over the life cycle and possibly how to mitigate them.

I now introduce the CLP, designed precisely to have this form. We follow the approach espoused by Manski (1990) and Dominitz and Manski (1997) in posing questions to uncover subjective beliefs about future earned income. We also take advantage of subsequent innovations focused on measuring conditional expectations about the future, for example, in relation to the choice of education (Arcidiacono *et al.*, 2014; Wiswall and Zafar, 2021). The specific innovation is to dig deeply into the prospects and risks associated with possible job transitions.

To set the stage and to aid in later panel analysis, we start by asking questions about work status in the past year. In the second round of the CLP, which was fielded in January 2021, our first question on labor market status related to their past status in January 2020. To classify their work status at that time, we first ask whether they were working for pay (either in employment or self-employment and working at least 10 hours per week). If the respondents say yes to this question, we further ask whether they were at that time employed or self-employed. If they say no, we ask whether they were looking for work for pay. Finally, if they say they were not looking for work, then they classify whether they were temporarily or permanently out of work. Respondents then report their current work status. They can again choose from among the same five options. The great majority of respondents were either employed or permanently out of the labor force: The sample of out-of-work job searchers was small.

After eliciting the current labor market status, we posed retrospective questions about any employment changes that may have occurred over the past year. We asked those who were working for pay in both periods whether or not they were working for the same employer as in January 2020. If they indicated that they were not, we asked for what reason they stopped working for the employer in January 2020, allowing the following options:

1. Laid off
2. Quit
3. Other

The numbers who changed employment were significant. Some 18% of those who were employed in January 2020 reported that they were separated from their employer between January 2020 and January 2021, with 5% being laid off, 11% quitting, and 2% other.

We then moved to the forward-looking questions. For those employed in January 2021, we asked them about the probabilities of undergoing future transitions during 2021. The survey question reads as follows:

- *Please think about your possible relationship with your current employer in 2021. Assign the probability in each possible case. The sum of the probabilities should be 100.*
  1. *Staying with your current employer during 2021.*
  2. *Being laid-off from your current employer at some point during 2021.*
  3. *Quitting from your current employer at some point during 2021.*
  4. *Separating from your current employer for some other reason during 2021.*

For those who reported their laid-off probability to be above zero, we followed up by posing questions about how long they would expect it to take before they were first reemployed at four different horizons: within 1 month, within 3 months, within 12 months, or within 24 months:

- *Suppose you were to be laid off from the current employer during 2021. What is the probability that you would start working for pay again within: 1/3/12/24 months of termination?*

For those who reported a positive probability of quitting or separating for other reasons during 2021, we asked a similar question, where the probabilities now refer to finding a job within each time horizon after quitting or other separation.

Finally, we focused on uncertainty about earnings in each possible transition. In fact, the key in the CLP is the branching structure: For each of the possible transitions during 2021, we build on the previous questions by collecting a complete subjective distribution of earnings for each respondent on each branch where they report positive probability. When the respondents get to the earnings part of the branch, they are asked in each condition to fill in a subjective distribution of annual earnings using a method developed by Delavande and Rohwedder (2008). They introduced the "balls in bins" elicitation device that is particularly intuitive and visually oriented: It is a version of this device that we implemented in our online survey. In our particular implementation, respondents are first asked to state the minimum and maximum values for possible future earnings, as in the pioneering work of Dominitz and Manski (1997). Then, the range between the stated minimum and maximum is divided into six equally sized bins. Respondents are then instructed to move 20 balls into the six bins to reflect how likely earnings are to fall in each of the ranges.

As noted, everyone who assigned a strictly positive probability to any type of transition during 2021 was asked to fill in a corresponding distribution of income. This is easiest in cases in which there is no change of job: Here, we ask about their beliefs about earned income in 2021. The precise question is a little harder to pose after a transition since we had already acknowledged the reality that many would expect to take time before returning to the work force. In these cases, the question was more delicate. Here is the basic design for the case of being laid off from the job during 2021.

- *Suppose you were to be laid off from the current employer during 2021 and to start to work for pay at some point in the following 2 years. Think about your possible earned income from the first 12 months of this earn from pay.*

The key subtlety is that the question effectively asks for the annual pay rate rather than earnings within the calendar year 2021 to separate this from the time out of the labor force.

Basic facts about transitions of currently employed workers are detailed in Caplin *et al.* (2023b). The most likely event by far is remaining with the current employer: Respondents report an average probability of 82%. Quitting is regarded as twice as likely as being fired. This quitting probability varies significantly over the life cycle, being far higher for younger than for older workers. Workers in the age group of 20–35 report on average a 20% chance of quitting compared to a roughly 8% chance in the 50–65 age group. By contrast, layoff probabilities are essentially flat at 6% across age groups. Together, these findings are consistent with the well-known fact that younger workers tend to exhibit more turnover in their labor market experiences that gradually settles down as they age. They are also well aligned with self reports of the transitions during 2020.

With regard to time out of the labor force, we find that respondents expect on average 4.4 (2.7) months to find a new job after being laid off (quitting). The time that respondents expect to spend without a job is longest for those in the age group of 50–65. On average, across all age groups, most workers expect small positive earnings growth if they stay with their employer. In the laid-off branch, there is a clear life-cycle pattern: It appears that the expectation of earnings decline after a layoff is much more prevalent among workers over 50. In contrast, a majority of younger workers expect their earnings to grow even after a layoff.

Of particular relevance to decision-making is the difference between the wage that is predicted from staying on the job and the wage that is predicted to be available upon quitting the job. On average, all age groups expect to earn a higher wage if they quit, with the gap being largest for the younger age groups. These beliefs appear decision relevant. The probability of quitting is correlated with possible earnings gain from quitting. We find that a 1% increase in relative earnings gain from quitting increases the quitting probability by 0.65%. This effect mainly comes from the younger and middle-aged workers. This results shows that younger and middle-aged workers with a higher predicted earnings gain after quitting are more likely to quit, which is consistent with the story of many search-theoretic models.

Much of the ground work of fielding and working with the CLP confirms the credibility of our measures of expectations. A striking example concerns our ability to put together a measure of holistic income risk that turns out to have striking similarities with the empirical distribution of income computed directly from registry data.

15.5 Late-in-Life Labor Supply

One interesting finding in the CLP concerns the large number of older workers who report that they would not expect to reenter the labor force quickly if they were to be laid off. This connects with an interesting open question on the mix of forces that end careers and, more broadly, on patterns in late-in-life work. In many advanced economies, the share of the population that is of standard working age group of 20–64 is projected to fall significantly in the coming decades. This shift poses several economic challenges, notably an increased financial strain on public pension and healthcare programs. In response, many countries are starting to enact or at least consider policies that encourage older workers to work longer. Yet, little is known about the opportunity sets generating observed retirement behavior, and many of the choices are confounded by shocks, such as to the physical health of workers or the financial health of firms.

Ameriks *et al.* (2020a) use questions on contingent behavior to find that older Americans have a strong willingness to work, especially in jobs with flexible schedules. These types of "strategic survey question" (SSQ) do not confound a desire to work with perceived job opportunities (see also Barsky *et al.*, 1997 and Ameriks *et al.*, 2020b, for SSQs on risk aversion and more). They directly control for job opportunities in hypothetical situations, which allows us to identify willingness to work independent from what workers expect to find available in the actual labor market. Indeed, we pose questions that allow us to estimate willingness to work in arrangements that may not currently be prevalent, involving, in particular, a flexible schedule. The SSQ approach is particularly useful in the context of late-in-life work where the gap between the desired and available opportunities may play an important role. In particular, we seek to answer whether older workers would take up jobs with flexible schedules even if that is not part of their current opportunity set.

The central finding by Ameriks *et al.* is that older individuals would work longer, especially if schedules were flexible. Based on the SSQs, many people would take the option to work fewer hours, even if it involved a more than proportionate reduction in earnings. Even those who are long retired have strong willingness to work, especially in a job with a flexible schedule, and this willingness to work becomes much stronger if they can choose the number of hours worked instead of having to work the same number of hours as in their previous job.

An important open question concerns the extent to which options for late-in-life work are understood by those of working age and by those whose career job ends for one reason or another. Is there a realistic understanding of the limited options available post retirement? This is an important issue to research. We are currently in the design phases of an instrument to explore the patterns of belief about late-in-life job opportunities. Of particular interest is whether there is a discrete change in beliefs at the point of retirement. Preliminary evidence suggests that there may indeed be such a shift, in the direction of increased pessimism about future employment opportunities. This is fertile ground for understanding the informational basis of beliefs in the pre-retirement phase, and possible mistakes made, in both savings decisions and labor market participation, as a result of poor such information.

15.6   Panel Data and Cognitive Instruments

One of the important research goals is to ensure, to the extent possible, that our survey of workers can enrich our understanding of the link between decision-making skills and patterns of lifetime income. While income patterns alone are not sufficient to empirically estimate the impact of decision-making skills, using them jointly with our survey instrument has high promise. That is why the emphasis is on developing an externally valid measure of decision-making skill and then tracking earnings. Overall, the ability the registries offer to access a wide array of life-course decisions and outcomes may be of great value in assessing decision-making skills. One long-run goal will be to identify markers (in the registry) for good decision-making skills, in general, and adaptability to shocks, in particular. We may find that the Danish registries contain far more information related to decision-making skills.

A particularly valuable aspect is what the panel nature of the CLP will teach us about the evolution of beliefs about future contingent wages and

job transitions as a function of experience. I close with the most specula-
tive aspect of the research, which relates to the specific cognitive skills that
can be measured that might show their importance in job transitions. The
proposed research path closely mirrors that involved in designing instruments to measure allocative skills. Again, there will be a need to test instruments in suitable experimental implementations before possible fielding.
Some issues relate to a multi-factor construct of search skill. Elements
include:

1. threat identification (e.g., impending layoff),
2. opportunity identification (e.g., searching while on job),
3. realism (e.g., accurately anticipating contingencies),
4. adaptability (e.g., adjusting strategy in light of experience).

There are also broader decision-making skills that may be needed to
navigate the labor market successfully. Here are three in particular that
may be worthy of investigation:

1. allocative skills, as outlined in the previous lecture;
2. financial skills, as introduced by Lusardi and Mitchell;
3. planning skills, as introduced by Ameriks *et al.* (2003) and since further
   refined.

15.6.1 *Measuring and modeling memory*

A critical issue in a panel of beliefs and outcomes is to understand the
informational basis for those beliefs as a key measure of decision quality.
One general aspect of expectations and updating is that it depends a great
deal on the structure of memory. Here, there are interesting research leads.
Of particular note is the work of Akerlof and Yellen (1985) on limited
recall of past experiences of unemployment. This gave rise to an interesting early literature on salience effects, fading of memories over time,
and even telescoping effects, in which far back events are recalled as more
recent (Topel, 1990). After a long lag, an exciting literature is now emerging, showing the importance of memory for beliefs about the future. Malmendier and Nagel (2011, 2015) have shown beliefs about the future to be
very strongly anchored in the past, particularly to what happened in for-
mative years. These beliefs appear resistant to change: Those who lived

through a stock market crash invest less in equities than do others even though all have access to the same historical data should they seek to learn about it. The psychological channels that drive this link are increasingly under study. This is an area that is increasingly of interest both theoretically and empirically. There are a number of prominent models that capture potentially rich interactions between memory and beliefs and that map to particular psychological theories of memory (da Silveira *et al.*, 2020; Bordalo *et al.*, 2017; Wachter and Kahana, 2019). Kuchler and Zafar (2019) link personal experiences and macroeconomic expectations.

Development of memory instruments is an exciting frontier. An ideal data set on past history and memory would include a battery of questions on past income, say for up to five years. One would expect the pooled data to reveal larger average errors further back in time. Beyond that, a panel might reveal links between current outcomes and beliefs about the past. Would an increase in income lead to an upward revision in estimates of prior income? Likewise, one could measure how memories of one and the same event change over time in light of current conditions; for example, does a past job loss come more to mind and impact beliefs more in a recession than in a boom? Note also that any reasonable theory of limited memory will involve stochasticity. The individual will, to some extent, be aware that their memory is imperfect. This means that the simplest model object that can capture memory is a subjective belief. Just as the introduction of well-designed instruments to measure expectations has revolutionized fields, from applied microeconomics to macroeconomics to finance, so well-engineered probabilistic questions about the past will shed new light on the link between history, memory, beliefs, and behavior, in particular helping us understand the role of memory in impacting uncertainty about the future.

Lecture 16

Communication Policies

Traditional policy tools operate through prices (e.g., taxes) or quantities (e.g., quotas). The theories guiding policy design are based on an essentially error-free understanding of these instruments. Yet, in a world of attentional constraints, thinking in these traditional terms is far too narrow. In fact, the rational inattention revolution was launched, in part, to capture the cognitive constraints relevant to monetary policy design and the perfect information fiction, suggesting that prices and wages would instantaneously adjust to increases in policy.

> In macroeconomic data we see few examples of variables that respond promptly to changes in other variables. Keynesian models recognize inertia in prices, but in their simpler forms translate this inertia in prices into prompt and strong responses of quantities to policy and to other disturbances. This implication of Keynesian models can be softened or eliminated by the introduction of adjustment costs, but such costs are usually modeled one variable at a time and have little support in either intuition or formal theory. A rational inattention approach implies pervasive inertial and erratic behavior, and implies connections across variables in the degree and nature of the inertia. (Sims, 2010, p. 156)

Important lessons have been learned in the monetary policy arena about the need for clear communication of policy intent (e.g., forward guidance). In this lecture, I outline research that broadens out from monetary policy to policy in general. The important central idea is that policy must be designed around actual limits in cognition. This is a road that has only just been opened and is of greatest long-run importance. I close with a particularly well-developed case study of the importance of clarity deriving from an intervention in the Mexican labor courts. A joint work with Andrei Gomberg and Joyce Sadka outlines a field study that demonstrably raised the quality of justice. At this stage we can confidently identify the channel through which this effect occurred. Obviously, more such studies are in order.

The applied analyses in this lecture are based on quite different measurement protocols than those in the earlier lectures. The analyses of monetary policy and social security policy make use of informational interventions to identify the limits of private comprehension. The analysis of cognitive decline is based on assessing beliefs about the decisions of future self. Finally, the judicial application makes critical use of the appeals court as a device for measuring mistakes. Each such method of identifying errors involves unique modeling challenges, which in turn suggest further possibilities for measurement. I discuss this issue, in particular, in relation to cognitive decline and the judicial application. Here is an overview of what is to come.

1. *Monetary Policy Communication and Information Treatments*: Given limited processing capacity, the idea that we all automatically know about a policy just because it is announced seems fanciful at best. This has been internalized by monetary policy makers, and communication is now an integral part of monetary policy design. In fact, they go further and place emphasis on measuring key expectations in relation to, for example, inflation. Following up on this, there is research on the determinants of these expectations and how various "information treatments" impact them. Some of these essentially act as "reminders" about inflation history, correcting apparently inaccurate prior beliefs.

2. *Confusion About Social Security Reform*: In the case of monetary policy, the policy tools are incomprehensible to the public at large, which makes communication inherently challenging. Yet, recent evidence suggests that people are uncertain about even the simplest and most personally salient policies, such as those relating to social security benefits (Ciani *et al.*, 2019). In a case study in Denmark, Caplin *et al.* (2022c) show that this form of uncertainty applies even to the simplest and most important aspect of social security: the age at which a worker can first

claim social security benefits. Empirically, many retire at precisely this age, indicating just what an important marker it is. Yet, as for other policies, we find great uncertainty about this claiming age, particularly for younger workers.

3. *Policy Uncertainty or Poor Communication?* In the Danish case, there are explicit plans to push back the social security claiming age in stages. The policy plans have been announced well in advance to allow younger workers to plan appropriately. Yet, in practice, the beliefs of younger workers exhibit not only high uncertainty but also a systematic gap from policy plans. They expect to be eligible at significantly younger ages than policy makers plan. The obvious open question is why beliefs and policy plans are so different. One possibility is policy uncertainty, as the policy can potentially be changed before it is implemented: Indeed, several such changes have been made. The other is inattention to policy and lack of awareness. While policy plans have been officially announced and details are available on various official websites, communication has largely been impersonal and passive. Is the gap between announced policy and beliefs largely a result of this inherent policy uncertainty, or is it due more to inattention? Caplin *et al.* (2022c) conduct an information treatment that actively communicates information that is freely available: currently announced policy intentions. We find that with active communication, the gap between plan and perception essentially disappears, yet uncertainty remains high. So, active communication significantly closes the gap between policy plan and public perception, which is presumably a policy goal. This highlights the widespread need to integrate communication strategies, including belief measurement and information treatments, into policy design.

4. *Cognitive Decline and Late-in-Life Welfare*: With population aging and the shift from defined benefit to defined contribution pensions, older households are becoming more responsible for managing their own finances during their retirement (Poterba, 2014). Ameriks *et al.* (2023) study mistaken decisions associated with cognitive decline. We show that those in the pre-decline phase are worried not only about possible future decline but also about possible future unawareness of that decline. Recent research reveals that many of us fear not only that we will go through such a decline but that we will not be sufficiently

aware of our deterioration to take effective remedial measures, such as handing over financial control to a relative. The link to errors is clear. One respondent during an online chat after a pilot Survey summarized the sources of worry succinctly:

> My mom, who is very old, was refused renewal of her driver's license because she failed the vision test. Her response was to sue the DMV for incompetence. I sincerely hope for self-driving cars before I get to that stage.

The policy challenge is for financial institutions and the authorities in charge of social security to develop communication strategies before decline has gone too far and to set in place appropriate protective measures.

5. *Clarity, Brevity, and Justice*: I outline an ongoing study in the Mexican labor courts showing that clear communication reduces apparent judicial errors (Caplin *et al.*, 2023a). These case files are complex: They might be on the scale of a small book, which has to be reviewed under great time pressure. The intervention was simple: addition of an index to make the file easier to navigate. The primary evidence of error reduction is a reduction in successful appeals. After diligent research into how the clarity of the case file improved the quality of justice, we now have an answer. Brevity.

6. As promised in the introduction and at the start of the applied part of the course, I close with a few comments on the definition of the state of the world as suitable to application.

16.1 Monetary Policy Communication and Beliefs

When people have limited information-processing capacity, policy makers cannot assume that the public immediately takes in a change in policy just because it is announced. Simple and salient communication is required to make people pay attention. Because of this, communication is now an integral part of monetary policy design. The European Central Bank states this explicitly:

Central bank communication has become a tool of policy in recent years. The ECB needs to be understood by markets and experts, but also by the wider public so that people can have trust in the institution and its policies.

Central banks now routinely announce inflation targets and their plans for achieving them in the form of "forward guidance." Communication strategies are designed to provide policy information in a digestible manner and thereby reduce both misunderstanding and uncertainty about future policy. Household and firm surveys of inflation expectations are conducted to identify the extent to which these announcements achieve their goal of being credible and comprehensible.

Information treatments and their impact on beliefs are of particular importance in macroeconomic policy design, given the centrality of inflation expectations in the monetary policy arena (Afrouzi and Yang, 2021; Armantier *et al.*, 2016; Coibion *et al.*, 2018, 2020). Expectations of both households and firms have been elicited in this manner. The corresponding information treatments operate in general by providing objective information on past inflation to a randomly chosen subset of subjects. There are by now many designs, some involving repeat treatment, with an increasing stress on linking to actual decisions, such as patterns of spending. An important open question involves better understanding why respondents appear to have such limited awareness of historical inflation.

Survey-based information treatments are now ubiquitous beyond the arena of monetary policy and are surveyed by Haaland *et al.* (2021). In the life-cycle context Wiswall and Zafar (2015a,b) use sequential surveys to understand how the provision of objective information on return to schooling alters beliefs. They study the determinants of college major choice using an experimentally generated panel of beliefs, which is obtained by providing students with information on the true population distribution of various major-specific characteristics. They find that students revise their beliefs in a reasonable manner in response to the information.

16.2   Confusion About Social Security Reform: Inattention or Policy Uncertainty?

Candia *et al.* (2020) address broad issues of communication as a form of policy. Yet, except when it comes to monetary policy, communication is rarely an integral part of policy design. Social security is a case in point. Policies that change social security eligibility and benefits are at the top of the agenda and are being implemented around the world. Social security and retirement reforms have been implemented in most European countries and in the U.S. The U.S. Social Security Amendments of 1983 raised the age of eligibility for unreduced retirement benefits to 67 by the year 2027. Russia also delayed the official retirement age in 2018, and China is currently planning to do so. These policies are a cornerstone in the attempt to make people work longer and to reduce public expenditures, following population aging. The importance of this topic is emphasized by the fact that an entire NBER program has been devoted to mapping and understanding the consequences of these programs (Börsch-Supan and Coile, 2018; Coile *et al.*, 2020).

Social security is a key determinant of late-in-life labor supply. and in large part, for that reason, social security reforms are often announced years in advance. One goal of such early announcements is to provide "forward guidance" to workers of all ages to allow them more effectively plan their labor force participation as well as spending and saving strategies more effectively. Yet, communication remains by and large passive, based on announcements at press conferences and making information available on possibly hard-to-navigate websites. Worryingly, but perhaps not surprisingly, studies have documented widespread ignorance about existing social security rules (e.g., Gustman and Steinmeier, 2005). Many view social security entitlements as uncertain, and the welfare cost of perceived policy uncertainty is high (Luttmer and Samwick, 2018).

Recent research raises further concerns about how many workers actively pursue up-to-date information about social security rules. Surveys of beliefs reveal widespread uncertainty about social security eligibility age, which is the most personally salient aspect of the system since it defines the age at which social security benefits first become available. There is typically a large spike in retirement at precisely this age, which explains why it is such a central feature of the policy. So strong is this effect that there is in fact an "excess employment sensitivity" puzzle: Labor market exits concentrate at social retirement ages even when the underlying incentives to do so are weak. Hentall-McCuish (2022) identifies mistaken beliefs about claiming age in U.K. data and models the underlying informational frictions in the form of costly attention, allowing for uncertain pension policy, in a dynamic life-cycle model of retirement. He studies this in the context of the U.K. female state pension age reform that increased eligibility age from 60 to 66 between 2010 and 2020.

Caplin *et al.* (2022c) study a particular reform of social security claiming age in Denmark, taking advantage of the registry and survey infrastructure. Social security is available to all Danish citizens who are above an age threshold. It is pay-as-you-go funded through the tax system, and concerns about fiscal stability led the parliament to decide on a major welfare reform package in 2006. This reform was simple and highly targeted: It changed **only the eligibility age**, without changing other features of the social security benefit system. The reform replaced a long-standing policy of universal social security eligibility at age 65 with longevity-based eligibility. This 2006 reform package and a subsequent modification in 2011 resulted in a gradual increase in the age threshold for social security eligibility by six months per year from 2019 to 2022 to move the social security eligibility age from 65 to 67. After that, the eligibility age is indexed to the life expectancy of those of age 60.

There are two primary sources of subjective uncertainty about the future social security claiming age in Denmark. One is that it is, in fact, a moving target. For example, in the Danish case in 2006, it was originally decided that this transition should take place over the period between 2024 and 2027, but in 2011, the parliament decided to speed up the increase such that it started in 2019. Further adding to policy uncertainty, it was announced that every five years, the age thresholds will be updated based on the development of life expectancy, with the decision to take effect 15 years later. The first revision was in 2015, and the latest was in 2020. In 2021, the current social security eligibility age was 66.5 years, and the parliament has now decided that the eligibility threshold will be 69 years by 2035. For cohorts born in 1971 or later, the social security eligibility age is currently an estimate.

In addition to this unavoidable policy uncertainty, there are many reasons to be concerned with how well informed the population is even about current policy plans. In large part, this is because communication has not been a priority and has not been a systematic focus of attention. The government communicated the policy change in 2006 and the revision in 2011 in press conferences and published the political agreement and information about its consequences on the home page of the Ministry of Finance. There was little in way of active communication with the affected age groups. The revisions in 2015 and 2020 were again published on the home pages of the Ministry of Employment and the Ministry of Finance with little fanfare. While there has been little in the way of active communication, future policies most certainly are not deliberately hidden. In fact, long-term projections of future social security eligibility ages were published as early as 2006 (and today, it is straightforward to search and find the information). It takes little in way of search for any interested Dane to go to the web page that contains up-to-date information on the actual or projected social security eligibility age. Given how personally important such information might be, one might be forgiven for assuming that the information is therefore well understood by most.

16.3   Active Communication Matters

From the viewpoint of policy, it is important not only to identify the general public's beliefs about social security eligibility but also to determine the extent to which any gap between policy plans and public beliefs results from limited attention, as opposed to inevitable policy uncertainty. This distinction is fundamental to the role of communication. If the gap is largely about fundamental future uncertainties, communicating current policies better will have little effect. If instead it is largely a result of passive learning by workers, then more active and better targeted communication has potentially large benefits. The goal of the work by Caplin *et al.* (2022c) is precisely to separately identify fundamental policy uncertainty associated with changing demographic and political factors from uncertainty that results from inattention to currently available information, in part because uncertainty might itself be a reason for inattention.

Our research design builds on the recent literature of information treatments (Haaland *et al.*, 2022) to tease apart fundamental uncertainty about the future from inattention to currently available information. In an ideal case, one would implement an information treatment that overcomes informational frictions altogether, leaving only the fundamental uncertainty in place. The 2006 Danish reform is close to ideal in this regard. The fact that it changed **only** the eligibility age, without changing other features of the social security benefit system, makes it an ideal case in point. It also allows us to implement a strikingly simple information treatment. Before posing questions about future eligibility age, we randomly select half of the survey respondents and provide them with the longevity-based plan that is currently available on the official website of the Danish Ministry of Employment. All this does is to overcome passive learning. For both groups we measure probabilistic beliefs using the balls and bins protocol of Delavande and Rohwedder (2008), which allows us to characterize the entire subjective probability distribution concerning social security eligibility and how active communication influences it.

Our first finding is that, as in other countries, there is in Denmark high subjective uncertainty. Workers are aware that they do not know the eligibility age, with younger workers in particular highly uncertain. There is also a systematic difference between the policy-announced eligibility age and what current workers believe. Younger workers, in particular, expect to become eligible for social security earlier than the published table indicates. There are projected to be real effects on retirement: Many believe that they will retire right around social security eligibility age. The gap between policy projection and subjective belief appears responsive to incentives: Those who report that social security claiming age greatly impacts the age of retirement have beliefs that align more closely with current projections.

How do beliefs differ as between those who do and those who do not see the current projections before providing us with their expectations? The impact of the information treatment is simple and striking. **It essentially eliminates the gap between the statutory eligibility age and the subjective mean beliefs.** It correspondingly affects beliefs about retirement. So, there indeed appears that those who are not provided with the table are ill-informed and that gaps in knowledge of current policy plans account by and large for their biased beliefs.

The effect of the information treatment on uncertainty is entirely different. **It has essentially no influence on subjective uncertainty**. This suggests that, unlike expectations, uncertainty about future social security is largely driven by unavoidable demographic and political uncertainties. As noted above, this irreducible uncertainty is not surprising since changes can and have been made since the initial announcement and because the Danish policy explicitly introduces fundamental demographic uncertainty since future eligibility ages depend on future life expectancy.

Another question we address in our research design is how long the information treatment is retained. One might anticipate a rapid deterioration in knowledge since the treatment is so brief, and there may be no immediate change in behavior for younger workers who are still decades away from claiming benefits. The finding is otherwise: The information is well retained. A follow-up survey one year later shows that the effect of the information treatment in the original survey dissipates only slowly. This reveals that our simple information treatment had a durable influence on beliefs and to a large extent broke the grip of the past. Our positive results on the value of active communication highlight the need to treat such communication as an integral part of policy design. Passively making information available online produces misunderstanding that could be avoided by a more deliberate communication policy. As part of such policies, the measurement of beliefs has a key role in providing the most direct window into the effectiveness of communication. Information treatments and belief measurement together are in that sense an important and complementary policy tools.

16.4   Cognitive Decline and Late-in-Life Welfare

An obvious source of mistakes in later life is cognitive decline. This surely raises the costs of comprehension and errors made in many settings. This is particularly important in financial contexts, given the important decisions at stake in relation, for example, to medical issues and long-term care. A major challenge is that cognitive decline may impact the quality of such decisions. For example, estimates suggest that about one-third of Americans 85 years or older (and 9% of those 65 years or older) have dementia (Plassman *et al.*, 2007). Cognitive decline appears to make older Americans less capable in terms of financial decision-making (Agarwal *et al.*, 2009) and vulnerable to financial fraud (DeLiema *et al.*, 2020). Nicholas *et al.* (2021) present evidence of deterioration in financial skills and increasing financial mistakes, such as missing payments, before a dementia diagnosis. For that reason, it is increasingly important for economists to understand how these households currently handle this issue and to examine room for improvement (Chandra *et al.*, 2020). Mazzona and Peracchi (2020) estimate that cognitive decline, of which subjects are unaware, results in 10% loss of wealth among wealthy stockholders.

Given the risks, many may plan to rely on a third party, such as a family member, to take over decisions when cognitive decline has set in. A first key question to address is how many older wealth-holders believe that they have a reliable agent and how many are concerned about the timing of their likely transfer of control. This is one subject of Ameriks *et al.* (2023). The focus of the research was influenced by a pilot survey. Most respondents in the pilot survey were confident in the ability of a trustworthy agent to make good financial decisions on their behalf. On the flip side, many appeared concerned about their own future behavior and the possibility that they might fail to transfer control at the right time. This fits with the reality that many who have watched loved ones age are struck by their failure to recognize their own decline. These are sophisticated issues of metacognition. Not all are aware of their state of decline, and many in the pre-decline phase are aware that they may later not be so aware.

Before posing questions on possible remedies, the survey opened by enquiring about subjective risks of undergoing cognitive decline. We specified this, as in the U.S. Health and Retirement Survey (HRS), as having significant difficulties in any of the following: remembering familiar things and recent changes, learning new things, following a story in a book or on TV, making decisions on everyday matters, handling financial matters, and using your intelligence to reason things through. We then asked respondents to report their subjective probabilities of having cognitive decline for at least one year and for at least five years. The respondents overall perceive a meaningful risk of experiencing cognitive decline for at least five years. The median probability is 15%, while the mean is 29%. This is fairly close to the 34% realized average chance of having cognitive decline for at least five years calculated from the realized path of cognitive decline in the HRS.

With the risk established, the survey dug further into how many older wealth-holders are aware not only that they might in future decline but that they might not recognize this immediately. The survey was designed also to quantify concerns about both the quality of an available agent and about the timing of the transfer of control.

In terms of agency, the key survey instrument is the following:

> Who do you think is most likely to make financial decisions on your behalf if you have significant cognitive decline if no spouse/partner were to be available?

Around 70% reported that a child would be the most likely agent and 10% a sibling, with the remaining essentially equally divided by a trustee or institution and a broad other category. We followed up with questions on how well the agent would perform in several respects:

1. understanding your needs and desires,
2. understanding your financial situation,
3. understanding financial matters in general,
4. pursuing your interest.

In broad terms, agents were assessed to be of high quality. Fully half of the respondents reported that they believed the agent would be excellent in all categories, increasing to 80% excellent or very good in all categories. This confirmed findings from the pilot survey that worries about the agent were on the whole second order.

Again, based on the pilot survey, we devoted much of the survey to deepening our understanding of concerns related to the timing of transfer of control to the agent. Note that our Vanguard Research Initiative survey sample is unusual in its tolerance for difficult questions. There is absolutely no way that one could place these questions in different and less research-oriented survey samples. That allowed us to provide respondents with a difficult hypothetical future scenario of which to base their answers:

1. Suppose that you are in the last five years of life. (If coupled, you have outlived your spouse/partner.)

2. You have mild cognitive decline in the first year.
3. You have your personal subjective beliefs about the progression of cognitive decline during ensuing years.
4. You have wealth of W (the nearest multiple of $500K$ to the actual wealth).
5. The following decisions will need to be made:

   (a) saving for the future and managing investments;
   (b) how to spend (routine spending, non-routine spending, long-term care, etc.);
   (c) giving to relatives, friends, or charities.

In this scenario we posed a first question on their current preferences as to when they would transfer control of resources to their agent:

1. Immediately at the onset of cognitive decline.
2. During further decline but before you completely lose the ability to manage your finances.
3. When you completely lose the ability to manage your finances.

More than 80% of respondents chose the second answer, with the remainder equally divided between the first and third options.

We followed this up with questions on the probability that, in practice, they would transfer control at this time as opposed to too early or too late relative to the current ideal. Responses revealed significant concern that the timing of transfer would not be ideal, with on average an approximately 35% chance of transferring control too late and 25% too early. As to which respondents were more worried about, more than 60% were more worried about a late rather than an early transfer.

We used several questions to quantify the primary concern (branching according to which mistake was more concerning). We designed a question to measure the compensating variation for making a transfer at the wrong time. For those more concerned with delay, we asked them to contrast Scenario 1, which involved transfer at the ideal time, with Scenario 2 referring to delayed transfer, and to specify a quantitative answer to the following question:

> At what level of resources would you be just as well off with the spending and saving decisions under Scenario 2 as with those under Scenario 1 with $500,000?

The average answer was around $600,000. This means that the risk is, on average, seen as quantitatively significant, amounting to nearly 20% of wealth at the onset of decline. We posed a second question concerning current willingness to pay for a guarantee of optimal timing of transfer, identifying a willingness to pay comprising some 2–3% of their current wealth.

The survey results show that many of us believe that our comprehension will deteriorate late in the life cycle and that, as a result, our decision-making ability will decline. We also believe that one aspect of such decline is that we might not recognize our own decline. This is a particularly interesting challenge for modeling and measurement. What precisely is the relationship between current self and anticipated cognitively declined future self? Is there perfect or imperfect empathy? And what of the view of cognitively constrained future self of past self? Would there be any ability to commit later self to an earlier agreed strategy of handing over at least partial control to a once-trusted agent?

Policy possibilities are much in need of research. Consider a quote from an online chat after the pilot survey:

> I would hope that financial institutions would take a responsible approach to abnormal changes in behavior by a long-term client.

Some policy possibilities involve financial institutions flagging agreed transactions as prompting an interaction to check that there is no fraud. In addition to obvious cases of wiring massive amounts of funds to previously unknown parties, there may be other cases that would warrant at least a check-in. A related issue is what to do if there are indeed good reasons to worry: Might it be time to inform a loved one, and might this too be agreed ahead of time? Would there be any role of agreed checks on cognition? Possibilities could be greatly enhanced with prior agreement about some forms of cognitive testing in lab-in-the-field style. But there may be no real ability to commit later self so the challenge is deep.

16.5 Clarity, Brevity, and Justice

A major role of the justice system is to decide cases correctly. The goal ideally is "determining what the facts are and what their legal significance is" (Posner, 2014). Of course, it is well understood that the costs of determining all facts and their legal significance in all cases may be prohibitive. How close legal systems come to achieving the ideal of error-free decision-making in practice is an open question. Cameron and Kornhauser (2006) and Stephenson (2010) argue that error reduction is a key element in the design of the legal systems, with appeals processes and liability suits a key case in point (Shavell, 1995). Typically, such appeals impose time and reputational costs on the responsible parties, in line with the broader argument that error reduction is a key element in the design of the legal system.

Caplin *et al.* (2023a) report the results of a field experiment on administration of justice that we conducted in a labor court in Mexico. This court, for the most part, dealt with cases involving firing disputes, with employees typically asking for reinstatement or compensation for illegal firing. In common with most Mexican courts during the period of study, the court operated without conducting a trial in the typical Anglo-American sense of the word. Rather, upon conclusion of hearings in which evidence was presented and its admissibility was ruled on, the resulting case file would be transmitted to an official in the court (whom we shall call a judge) charged with composing the opinion for the court. They are tasked with reducing a long and complex trial transcript to a standardized record of "legal facts." The official in question would not have been present during the evidence presentation hearings but, rather, would solely base her opinion on the written file containing all the evidence in the case. The job is effectively impossible to do perfectly given the great complexity and essential disorganization of the case files.

Once issued, this decision could be appealed to a higher court, alleging a violation of a party's constitutional rights. The grounds for a successful appeal is an assessment that errors were made in translating the trial transcript into legal facts. In cases in which the appeal is granted, the original-opinion author is put in charge of the revision and must respond to the claims in the appeal and reassess the legal facts. That task is in addition to that judge's other workload, and she would have to assign it a high priority. Given the high volume of opinions judges had to produce, this additional work would certainly be unwelcome. Hence, though the trial court judge may not be fully internalizing the costs of possible errors, she is effectively incentivized to avoid being overturned on appeal. Appeals, if granted, are not only time-consuming but also damaging to the reputation of the judge.

In an all-too-rare demonstration of a desire to improve, and by an arrangement with the court, we were able to gain access to the case files and code their content before the judges themselves could read them. We thus possessed the same information the judges themselves did when preparing their opinions. What is more, we were able to randomly vary the ease with which the judge could navigate a case file by providing a summary (similar to an index of a book) that included basic information about the case, including the list of major evidence items admitted and their location in the case file. Though all case files were indexed in this manner, we randomized whether the index page would be included in the submission to the judge. Without this index, the judges had little guidance on where to look for the important legal facts buried in the file. With it, there is reason to believe that they were better able to read the file in order of importance.

The fact that stands out is the reduction in successful appeals for those cases in which indices were added. Since the research team did not interfere with the appeals process, this reduction in successful appeals is *prima facie* evidence of reduced errors. The effect was both statistically and quantitatively significant. Our intervention lowered the reversal rate by about a third from 16% to less than 11%. Given that we did not affect the content of the case file, but only the ease with which evidence in it could be accessed by the judge, we interpret this result as demonstrating that simplifying the attentional task the judge is facing by itself improves the quality of her decision, at least as far as it can be measured by the appeals process. This strongly suggests a role of informational constraints in producing verdicts that are subject to a successful appeal.

A particularly scientifically valuable aspect of this field study is that we have been able to pin down the attentional channel more precisely. The first step was to provide a basic classification of case files into two large and quite distinct categories. These are all cases in which the plaintiff is always the worker suing for wrongful treatment. The defendants are the employers they claim to have been working for. A key distinction between cases is that in roughly half the cases, defendants **denied existence of labor**

relationship outright. They therefore submitted no evidence. Of course, in these cases, the law puts the burden of proof on the plaintiff, who has to demonstrate existence of an employment relationship. In a sense, these are simple cases since the entire case rests on whether or not the worker can establish existence of a relationship.

The remaining cases are more complex. They are cases in which the labor relationship is acknowledged by both sides, and it is the legality of its termination that is at issue. In general, by Mexican law the burden of proof in those cases is placed largely on the defendant. These are the more complex cases in which both sides are generally required to present evidence in support of their claims and where the claims themselves maybe more complicated.

Where was our treatment more effective, or was it equally effective in both types of cases? Here, the result is remarkably clean. Our treatment effect is entirely concentrated on the **complex cases**, in which there is an acknowledged labor relationship, and in these cases, it was very effective in reducing the rate of successful appeals. This highlights the importance of better understanding the sources of complexity (Oprea, 2021).

Our arrangement with the court let us dig deeper to identify the channel responsible for this large treatment effect. In over 60% of the cases in our study, we were able to obtain the texts of the original opinions produced by judges (before appeals). We were therefore able to compare the content of the case files with the texts of these opinions. By exploring the files, we were able to address two more open questions. First, what are the key differences between the opinions written with and without the clarifying index? Does the index lead to the identification of more pieces of evidence that might have been missed without the index or fewer and more targeted pieces of evidence? Does the effect operate through a closer reading of both plaintiff and defendant cases, or is it more one-sided, and if so, which?

The answers again are surprisingly clean. In the treated case files, the judges listed **fewer** pieces of evidence in their judgments. This reduction was only found in the cases in which the labor relationship itself was acknowledged by both sides, the same cases in which we found our treatment effective in preventing successful appeals. Moreover, the effect was asymmetric as between defendant and plaintiff. **It was only the evidence presented by the defendants that got shortened**. Controlling for the number of documental pieces of evidence presented by the defendant, opinions in treated cases on average contain mentions of some seven documents fewer than those in untreated cases. We observe no statistically significant effects of this sort in the cases where the burden of proof is on the plaintiff, nor is there any significant effect on evidence presented by plaintiffs in any cases.

The field study shows that treated opinions in the impacted cases are shorter and more "on point." These same cases are also less likely to be overturned on appeal. It appears that the judges were able to use the case summaries we provided to settle on a legal theory of the case which would be supported by a subset of evidence. This, perhaps, left appeals courts with fewer targets for a potential overturn.

16.6   Closing Remarks on Applications

The legal case study is of particular value in thinking about how to define the states of the world in applied settings. The first point is that there is much researcher discretion in defining the state of the world, and this can be used to expand the reach of the corresponding analytic methods. When theorists think of a state of the world, they generally have in mind as full a description of the universe as necessary. The psychometric tradition is entirely different. The state is identified by which hand holds the heavier weight or which of two sounds is louder and by how much. In economic experiments that elicit SDSC data, the state is, likewise, something that is readily measurable, such as whether a rectangular array contains more red or blue dots. Particularly in the latter cases, one might worry that there are very different such arrays, with some making counting easy, others difficult. Even in the case of weight or sound, each case is subtly different, and one might wish to say that there are no objectively identical states.

Of course, in applications, there are limits to how far we wish to go in separating states, and these tend to be agreed upon among researchers. The test for whether or not a classification was successful is to some extent empirical: Does a theory based on the proposed classification of states allow progress in understanding patterns in data? If so, this is part (possibly not the end) of a progressive research agenda. If not, back to the drawing board.

What about outside laboratory settings in which not only are all cases unique but also we do not really know the classification of payoff-relevant states in the eyes of the DM? The last case, that of judicial decisions, illustrates issues well. It is typical to model judges as seeking the truth (e.g., Kamenica and Gentzkow, 2011). That certainly seems likely to be part of the motivation for reviewing case files carefully. Of course, if we use this definition, then it may be effectively impossible to get the corresponding SDSC data. Effectively, the best we could do might be to merge opinions of various experts to arrive at a probabilistic classification. I believe that this is an important effort to undertake, but it is not the only path forward.

An alternative applicable to the Mexican labor courts is to treat the relevant state as whether or not the verdict is successfully appealed. Avoiding such appeals may or may not be precisely what is guiding the judges. But it has two advantages. First, it is clearly payoff relevant, possibly more than the judge's subjective belief that she arrived at the correct verdict. Second, it is available in the data so that, essentially, one can build an operational model of mistakes made by having cases reviewed and the verdicts reconsidered. There is then the interesting modeling challenge of connecting this version of the state with an overarching model of the legal system as involving the desire to reduce errors in the original sense of not making Type 1 and Type 2 errors, but that is to some extent a separate issue.

The broad point of this discussion is to make clear that one should not use the purely theoretical notion of a state of the world in judging the value of the methods of the book in modeling and measuring mistakes. They may be more broadly applicable than currently understood.

Epilogue

As noted in the introduction, early in my academic career, I noticed the rigid boundaries within and between social scientific disciplines. Of particular relevance to the science of mistakes is the extent to which theory and measurement advance in separate silos. This book is by and large a result of my deliberate decision to reject this approach and try to cut a different path. As a result, the work has a large personal component. It expresses my research aesthetic more accurately than anything I can write by way of conclusion. So, instead of trying to summarize, I will conclude instead by expressing a wish for the future of the forms of social scientific research that most excite me.

The key to this fictional future is continued reduction in the cost of forming effective research teams. A wonderful feature of the past few decades is that the cost of forming links has dropped by orders of magnitude. That has allowed me and others to build durable academic relationships across the theory/application divide. Yet, for all that barriers to team formation have been reduced, the formation of effective learning teams operates on a scale of years and decades, not days, weeks, or months. There is a kind of "match-making" process that is at present completely decentralized and disorganized. Any individual or institution that could change this would do orders of magnitude more to advance social science, in general, and the science of mistakes, in particular, than any of us engaged in the research game can do alone.

One mode of advance involves increasing our focus on research into teamwork itself. How effective teams form and how to stimulate teamwork more effectively are hugely important research subjects in their own right. Some theoretical guidance derives from team-theoretic constructs, such as those introduced by Marschak and Radner (1972). Some applied insights derive from recent research by Weidmann and Deming (2021) on team-work outlined in Lecture 14.

Positive as it would be for social scientists to better understand constraints on team formation, left to our own devices, we will only make incremental progress. Outside intervention of some form is needed. The larger open question is how to design team-friendly research institutions in the social sciences. Does this require a physical entity: a social scientific MIT or, better yet, a Caltech? An Institute for Advanced Social Science perhaps? Or might the ideal be almost entirely virtual with appropriately timed meet-ups? Do we need a social scientific "dating" app? Whatever is called for, I believe that with appropriate leadership and institutional change, advances in the science of mistakes would accelerate by orders of magnitude.

Bibliography

Acemoglu, D. and Autor, D. 2011. Skills, tasks and technologies: Implications for employment and earnings. In *Handbook of Labor Economics* (Vol. 4, pp. 1043–1171). Elsevier, Amsterdam.

Afrouzi, H. and Yang, C. 2021. Selection in Information Acquisition and Monetary Non-Neutrality.

Agarwal, S., Driscoll, J.C., Gabaix, X. and Laibson, D. 2009. The age of reason: Financial decisions over the life cycle and implications for regulation. *Brookings Papers on Economic Activity*, 2009(2), 51–117.

Agranov, M., Caplin, A. and Tergiman, C. 2015. Naive play and the process of choice in guessing game. *Journal of the Economic Science Association*, 1, 1–12.

Aguiar, M. and Hurst, E. 2005. Consumption versus expenditure. *Journal of political Economy*, 113(5), 919–948.

Akerlof, G.A. and Yellen, J.L. 1985. Unemployment through the filter of memory. *The Quarterly Journal of Economics*, 100(3), 747–773.

Alos-Ferrer, C., Fehr, E. and Netzer, N. 2021. Time will tell: Recovering preferences when choices are noisy. *Journal of Political Economy*, 129(6), 1828–1877.

Amari, S.I. 2016. *Information Geometry and Its Applications* (Vol. 194). Springer, Berlin.

Ameriks, J., Briggs, J., Caplin, A., Lee, M., Shapiro, M. and Tonetti, C. 2020a. Older Americans would work longer if jobs were flexible. *American Economic Journal: Macroeconomics*, 12(1), 174–209.

Ameriks, J., Briggs, J., Caplin, A., Shapiro, M.D. and Tonetti, C. 2020b. Long-term-care utility and late-in-life saving. *Journal of Political Economy*, 128(6), 2375–2451.

Ameriks, J., Caplin, A. and Leahy, J. 2003. Wealth accumulation and the propensity to plan. *The Quarterly Journal of Economics*, 118(3), pp. 1007–1047.

Ameriks, J., Caplin, A., Leahy, J. and Tyler, T. 2007. Measuring self-control problems. *American Economic Review*, 97, 966–972.

Ameriks, J., Caplin, A., Lee, M., Shapiro, M.D. and Tonetti, C. 2023. *Cognitive Decline, Limited Awareness, Imperfect Agency, and Financial Well-being*. Forthcoming, American Economic Review, Insights.

Andersen, H.Y. and Leth-Petersen, S. 2021. Housing wealth or collateral: How home value shocks drive home equity extraction and spending. *Journal of the European Economic Association*, 19(1), 403–440.

Angeletos, G.M. and Sastry, K. 2019. Inattentive economies, National Bureau of Economic Research Working Paper 26413, Cambridge, Mass.

Apesteguia, J. and Ballester, M.A. 2018. Monotone stochastic choice models: The case of risk and time preferences. *Journal of Political Economy*, 126(1), 74–106.

Archsmith, J.E., Heyes, A., Neidell, M.J. and Sampat, B.N. 2021. The Dynamics of Inattention in the (Baseball) Field. National Bureau of Economic Research Working Paper 28922.

Arcidiacono, P., Hotz, V.J. and Kang, S. 2012. Modeling college major choices using elicited measures of expectations and counterfactuals. *Journal of Econometrics*, 166(1), 3–16.

Arcidiacono, P., Hotz, V.J., Maurel, A. and Romano, T. 2014. Recovering *ex ante* returns and preferences for occupations using subjective expectations data. National Bureau of Economic Research Working Paper 20626.

Armantier, O., Nelson, S., Topa, G., Van der Klaauw, W. and Zafar, B. 2016. The price is right: Updating inflation expectations in a randomized price information experiment. *Review of Economics and Statistics*, 98(3), 503–523.

Armantier, O. and Treich, N. 2013. Eliciting beliefs: Proper scoring rules, incentives, stakes and hedging. *European Economic Review*, 62, pp. 17–40.

Autor, D.H., Levy, F. and Murnane, R.J. 2003. The skill content of recent technological change: An empirical exploration. *The Quarterly Journal of Economics*, 118(4), 1279–1333.

Avoyan, A. and Romagnoli, G. 2019. Paying for Inattention. Available at SSRN 3427147.

Bagger, J., Fontaine, F., Postel-Vinay, F., and Robin, J.-M. 2014. Tenure, experience, human capital, and wages: A tractable equilibrium search model of wage dynamics. American Economic Review 104 (6), 1551–96.

Barsky, R.B., Juster, F.T., Kimball, M.S. and Shapiro, M.D. 1997. Preference parameters and behavioral heterogeneity: An experimental approach in the health and retirement study. *Quarterly Journal of Economics*, 112(2), 537–579.

Bartel, A., Ichniowski, C. and Shaw, K. 2007. How does information technology affect productivity? Plant-level comparisons of product innovation, process improvement, and worker skills. *The Quarterly Journal of Economics*, 122(4), 1721–1758.

Bayer, H.M. and Glimcher, P.W. 2005. Midbrain dopamine neurons encode a quantitative reward prediction error signal. *Neuron*, 47(1), 129–141.

Ben-Simon, A., Budescu, D.V. and Nevo, B. 1997. A comparative study of measures of partial knowledge in multiple-choice tests. *Applied Psychological Measurement*, 21(1), pp. 65–88.

Bernheim, B.D. and Rangel, A. 2009. Beyond revealed preference: choice-theoretic foundations for behavioral welfare economics. *Quarterly Journal of Economics*, 124(1), 51–104.

Bertrand, M. and Schoar, A. 2003. Managing with style: The effect of managers on firm policies. *The Quarterly Journal of Economics*, 118(4), 1169–1208.

Bhargava, S., Loewenstein, G. and Sydnor, J. 2017. Choose to lose: Health plan choices from a menu with dominated option. *The Quarterly Journal of Economics*, 132(3), 1319–1372.

Bhattacharya, V. and Howard, G. 2021. Rational inattention in the infield. *American Economic Journal: Microeconomics*.

Bickel, J.E. 2010. Scoring rules and decision analysis education. *Decision Analysis*, 7(4), pp. 346–357.

Blackwell, D. 1953. Equivalent comparisons of experiments. *The Annals of Mathematical Statistics*, 265–272.

Block, H.D. and Marschak, J. 1959. *Random Orderings and Stochastic Theories of Response*. No. 66. Cowles Foundation for Research in Economics, Yale University.

Bloedel, A.W. and Zhong, W. 2020. The cost of optimally-acquired information. Unpublished Manuscript, November.

Bloom, N., Sadun, R. and Van Reenen, J. 2012. The organization of firms across countries. *The Quarterly Journal of Economics*, 127(4), 1663–1705.

Bordalo, P., Gennaioli, N. and Shleifer, A. 2017. Memory, attention, and choice. *The Quarterly Journal of Economics*.

Borsch-Supan, A.H. and Coile, C. 2018. Social security programs and retirement around the world: reforms and retirement incentives: Introduction and summary. National Bureau of Economic Research Working Paper 25280.

Bronchetti, E.T., Kessler, J.B., Magenheim, E.B., Taubinsky, D. and Zwick, E. 2020. Is Attention Produced Rationally? National Bureau of Economic Research Working Paper 27443.

Brown, J.R., Kapteyn, A., Luttmer, E.F. and Mitchell, O.S. 2017. Cognitive constraints on valuing annuities. *Journal of the European Economic Association*, 15(2), pp. 429–462.

Bucher, S.F. and Caplin, A. 2021. Inattention and Inequity in School Matching. National Bureau of Economic Research Working Paper 29586.

Callaway, F., Rangel, A. and Griffiths, T.L. 2021. Fixation patterns in simple choice reflect optimal information sampling. *PLoS Computational Biology*, 17(3), p.e1008863.

Camerer, C.F. and Hogarth, R.M. 1999. The effects of financial incentives in experiments: A review and capital-labor-production framework. *Journal of Risk and Uncertainty*, 19(1), 7–42.

Cameron, C.M. and Kornhauser, L.A. 2006. Appeals mechanisms, litigant selection, and the structure of judicial hierarchies. Institutional Games and the US Supreme Court, 173.

Candia, B., Coibion, O. and Gorodnichenko, Y. 2020. Communication and the beliefs of economic agents. National Bureau of Economic Research Working Paper 27800.

Caplin, A. 2021. Economic Data Engineering. National Bureau of Economic Research Working Paper 29378.

Caplin, A., Csaba, D., Leahy, J. and Nov, O. 2020. Rational inattention, competitive supply, and psychometrics. *The Quarterly Journal of Economics*, 135(3), 1681–1724.

Caplin, A. and Dean, M. 2011. Search, choice, and revealed preference. *Theoretical Economics*, 6(1), 19–48.

Caplin, A. and Dean, M. 2013. Behavioral implications of rational inattention with shannon entropy. National Bureau of Economic Research Working Paper 19318.

Caplin, A. and Dean, M. 2015. Revealed preference, rational inattention, and costly information acquisition. *American Economic Review*, 105(7), 2183–2203.

Caplin, A., Dean, M., Glimcher, P.W. and Rutledge, R.B. 2010. Measuring beliefs and rewards: A neuroeconomic approach. *The Quarterly Journal of Economics*, 125(3), 923–960.

Caplin, A., Dean, M. and Leahy, J. 2017. Rationally inattentive behavior: characterizing and generalizing shannon entropy. National Bureau of Economic Research Working Paper 23652.

Caplin, A., Dean, M. and Leahy, J. 2019. Rational inattention, optimal consideration sets, and stochastic choice. *Review of Economic Studies*, 86(3), 1061–1094.

Caplin, A., Dean, M. and Leahy, J. 2022a. Rationally inattentive behavior: Characterizing and generalizing Shannon entropy. *Journal of Political Economy*, 130, 1676–1715.

Caplin, A., Dean, M. and Martin, D. 2011. Search and satisficing. *American Economic Review*, 101: 2899–2922.

Caplin, A., Gomberg, A. and Sadka, J. 2023a. Measuring, modeling, and minimizing judicial errors. Working Paper.

Caplin, A., Gregory, V., Leth-Petersen, S., Lee, E. and Saeverud, J. 2023b. Subjective earnings risk. National Bureau of Economic Research Working Paper 31019.

Caplin, A. and Leahy, J. 1994. Business as usual, market crashes, and wisdom after the fact. *The American Economic Review*, 548–565.

Caplin, A. and Leahy, J. 2001. Psychological expected utility theory and anticipatory feelings. *Quarterly Journal of Economics*, 55–80.

Caplin, A. and Leahy, J. 2004. The supply of information by a concerned expert. *Economic Journal*, 487–505.

Caplin, A. and Leahy, J.V. 2019. Wishful thinking. National Bureau of Economic Research Working Paper 25707.

Caplin, A., Leahy, J. and Matejka, F. 2015. Social learning and selective attention. National Bureau of Economic Research Working Paper 21001.

Caplin, A., Leth-Petersen, S., Lee, E. and Saeverud, J. 2022c. Communicating social security reform. National Bureau of Economic Research Working Paper 30645.

Caplin, A. and Martin, D. 2011. A Testable Theory of Imperfect Perception. National Bureau of Economic Research Working Paper 17163.

Caplin, A. and Martin, D. 2015. A testable theory of imperfect perception. *Economic Journal*, 125(582), 184–202.

Caplin, A. and Martin, D. 2021. Comparison of decisions under unknown experiments. *Journal of Political Economy*, 129, 3185–3205 129(11).

Caplin, A., Martin, D. and Marx, P. 2022b. Modeling Machine Learning. National Bureau of Economic Research Working Paper 30600.

Caplin, A., Martin, D. and Marx, P. 2023c. Rationalizable Learning. National Bureau of Economic Research Working Paper 30873.

Carrasco, M. 2011. Visual attention: The past 25 years. Vision research, 51(13), pp. 1484–1525.

Carrington, W.J. 1993. Wage losses for displaced workers: is it really the firm that matters? *Journal of Human Resources*, 435–462.

Carvalho, A. 2016. An overview of applications of proper scoring rules. Decision Analysis, 13(4), pp. 223–242.

Carvalho, L. and Silverman, D. 2019. Complexity and sophistication. National Bureau of Economic Research Working Paper 26036.

Chan, S. and A.H. Stevens 1999. Employment and retirement following a late-career job loss. *American Economic Review* 89 (2), 211–216.

Chandra, A., Coile, C. and Mommaerts, C. 2020. What Can Economics Say About Alzheimer's Disease? National Bureau of Economic Research Working Paper 27760.

Chen, Y. and He, Y. 2021. Information acquisition and provision in school choice: An experimental study. *Journal of Economic Theory*, 197, 105345.

Chentsov, N.N. 1982. Statistical decision rules and optimal inference. *Monog*, 53.

Chetty, R., Looney, A. and Kroft, K. 2009. Salience and taxation: Theory and evidence. *American Economic Review*, 99, 1145–1177.

Ciani, E., Delavande, A., Etheridge, B. and Francesconi, M. 2019. Policy uncertainty and information flows: Evidence from pension reform expectations.

Coibion, O., Gorodnichenko, Y. and Kamdar, R. 2018. The formation of expectations, inflation, and the phillips curve. *Journal of Economic Literature*, 56(4), pp. 1447–91.

Coibion, O., Gorodnichenko, Y. and Ropele, T. 2020. Inflation expectations and firm decisions: New causal evidence. *The Quarterly Journal of Economics*, 135(1), pp. 165–219.

Coile, C.C., Milligan, K. and Wise, D.A. (Eds.) 2020. Social Security Programs and Retirement around the World: working longer. University of Chicago Press.

Conlon, J.J., Pilossoph, L., Wiswall, M. and Zafar, B. 2018. Labor market search with imperfect information and learning. National Bureau of Economic Research Working Paper 24988.

Cover, T.M. and Thomas, J. 1999. *Elements of Information Theory*. John Wiley & Sons. New York.

Csaba, D. 2021. Attention elasticities and invariant information costs. arXiv preprint arXiv:2105.07565.

Currie, J. and MacLeod, W.B. 2017. Diagnosing expertise: Human capital, decision-making, and performance among physicians. *Journal of Labor Economics*, 35(1), 1–43.

da Silveira, R.A., Sung, Y. and Woodford, M. 2020. Optimally imprecise memory and biased forecasts. National Bureau of Economic Research Working Paper 28075.

Davidson, D. and Marschak, J. 1959. Experimental tests of a stochastic decision theory. Measurement: Definitions and theories, 17, 2

De Finetti, B. 1965. Methods for discriminating levels of partial knowledge concerning a test item. *British Journal of Mathematical and Statistical Psychology*, 18(1), 87–123.

De Oliveira, H., Denti, T., Mihm, M. and Ozbek, K. 2017. Rationally inattentive preferences and hidden information costs. *Theoretical Economics*, 12(2), 621–654.

Dean, M. and Neligh, N. 2017. Experimental tests of rational inattention. Columbia University Working Paper.

Debreu, G. 1951. The coefficient of resource utilization. *Econometrica: Journal of the Econometric Society*, 273–292.

Delavande, A. and Rohwedder, S. 2008. Eliciting subjective probabilities in internet surveys. *Public Opinion Quarterly*, 72(5), 866–891.

DeLiema, M., Deevy, M., Lusardi, A. and Mitchell, O.S. 2020. Financial fraud among older Americans: Evidence and implications. *The Journals of Gerontology: Series B*, 75(4), 861–868.

Deming, D.J. 2021. The Growing Importance of Decision-Making on the Job. National Bureau of Economic Research Working Paper 28733.

Denti, T. 2022. Posterior separable cost of information. *American Economic Review*, 112(10), pp. 3215–59.

Dominitz, J. and Manski, C.F. 1996. Eliciting student expectations of the returns to schooling. *Journal of Human Resources*, 31, 1–26.

Dominitz, J. and Manski, C.F. 1997. Using Expectations Data to Study Subjective Income Expectations. *Journal of the American Statistical Association*, 92, 855–867.

Ehlers, L. 2008. Truncation strategies in matching markets. *Mathematics of Operations Research*, 33(2), pp. 327–335.

Ellis, A. 2018. Foundations for optimal inattention. *Journal of Economic Theory*, 173, pp. 56–94.

Enke, B. and Graeber, T. 2019. Cognitive uncertainty. National Bureau of Economic Research Working Paper 26518.

Ericsson, K.A. and Simon, H.A. 1980. Verbal reports as data. *Psychological Review*, 87(3), 215.

Farber, H.S., Hall, R., and Pencavel, J. 1993. The incidence and costs of job loss: 1982–91. Brookings papers on economic activity. *Microeconomics* 1993 (1), 73–132.

Farrell, M.J. 1957. The measurement of productive efficiency. *Journal of the Royal Statistical Society: Series A (General)*, 120(3), 253–281.

Fehr, E. and Rangel, A. 2011. Neuroeconomic foundations of economic choice – recent advances. *Journal of Economic Perspectives*, 25(4), 3–30.

Frankel, A. and Kamenica, E. 2019. Quantifying information and uncertainty. *American Economic Review*, 109(10), 3650–3680.

Frantz, R.S. 2013. *X-efficiency: Theory, Evidence and Applications* (Vol. 2). Springer Science & Business Media, Berlin.

Frederick, S. 2005. Cognitive reflection and decision-making. *Journal of Economic Perspectives*, 19(4), 25–42.

Fudenberg, D., Strack, P. and Strzalecki, T. 2018. Speed, accuracy, and the optimal timing of choices. *American Economic Review*, 108(12), 3651–3684.

Gneiting, T. and Raftery, A.E. 2007. Strictly proper scoring rules, prediction, and estimation. *Journal of the American statistical Association*, 102(477), pp. 359–378.

Green, D.M. and Swets, J.A. 1966. *Signal Detection Theory and Psychophysics* (Vol. 1, pp. 1969–2012). Wiley, New York.

Gregory, V. 2020. Firms as learning environments: Implications for earnings dynamics and job search. FRB St. Louis. Working Paper (2020-036).

Griffiths, T.L., Lieder, F. and Goodman, N.D. 2015. Rational use of cognitive resources: Levels of analysis between the computational and the algorithmic. *Topics in Cognitive Science*, 7(2), 217–229.

Ghosh, S. 2023. *Strategic Communication and Scientific Learning*, Forthcoming.

Gul, F. and Pesendorfer, W. 2001. Temptation and selfcontrol. *Econometrica*, 69(6), 1403–1435.

Guo, C., Pleiss, G., Yu, S. and K. 2017. On calibration of modern neural networks. *International Conference on Machine Learning*, 1321–1330. PMLR.

Gustman, A.L. and Steinmeier, T.L. 2005. Imperfect knowledge of social security and pensions. *Industrial Relations: A Journal of Economy and Society*, 44(2), 373–397.

Guvenen, F., Karahan, F., Ozkan, S. and Song, J. 2015. What do data on millions of US workers reveal about life-cycle earnings risk? National Bureau of Economic Research Working Paper 20913.

Haaland, I., Roth, C. and Wohlfart, J. 2023. Designing information provision experiments. *Journal of Economic Literature*. Forthcoming.

Haavelmo, T. 1944. The probability approach in econometrics. *Econometrica: Journal of the Econometric Society*, iii–115.

Hastings, J.S. and Weinstein, J.M. 2008. Information, school choice, and academic achievement: Evidence from two experiments. *The Quarterly Journal of Economics*, 123(4), 1373–1414.

Hayek, F.A. 1937. Economics and knowledge. *Economica*, 33–54.

Hayek, F.A. 1945. The Use of Knowledge in Society. *American Economic Review*, 35(4), 519–553.

Hebert, B.M. and Jennifer, La'O. 2020. Information Acquisition, Efficiency, and Non-Fundamental Volatility. National Bureau of Economic Research Working Paper 26771.

Hebert, B.M. and Woodford, M. 2019. Rational Inattention When Decisions Take Time. National Bureau of Economic Research Working Paper 26415.

Hebert, B.M. and Woodford, M. 2020. Neighborhood-based Information Costs. National Bureau of Economic Research Working Paper 26743.

Hendren, N. 2017. Knowledge of future job loss and implications for unemployment insurance. *American Economic Review*, 107(7), 1778–1823.

Hoxby, C.M. and Turner, S. 2015. What high-achieving low-income students know about college. *American Economic Review*, 105(5), 514–517.

Jacobson, L.S., LaLonde, R.J. and Sullivan, D.G. 1993. Earnings losses of displaced workers. *The American Economic Review*, 685–709.

Johnson, E. J., Camerer, C., Sen, S. and Rymon, T. 2002. Detecting failures of backward induction: Monitoring information search in sequential bargaining. *Journal of Economic Theory*, 104, 16–47.

Jovanovic, B. and Nyarko, Y. 1994. The Bayesian Foundations of Learning by Doing. National Bureau of Economic Research.

Kamenica, E. and Gentzkow, M. 2011. Bayesian persuasion. *American Economic Review*, 101(6), 2590–2615.

Kang, M.J. and Camerer, C. 2018. Measured anxiety affects choices in experimental clock games. *Research in Economics*, 72(1), 49–64.

Kaur, S., Mullainathan, S., Oh, S. and Schilbach, F. 2021. Do Financial Concerns Make Workers Less Productive? National Bureau of Economic Research Working Paper 28338.

Khaw, M.W., Li, Z. and Woodford, M. 2017. Risk Aversion as a Perceptual Bias. National Bureau of Economic Research Working Paper 23294.

Kool, W. and Botvinick, M. 2018. Mental labour. *Nature Human Behaviour*, 2(12), 899–908.

Koopmans, T.C. 1949. Identification problems in economic model construction. *Econometrica*, 125–144.

Koopmans, T.C. 1962. On flexibility of future preference (No. 150). Cowles Foundation for Research in Economics, Yale University.

Koopmans, T.C. and Beckmann, M. 1957. Assignment problems and the location of economic activities. *Econometrica: Journal of the Econometric Society*, 53–76.

Krajbich, I. and Rangel, A 2011. Multialternative drift-diffusion model predicts the relationship between visual fixations and choice in value-based decisions. *Proceedings of the National Academy of Sciences*, 108(33), 13852–13857.

Kreiner, C.T., Lassen, D.D. and Leth-Petersen, S. 2014. Measuring the accuracy of survey responses using administrative register data: Evidence from Denmark. In *Improving the Measurement of Consumer Expenditures*, pp. 289–307. University of Chicago Press, Chicago.

Kreps, D.M. 1979. A representation theorem for "preference for flexibility". *Econometrica*, 47(3), 565–577.

Kreps, D. 2018. *Notes on the Theory of Choice*. Routledge, London.

Kuchler, T. and Zafar, B. 2019. Personal experiences and expectations about aggregate outcomes. *The Journal of Finance*, 74(5), 2491–2542.

Lazear, E.P., Shaw, K.L. and Stanton, C.T. 2015. The value of bosses. *Journal of Labor Economics*, 33(4), 823–861.

Leibenstein, H. 1966. Allocative efficiency vs. "X-efficiency". *The American Economic Review*, 56(3), 392–415.

Lieder, F. and Griffiths, T.L. 2020. Resource-rational analysis: Understanding human cognition as the optimal use of limited computational resources. *Behavioral and Brain Sciences*, 43.

Lu, J. 2016. Random choice and private information. *Econometrica*, 84(6), 1983–2027.

Luce, R.D. 1956. Semiorders and a theory of utility discrimination. *Econometrica*, 178–191.

Luce, R.D. 1958. A probabilistic theory of utility. *Econometrica*, 193–224.

Lusardi, A. and Mitchell, O.S. 2008. Planning and financial literacy: How do women fare?. *American Economic Review*, 98(2), pp. 413–17.

Lusardi, A. and Mitchell, O.S. 2014. The economic importance of financial literacy: Theory and evidence. *Journal of Economic Literature*, 52(1), pp. 5–44.

Luttmer, E.F. and Samwick, A.A. 2018. The welfare cost of perceived policy uncertainty: evidence from social security. *American Economic Review*, 108(2), pp. 275–307.

MacCuish, J.H. 2019. Rational inattention and retirement puzzles. arXiv preprint arXiv:1904.06520.

Maćkowiak, B., Matějka, F. and Wiederholt, M. 2021. Rational inattention: A review.

Malmendier, U. and Nagel, S. 2011. Depression babies: Do macroeconomic experiences affect risk taking? *Quarterly Journal of Economics*, 126, 373–416.

Malmendier, U. and Nagel, S. 2015. Learning from inflation experiences. *Quarterly Journal of Economics*, 131(1), 53–87.

Mani, A., Mullainathan, S., Shafir, E. and Zhao, J. 2013. Poverty impedes cognitive function. *Science*, 341(6149), pp. 976–980.

Manski, C.F. 1990. The use of intentions data to predict behavior: A best-case analysis. *Journal of the American Statistical Association*, 85(412), 934–940.

Manski, C.F. 2004. Measuring expectations. *Econometrica*, 1329–1376.

Manzini, P. and Mariotti, M. 2007. Sequentially rationalizable choice. *American Economic Review*, 97(5), 1824–1839.

Manzini, P. and Mariotti, M. 2014. Stochastic choice and consideration sets. *Econometrica*, 89(3), 1153–1176.

Marschak, J. 1953. Economic measurements for policy and prediction. In W. Hood, T.K. (Eds.), *Studies in Econometric Method*, New York: Wiley, pp. 1–26.

Marschak, J. and Radner, R. 1972. Economic Theory of Teams. Cowles Foundation Monograph 22. New Haven, Ct.

Matĕjka, F. and McKay, A. 2015. Rational inattention to discrete choices: A new foundation for the multinomial logit model. *American Economic Review*, 105(1), 272–298.

Mattsson, L.G. and Weibull, J.W. 2002. Probabilistic choice and procedurally bounded rationality. *Games and Economic Behavior*, 41(1), 61–78.

Mazzonna, F. and Peracchi, F. 2017. Unhealthy retirement? *Journal of Human Resources*, 52(1), pp. 128–151.

Menzio, G., Telyukova, I.A. and Visschers, L. 2016. Directed search over the life cycle. *Review of Economic Dynamics*, 19, 38–62.

Miao, J. and Xing, H. 2020. Dynamic discrete choice under rational inattention.

Minderer, M.J. Djolonga, R., Romijnders, F., Hubis, X., Zhai, N., Houlsby, D., Tran, D. and Lucic, M. 2021. Revisiting the Calibration of Modern Neural Networks, Neural Information Processing Systems (NeurIPS).

Montanari. 2022. Attention, inertia and switching costs as endogenous drivers of dynamic insurance choice. Mimeo.

Moore, D.A. and Healy, P.J. 2008. The trouble with overconfidence. *Psychological Review*, 115(2), p.502.

Morris, S. and Strack, P. 2019. The wald problem and the relation of sequential sampling and ex-ante information costs. Available at SSRN 2991567.

Mueller, A.I., Spinnewijn, J. and Topa, G. 2021. Job seekers' perceptions and employment prospects: Heterogeneity, duration dependence, and bias. *American Economic Review*, 111(1), 324–363.

Musslick, S., Cohen, J.D. and Shenhav, A. 2018. Estimating the Costs of Cognitive Control from Task Performance: Theoretical Validation and Potential Pitfalls. In CogSci.

Musslick, S., Cohen, J.D. and Shenhav, A. 2019. Decomposing Individual Differences in Cognitive Control: A Model-Based Approach. In CogSci, pp. 2427–2433.

Nagel, R. 1995. Unraveling in guessing games: An experimental study. *The American Economic Review*, 85(5), 1313–1326.

Nicholas, L.H., Langa, K.M., Bynum, J.P. and Hsu, J.W. 2021. Financial presentation of Alzheimer disease and related dementias. *JAMA Internal Medicine*, 181(2), 220–227.

Nyarko, Y. and Schotter, A. 2002. An experimental study of belief learning using elicited beliefs. *Econometrica*, 70(3), pp. 971–1005.

Okonkwo, O.C., Wadley, V.G., Griffith, H.R., Belue, K., Lanza, S., Zamrini, E.Y., Harrell, L.E., Brockington, J.C., Clark, D., Raman, R. and Marson, D.C. 2008. Awareness of deficits in financial abilities in patients with mild cognitive impairment: Going beyond self-informant discrepancy. *The American Journal of Geriatric Psychiatry*, 16(8), 650–659.

Oprea, R. 2020. What makes a rule complex?. *American Economic Review*, 110(12), pp. 3913–51.

Payne, J.W., Bettman, J.R. and Johnson, E.J. 1993. *The Adaptive Decision Maker*. Cambridge University Press, Cambridge.

Plassman, B.L., Langa, K.M., Fisher, G.G., Heeringa, S.G., Weir, D.R., Ofstedal, M.B., Burke, J.R., Hurd, M.D., Potter, G.G., Rodgers, W.L. and Steffens, D.C. 2007. Prevalence of dementia in the United States: The aging, demographics, and memory study. *Neuroepidemiology*, 29(1–2), 125–132.

Pomatto, L., Strack, P. and Tamuz, O. 2018. The Cost of Information. arXiv preprint arXiv:1812.04211.

Posner, R.A. 2014. Economic analysis of law. Wolters Kluwer.

Poterba, J.M. 2014. Retirement security in an aging population. *American Economic Review: Papers and Proceedings*, 104, 1–30.

Rajpurkar, P., Irvin, J., Zhu, K., Yang, B., Mehta, H., Duan, T., Ding, D., Bagul, A., Langlotz, C., Shpanskaya, K., Lungren, M., and Ng, A. 2017. Radiologist-Level Pneumonia Detection on Chest X-rays with Deep Learning. arXiv preprint arXiv:1711.05225.

Ratcliff, R. and McKoon, G. 2008. The diffusion decision model: Theory and data for two-choice decision tasks. *Neural Computation*, 20: 873–922.

Rockafellar, R.T. 2015. *Convex Analysis*. Princeton University Press, Princeton, NJ.

Rohwedder, S. and Willis, R.J. 2010. Mental retirement. *Journal of Economic Perspectives*, 24(1), 119–138.

Roth, A.E. and Sotomayor, M. 1992. Two-sided matching. *Handbook of Game Theory with Economic Applications*, 1, 485–541.

Roth, C. and Wohlfart, J. 2020. How do expectations about the macroeconomy affect personal expectations and behavior? *Review of Economics and Statistics*, 102(4), 731–748.

Salcher, I. 2023. Interruptions and Productivity. Forthcoming.

Samuelson, P.A. 1938. A note on the pure theory of consumer's choice. *Economica*, 5, 61–71.

Savage, L.J. 1971. Elicitation of personal probabilities and expectations. *Journal of the American Statistical Association*, 66(336), 783–801.

Schotter, A. and Trevino, I. 2014. Belief elicitation in the laboratory. *Annu. Rev. Econ.*, 6(1), pp. 103–128.

Schultz, W., Dayan, P. and Montague, P.R. 1997. A neural substrate of prediction and reward. *Science*, 275(5306), 1593–1599.

Shannon, C.E. 1948. A mathematical theory of communication. *The Bell System Technical Journal*, 27(3), 379–423.

Shavell, S. 1995. The appeals process as a means of error correction. *The Journal of Legal Studies*, 24(2), 379–426.

Shaw, M.L. and Shaw, P. 1977. Optimal allocation of cognitive resources to spatial locations. *Journal of Experimental Psychology: Human Perception and Performance*, 3(2), 201.

Shenhav, A., Cohen, J.D. and Botvinick, M.M. 2016. Dorsal anterior cingulate cortex and the value of control. *Nature neuroscience*, 19(10), pp. 1286–1291.

Sims, C.A. 1998. Stickiness. *Carnegie-Rochester Conference Series on Public Policy*, 49, 317–356.

Sims, C.A. 2003. Implications of rational inattention. *Journal of Monetary Economics*, 50, 665–690.

Sims, C.A. 2010. Rational inattention and monetary economics. In Handbook of monetary economics (Vol. 3, pp. 155-181). Elsevier.

Spurlino, E. 2022. Equilibria in Simultaneous Information Acquisition Games. Working Paper.

Spurlino, E. 2023. *Rationally Inattentive but Strategically Unsophisticated*. Forthcoming.

Steiner, J., Stewart, C. and Matějka, F. 2017. Rational inattention dynamics: Inertia and delay in decision-making. *Econometrica*, 85(2), 521–553.

Stephenson, M.C. 2010. Information acquisition and institutional design. *Harvard Law Review*, 124, 1422.

Stigler, G.J. 1961. The economics of information. *Journal of Political Economy*, 213–225.

Stigler, G.J. 1976. The existence of x-efficiency. *The American Economic Review*, 66(1), 213–216.

Syverson, C. 2011. What determines productivity? *Journal of Economic Literature*, 49(2), 326–365.

Thaler, R.H. and Sunstein, C.R. 2009. *Nudge: Improving Decisions About Health, Wealth, and Happiness*. Penguin.

Thurstone, L.L. 1927. A law of comparative judgement. *Psychological Review*, 34, 273–286.

Thurstone, L.L. 1931. The indifference function. *Journal of Social Psychology*, 2, 139–167.

Topel, R. 1990. Specific capital and unemployment: Measuring the costs and consequences of job loss. *Carnegie-Rochester Conference Series on Public Policy*, 33(September), 181–214.

Topel, R.H. and Ward, M.P. 1992. Job mobility and the careers of young men. *The Quarterly Journal of Economics* 107 (2), 439–479.

Toussaert, S. 2018. Eliciting temptation and self-control through menu choices: A lab experiment. *Econometrica*, 86(3), 859–889.

Von Wachter, T., Handwerker, E.W. and Hildreth, A.K. 2009. Estimating the'True' Cost of Job Loss: Evidence Using Matched Data from California 1991–2000. US Census Bureau Center for Economic Studies Paper No. CES-WP-09-14.

Wachter, J.A. and Kahana, M.J. 2019. A retrieved-context theory of financial decisions. National Bureau of Economic Research Working Paper 26200.

Weber, E.H. 1834. *On the Tactile Senses*. H.E. Ross and D.J. Murray (Trans. and Eds.) New York: Experimental Psychology Series.

Weidmann, B. and Deming, D.J. 2021. Team players: How social skills improve team performance. *Econometrica*, 89(6), 2637–2657.

Welch, F. 1970. Education in production. *Journal of Political Economy*, 78(1), 35–59.

Wiswall, M. and Zafar, B. 2015a. Determinants of college major choice: Identification using an information experiment. *Review of Economic Studies*, 82(2), 791–824.

Wiswall, M. and Zafar, B. 2015b. How do college students respond to public information about earnings? *Journal of Human Capital*, 9(2), 117–169.

Wiswall, M. and Zafar, B. 2021. Human capital investments and expectations about career and family. *Journal of Political Economy*, 129(5), 1361–1424.

Woodford, M. 2020. Modeling imprecision in perception, valuation, and choice. *Annual Review of Economics*, 12, 579–601.

Yeung, N. and Summerfield, C. 2012. Metacognition in human decision-making: Confidence and error monitoring. *Philosophical Transactions of the Royal Society B: Biological Sciences*, 367(1594), pp. 1310–1321.

Index

A

Acemoglu, Daron, 328
affine independence, 217
Afrouzi, Hassan, 357
Agarwal, Sumit, 363
Agranov, Marina, 16
Aguiar, Mark, 313
Akerlof, George, 351
allocative skill, 324–325, 327–328, 335
Alos-Ferrer, Carlos, 320
Amari, Shun-ichi, 197
Ameriks, John, 23, 153, 340, 349, 351, 355, 363
Andersen, Henrik, 325
Angeletos, George-Marios, 19
Apesteguia, Jose, 11
Archsmith, James, 315
Arcidiacono, Peter, 345
Armantier, Olivier, 303, 357
attention cost function, 187
Autor, David, 328
Avoyan, Ala, 316

B

Bagger, Jesper, 343
Bagul, Aarti, 291, 299
Ballester, Miguel, 11
Barsky, Robert, 349
Bartel, Ann, 325

basic observations, 9
Bayer, Hannah, 14
Beckmann, Martin, 330
Ben-Simon, Anat, 311
Bernheim, Douglas, 162, 173
Bertrand, Marianne, 325
Bettman, James, 15
Bhargava, S., 160
Bickel, J. Eric, 307–309, 312, 314
Blackwell experiment, 20, 28, 54, 118
Blackwell model, 27–31, 34, 41, 52, 288
Blackwell order, 100, 102, 131, 156, 158, 164–165, 167–168
Blackwell theorem, 122
Blackwell, David, 3–4, 12, 17, 19, 40, 155, 161
Block, Howard, 7–11, 15–17, 30–32, 52
Bloedel, Alexander, 19, 205, 320
Bloom, Nicholas, 325
Bordalo, Pedro, 352
Borsch-Supan, Axel, 358
Botvinick, Matthew, 147, 318
Bregman divergence, 305
Brier, Glenn, 303
Briggs, Joseph, 349
Bronchetti, Erin, 315
Brown, Jeffrey, 324
Bucher, Stefan, 19, 247, 254–255, 257, 260, 262–263, 269, 271, 273, 275, 331
Budescu, David, 311

Burke, James, 363
Bynum, Julie, 363

C

calibration, 21, 280, 288, 291, 308–309,
    313–314, 317, 341
Callaway, Fred, 320
Camerer, Colin, 14
Cameron, Charles, 367
Candia, Bernardo, 358
capacity-constrained representation
    (CCR), 101, 103–106, 108, 111, 113,
    116, 132, 281, 284, 292, 294
Caplin, Andrew, 10, 14, 16–19, 23, 39–41,
    45–46, 54, 56, 75–76, 83, 87–88, 101,
    104, 118, 122, 137, 140, 153, 155, 160,
    167, 173, 175, 177, 185, 192–193, 204,
    206, 215–217, 233, 247, 251, 254–255,
    257, 260, 262–263, 269, 271, 273, 275,
    279, 283–284, 298, 320, 331, 340,
    348–349, 351, 354–356, 359–360, 363,
    367
Carrasco, 320
Carrington, William, 343
Carvalho, Leandro, 281, 303, 316
CCLN, 137, 138, 140–141, 145–147
CCR utility cone, 102, 108, 110, 115,
    132–133
CDL, 185–186, 188, 194–195, 197,
    200–201, 203–204, 237–239, 241,
    243–244
Chan, Sewin, 343
Chandra, Amitabh, 363
Chen, Yan, 272
Chentsov, Nikolai, 196
Chetty, Raj, 33
CheXNeXt, 299
choice process, 17
choice process data, 16
Ciani, Emanuele, 354
CIR utility cone, 102, 110, 113, 115, 132
CMM, 299–300
cognitive control, 309, 324
cognitive decline, 23, 355, 362, 364–365
cognitive economics, 1

cognitive reflection task, 324
Cohen, Jonathan, 318–319
Coibion, Olivier, 357–358
Coile, Courtney, 358, 363
communication policies, 23, 353
Conlon, John, 344
consideration sets, 19
Copenhagen Life Panel (CLP), 22, 340,
    345, 347–350
cost of revealed learning, 116
cost-based machine learning, 20, 293
cost-based representation, 297
costly control, 318
costly information acquisition, 56
costly information representation (CIR),
    17, 53, 56–58, 60, 63–64, 67, 72, 74,
    77–81, 83, 86, 89, 93, 96–98, 100–101,
    103–106, 108, 112, 116, 131, 138,
    140–142, 178, 181, 194, 281, 284,
    293–294
costs of learning, 2–3, 18
Cover, Thomas, 213
cross-loss, 299
cross-loss matrix, 294
Csaba, Daniel, 137, 205, 257, 276, 320,
    334
Currie, Janet, 21, 309, 312

D

da Silveira, Rava, 352
Danish population registries, 325, 340
data engineering, 10, 13
data envelope analysis, 326
Davidson, Donald, 7
Dayan, Peter, 14
De Finetti, Bruno, 21, 281, 307–308, 310
De Liema, Marguerite, 363
De Oliveira, Enrique, 153
Dean, Mark, 16, 18–19, 40, 54, 56, 75, 83,
    87–88, 104, 118, 122, 140, 185,
    191–193, 204, 206, 215–217, 233
Debreu, Gerard, 326
decision-making skills, 22, 337–338, 340,
    342, 350
deep learning, 286

Deevy, Martha, 363
Dekel, Eddie, 153
Delavande, Adeline, 347, 354, 361
Deming, David, 21–22, 324, 336–337,
    341–342, 374
Denti, Tomasso, 153, 194
Ding, Daisy, 291, 299
direct loss difference matrix, 295
direct value difference matrix, 76
direct value switch, 82–83
direct value switch matrix, 79
Dixit, Avinash, 5
Djolonga, Josip, 292
Dominitz, Jeff, 345, 347
Driscoll, John, 363
Duan, Tony, 291, 299

E

economic data engineering, 1–2, 10
economics of attention, 1
efficient coding, 103
Ehlers, Lars, 261
Ellis, Andrew, 54
Enke, Ben, 309, 316
Ericsson, Karl, 15
Etheridge, Ben, 354
Eungik Lee, 340
exchangeability, 19, 247–248, 258

F

Farrell, Michael, 326
feasibility-based machine learning, 20,
    293
feasibility-based representation, 297
Fehr, Ernst, 205, 320
financial skill instrument, 323
Fisher, Gwenith, 363
fixed information representations (FIRs),
    101–103, 106, 108, 133
Floyd–Warshall, 98
Floyd–Warshall algorithm, 97, 296
Fontaine, François, 343
Francesconi, Marco, 354
Frankel, 173
Frantz, Roger, 327

Frederick, Shane, 324, 336
Fudenberg, Drew, 320

G

Gabaix, Xavier, 363
garbling matrix, 120
garblings, 102, 121
Gennaioli, Nicola, 352
Gentzkow, Matthew, 28, 193, 200, 233,
    371
Ghosh, Srijita, 245
Glimcher, Paul, 14
Gneiting, 281, 304
Gneiting, Tilmann, 302–304
Gomberg, Andrei, 23, 354, 356, 367
Gorodnichenko, Yuriy, 357–358
Graeber, Thomas, 309, 316
Grahek, Ivan, 319
Gregory, Victoria, 23, 340
Griffiths, Tom, 320
Gul, Faruk, 153
Guo, Chuan, 292
Gustman, Alan, 358
Guvenen, Fatih, 343

H

Hébert, Ben, 192–193, 196, 205
Haaland, Ingar, 357, 361
Haavelmo, Trygve, 10
Handwerker, Elizabeth, 343
Hastings, Justine, 33
Hayek, Friedrich, 3, 53
He, Yinghua, 272
Health and Retirement Survey (HRS), 363
Healy, Paul, 314
Hebert, Ben, 19, 192, 320
Heeringa, Steven, 363
Hendren, Nathaniel, 344
Hentall-McCuish, Jamie, 359
Heyes, Anthony, 315
Hildreth, Andrew, 343
Hotz, V. Joseph, 345
Houlsby, Neil, 292
Hoxby, Caroline, 33
Hsu, Joanne, 363

Hubis, Frances, 292
Huff Stevens, Ann, 343
Hurd, Michael, 363
Hurst, Erik, 313

I

Ichniowski, Casey, 325
ILR conditions, 216, 239–240
ILR hyperplane, 233, 240–242
immediate acceptance (IA) algorithm, 272
inattention is free, 88
indirect loss difference matrix, 296
indirect loss-difference, 299
indirect value difference matrix, 73, 76, 84
indirect value switch, 79
information monotonicity, 197
information treatments, 354, 357
invariance under compression, 203
invariant cost function, 196, 198
invariant likelihood ratio (ILR), 233, 235,
    332
invariant likelihood ratio (ILR) equations,
    215
invariant posterior separable, 198
invariant posterior-separable
    representation, 201, 203–204
Irvin, Jeremy, 291, 299

J

Jacobson, Louis, 343
job transitions, 22, 337, 340, 343
Johnson, 15
Johnson, Eric, 15
Jovanovic, Boyan, 326
Juster, Thomas, 349

K

Kahana, Michael, 352
Kamdar, Rupal, 357
Kamenica, Emir, 28, 173, 193, 200, 233,
    371
Kang, Min, 14
Kapteyn, Arie, 324
Karahan, Fatih, 343
Kaur, Supreet, 315

Kessler, Judd, 315
Khaw, Mel Win, 8
Kimball, Miles, 349
Kool, Wouter, 147
Koopmans, Tjalling, 10, 153, 330
Kornhauser, Lewis, 367
Krajbich, Ian, 320
Kreiner, Claus, 325
Kreps, David, 153, 247
Kuchler, Theresa, 352

L

La'O, Jennifer, 19, 196
Lagrangean lemma, 99, 118, 200
Laibson, David, 363
LaLonde, Robert, 343
Langa, Kenneth, 363
Langlotz, Curtis, 291, 299
Lassen, David, 325
Laura Bustamente, 319
Lazear, Edward, 325
Leahy, John, 13–14, 19, 118, 137, 140,
    153, 185, 192–193, 204, 206, 215–216,
    233, 251, 316, 320, 351
learning cost polyhedron, 93
Lee, Eungik, 23, 340, 354–355, 359–360
Lee, Minjoon, 23, 340, 355, 363
Leth-Petersen, Soren, 22–23, 324–325,
    340, 354–355, 359–360
Levy, Frank, 328
Li, Ziang, 8
Liebenstein, Harvey, 327
likelihood ratio inequalities, 216
linear family of decision problems,
    139
Lipman, Barton, 153
locally invariant posteriors (LIP), 201,
    204–205, 221–222
loss adapted, 296
loss calibrated, 290, 294–295
loss calibration, 289
loss function, 282, 285, 287, 290
Lu, Jay, 138, 147–148
Luce, Duncan, 8
Lucic, Mario, 292

Lungren, Matthew, 291, 299
Lusardi, 323
Lusardi, Annamaria, 21, 323, 336, 351, 363
Luttmer, Erzo, 324, 358

M

Machina triangle, 169
machine learning, 20, 279–280, 282, 287, 291, 317
Mackowiak, Bartosz, 246, 206
MacLeod, Bentley, 21, 309, 312
Magenheim, Ellen, 315
Malmendier, Ulrike, 351
management skills, 21–22, 323, 325, 335
Mani, Anandi, 315
Mankiw, Greg, 53
Manski, Charles, 345, 347
Manzini, Paola, 6–7, 12, 15
Mariotti, Marco, 6–7, 12, 15
Marschak, Jacob, 7–11, 15–17, 30–32, 52, 374
Martin, Daniel, 16–17, 19–20, 39, 41, 45–46, 76, 101, 122, 155, 160, 167, 173, 175, 177, 279, 282–284, 298
Marx, Philip, 20, 76, 101, 122, 279, 282–284, 298
Matejka, Filip, 19, 37, 206, 213–214, 231, 246, 251, 254, 265
Matejka–Mckay, 331
Mattson, Lars-Göran, 19, 213
Maurel, Arnaud, 345
Mazzona, Fabrizio, 363
McFadden, Daniel, 7, 11
McKay, Alexander, 19, 37, 246
McKay, Alisdair, 206, 213–214, 231, 254, 265
McKoon, Gail, 205, 320
mean- and optimality-preserving spread (MOPS), 102, 126–128, 130–134
mean-preserving spreads (MPSs), 102, 121, 123–124, 127, 134
Mehta, Hershel, 291, 299
memory, 351, 352

Menzio, Guido, 343
Meuller, Andreas, 339, 344
Miao, Jianjun, 233, 246
Mihm, Max, 153
Milligan, Kevin, 358
Minderer, Matthias, 292
Mitchell, Olivia, 21, 323–324, 336, 351, 363
Mommaerts, Corina, 363
Montague, Read, 14
Moore, Don, 314
Morris, Steven, 19, 205, 320
Mueller, 344
Mullainathan, Sendhil, 315
Murnane, Richard, 328
Musslick, Sebastian, 319

N

Nagel, Rosemarie, 16
Nagel, Stefan, 351
Neidel, Matthew, 315
Neligh, Nate, 192–193
Nelson, Scott, 357
Netzer, Nick, 320
Nevo, Baruch, 311
Ng, Andrew, 291, 299
NIAS utility cone, 158, 160, 171–172, 175–177
Nicholas, Lauren, 363
no improving action switch (NIAS), 17, 27, 46, 50–52, 57, 59–60, 62, 65–67, 72, 73, 77–79, 81, 83, 86–88, 103–105, 112–115, 155–156, 158, 161, 164, 168, 170, 174, 176–180, 182, 194, 281, 335
no improving attention cycles (NIAC), 18, 83, 86–88, 98, 103–105, 112, 115–116, 140, 179, 181–182, 194, 281, 296, 334–335
Nov, Oded, 137, 320
Nyarko, Yaw, 303, 326

O

Ofstedal, Mary Beth, 363
Oh, Suanna, 315
only payoffs matter, 201–204

Oprea, Ryan, 316, 369
optimal consideration sets, 233
optimal sequential search, 273
Oster, Emily, 14
Ozbek, Kamal, 153
Ozkan, SerdarSon, Jae, 343

P

Payne, John, 15
Peracchi, Franco, 363
Pesendorfer, Wolfgang, 153
Pilossoph, Laura, 344
Plassman, Brenda, 363
Pleiss, Geoff, 292
Pomatto, Luciano, 193, 205
Posner, Richard, 367
Postel-Vinay, Fabien, 343
posterior separable, 117, 193
posterior-based optimality conditions, 215
posterior-separable, 200
posterior-separable cost function, 185,
    193–195
posterior-separable representation,
    194–195, 203–204
Poterba, James, 355
prediction function, 288
proper loss function, 288, 301
proper scoring, 306
proper scoring rules, 302–303, 310
psychometric, 137, 147, 324
psychometric curve, 8, 33–34

Q

qualifying costs of revealed learning, 57,
    76–77, 85, 297

R

Radner, Roy, 374
Raftery, Adrian, 281, 302–304
Rajpurkar, Pranav, 291, 299
random utility, 7, 12
Rangel, Antonio, 162, 173–174, 205, 320
Ratcliff, Roger, 205, 320

rational inattention, 3, 18–19, 53–54, 103,
    209, 211, 255, 274, 306–307, 317, 324,
    353
rationally inattentive strategies, 55
receiver operating curve (ROC), 301
reinforcement learning, 314
Reis, Ricardo, 53
reservation wages, 344
revealed action probabilities, 40
revealed attention strategy, 58, 61
revealed Blackwell more informative, 161
revealed experiment, 40, 49, 155, 160, 179
revealed information structure, 132–133
revealed posteriors, 40, 45, 47, 51, 65–66,
    68–70, 107, 126, 135–136, 163, 168
revealed prior, 35
revealed strategy, 40, 47
revealed value, 42
Richter, Marcel, 187
Robin, Jean-Marc, 343
Rockafellar, Ralph, 18
Rockafellar, Rodney, 118, 150, 199,
    303–304
Rohwedder, Susann, 347, 361
Romagnoli, Giorgia, 316
Romano, Teresa, 345
Romijnders, Rob, 292
Roth, Al, 8
Roth, Christopher, 361
Rustichini, Aldo, 153

S

Sadka, Joyce, 23, 354, 356, 367
Sadun, Raffaella, 325
Saeverud, Johan, 23, 340, 354–355,
    359–360
Salcher, Isabelle, 316
Sampat, Bhaven, 315
Samuelson, Paul, 5, 11, 31, 33
Samwick, Andrew, 358
Sastry, Kartik, 19
Savage, Leonard, 21, 281, 302–303, 305,
    307–312, 314
Schilbach, Frank, 315
Schoar, Antoinette, 325

Schotter, Andrew, 303
Schulz, Wolfram, 14
science of mistakes, 1, 3, 9, 373
SDSC optimality conditions, 214
SDSC strategies, 221, 231, 255
SDSC-based optimality conditions, 221, 225, 230, 231
search skill, 341, 351
sequential search, 274
Shafir, Eldar, 315
Shannon, Claude, 189
Shannon cost function, 191, 204, 212, 252, 273, 335
Shannon entropy, 185, 189–190, 304
Shannon model, 17, 19, 185, 191–193, 205–207, 209, 211, 214, 240, 247, 251, 254
Shannon representation, 204
Shapiro, Matthew, 23, 340, 349, 355, 363
Shavell, Stephen, 367
Shaw, 192
Shaw Peter, 192
Shaw, Katherine, 325
Shaw, Marilyn, 192
Shenhav, Amitai, 318–319
Shleifer, Andrei, 352
Shorrocks, Anthony, 193
Shpanskaya, Katie, 291, 299
signal-based representation (SBR), 281, 289–290, 292, 294, 296–297, 301
Silverman, Daniel, 316
Simon, Herbert, 15
Sims, Christopher, 3, 19, 23, 54, 103, 185, 189, 193, 246, 353
social security reform, 354
Sotomayor, Marilda, 8
Spinnewijn, Johannes, 339, 344
Spurlino, Eric, 230
Stanton, Christopher, 325
state-dependent stochastic choice (SDSC), 18, 20, 27, 33–36, 39, 42, 45, 47, 52–53, 56, 62, 64, 101, 137, 141, 145, 148–149, 152, 161, 173, 186–187, 203, 213–214, 216, 277, 282, 307–308, 323, 325, 334, 370
Steiner, Jakub, 246

Steinmeier, Thomas, 358
Stephenson, Matthew, 367
Stewart, Colin, 246
Stigler, George, 3, 15, 53, 327
stochastic choice, 8
Strack, Philipp, 19, 193, 205, 320
strategic survey question (SSQ), 349
strict NIAS, 46–47
strong axiom of revealed preference, 6
strongly loss adapted, 295, 297
Stroop task, 35, 318
Strzalecki, Tomas, 320
Sullivan, Daniel, 343
Summerfield, Christopher, 309, 316
Sun, Yu, 292
Sung, Yeji, 352
Sunnstein, Cass, 156
survey of consumer expectations, 344
Sydnor, J., 160
Syverson, Chad, 325

T

Tamuz, Omer, 193, 205
task literature, 328
task skill, 313, 338
Taubinsky, Dmitry, 315
Telyukova, Irina, 343
Tergiman, Chloe, 16
Thaler, Richard, 156
Thurstone, Louis, 8
Till, Von Wachter, 343
Tonetti, Christopher, 23, 340, 349, 355, 363
Topa, Giorgio, 339, 344, 357
Topel, Robert, 343, 351
Toussaert, Severine, 153
tracking problem, 42, 47
Tran, Dustin, 292
Treich, Nicolas, 303
Trello task, 336
Trevino, Isabelle, 303
Trueblood, Jennifer, 319
Tsallis entropy, 192
Tsallis, Constantino, 192

Turner, 33
Tyler, Tom, 153

U

uniformly posterior-separable cost
   function, 193, 195–196
uniformly posterior-separable
   representation, 201
UPS, 205–206, 257

V

value of information, 173, 271
value switch, 76, 81
Van Reenen, John, 325
Vand der Klauuw, Wilbert, 357
variational lower bound, 117
variational lower bound on costs,
   98–100
Verrechia, Robert, 54
Visschers, Ludo, 343

W

β-weighted cross-entropy, 285, 299
Wachter, Jessica, 352
Ward, Michael, 343
weak Blackwell property, 88, 193
Weber, Ernst, 1, 33
Weber–Fechner laws, 8
Weibull, Jörgen, 19, 213
Weidmann, Ben, 22, 324, 336, 374

weighted cross-entropy, 295
Weinberger, Kilian, 292
Weinstein, 33
Weir, David, 363
Welch, Finis, 324, 327
Wiederholt, Mirko, 206, 246
Wise, David, 358
Wiswall, Matthew, 344–345, 357
Wohlfart, Johannes, 361
Woodford, Michael, 8, 103, 192–193, 205,
   320, 352

X

X-efficiency, 326–327
Xing, Hao, 233, 246

Y

Yang, Brandon, 291, 299
Yang, Choongryul, 357
Yellen, Janet, 351
Yeung, Nick, 309, 316

Z

Zafar, Basit, 344–345, 352, 357
Zhai, Xiaohua, 292
Zhao, Jiaying, 315
Zhang, Weijie, 320
Zhong, Weijie, 19, 205, 320
Zhu, Kaylie, 291, 299
Zwick, Eric, 315

Printed in the United States
by Baker & Taylor Publisher Services